But There Was No Peace

BUT THERE WAS NO PEACE

The Role of Violence in the Politics of Reconstruction

GEORGE C. RABLE

THE UNIVERSITY OF GEORGIA PRESS   ATHENS & LONDON

© 1984 by The University of Georgia Press
Preface to the new edition
© 2007 by The University of Georgia Press
Athens, Georgia 30602

Designed by Sandra Strother Hudson
Set in Linotron 202 Century Schoolbook

Printed digitally in the United States of America

The Library of Congress has cataloged
an earlier version of this book as follows:

Library of Congress Cataloging-in-Publication Data

Rable, George C.
But there was no peace : the role of violence
in the politics of Reconstruction / George C. Rable
xiii, 257 p. ; 24 cm.
Bibliography: p. [247]–251.
Includes index.
ISBN 0-8203-0703-3 (hardcover)
ISBN 0-8203-0710-6 (paperback)
1. Reconstruction (U.S. history, 1865–1877).
2. Violence—Southern States—History—19th century.
3. Southern States—History—1865–1877. I. Title.
E668.R13 1984
973.8—dc19   83-17883
2007 Paperback ISBN-13: 978-0-8203-3011-2
ISBN-10: 0-8203-3011-6

British Library Cataloging-in-Publication Data available

www.ugapress.org

For my mother and father and Kay and, of course, Annie

Contents

Preface to the New Edition

T Harry Williams used to say that no historian should ever be held responsible for what he writes in his first book. To a graduate student struggling to finish a dissertation, the remark struck me as amusing but odd. Now it seems that the wisecrack may also have been wise.

Looking back over a book—most of it written over twenty-five years ago—can (and probably should) be a humbling experience. Now it is easy to see what might have been done differently. Racial and political violence during the Reconstruction period is a vast and complex subject—perhaps too much so for one short book. Even when I began the project, there was substantial historical literature on various phases of the topic, including the Ku Klux Klan and violent incidents in various states.[1] In many ways the whole subject of political terrorism has been and remains important for understanding the course of Reconstruction, and it continues to receive attention in more general works on the period as well as in American history textbooks.

In presenting a comprehensive account of violence during Reconstruction, I couched the story in a framework of revolution/counter-revolution. Once-powerful white southerners perceived the federal government's Reconstruction policies as "revolutionary," and violence became an important feature of a "counterrevolution," which led to the eventual collapse of Republican-controlled state governments and more broadly the collapse of Reconstruction itself. Here perceptions of a society in the throes of political, economic, social, and especially racial upheaval became the starting point for understanding the furious and often violent response to what historians have seen as moderate if not conservative efforts to reunite the country, build a southern Republican party, and guarantee certain basic rights for the recently freed slaves. Emphasizing white southern resistance and to a lesser extent the Republicans' response rather than probing the more general strengths and weaknesses of national reconstruction policies, the book partly recasts debates about the "failure" of Reconstruction.

Much Reconstruction violence was "instrumental" in that it had a strongly political purpose, beginning with the 1866 New Orleans riot. From 1868 on, the goal was to drive southern Republicans from power in state and local governments while at the same time reestablishing "race control." *But There Was No Peace* explores Reconstruction as a crisis in political legitimacy by analyzing the response of white southern conservatives to military reconstruction and the emergence of a southern Republican party. What role did violence play in the political strategies of a resurgent southern Democracy? How did leading politicians and newspaper editors justify or explain away the use of violence? Aside from sifting through contradictory evidence and sorting out what happened in various incidents, I highlighted the role of this resistance and violence in subverting Reconstruction.

The results of all the bloodshed were decidedly mixed in national, state, and local politics. In 1868, night-riding and intimidation helped put Georgia and Louisiana in the Democratic column but failed to prevent Ulysses S. Grant from being elected president. Ku Klux Klan terrorism could be frighteningly effective at the local level yet never achieved its larger objective of overthrowing Republican state governments. After Federal prosecutions under the Enforcement Acts helped suppress the Klan, an emphasis on white unity and the selective use of violence became standard campaign tactics in those states remaining under Republican control. Political terrorism played a significant role in the "redemption" of Alabama, Mississippi, Louisiana, and South Carolina.

Were I starting the project over again, I might have focused almost entirely on post-Klan violence in those states, a subject that still needs more intensive study. As for regrets, like Frank Sinatra, "I've had a few." The application of frustration, aggression, and other psychological notions from the social sciences to political violence during Reconstruction won mixed reviews, and deservedly so. Admittedly, the book exaggerates the degree of white unity and places too much weight on racial motives. On specific incidents, more careful attention to the social, economic, and cultural context would have yielded some additional insights; by the same token, more detailed research on both the perpetrators and victims of violence might have been a fruitful line of inquiry; so too, a more comparative look at events across the region could have revealed some new patterns in the use of violence as a political tactic. For the most part, generous reviewers not only offered legitimate criticisms but also pointed to some useful alternative approaches that should be pursued in future studies.

On the whole, I stand by the major interpretative points made in the book, though I would no longer be so quick to apply the word *inevitable* to the failure of Reconstruction. Perhaps *highly probable* would be more reasonable. The difficulties faced by the Congress, the presidents, the army, and the southern state governments were formidable. The policy alternatives were tantalizing but fraught with perils of their own. Resistance to "military reconstruction" and to the new Republican regimes seems an especially timely topic.[2] Questions of legitimacy and security bedeviled politicians and ordinary citizens throughout the Reconstruction period, and the norms of electoral politics and necessary compromise often did not apply.

Reconstruction is a complex and generally cheerless story, a subject much more attractive to scholars than to general readers, and even academic interest in the period languished for a time before reviving recently. Since the original publication of *But There Was No Peace*, a few historians have tackled the subject from new angles. Two books on the Ku Klux Klan probed the connections between Klan raids and railroad construction as well as the constitutional and legal limitations on Federal prosecutions under the Enforcement Acts. Richard Zuczek's book *State of Rebellion* argues that white resistance in South Carolina was not only critical to the overthrow of Reconstruction but also marked a continuation of the Civil War.[3] More recently two studies—one by an able young scholar and the other by a talented journalist—have recounted sobering stories of violence in Reconstruction Louisiana and Mississippi.[4] And there is clearly room for much more work. To cite just one example, the voluminous "outrage" reports in the Freedmen's Bureau records await systematic analysis. Given the vast array of published and unpublished materials, largely untapped local sources including rural newspapers, the discovery of Reconstruction by social historians, the rich scholarship in African American history, and revived interest in political economy and state authority, the subject of violence during Reconstruction remains far from exhausted.

GEORGE C. RABLE
Tuscaloosa, Alabama
December 13, 2006

NOTES

1. For a perceptive historiographical overview, see Michael Perman, "Counter Reconstruction: The Role of Violence in Southern Redemption," in *The Facts of Reconstruction: Essays in Honor of John Hope Franklin*, ed. Eric Anderson and Alfred A. Moss Jr. (Baton Rouge: Louisiana State University Press, 1991), 121–40.

2. For an intelligent look at some of the "lessons" of Reconstruction in terms of American foreign policy and the promotion of democracy, see Edward L. Ayers, "Exporting Reconstruction," in *What Caused the Civil War? Reflections on the South and Southern History* (New York: W. W. Norton, 2005), 145–66.

3. Scott Reynolds Nelson, *Iron Confederacies: Southern Railways, Klan Violence, and Reconstruction* (Chapel Hill: University of North Carolina Press, 1999); Lou Falkner Williams, *The Great South Carolina Ku Klux Klan Trials, 1871–72* (Athens: University of Georgia Press, 1996); Richard Zuczek, *State of Rebellion: Reconstruction in South Carolina* (Columbia: University of South Carolina Press, 1996).

4. James K. Hogue, *Uncivil War: Five New Orleans Street Battles and the Rise and Fall of Radical Reconstruction* (Baton Rouge: Louisiana State University Press, 2006); Nicholas Lemann, *Redemption: The Last Battle of the Civil War* (New York: Farrar, Strauss and Giroux, 2006).

Acknowledgments

The only unalloyed pleasure in writing a book is thanking those who helped along the way. These few words must serve as the author's meager thanks for much generous assistance.

On several research trips, I met with almost unfailing helpfulness and courtesy from scores of librarians and archivists. The staffs at the Southern Historical Collection at the University of North Carolina, the Perkins Library at Duke University, the Alabama Department of Archives and History in Montgomery, and the Rutherford B. Hayes Memorial Library in Fremont, Ohio, deserve special commendation for extraordinary services.

Two of my colleagues at Anderson College, Glenn Nichols and J. Douglas Nelson, provided good humor and much-needed encouragement in the latter stages of this project. My good friend "Coach" A. Wilson Greene of the National Park Service was a source of generous hospitality and abusive humor on several research trips.

Professors Terry Seip of the University of Southern California and Randy Roberts of Sam Houston State University each read several chapters and made many important suggestions for improvement. Joseph G. "Chip" Dawson III of Texas A&M University at Galveston also critiqued several chapters and shared much useful information on Louisiana affairs. Thomas E. Schott of the United States Air Force generously gave me access to his voluminous notes on Alexander H. Stephens, answered many questions on Georgia politics and proved to be a boon companion on two lengthy research expeditions. Through their interest and encouragement, all four of these individuals demonstrated a commitment to friendship that is all too rare in academic circles.

John L. Loos of Louisiana State University was a constant source of wry humor and useful advice during my graduate school days. He has remained a trusted friend, valued counselor, and dependable source of assistance.

Trudie Calvert edited the manuscript for the University of Georgia Press with great care and made numerous stylistic improvements.

There are five individuals without whom this book could never have been completed.

Charles East, editor of the University of Georgia Press, willingly read what proved to be a very rough early version of the work, selected outside readers who made invaluable suggestions for revision, and had more faith in this neophyte author than was often warranted.

William J. Cooper, Jr., of Louisiana State University read an earlier draft of the work, discussed each chapter with me at some length, and spurred me through his probing questions to make numerous interpretive changes. More important, his advice and good cheer at several difficult points were crucial for its successful completion.

The late John D. Unruh, Jr., of Bluffton College initiated me into the serious study of history and taught me the value of thorough research and tough questioning of one's own work. His brilliance, humility, and superb example of humane scholarship will always serve as the epitome of the best this profession has produced.

The late T. Harry Williams of Louisiana State University directed my original research with constant prodding, unfailing wit, and warm generosity. His careful reading of each page improved the writing style and saved me from many embarrassing solecisms.

My long-suffering wife Kay obviously deserves more than this small paragraph of appreciation. She not only was an invaluable assistant and cheerful companion on several research trips, but she proofread, copied information, and typed several versions of the manuscript. She uncomplainingly tolerated a husband who was often obsessed with another time and other places. Her faith and love sustained me through some rough times and made the good times worth celebrating.

Anderson, Indiana   GEORGE C. RABLE

Introduction

A study of selected race riots during Reconstruction begun ten years ago formed the genesis for the analysis of violence during that period that is the focus of this book. At first glance, bloodshed in the South after the Civil War seemed endemic, but closer examination uncovered complex patterns. Civil wars produce political, social, and economic upheaval, leaving in their wake deep bitterness among both victors and vanquished. After Appomattox the South's political leaders saw themselves entering an era of revolutionary changes imposed by the national government, which many viewed as an outside power. Continuing a long pattern of American, and particularly southern, behavior, many whites found an outlet for their frustration by attacking those deemed responsible for their suffering: white Republicans and blacks. The numerous "outrages" reported by the Freedmen's Bureau and army officers and a bloody race riot at Memphis, Tennessee, in 1866 are symbolic of the tensions that boiled within the former Confederate states.

By 1867 civil disorder was taking on an increasingly political character. Interpreting the passage of the Reconstruction Acts as the final triumph of Jacobinical radicalism, veteran politicians and newspaper editors unleashed vehement attacks on the new Republican state governments. Conservative leaders adopted a variety of peaceful strategies to stem the Republican tide, ranging from courting black voters to legalistic obstructionism, but to no avail. Frustrated at their inability to bring their states back to Democratic control, some southerners turned to the Ku Klux Klan and other white supremacist organizations, using terrorism to eliminate opposition leaders and to strike fear into the hearts of rank-and-file Republicans, both black and white. The poverty and economic instability that were universal in the postwar South heightened political conflict and worsened race relations.

Factional disputes within the Republican party, weaknesses in the southern state governments, and the halting and inefficient federal campaign against terrorism encouraged impatient whites to use force against their political foes.

A counterrevolutionary tide began sweeping through the South in the early 1870s, sending state after state back into Democratic hands. Conservative leaders acquired great skill at selectively employing armed force to win state and congressional elections. Violent canvasses in Alabama, Louisiana, Mississippi, and South Carolina exposed the impotence of the Republican party in the South and the determination of Democrats to defeat their opponents by any means necessary. The final triumph of the counterrevolution awaited the withdrawal of northern Republican support from the so-called "carpetbag regimes" in 1877. The inconsistency of federal Reconstruction policy and the strength of southern resistance seem to have doomed the Reconstruction experiment to inevitable collapse. Although Americans have often been loathe to concede that violence may bring about needed change, terrorism in the Reconstruction era was instrumental in achieving the ends desired by its perpetrators.

Building upon the massive outpouring of Reconstruction scholarship in the past several decades, this study examines the political, social, economic, and psychological fissures in southern society that led to racial and political warfare. Although the lack of statistical information on violent outbreaks prevented any quantitative analysis of the demographic, economic, and social characteristics of the rioters and their victims, contemporary documents and testimony contained valuable clues for analyzing the causes of social and political disorder. Such psychological and sociological concepts as the theory that frustration often produces aggression proved useful for placing Reconstruction violence into a wider perspective. Important studies of modern revolutionary violence by historians, political scientists, and sociologists provided the revolution-counterrevolution metaphor as a device to explain the response of many southern whites to the problems of Reconstruction. Studies of European mob behavior along with several detailed works on twentieth-century American racial disturbances revealed the purposefulness and calculation of social violence.

An imposing number of manuscripts, newspapers, diaries, memoirs, and government documents containing references to Reconstruction violence may be found; the research for this book was exhausting but hardly exhaustive. Local records, for example, contain much new information, and studies of violence in particular states, especially Louisiana and South Carolina, would be valuable.

Works published in the past several decades have provided a foundation for extending the study of Reconstruction beyond the increasingly weary and unfruitful debate between traditional, revisionist, and neo-revisionist interpretations. The study of violence in Reconstruction reveals the sterility of attempts to treat the period as a morality play. The powerful nature of the southern counterrevolution against Reconstruction and the complex motives of the actors involved should give pause. We can no longer hold forth with brash certitude about the tantalizing might-have-beens or write in stentorian tones of the mistakes of the much-abused postwar generation.

1. American Violence, Southern Violence, and Reconstruction

In the context of world history, the American Civil War is a singular event. In four years more than six hundred thousand men died, the Union was preserved, and slavery was destroyed, but no formal peace settlement was ever made. The country miraculously avoided the bloody reprisals that commonly follow civil wars. The victors were amazingly lenient and executed but one rebel, Henry Wirz, commandant of the infamous Andersonville prison. The leaders of the southern "rebellion" not only saved their necks but after a brief period of "reconstruction" regained their dominant social, economic, and political positions. Yet more ironic, the losers in the conflict—the white southerners—committed numerous acts of violence against the winners. Individuals and groups, organized and unorganized, intimidated, whipped, hanged, and shot Union men, blacks, and Republicans of both races. By the time the federal government retreated from its reconstruction of the South, former Confederates had achieved through political terrorism what they had been unable to win with their armies—the freedom to order their own society and particularly race relations as they saw fit.

The Civil War marked a unique though short-lived triumph of liberalism and nationalism.[1] This is not to say that the ideas of classical liberalism did not prevail during the postwar era. They did. But these doctrines were distorted for conservative purposes by businessmen and Republican politicians as well as by white southerners attempting to preserve their most sacred values. Even more than the war, this cultural struggle would forge a "national" unity in the South that had eluded the Confederates.

Not unexpectedly, some white southerners readily employed violence to achieve their goals. As Americans, and particularly as southerners, they were heirs to a long tradition of violence. From the conquest of the Indians and the riots of the Revolution to the ethnic, religious, and racial conflicts of the Jacksonian period, Americans had willingly, sometimes eagerly, shed large quantities of blood.[2] Nowhere was violence more acceptable as a normal part of life than in the southern states. The South early acquired a reputation as the nation's most violent section, and what fragmentary statistical evidence is available on regional murder rates in the antebellum period substantiates this generalization.[3]

Explanations for southern violence have been diverse but unpersuasive. Wilbur Cash believed the antebellum southerner's penchant for fighting was a carryover from frontier conditions. Inhabitants of a thinly settled region, where the bonds of social convention were loosened and government barely existed, southerners displayed an often maniacal individualism that inevitably produced bloodshed. Carrying the argument one step further, Richard Slotkin has asserted that "civilized" man tames the frontier by destroying the wilderness and subduing its inhabitants (in this case, the Indians).[4] Such extreme reactions to adverse conditions are ingrained in the settled life of the community long after the forest has disappeared and the savages have been shoved westward. Even if one accepts this explanation, questions remain unanswered. Why, for example, did a frontier mentality survive in the South after the Civil War?

Dickson D. Bruce, Jr., interprets violence within the context of more general cultural values. Bruce argues that southerners were obsessed by the idea of passion and the need to subdue man's selfish instincts in order to maintain social order. Their essentially pessimistic view of human nature led southerners to accept violence as an unfortunate if unavoidable element of society. If violence could never entirely be eliminated, it could be controlled, and maintaining such a balance became the central philosophical and practical dilemma for thoughtful men. From childrearing to the governance of social relations, southerners sought to keep emotion and particularly passion within narrow bounds.[5]

Their failure soon became obvious. Southerners exhibited violent tendencies regardless of their race or social class. Some comfort could be gained by picturing the North as even more unstable—indeed as a society without structure ruled by the whims and excesses of sansculotte mobs.[6] Yet slave insurrections, dueling, fighting, brawling, and general rowdiness gave a hollow ring to southern claims that their civilization was superior.

The cultural argument, then, says both too much and too little. If an obsession with controlling passion somehow caused southerners to embrace violence, is this a characteristic common to other violent societies? Not only were there many bloody affrays in the North both before and after the Civil War, but that region's culture was thought to be different from that of the South. Some cultural continuity is presumed to exist within the South, yet if so, why were there changes in the pattern of disorder over several decades? Such an overarching explanation for southern violence has a certain plausibility but neglects the historical context. The student of violence during Reconstruction must recognize not only the social structure and mores of the South but also the conditions of time and place.[7]

The problem of violence in turn raises important questions about the nature of recent work on Reconstruction. The trend for the past decade has been to interpret the era as an age of conservatism.[8] This thesis appears self-evident from the perspective of our own time, but it would have seemed peculiar if not absurd to Americans, and especially to southerners, living in the 1860s and 1870s. For both northerners and southerners, the war had wrought radical changes; economic, social,. and political upheaval followed in the wake of the conflict. The extraordinary violence of the Reconstruction period therefore erupted because white southerners in 1865 found their world turned upside down.

Sacrifice, suffering, and defeat had rubbed emotions raw. The physical devastation of four years of fighting could be more easily repaired than the psychological damage. The South drifted outside of the American mainstream—a striking counterpoint to the national myths of success and innocence.[9] The repressive experience of suffering military conquest and occupation and the obsession with lost causes and shattered dreams would shape southern attitudes and actions for many years.

The collapse of the Confederacy produced an intense fear of the future. If reality belies this feeling of panic, reality went unrecognized. Mail service was either unreliable or nonexistent; newspapers printed horrible stories of Yankee intentions that later proved fallacious. Even after the restoration of communication and transportation facilities, southerners received distorted information about federal policy and few reliable assessments of northern public opinion.

Frightening and contradictory rumors led to the fear that the end of the war did not mean an end to the bloodshed. Henry Ravenel, a South Carolina planter, worried that the war would be just another unsuccessful rebellion and that the Confederates would be hanged as traitors. Uncertainty haunted the southern mind. What forms would northern vengeance take? Who would control the Reconstruction policies of the federal government? The very precariousness of the South's future fed already fevered imaginations.[10]

Other southerners thought they saw the course of events more clearly. Former Confederate Vice-President Alexander H. Stephens believed that American history was moving toward "complete Centralism" in government under the guidance of the radical Republicans. Stephens's bitter political enemy Benjamin H. Hill agreed that the northern Jacobins were about to "fix upon the whole country, by repeated amendment, a new Constitution suited to their fanatical vagaries." Both men feared a despotism that would destroy democracy and southern society.[11]

More terrifying than the shrouded future was the present powerlessness of the South. Unable to control the course of events, southerners awaited their fate at the hands of a "hostile" president and a Republican Congress. The Union would be restored on terms dictated by the victors and at an uncertain date. Periods of concentrated and prolonged frustration commonly produce aggression in humans, leading them to strike out against those they perceive to be responsible for their predicament.[12] In studying a variety of civil disturbances around the world, Ted Robert Gurr concluded that "frustration-induced anger" is largely responsible for causing internal strife.[13]

Such frustration subsided temporarily when Andrew Johnson announced his liberal pardon policy and provided for setting up provisional state governments in the South. Some veteran politicians eagerly sought positions of power in the new governments, but others hung back, adopting a policy of "masterly inactivity." Governor Charles J. Jenkins of Georgia advised the people of his state to observe the political struggle in the North with "calm and resolute dignity." Lacking influence, conservative politicians could see no gain in sectional agitation that would further call southern loyalty into question. The only safe course seemed to be to rebuild their fortunes and wait.[14]

In the fall and winter of 1865 the southern people as a whole were described by some northern visitors as "crushed and submissive." Former Confederates told Yankee travelers that they had been thoroughly whipped and had had enough of war. Men and women quietly went about their business and shunned political discussion.[15] Beneath this seemingly placid surface lay the shock, anger, confusion, apathy, and despair engendered by defeat. No consensus seemed to exist in either region as to how to rebuild and reshape a war-shattered society. Southerners were certain, however, about what they wished to avoid.

When white southerners raised their voices, it was to affirm that they had accepted the results of the war unconditionally. But their promises of conciliation and forebearance were vague and often contradictory. On February 22, 1866, Alexander H. Stephens addressed a joint session of the Georgia General Assembly and defined more clearly the drift of southern sentiment. Stephens called for the nation to stand reunited on the single foundation of the Constitution. The South might then resume in good faith her loyalty to the Union. Yet for all his words of reconciliation and conservative statesmanship, Stephens was unwavering in his insistence that the southern states must be restored to their former relations with the national government; both sections must conquer old prejudices. In short, acquiescence did not mean submission. Southerners spoke of the need for sectional compromise and in the same breath pledged acceptance of the results of the war. Even James Lusk Alcorn, a leading Mississippi Whig who later became a Republican, believed the South must have a voice in deciding its future and should be consulted as to how and when slavery would be abolished.[16]

A substantial number of southerners mistakenly imagined they could both rejoin the nation and enjoy their former status. The South's only desire, said Robert E. Lee, was to preserve the Union "as established by our forefathers." Several Confederate state governors attempted to act as if nothing had changed. Governor Joseph E. Brown of Georgia called a meeting of his state's General Assembly, and when Secretary of War Edwin Stanton forbade it, Brown took his case to the local Union commander, General James Harrison Wilson. Brown told Wilson that signing a parole would mean the end of his political career in Georgia, whereupon the general bluntly asked the governor if he faced any future in the country other than being hanged. Struck by this forceful logic, Brown replied that he had not thought about it and agreed to sign the parole.[17]

Brown's actions illustrated the limits of southern loyalty. Former rebels vehemently proclaimed their "acceptance of the situation" yet sought to turn events to their own advantage.[18] Northern newspaper accounts of southern intransigence and the "bloody shirt" harangues of Republican politicians were not entirely groundless. Southerners who still hoped for a Confederate triumph were like the unreconstructed Robert Toombs, who, Stephens said, "talks of things as he would have them and not as they are." A few noncombatants, particularly women, even spoke of renewing the contest shortly after the surrender of the Confederate armies.[19] Faced with the bitter reality of their position, many men sought refuge in what Cash has described as a tendency toward hedonism and romanticism.[20] Fantasizing about past glories or building imaginary castles for the future allowed temporary escape from the harsh present. Only the ever-present Yankee intruded into these pleasant dreams.

Expressions of bitter contempt fell on those who sought to propitiate the Yankees. The preservation of both dignity and self-respect decreed that honest men need not whine at the feet of their oppressors or curry favor by kowtowing to the enemy. The still fiery Jubal Early wrote from Cuba: "The history of the world does not afford an instance in which a conquered people have submitted with good will to the rule of their conquerors."[21]

Surrender did not signify an admission of guilt. The justness of their cause was unquestioned; repentence therefore was inappropriate. Georgia humorist Charles H. Smith ("Bill Arp"), for example, announced he would never apologize for his participation in the war. Mothers sought to instill in their sons' minds the sacredness of the "Lost Cause." Louisiana historian Charles Gayarré spoke for many former Confederates: "We repudiate the idea that we ever ceased to be good Americans. We honestly believed that we were supporting the holiest of all causes, and we still think so."[22]

Along with the survival of Confederate loyalty, there also persisted a hypersensitiveness on points of honor, both personal and regional. The heightened individualism and fierce pride of the antebellum southerner had frequently produced aggressive acts such as fighting and dueling. These social attitudes readily carried over into politics, as William J. Cooper, Jr., has ably demonstrated, and southerners responded as though antislavery attacks were personal insults.[23]

If anything, these emotions were intensified by military defeat. In September 1866, Wade Hampton exhorted his fellow citizens not to "cover ourselves with eternal infamy by branding as traitors the men who died for us" but to cling to that most precious of all commodities, "our honor." The requirements of honor made southerners reluctant to grant further concessions to their foes. Most editors and politicians saw capitulation as a sign of weakness that would dissipate the South's remaining strength and encourage the northern politicians to insist on harsher conditions of settlement. Failing to understand northern needs for at least a symbolic acceptance of defeat, some southerners objected to Andrew Johnson's conservative restoration policy. A few Jesuitical obstructionists higgled over repealing the ordinances of secession, and others questioned the validity of the newly drafted state constitutions. Acts the North interpreted as brazen effrontery were to the South legitimate means of defending honor and asserting the section's rightful place in the American Union.[24]

Moderates feared this smoldering resentment might boil over in the 1865 state elections. Prudent men, they cautioned, must be sent to the constitutional conventions and state legislatures to demonstrate southern loyalty. Although for many of the contests the evidence is fragmentary, the voters apparently elected a substantial number of former Whigs and original Unionists.[25] Still, most of those elected, regardless of background, had sided with the Confederacy during the war. The southern electorate sent to the Thirty-Ninth Congress the vice-president of the Confederacy, four Confederate generals, four Confederate colonels, and nine former Confederate congressmen. Oblivious to the northern reaction, many citizens found nothing wrong with electing their "natural" leaders to state and national offices. As Chief Justice Salmon P. Chase had discovered during his tour of the South in the spring of 1865, the old politicos were eager to wield their accustomed influence.[26]

Politicians who deviated from the narrow confines of southern orthodoxy on Reconstruction paid a dear price. When Georgia's Joe Brown traveled to Washington in late 1866, he discovered that suffrage for southern blacks was no longer a debatable question and that adoption of the proposed Fourteenth Amendment and universal suffrage might avert white disfranchisement. Brown's public letter advocating this course opened him to a fusillade of angry protest. Even less bold statements elicited cries of "traitor" and "Judas." During his brief imprisonment after the war in Fort Warren in Boston Harbor, former Confederate Postmaster General John H. Reagan wrote a letter to the people of his native Texas urging them to adopt at least a qualified form of Negro suffrage to mollify the North. After Reagan's release from prison, the "Fort Warren letter" made him a pariah in his home state. Southerners who counseled moderation or making the smallest concessions found themselves publicly reviled and privately scorned.[27]

When Congress refused to admit members from the former Confederate states in December 1865, editors and politicians accused northern Republicans of bad faith. How could they have lectured throughout the war that the Union was indissoluble and then, once the war was over, refuse to allow the southern states representation in the Union? The South had disbanded her armies in good faith and asked only that the North abide by the "terms of surrender."[28]

Conservatives attributed the unprincipled behavior of Republican politicians to their revolutionary desire to subvert the American republic and establish a centralized despotism. Drawing a historical analogy to France under the Jacobins, newspaper editors predicted that the radicals would soon set up the guillotines and begin a reign of terror. Would Charles Sumner or Thaddeus Stevens become the American Robespierre?[29] Duff Green, a veteran of Jacksonian party battles, described radical Republicanism as the culmination of a monarchist conspiracy dating from the days of John Adams. Another commentator compared the reign of radicalism to mob rule in ancient Constantinople. The military occupation of the South, a Richmond editorialist claimed, bore a striking resemblance to conditions in England between the reigns of King John and Charles II. Others found a closer parallel with Ireland under the British. Randolph Shotwell angrily wrote from his prison cell in Fort Delaware: "The South is no more a real partner in the so-called Union than Poland is a part of Russia, or India of England, or Cuba of Spain. Why then should this country be called a Union? The very term signifies equality of parts. Let it be called Yankeeland."[30]

Though eager polemicists plumbed the depths of vituperation to characterize Yankee oppression, some feared the radical Republicans more for their political opportunism than for their fanaticism. Radicals in both sections had but one fixed principle: self-interest. The Republicans, Herschel Johnson predicted, intended to keep the South out of the Union until after the presidential election of 1868. Once a Republican partisan was ensconced in the executive mansion, the party could approach the question of national reunion.[31]

Besides impugning the motives of the radical Republicans, the South underestimated their political strength, dismissing them as an insignificant minority of the northern electorate. Some hoped that a financial crisis might arise to unseat the radicals; others expected an eventual political reaction in the North and a renewal of the old alliance between the South and West.[32]

After Republican victories in the 1866 elections dashed these hopes, a deep gloom spread over the South. Herschel Johnson grieved that the country was now "at the mercy of the maddened tide of fanaticism and being drifted to irretrievable ruin." Southerners were powerless, Johnson lamented: "We are undone and constitutional liberty gone forever." For a time a proposal circulated with the tacit support of President Johnson calling for a compromise version of the proposed Fourteenth Amendment without the objectionable section disqualifying former Confederates from holding office, but it won little support. Mississippi's provisional governor, William L. Sharkey, informed a group of southern politicians in Washington that nothing could be gained by compromise at this late hour and that the government had "gone to hell."[33]

Southern opinion was not monolithic; a few prescient politicians read impending disaster in the recent election results and counseled moderation. Alcorn advised a group of Mississippi leaders that their state had made a grave mistake in refusing to ratify the Fourteenth Amendment. Unionist Governors Isaac Murphy of Arkansas and James Madison Wells of Louisiana vainly sought to awaken their respective legislatures to reality. Murphy described the dire consequences that would surely follow southern rejection of the amendment, and Wells warned that Louisiana would never receive more favorable terms for readmission to the Union.[34]

Such admonitions fell on unreceptive ears. Few southerners could approve a measure that disqualified former Confederates from political office; others saw ratification as leading to universal Negro suffrage. Furthermore, as a constitutional proposition, to submit an amendment to unrepresented states was absurd. How could the South be in the Union for the purpose of ratification but out when it came to representation in Congress? Moreover, many southerners doubted that ratification would assuage northern hatred. There was no guarantee that Congress would admit southern representatives without imposing additional requirements. Therefore, any concession might be misinterpreted and lead to still harsher terms.[35]

The question of ratification impinged on the concept of honor because former rebels drew a sharp distinction between submitting to necessity and assisting in their own degradation. South Carolina's provisional governor, Benjamin F. Perry, pointed out that Congress might well impose worse measures on the southern states but that such conditions would never be "voluntarily accepted." The South would therefore go quietly about her business, come what may.[36] As a direct result of southern intransigence on the Fourteenth Amendment, on March 2, 1867, Congress passed the first of the military Reconstruction acts.

The effects of defeat extended far beyond economic stagnation and political uncertainty. Frustrated by the delay in national reunion and the refusal of northern politicians to accept what seemed to be reasonable conditions for reconciliation, southern whites examined the sources of their discontent. Conditions that a twentieth-century psychologist might describe as a combination of alienation and anomie resulted in anger among the region's traditional leaders.

As Hannah Arendt has pointed out, rage is not a usual response to incurable diseases or seemingly unchangeable social conditions. Rage occurs when people suspect that a situation could be changed and their sense of justice is offended.[37] Every society cultivates its own myths, and for white southerners one of the most useful was the myth of southern innocence—or, perhaps more accurately, wounded innocence. There was a growing belief that peace and sectional reconciliation were possible if only the selfish and despotic northern radicals did not seek delay for their own evil purposes. Thus the frustration experienced by former Confederates could be called "arbitrary" and therefore likely to elicit an aggressive response.[38]

The key element in understanding this aggressive response is perception, and this, too, raises a difficult issue in the interpretation of Reconstruction.[39] From the viewpoint of the late twentieth century, the demands made on the South by the president, Congress, and the northern people seem reasonable, even conservative, if ill-defined. The southern frame of reference, however, was radically different, and this attitudinal chasm between the regions in part explains not only the failure to compromise outstanding political differences but also the willingness of both sides, though certainly the South to a greater degree, to use force to ensure that their own views prevailed. Psychological, not actual, reality governed these sectional responses.

Feeling betrayed, oppressed, and confused, many southerners could not conceal their anger, which naturally was expressed against those they considered responsible for their plight—the Yankees. Northern travelers sensed seething resentment beneath a façade of professed loyalty. They had been "whipped by numbers," former Confederates asserted; the coming of peace only intensified hatred of the "enemy." A woman in Savannah, Georgia, complained that she could hardly step outside her door for a breath of fresh air without seeing Union soldiers of both races parading about the streets. One citizen of Vicksburg, Mississippi, told a British visitor that he looked forward to "cleaning out all the Yankees from that section." The now familiar cry, "The South will rise again," rose from the ashes of war.[40]

The South's traditional siege mentality accounts for part of this reaction. Before the war, southerners reacted to abolitionist attacks by exaggerating the virtues and adopting extreme defenses of their society. This apologia turned increasingly to paranoia, and the South saw itself ringed by enemies.[41] This attitude intensified after 1865, when conservatives believed vile conspiracies were being hatched against them in Washington.

The same attitude appeared in the deep suspicion of and hostility toward northern men who came south after the war. Railway and steamboat passengers shunned contact with Yankee travelers and occasionally made loud and insulting comments. A New Orleans hotel that refused to accommodate northern men or United States soldiers became the most popular such establishment in the city. Wade Hampton poured out his frustration to General Lee: "I am not reconstructed yet, and in what I shall write every word will be dictated by Southern feelings and from a Southern heart." Jubal Early agreed that "if my salvation depends on being able to love them [Yankees], I fear I shall be lost. . . . There is scarce a night of my life I do not dream of being engaged in battle with the Yankees. I wish it was not all a dream."[42] Such expressions of anger obviously had a certain cathartic effect, but they could never entirely release deep-seated emotions.

The words of defiance added up to a rejection of American nationalism and an affirmation of southern distinctiveness. Despite professions of loyalty, it was difficult to renew former allegiances.[43] The public display of the American flag became an occasion for venting rebel sentiments. An old woman and her daughter, seeing the flag flying in front of a local army headquarters, stepped to the middle of the street to avoid the dishonor of passing under it. The commandant had them arrested and forced them to march back and forth under the flag while an army band played the "Star Spangled Banner" and "Yankee Doodle." A theater audience in Chattanooga, Tennessee, loudly hissed the stars and stripes. Bolder citizens took special pleasure in waving the Confederate flag in front of federal troops and shouting rebel slogans.[44]

The commemoration of patriotic holidays became anathema to some southerners. The Fourth of July seemed more an occasion for mourning than for celebration. Governor James W. Throckmorton of Texas flew no American flags on state buildings, but he proudly displayed portraits of Robert E. Lee and Jefferson Davis in the executive mansion. There was a bull market in Confederate memorabilia, with likenesses of Lee and Stonewall Jackson adorning the walls of many homes. Local organizations regularly decorated Confederate graves, and the Arkansas General Assembly passed a law extending aid to wounded soldiers and widows and for the purchase of artificial limbs for maimed Confederate veterans.[45]

This reverence for the heroes in gray made the contrasting presence of federal occupying troops all the more infuriating. These "blue coated dogs of despotism," as one woman described them, were a striking reminder of defeat. Echoing the Declaration of Independence, strident editorial writers charged that soldiers were being kept among the people in a time of peace. The troops frequently faced cold stares or open contempt on the streets of the cities and towns. Aristocratic women heatedly condemned these Yankee satraps for expecting a warm welcome into the highest social circles. Although some intersectional marriages took place, soldiers who sought the company of local belles often found doors slammed in their faces.[46]

If the sight of Union soldiers stirred resentment, the seeming arbitrariness of military practice caused greater anger, particularly for civilians unused to martial law. A Charleston clergyman wrote of his horror at seeing former Confederate Treasury Secretary George A. Trenholm sent to jail like a common felon and guarded by a Negro. Citizens in Austin and Millican, Texas, denounced the confinement of leading citizens in large circular stockades exposed to all the ravages of the weather. Yet southerners were hardly helpless. A provost marshal in Lamar County, Texas, told congressional investigators of being assaulted by two to three hundred men during the military trial of a local desperado.[47]

The actions of federal soldiers contributed to arousing local ire. While troops were billeted on the University of Georgia campus, they removed seats from the chapel, dumped their rubbish inside, and chipped the building's columns during bayonet drills and rifle practice. Some soldiers stole civilians' horses, cattle, and cash and made raids on melon patches. The troops in Macon, Georgia, shocked residents there by swimming one Sunday afternoon in a public park without proper attire.[48] Behaving like Visigoths, as some southerners referred to them, may have been the federal soldiers' way of displaying their contempt for their defeated foes.

Cultural encounters between victors and vanquished could become deadly serious. When soldiers got drunk, bloody clashes with citizens and police regularly ensued. A typical row took place in Nashville during the 1866 Christmas holidays. While some bluecoats were drinking in a saloon, a policeman let out a cheer for Jefferson Davis, and a fight broke out. One soldier was shot to death, but the policeman involved later received a promotion in rank.[49]

The primary duty of federal forces in the South was to maintain order—a task that would prove difficult throughout the Reconstruction period. Federal forces filled the role of police; but effective police control depends on the unwritten law that a needed public function is being served and the police should be obeyed. Southerners refused to recognize the legitimacy of this function and therefore were reluctant to obey. As a result, the army in the South faced a variety of disorders. Reconstruction violence tends to conjure up the image of Ku Klux Klan night riders descending on a hapless victim in a small cabin. Reality, however, was much more complex. It is easy to forget that political violence was accompanied by ordinary crime.

These disorders must be examined in their historical context in the aftermath of a long and bloody war. Wars always leave a residue of violent men (for example, the James brothers in Missouri), who cannot return to peaceful pursuits. They find it difficult, as Eric Hoffer says, to "recapture the rhythm of their prewar lives. The readjustment to peace and home is slow and painful, and the country is flooded with temporary misfits."[50] Southern newspaper editors attributed the postwar "crime wave" to the loosening of moral bonds by the war. Demobilization had released on society men accustomed to solving their problems by physical force.[51] It is, of course, impossible to make precise judgments about the effects of the war on southern violence. With no reliable statistics on crime rates and only very sketchy impressionistic evidence, the causal link remains unclear.

Unquestionably, there were enough weapons in the postwar South to wreak havoc. Before the war southerners had put a premium on ability to use firearms—a regional characteristic that survives in the twentieth century.[52] Students of social violence are divided over whether the mere presence of weapons stimulates aggressive behavior,[53] but there is little doubt that many southerners were not only able but willing to use their guns. One federal soldier described the typical Texan, who carried "a large bowie knife and revolver strapped to him." Persons traveling on steamboats or by rail casually packed guns. Young boys and men alike went about with revolvers bulging beneath their coats. In Mississippi, even prisoners entered courtrooms heavily armed, which may give some indication of the quality of justice in that state.[54]

Outlaws and bands of desperadoes infested many areas. Some claimed to be "regulators" attempting to restore law and order, but in fact they exploited the turbulent condition of postwar society for their own advantage. Livestock and agricultural produce were favorite targets of these bands. In Louisiana and Texas, outlaws roamed unchecked because communities there lacked even a semblance of government. Thieves and cutthroats attacked and killed law enforcement officers with impunity.[55]

Whether this random, criminal violence had any connection with politics is hard to determine. Crimes of passion and revenge had not been uncommon in the antebellum era, and the war created new scores to settle. Union men and former Confederates alike appeared willing to continue their blood feuds after Appomattox. As a minority in most parts of the former Confederacy, natives with Union sympathy were subject to persecution. They claimed that traitors were again in control and that they now had no more freedom to express their views in public or even quietly go about their business than during the heyday of the rebellion. They charged rebel officeholders with driving them from their homes and failing to protect them from bandits and marauders, and they pleaded with northern politicians to reduce the southern states to territories for the immediate future.[56]

Union loyalists claimed it was unsafe for them to live in the South. Provisional Governor Andrew Jackson Hamilton of Texas reported persecution so fierce that "human life in Texas is not to day worth as much, so far as law or protection can give value to it, as that of domestic cattle." A Florida minister told of a class of young boys who "would put a bowie-knife or a bullet through a northern man as soon as they would through a mad dog." Some Union men visited Washington, where they filled the ears of sympathetic congressmen with gruesome tales of suffering and woe. But lodging complaints could be dangerous. In September 1866, Albion W. Tourgée, an Ohioan who had recently settled in North Carolina, graphically described to a convention of southern loyalists meeting in Philadelphia how the bodies of fifteen

Negroes had been dragged from a pond in Guilford County. He added that twelve hundred former Union soldiers had been forced to sell their property and flee the state. On his return to North Carolina, Tourgée was subjected to verbal abuse and threats against his life.[57]

Tennessee in particular remained a running battleground between Unionists and rebels with armed bands patrolling various sections of the state. If the federal troops were withdrawn, Governor William G. "Parson" Brownlow predicted, no loyal man would be safe. Union men brought damage suits against former Confederates with Brownlow's encouragement and in some cases ambushed and killed southern sympathizers. The governor sought to organize a state militia to protect "loyal" men from "rebel" persecution, but his opponents suspected that the "Parson" intended to use these forces to harass his political enemies.[58]

Warnings by Union men of an impending blood bath in the South went largely unheeded. The state governments established under the Johnson administration were either unwilling or unable to stop the outrages. Few persons were prosecuted for crimes against loyal men except in Tennessee. Disputes erupted between state officials and the military over the the extent of martial law, and the reestablishment of civil courts left Unionists with little protection. Local authorities had even less power or inclination to arrest the perpetrators of violence, particularly where well-organized gangs operated.[59]

Federal troops likewise proved to be no panacea for the Unionists' ills. By the time detachments reached places where disturbances had been reported, they found everything quiet, thus raising doubts about the authenticity of the reports. Infantry units were ineffective against mounted criminal bands. Nor was the mere presence of troops an effective deterrent to violence. In isolated instances, desperadoes fired on soldiers and drove them off. Officers sometimes listened sympathetically to former rebels and gave little weight to loyalist pleas for protection.[60]

The extent to which Union men suffered from "rebel" persecution remains controversial. Undoubtedly, some loyalists greatly embroidered their stories for northern consumption and for political purposes. Indeed, the running debate over outrages against loyal men set a pattern of response for the rest of the Reconstruction period. Conservative spokesmen consistently denied the truth of tales of intimidation and violence against Unionists and northern immigrants, claiming that anyone could travel from Virginia to Texas without danger of molestation. They feared that the northern people would never learn the truth from radical newspapers and periodicals such as the *New York Tribune* and *Harper's Weekly*. The *New Orleans Picayune* estimated that only one in twenty reports of southern outrages had any basis in fact and that one had been significantly exaggerated.[61]

The South in the early years of Reconstruction remained sullen and defiant, her leaders convinced that they had met all the terms of surrender and were entitled to readmission to the Union. A North Carolina editor trumpeted the need for a "union of equals" in which the South's rights were respected by the rest of the country. Conservatives accused northerners of bad faith and hypocrisy in singing paeans to the integrity of the Union and then doing their best to keep the South out of the national compact. The South had acted, Wade Hampton informed President Johnson, in good faith and would abide by all the laws of the land and fulfill all the terms of restoration, but she could not declare that her cause had been unjust. However many sacrifices the South might make, she would not disgrace herself by entering any "left-handed alliance" with the North in which she was a distinctly inferior partner.[62]

Hampton spoke for a majority of white southerners whose surrender to federal authority was qualified at best. To dwell on differences between so-called moderates and diehard supporters of the "Lost Cause" is to miss the point. A careful dissection of the statements of both groups reveals an underlying consensus in favor of making as few concessions to the Yankees as possible. As heirs to a long tradition of violent action, frustrated by the "oppressive" and "arbitrary" policies of the Congress, southerners stood ready to resist any fundamental restructuring of their society. This resistance, in addition to its disruptive effects on the process of political readjustment, created new tensions in southern society that along with the explosive race question led naturally to bloodshed. To alter Clausewitz's famous dictum, for the South, peace became war carried on by other means.

2. The Specter of Saint-Domingue

The two men could not have been more unlike. Alexander H. Stephens, vice-president of the Confederacy, had been the leading constitutional thinker in the South since the death of John C. Calhoun; Lieutenant George O. Sanderson, a native of Massachusetts, had come south with the federal army and became a Freedmen's Bureau agent in North Carolina. Yet Stephens's heritage and Sanderson's experiences reveal a great deal about the most critical problem of the postwar South. On March 21, 1861, in Savannah, Georgia, Stephens delivered what became known as his "Cornerstone" speech. In discussing the new Confederate constitution, Stephens argued that the South had abandoned the founding fathers' ideas about the equality of man: "Our new government is founded upon exactly the opposite idea; its foundations are laid, its cornerstone rests upon the great truth, that the negro is not equal to the white man; that slavery—subordination to the superior race—is his natural and normal condition." In his official position after the war Sanderson experienced the practical application of Stephens's truism in southern life. One morning an enraged county judge stormed into his office. The judge asked the northerner how much effrontery he would have to stand from the freedmen. Sanderson sought to calm his visitor and learn the cause of his anger. The man stated that one of Sanderson's black soldiers, an "infernal nigger," had marched past his home and had said "good morning" to him. Sanderson naturally wondered why a simple, courteous greeting had evoked such a heated response. The judge then gave the Yankee a pointed lesson in racial etiquette. He told Sanderson that his slaves had never addressed him unless spoken to and that he would not submit to the outrage of a black man speaking to him first. Both Stephens's speech and Sanderson's story capture the essence of southern racial ideology: the black man must always remain in a subservient position, and the most trivial incident could provoke a vigorous reaction.[1]

The consensus on the question was unswerving and unequivocal. If the central theme of southern history, as U. B. Phillips argued, was the persistent effort to keep the South a white man's country, then Reconstruction marked the continuation and expansion of this crusade. Former Confederates, still reeling from their recent military collapse, repeated to themselves the familiar catechism of white supremacy. They called forth all of American history to prove that the nation and the government rested on a firm foundation of white hegemony. Governor Benjamin F. Perry drove the point home in a message to the South Carolina legislature. The radical Republicans, he said, forgot that the United States always had been and forever would be a white man's country and that even the Supreme Court in its landmark Dred Scott decision had declared that the Negro was not and could not become a citizen. So far as many white southerners were concerned, the Civil War had not altered this arrangement.[2]

Despite such agreement, the discussion of the race question was unceasing. In the words of northern reporter Sidney Andrews, "Everyone talks about the negro, at all hours of the day, and under all circumstances. . . . Let the conversation begin where it will, it ends with Sambo." That the most pressing concern among southern whites was the future status of southern blacks should not have been surprising to anyone familiar with the region. Long before the war, that prescient observer of America, Alexis de Tocqueville, had predicted: "The most formidable of all ills that threaten the future of the Union arises from the presence of a black population upon its territory."[3] Slavery had dominated the thoughts, actions, and dreams of the antebellum South and had loomed like a colossus over southern politics. The institution that had seemed immutable was gone in 1865, but the black people remained.

Deep passions overrode rationality. Even slaveholders who accepted the reality of emancipation thought they could expect compensation for their loss. One wildly optimistic North Carolinian believed that the South could easily convince Congress to appropriate $400 million to cover the loss of her slave property. As late as 1869, planters near Port Hudson, Louisiana, kept careful records of the number and value of their slaves lost in the war, waiting for the government to decide to pay off their claims.[4]

For many whites it was an article of faith that much of the old order could be preserved. In particular this meant a paternalistic racial ideology whose roots ran deep in southern society.[5] Proslavery spokesmen had long rejected the idea that an irrepressible conflict existed between capital and labor in favor of an organic view of social relationships. Under a free labor system after emancipation, black labor and white capital shared a common interest in agriculture, and each group remained dependent on the other. Whites and blacks lived in the same country, shared the same climate, spoke the same language, worshiped the same God, ate the same food, and worked in daily contact. If the two races acted properly, they could create a harmonious social structure. James Lusk Alcorn advised whites to avoid racial conflict and to attempt to retain the paternalistic features of the slave system while modifying their ideas and practices to meet the requirements of free labor.[6] Such an ideal required a delicate balancing of conflicting ideas, instincts, and interests that eventually collapsed under the weight of its own contradictions.

Many southerners sincerely avowed that they were the Negro's best friend. They believed their two centuries of dealing with blacks made them experts on the race. Yankee politicians might use the southern Negro for partisan ends, Freedmen's Bureau officials might see the southern blacks as a source of employment for themselves, and fanatical philanthropists might shed crocodile tears over the sufferings of their black brothers—but only white southerners could act in the best interest of both races.[7]

Such assertions ran against the common assumption that free black labor could not succeed. The freedmen, whites quickly informed northern visitors, would never become industrious citizens. Although southerners accepted a social cosmology which, by divine edict, reduced black people to "hewers of wood" and "drawers of water," they could no longer assume that the Negroes accepted this lowly status. By 1866 planters reported that free blacks were of little use on farms and plantations, and some despaired of the South ever recovering her agricultural prosperity.[8]

The missing element in free labor, most farmers agreed, was compulsion. After touring the region for President Johnson, Carl Schurz estimated that nineteen out of twenty southern whites believed that only physical force could make the Negro into a productive worker. William M. Browne caustically commented that "moral elevation, social equality and political superiority do not increase the African's capacity to weed a row." On the basis of his observations of free labor in Texas, Charles Mitchell concluded that the blacks consumed all they made, stole from others, and thereby added nothing to the wealth of the country.[9] However defective these statements were as economic analysis, they carried the force of unswerving conviction.

The southern pessimism about black workers rested on a firm foundation of racism. Prejudice generates its own language. To white southerners, "black" and "Negro" were what Gordon Allport has called "labels of primary potency," that is, words that by themselves conjured up a variety of irrational emotions and fears. The stereotyping produced by prejudice further widened the chasm between blacks and the dominant white society. A prime example is a description by a delegate to the South Carolina constitutional convention of 1865 of the Negro as an animal, "a higher sort of animal, to be sure, than the dog or the horse, but, after all, an animal." In this view, the black was by nature a lazy creature with only hazy ideas about anything except physical comfort. Some commentators questioned whether this distinctly inferior race could ever be assimilated into southern society, and a few still favored black colonization to Africa, Mexico, or the desert regions of the United States.[10]

Using arguments that were at once sincere and self-serving, conservatives maintained that emancipation had caused a deterioration of the black race. Refurbishing the old rationalizations of proslavery ideology, whites contended that of all men the free Negro was the most miserable. Freedom had proved a curse rather than a blessing to the once happy slaves. The free blacks, by this line of exposition, were incapable of fulfilling their own needs and would either lapse into barbarism or sicken and die, thus becoming the unwitting victims of the abolitionists' unworkable social theories.[11]

Although most planters reluctantly experimented with free labor and some even praised the efficiency of the freedmen, most were psychologically unable to deal with blacks as autonomous individuals. They expected the same humble obedience from the freedmen that they had demanded from their slaves. Accustomed to having their slightest whim satisfied by their bondsmen, they were appalled at the "insolence" of free blacks. A few hot-tempered whites shot blacks who did not show the proper subordination, and most insisted the blacks receive harsh treatment without murmur, protest, or resistance. A Freedmen's Bureau officer reported that whites drafted labor contracts containing provisions for fines against Negroes who were disrespectful or impolite and prohibitions against their leaving the fields without the employer's permission.[12]

Whites saw emancipation as the beginning of a revolutionary upheaval in society and a breakdown in the structure of race relations. Allen Grimshaw, one of the most perceptive students of modern racial violence, has pointed out that systems of racial subordination such as existed in the antebellum South are "fundamentally unstable" and therefore subject to periodic challenge. When the accommodative structure of race relations comes under serious attack, as it obviously did during the early years of Reconstruction, the probability of violence increases.[13] The hypersensitivity of conservatives to any change in the pattern of race relations and their determination to restore white hegemony gave enormous significance to every alteration in traditional folkways.

Apparently minor incidents often illustrated the wrenching nature of the revolution. A South Carolina minister returned to his home to find it guarded by a black soldier who denied his right to enter. When the preacher ordered the soldier to give way under threat of force, the sentry scratched his head, scraped his feet, and said, "Yes, boss, go in." An Alabama planter whose black workers greeted him as "General" reflected that only a short time earlier they would have said, "Good morning, master." Shortly thereafter, he hailed a freedman on the highway, calling, "Howdy, uncle." The black replied, "I ain't no 'uncle,' sah, I'se your ekal [equal]." Loss of the amenities of former days often infuriated whites. In East Tennessee blacks who resented being called "boy" or "Buck" had pistols shoved against their heads and were forced to assume a more humble demeanor.[14]

Fearful of a possible racial war, a few planters refused to recognize emancipation or to allow their former slaves to leave the plantations. Freedmen attempting to flee were beaten, mutilated, and in a few instances killed. Some landowners declined to make contracts with blacks, threatened them with reenslavement, forbade their departure from their employers' lands, and kept the most recalcitrant ones in chains. Federal military and Freedmen's Bureau officials reported the kidnapping of black children, the use of Negroes in county chain gangs, and the arrest of blacks for trifling offenses so they could be leased out to whites.[15]

The social instability of the postwar South was exacerbated by economic uncertainty because southern agriculture entered a chronic depression that would continue for the rest of the century. The sharecropping system was a compromise between the demands of whites for control over black labor and the desire of blacks for independence from direct white supervision. This settlement, however, satisfied neither party. Southern agriculture was not competitive in world markets, and blacks failed to obtain an economic stake in the New South. Yet as Jonathan Wiener has demonstrated, the planter class persisted and maintained its economic, political, and social hegemony.[16]

Labor contracts, sharecropping agreements, and black codes were a result of economic hardship and instability but were also the logical culmination of years of proslavery polemics and paternalistic rhetoric. But, though reflecting social consensus among whites, these laws did not always mirror the reality of southern race relations. Although only a few states allowed even limited corporal punishment by employers, some whites were loath to give up the lash as a tool of labor discipline.

They continued to flog unruly blacks with cowhide whips and punished infractions by chains, the pillory, and hanging by the thumbs. In the Louisiana interior, black women were still stripped naked and whipped by white men. Planters who used such methods to keep "their" Negroes in line became enraged when the freedmen had the temerity to complain to federal provost marshals.[17]

Local officials joined planters in authorizing physical penalties for black criminals. In some communities the courts decreed a public whipping as the proper punishment for blacks convicted of petty larceny, whereas whites found guilty of the same offense paid only a small fine. Magistrates sentenced black offenders to work on chain gangs, to be pilloried, or to stand in a public square with a placard reading "thief" hanging around their necks. Blacks could find little justice in local courts, and the Freedmen's Bureau and the army were often unwilling or unable to intercede on their behalf.[18]

Justice appeared to be blind to crimes by whites against blacks. Courts seldom heard complaints involving white assaults on blacks because officials helped white defendants escape prosecution. Local authorities did little to apprehend roving bands of whites who killed freedmen, and in many communities the murder of a black person was not considered a serious crime. If arrests were made, white mobs released the guilty parties, and in the rare conviction of a white man for an assult on or murder of a freedman, the punishment was usually minimal or ludicrous. John Bate of Marianna, Florida, guilty of a vicious attack on a black woman, was sentenced only to pay court costs and a fine of five cents. The combination of public apathy, uneven justice, and inefficient or prejudiced officials made prosecuting whites for crimes against blacks almost impossible. General Philip Sheridan summed up the situation: "My own opinion is that the trial of a white man for the murder of a freedman in Texas would be a farce."[19]

One could gain the impression that the entire South was an armed camp with murders an everyday occurrence. Certainly large areas of the former Confederacy were relatively peaceful and enjoyed reasonably diligent and efficient law enforcement. Many white citizens must have privately deplored persecution of the freedmen, but their failure to denounce such acts publicly virtually ensured federal intervention.

Blacks as well as southern Union men saw the army as their only source of protection. Scores of witnesses testified before the Joint Committee on Reconstruction that the withdrawal of federal troops from the South would lead to a racial massacre. But the soldiers could provide only limited assistance. Commanders did not have enough men at their disposal to respond to all requests for help, and in remote areas of many states, no soldiers were available.[20]

Because many of the outbreaks of violence in the early Reconstruction period seem random and capricious, analysis is difficult. Allen Grimshaw has categorized racial violence into four types: spontaneous brawls, attacks by groups of one race on isolated members of the other, a full-scale assault of one race on the other, and random assaults and stabbings.[21] Although he applies these categories primarily to urban disturbances, they fit the patterns of racial conflict in the rural South. To connect each incident with the politics or the social upheaval of Reconstruction, however, would oversimplify a complex series of events. Besides ordinary criminal activity, grisly episodes of psychotic and sadistic violence, sometimes involving mutilation, occurred. Race may not have been the motivating factor in all cases of white assaults on blacks; indeed, experimental evidence indicates that some demented individuals are stimulated by the terror and pain of their victims to commit additional acts of cruelty.[22]

Yet most of the outrages whites committed against blacks were related to race control. Whites were determined, as one man told Whitelaw Reid, to keep the freedmen from becoming "saucy." A citizen of Concord, North Carolina, overheard blacks bragging that someday they would rule whites: "The niggers that talk like that'll get killed certain," he commented, "the people won't stan' that kind o' talk." Violations of minor points of racial etiquette raised the hackles of sensitive southerners. In Greenville, South Carolina, a black man, walking with a woman on the sidewalk, refused to step aside when he met several young white men. This breach of southern racial customs led the whites to chase the Negro and stab him twice. The violence quickly escalated. Blacks armed with clubs roamed the streets, a fire of mysterious origin broke out that night, and white citizens formed a volunteer company to patrol the streets.[23] This sense of punctilio combined with the southern concept of individual honor made each such confrontation potentially bloody.

Raw emotions readily translated into the political conviction that white men must always govern the South, and there was no more explosive question in postbellum politics than black suffrage. Alarmed former Confederates predicted social and political chaos in the wake of Negro enfranchisement. Blacks could vote freely, candid men admitted, only if United States troops were stationed at every polling place in the South. Angry whites raised the old chimeras of social equality and a war of the races as the probable consequences of black suffrage, and polemicists conjured up the familiar phantoms of Negro rule and the amalgamation of the races. A few southerners admitted that they would rather see blacks dead than share the vote with them.[24]

Nevertheless, southern leaders knew that northern politicians were likely to make Negro suffrage a precondition for readmission to the

Union. Southern politicians exhorted the people to stand by the Constitution and resist all Republican attempts to shackle the South with a black electorate. A restored Union, they argued, should not be purchased at the price of dishonor; the South should never voluntarily participate in her own degradation. Governor David S. Walker advised the Florida legislature that it would be better for the state to remain out of the Union than "go back 'eviscerated of her manhood,' despoiled of her honor, recreant of her duty, without her self-respect; and of course without the respect of the balance of mankind—a miserable thing, with seeds of moral and political death in herself, soon to be communicated to all her associates." Ninety-nine out of every one hundred whites, a Richmond editor estimated, preferred military rule to black suffrage.[25]

Conservatives prophesied that if the doctrines of Thaddeus Stevens and his radical cohorts prevailed, a race war would begin. As one North Carolinian put it, the sudden unleashing of the Negro hordes on the South and the attempt to elevate them to a level of political equality with their former masters would create a "spirit of exterminating violence toward the black race." The weaker race would be destroyed, and Negroes would become as rare in the South as Indians or buffaloes. Northerners might chide and scoff as southerners raised the ancient cry of racial warfare, but, however unrealistic such a danger was in fact, the specter loomed real in the minds of many.[26]

The struggle for political supremacy was in part a contest to control southern wealth—a wealth consisting primarily of land. During and shortly after the war, the army and the Freedmen's Bureau had turned over to the freedmen lands deserted by rebels, mainly on the Sea Islands of South Carolina. Later the government restored the confiscated lands to their former owners. Nevertheless, this brief period of land-ownership led some blacks to believe that the promise of "forty acres and a mule" was more than a mirage. Yankee sharpers took advantage of this faith and sold Negroes painted sticks that they purported would give a person the plot of ground on which he stuck the stick. Other con men peddled phony deeds.[27]

Firmly convinced that the government would give them land at Christmas time, many blacks in late 1865 refused to sign contracts for the coming year. Planters complained that freedmen believed false rumors and were holding out for higher wages to test their overblown expectations of freedom's bonanza. The blacks remained wary of their old masters and waited for months before making any permanent work arrangements. Whites expected the Negroes to labor more willingly once their hopes of receiving free land were dashed.[28]

The freedmen's increasingly sullen manner and their oft-expressed desire to acquire their masters' lands stirred up old fears of a black insurrection. Although many whites scoffed at the idea of blacks seizing land by force, others prepared for the worst. Nervous southerners listened to every half-baked tale about idle and turbulent Negroes roaming the countryside and gathering at military posts awaiting the day of revolution. The alarm spread quickly in the South Carolina lowcountry, where whites had reason to suspect that the freedmen might attempt to expel them from their property. In portions of the state, federal troops forcibly ejected from the plantations blacks who refused to work or sign contracts.[29]

Although the Freedmen's Bureau sought to dispel rumors of a land giveaway, southerners accused its agents and black soldiers of spreading such promises, circulating radical propaganda, and encouraging insurrection. These men supposedly prevented the freedmen from working and convinced them of their right to live in luxuriant idleness.[30]

The inclusion of black troops in the list of southern bogeymen was no afterthought. Whites resented the Negro soldiers more than any other group of "aliens" and condemned them in unmeasured terms. One elderly man in Wilmington, North Carolina, on seeing a column of Negro soldiers parading down a street, expressed his outrage and detestation by calling for the angel Gabriel to blow his trumpet and sound the coming of the Apocalypse. The stationing of black troops in the South, Carl Schurz argued, would have the salutary effect of driving home to the whites the realization that their former slaves were now free, but most southerners interpreted placing these soldiers in their communities as a deliberate and premeditated insult. Editors and politicians vented their anger against the policy in vitriolic and often incoherent tirades. To see their former slaves marching about armed, lording it over white people, was more than the calmest white man could stomach. The ubiquitous Negro troops became a painful reminder of the South's humiliation. Projecting their own emotions onto the objects of their wrath, conservatives accused the black soldiers of stirring up racial hatred and harboring a secret passion to avenge themselves against the former slaveholders.[31]

Black soldiers supposedly had a pernicious influence on the freedmen, encouraging their suspicions against their employers and disinclination to work. These uniformed blacks were transforming orderly and contented servants into surly and violent vagabonds, luring idle freedmen to their camps, and recruiting valuable field hands into their regiments. Describing at length the nearly total demoralization of black labor in areas garrisoned by the Negro soldiers, southern governors pleaded with President Johnson for their immediate removal. Planters upbraided the army for deliberately enlisting the most vicious former slaves and sending them into the countryside to pillage and intimidate peaceful citizens.[32]

White accounts held that the black soldiers greatly contributed to local crime. The most common complaint was that, reflecting the congenital defects of their race, these troops were persistent thieves. Livestock, foodstuffs, and any portable goods were unsafe in their vicinity. They frequently got drunk and made noisy forays into towns, firing their guns and threatening lives. Fights often broke out near saloons between Negro troops and whites when members of both parties were well fortified with alcohol. Perhaps exploiting their new position of authority, the bluecoats treated citizens rudely on the streets, insulted women and children, and drove people off the sidewalks. Such confrontations led to angry words and occasional bloodshed. Black soldiers were no doubt sometimes harsh and undiplomatic when arresting whites, but whites often shot at Negroes who were peacefully performing their duty. Most whites were so outraged by the mere appearance of these black troops in their midst that a trivial incident could spark a serious disturbance.[33]

Investigations of the many white attacks on black soldiers seldom revealed any discernible motive other than resentment. Clashes between local police and militia units and black soldiers usually took place near saloons when police attempted to disarm the Negroes. In Knoxville, Tennessee, a black private halted one Colonel Dyer (apparently a former Confederate officer). When Dyer reached into his pocket for identification papers, the black sentry, assuming he was reaching for a weapon, shot and killed him. An angry mob seized the black man, strung him up in front of the Freedmen's Bureau office, then cut him down, carried him to the local army commander's office, and hanged him again. The soldier died after forty minutes of agony. The mob draped a placard on the body that read: "Hung to show the niggers and Freedmen's Bureau Nigger Officers what it takes to make a true Tennessean and whether they'd be run over or not."[34]

Rumors of land distribution, the presence of black soldiers, and numerous local disturbances all created fear of an insurrection among southerners in the summer and fall of 1865. Following the pattern of earlier slave revolt scares, this new series of alarms focused on incendiary outsiders ("radical emissaries") and aggressive blacks (particularly soldiers).[35] Whether these fears were realistic is less important than the perception of danger. The belief that a black revolt was possible illustrates the schizophrenic aspect of the white evaluation of black character and personality. On the one hand, planters traditionally portrayed their black slaves as shuffling, childlike Sambos, who in their limited way had fully accepted the system of white paternalism.

On the other hand, in times of crisis, whites were convinced that even a quiet Negro was a potential Nat Turner, ready to raise the red flag of revolt and begin a general slaughter of the whites. They feared that their homeland might become a new Saint-Domingue with a native Toussaint L'Ouverture establishing a black republic.[36]

Several signs indicated impending revolution: freedmen were buying arms, forming military companies, and drilling late into the night. Rumors spread that large arms caches were being stored for the day of the uprising. In rural communities, farmers complained of armed black marauders stealing and slaughtering livestock and in some cases shooting women and children.[37]

Conservatives charged radical incendiaries with inciting the blacks to revolt by spreading false rumors of their eventual reenslavement. According to newspaper reports, northern Jacobins drilled armed blacks and trained them to slaughter whites. Editors charged that native Union men, such as William W. Holden in North Carolina, encouraged political agitation among blacks and fomented bad blood between the races for their own benefit.[38]

This paranoia sometimes produced ludicrous denouements. In August 1865 frightening rumors spread through the South Carolina low-country when a group of freedmen united to defend their watermelon patches against thieves. One Tennessee preacher sat up all night with a gun by his side until frightened by the appearance of a solicitous Negro who wondered why he was still awake. When a detachment of federal troops investigated reports of a planned uprising in the Teche country of Louisiana, the only incendiary organization they could find was a group of black children playing with wooden swords. Army commanders found much of their time wasted by receiving delegations of anxious whites with bloodcurdling tales. Some whites blanched at a sullen look on the face of a freedman, jumped at every mysterious noise, and interpreted any sign of disobedience as the beginning of the revolution.[39]

Many southerners, of course, discounted such apocalyptic fears. The wild stories clashed with their conception of the docile and subservient Negroes. Others thought that the blacks had more sense than to rise against overwhelming odds. Rational and temperate citizens demanded proof of danger before following the lead of timid rumormongers. Yet even those whites who scoffed at the reported plots and ridiculed those fainthearted souls who believed in them advised vigilance and preparation for any contingency.[40]

Under persistent white pressure, Freedmen's Bureau agents and army officers investigated many insurrection reports. Most of them were found to be based on hearsay or the exaggerations of fevered imaginations. Clinton B. Fisk, an assistant commissioner in the bureau, carefully checked on several terrifying reports in Tennessee and northern Mississippi. His talks with members of both races revealed no evidence of an uprising, but he learned that the Mississippi panic began when whites saw a Negro marching through the woods shooting squirrels with a fowling piece. Whites, who were themselves heavily armed, became fearful at the sight of a black carrying a gun.[41]

Southerners responded to the rumors by forming county patrols and "home guards" to ferret out black rebels and crush any incipient rebellion by picketing the roads and disarming passing blacks. Negroes' weapons were seized, including hunting pieces and useless old guns. Going far beyond precautionary measures, the vigilantes forcibly entered freedmen's homes, stole their money, and assaulted them. Black petitioners protested that local authorities in Florida confiscated their weapons and required any black who wished to own a gun to get a pass from a white man signed by a probate judge. These freedmen asked Secretary of State William H. Seward how they could truly be free under such conditions. The local patrol, one Virginian admitted, "keeps perfect order and makes them [the blacks] stand in some fear."[42]

In many places quasi-military organizations were not deemed adequate to keep the peace, and southerners wanted to revive their old state militias. Pointing to increasing black crime and disorder, Mississippi Governor William L. Sharkey began to organize state militia units in August 1865. Sharkey assured President Johnson that this could be done with "perfect safety" and that it "would have a good effect in the other states and certainly here." On August 24, Major General Henry W. Slocum, commander of the Department of Mississippi, issued a general order forbidding the formation of militia in the state. Slocum, obviously piqued that Sharkey had not consulted him, stated that he could not allow young former Confederates to patrol counties garrisoned by black troops and to defy army orders on the treatment of the freedmen. Most victims of violence, the general claimed, were Union men and blacks. Johnson at first upheld Slocum, but Sharkey objected that the troops in Mississippi, especially the black soldiers, were unable or unwilling to maintain order. On August 30, Johnson wrote to Carl Schurz that he favored militia organizations in the southern states and that the military authorities could easily prevent their committing any outrages. Over the protests of Schurz, who said the militia was being used to oppress loyalists and freedmen, the president rescinded Slocum's order. Sharkey triumphed, and his successor, Benjamin G. Humphreys, organized militia units in anticipation of a black insurrection during the Christmas holidays.[43]

Other states quickly followed Mississippi's lead, and letters poured into the offices of southern governors asking for permission to organize militia units or stating that companies had already been established. Planters asked for militiamen to force Negroes to sign labor contracts and to quell possible insurrections. If the blacks pursued a course of vengeance against the whites, Governor William W. Holden of North Carolina warned, they would "be visited with swift and condign punishment."[44]

Many militia companies marched through the countryside and illegally seized arms, offering the excuse that they were preventing a rebellion. Army commanders saw through this smoke screen and issued orders forbidding any further confiscation of weapons. Militiamen engaged in personal vendettas, robbed Negroes of their private property, and shot freedmen who attempted to stop these depredations. Schurz, with some justification, pointedly described the militia in the South as having but one purpose: "the restoration of the old patrol system which was one of the characteristic features of the regime of slavery."[45]

The 1865 holiday season passed quietly without the greatly feared Negro insurrection. Disturbances generally arose only when whites disarmed and assaulted Negroes. Were the cries of a new Saint-Domingue mere pretext to justify the persecution of the freedmen? It may have been for some whites, but others sincerely believed that their former slaves were ready to wreak vengeance for their years of bondage. Their response was a brutal suppression of freedmen that gave new and striking evidence of white southerners' determination to maintain racial control.

Besides militia units and county patrols, irregular bands of marauders and desperadoes preyed on blacks. Such attacks were often unprovoked and against inoffensive individuals. Mounted outlaws and "regulators" rode about the countryside whipping, hanging, and murdering blacks, immune to capture by local authorities or federal soldiers. Driving freedmen from their homes and threatening witnesses with swift retribution, they perpetrated such punishments as lashing their victims on their bare backs with cowhide whips. In Pitt County, North Carolina, a group of former Confederate soldiers met a black man on the road, castrated him, and later killed him. A ruffian in Edgefield, South Carolina, claimed to have cut ears off eight Negroes and carried the lobes in an envelope to display to friends and acquaintances.[46]

The mutilations, burnings at the stake, drownings, and display of limbs and skulls as "trophies" of battle created what some whites termed a "healthy" fear in black communities. Rowdies in Chapel Hill, North Carolina, pummeled an old black man for exhibiting "magic lantern pictures" that had abolition themes. Mobs, sometimes assisted by police, attacked Negro parades. In Texas, blacks were killed for failing to remove their hats when passing a white man, for carrying letters to the Freedmen's Bureau, and for resisting whippings of themselves or their wives. One brute enjoyed watching the Negroes "kick" after they were shot and thought the freedmen should be "thinned out."[47]

The black response to these incidents has been virtually unexplored. Obviously, the freedmen were aware that resistance to outrages would lead to swift and strong retaliation. Black retribution shocked even sympathetic whites, who generally counseled blacks to restraint if not acquiescence. Yet against great odds and under great provocation, some blacks did fight back. When students at the University of North Carolina joined with other citizens to attack a Negro meeting, they discovered that some freedmen were not the obsequious, shuffling Sambos of plantation legend. The blacks counterattacked with sticks until the students and townspeople beat a hasty retreat.[48] Although the extent of black resistance during Reconstruction is impossible to determine, there were enough incidents to reaffirm white convictions that emancipation was leading to revolution.

Southern apologists have normally minimized the extent of violence against blacks, whereas revisionist historians have emphasized it as a major characteristic of the period. Incomplete data preclude a numerical analysis of the incidents. Army officers and Freedmen's Bureau agents reported numerous outrages against blacks from the end of the war up to the passage of the first Reconstruction Act, but not all attacks were included, and some probably were reported erroneously.[49] Regardless of the exact figures, a substantial number of robberies, assaults, rapes, and murders were committed against freedmen, and little or no action was taken against the guilty parties.[50]

The quantity of violence is certainly of less significance than the causes. There is no doubt that the economic, social, and psychological impact of emancipation and the whites' determination to maintain the racial upper hand contributed to the bloodshed, but a more fundamental aspect of racism was at work. The common belief among whites that black people were not fully human has traditionally served as a powerful justification for aggression against Negroes. In any society, the devaluation of human life can lead to violence.[51]

Northern visitors to the postwar South were shocked to hear whites talk of killing a Negro in the same tone they would have used to discuss killing a dog. In certain quarters, murdering a freedman became a matter of pride, and men spoke freely of their desire to see the black race exterminated. One Tennessean casually remarked in the middle of a personal letter that although the Negroes in his neighborhood were working fairly well, "they have had to be shot sometimes." A Jackson, Mississippi, newspaper reported two murders in one day, one of a white man by a freedman and the other of a black by a white. In the first instance, the editor commented, "No efforts will be spared to bring the black fiend to a certain and summary death." In the second case, the reporter simply noted that the provocation for the killing must have been "very great."[52] Such extreme views probably did not represent the preponderance of white opinion, but a silent majority too often let its more extreme elements speak for it. When whites excused atrocious crimes, they made the victims responsible for their own suffering. By assigning all culpability to the blacks, whites could escape responsibility and justify their own aggressive behavior.[53]

Southern conservatives have traditionally argued, and historians have agreed, that lower-class whites were more hostile to Negroes and therefore more likely to commit acts of violence against them than were members of the old slaveholding class. The poor whites feared that the elevation of the blacks from slaves to citizens would give them new privileges at the whites' expense. As members of the master race, at least in proslavery ideology, lower-class whites possessed an intense racial pride and sense of superiority. No matter how low his economic status or how great the social distance from his planter neighbor, the poor white knew, in the words of Wilbur Cash, that "come what might, he would always be a white man."[54] Yet to accuse common whites of a particular animus against blacks would be both a rationalization and an oversimplification of a complex social situation. Even among the so-called aristocracy, habit and prejudice often triumphed over humanitarian or paternalistic impulses, and upper-class whites condoned if they did not participate in attacks on the freedmen. The pulpit, the press, and the upper echelons of southern society occasionally issued mild condemnations of the outrages but took no effective action to stop them. One North Carolina editor warned of the danger of unleashing the aggressive instincts of the nonslaveholding classes and pledged the best efforts of the southern elite to protect the rights of both the common whites and the Negroes. He concluded, however, that the southern leadership would stand by its own race in a crisis: "In this matter, the South is a unit, and will remain so."[55]

The indistinction of class lines on racial matters demonstrates how social norms contributed to violence. The outrages persisted because the dominant elements of white society at least tacitly approved them. As disorders multiplied, each new incident shored up society's rationalizations for violence as a legitimate method of control.[56] The cycle of frustration followed by aggression clearly operates differently in different cultures, and in the South cultural forces stimulated a violent response, particularly to racial frustration.[57] During the early years of

Reconstruction, the South was wracked by potential and actual racial conflict, and her very existence seemed threatened by wanton acts of terrorism.

It became only a question of time before tensions exploded into a full-scale racial conflagration. In Norfolk, Virginia, a busy port, a naval yard, and a large number of saloons resulted in disorder under normal circumstances. The influx of blacks from the countryside added another explosive element. Norfolk was rocked both by racial conflict and by bloody clashes between Union men and former Confederates. In April 1866, the freedmen planned a parade to celebrate congressional passage of the Civil Rights Act. Many white citizens saw the event as one more in a series of public humiliations. Acutely sensitive about their loss of power and control over the black population, the whites found this new display of assertiveness intolerable. The local army commander, Major F. W. Stanhope, heard rumors that a group of whites planned to attack the procession and alerted his men.[58]

In spite of rainy weather, blacks marched through Norfolk's streets on the morning of April 16. Eyewitnesses estimated that the crowd numbered from two hundred to a thousand, and some were armed. As the Negroes moved toward a speaker's stand to start the festivities, whites hiding behind a wall threw bricks and bottles at them. When the blacks reached the stand, a policeman cursed them and apparently shot a young man. More shooting erupted, and some of the Negroes assaulted white onlookers with sticks and boards. Although whites later testified that the blacks had fired first, they probably began their attack after the policeman had shot the black youth. Witnesses identified one of the white rioters as Robert Whitehurst, a young man who had recently quarreled with some blacks. Whitehurst came out of his house shooting at the blacks, but the mob chased him back inside. Whitehurst's mother begged her son to stop firing, but in a struggle for his gun she was shot dead. Later in the day some Negroes killed Whitehurst.[59]

That night, roving bands of whites, including police and firemen, vowing vengeance on Whitehurst's murderers, nearly started another riot. Major Stanhope's troops patrolled the streets and kept an uneasy peace. Altogether, three whites and two blacks died in the day's rioting. The civil authorities arrested some blacks on flimsy charges, but they were later acquitted. An army board set up to investigate the affair placed equal blame on both races and recommended that Norfolk remain under military occupation for the immediate future. White conservatives declared that the incendiary teachings of radicals and the laxness of the military authorities in allowing the Negroes to march had caused the trouble.[60]

The violence at Norfolk and elsewhere illustrated what some scholars have called the "preservative" nature of American racial violence. Many disorders of the Reconstruction period were attributable to white efforts to maintain the racial status quo. Southern violence before and after Reconstruction was conservative; its goal was to protect the dominant political, economic, social, and psychological position of the white race.[61] The outbreaks of violence during that era also follow a pattern similar to that of twentieth-century racial conflicts. Violence occurred in a transitional period (after a long and bloody Civil War), involved a subordinate social group (blacks), received official sanction (by law enforcement officials, political leaders, and newspaper editors), and often involved organized groups ("regulators" or later the Ku Klux Klan).[62] These patterns changed over time. In the Reconstruction disorders and the race riots of the early twentieth century, whites were the aggressors, but after World War II the rioters were black. The expansion of metropolitan areas made the causes of racial outbreaks more complex and their occurrence less predictable. Likewise, twentieth-century riots have been less overtly political than many of the Reconstruction outbreaks. Yet all of this violence bespeaks the breakdown of authority and the fragmentation of society.

The South seemed to be in a state of rapid decay. Increasing disorder and bloodshed appeared symptomatic of a society in the process of being torn apart. The growing signs of social chaos were unmistakable, but white southerners, always masters of self-delusion, sought to deny the obvious. Newspaper editors accused northern radicals of exaggerating the number of outrages in the South for political effect and asserted that most of the violence was perpetrated by freedmen, white vagabonds (the term "carpetbagger" was not yet in common use), or federal soldiers. Adding that the North was hardly a land of tranquillity, an Alabama editorialist, tongue at least partially in cheek, suggested that a federal bureau be created to investigate murders and other violence in the North. In light of the great upheaval of the Civil War, southerners maintained that the number of crimes and disturbances in the former Confederate states was surprisingly small.[63]

Rationalizations unfortunately could not eliminate the region's endemic racial problems. The uncertain future of southern agriculture and free labor, a hypersensitivity on all racial matters, a continuing paranoia about potential insurrections, and an unbending faith in white supremacy guaranteed that racial disturbances would continue. As William Faulkner has Bayard Sartoris's black companion Ringo observe after learning of his own freedom, "This war ain't over. Hit just started good."[64]

3. The Memphis Race Riot

Racial violence in the Reconstruction South not only reflected the underlying political, economic, social, and psychological tensions of the era but also established patterns for later disturbances. The 1866 race riot in Memphis, Tennessee, became the prototype for twentieth-century race riots.[1] Like many future disorders, the Memphis outbreak took place because the black population in the city had suddenly increased, blacks and whites (in this case Irishmen) competed for scarce jobs, the press greatly exaggerated the extent of black crime, and police often clashed with Negroes.[2]

The Mississippi port of Memphis had a long and well-deserved reputation for disorder. The city was infested with gamblers, prostitutes, thieves, and river pirates and was widely known as a hard-drinking and hard-fighting river town. After suffering only minor damage during the Civil War, Memphis was on the road to economic recovery, and the infusion of northern capital and capitalists would one day make it a leading commercial center of the New South. Even shortly after the surrender, steamboats lined the waterfront, the docks hummed with activity, and the levee was crammed with casks and cotton bales.[3]

Yet this surface prosperity could not obscure deep social conflicts. By the summer of 1865 rebel soldiers were returning to their homes, anxious to resume their former sway in local affairs. Whatever economic benefits northern businessmen might bring to the city, native Memphians resented them as painful reminders of their recent defeat. Old citizens outspokenly condemned the Yankee "invaders" and affirmed their loyalty to the Confederate cause. One malcontent stopped a respectable man on the street, cursed him for having rejoiced in the fall of Atlanta to the federal armies, and thrust a pistol into his face. The citizen felt compelled to give the ruffian a sound caning. Other former

Confederates made similarly sanguinary threats to northern school-teachers and preachers.[4]

The demographic character of Memphis changed dramatically as large numbers of freedmen flocked to the city, leaving some farmers and planters without laborers. The census of 1860 listed 3,882 Negroes in Memphis (17 percent of the total population), but the 1870 enumeration counted 15,741 (39 percent of the total population). Many blacks settled near Fort Pickering in south Memphis either for military protection or in expectation of federal largesse. There a collection of ramshackle houses became a center for contagious disease, vice, and crime and a forerunner of the twentieth-century racial enclave. Freedmen's benevolent societies sought to care for these people but lacked the resources to aid such large numbers. In August 1865, when the Negro population of the city had swelled to between 20,000 and 25,000 persons, whites began to fear insurrection and became seriously alarmed about the overcrowding and crime in the area.[5]

Whites charged the military and the Freedmen's Bureau with supporting idle blacks by providing them with full rations and discouraging them from working for their former owners. Newspapers reported that lazy Negroes roamed the streets, robbed local businesses, and shot off their guns at all hours of the day and night. Editors routinely cited blacks' depredations as evidence of the need for more vigorous law enforcement. Conservatives concluded that some Negroes had become drunk with freedom (if not with liquor) and had not yet learned the difference between liberty and license. The discovery of two black men living with two white women in a shanty in south Memphis turned the whites' worst nightmare into reality. Inflammatory reports of black behavior aroused white citizens and readied them for aggression.[6]

Even under ordinary conditions, Memphis was crime-ridden. The city harbored thieves, gamblers, and prostitutes; public drunkenness, robberies, and murders were on the rise. Because rowdies roamed about the river front, the city council passed a resolution levying heavy fines against persons caught wielding slingshots and brass knuckles. The widespread practice of carrying firearms made strolling the streets a dangerous pastime. Irate citizens claimed they were unable to sleep because gunshots were heard throughout the night. Even juveniles went about heavily armed, a habit that sometimes resulted in tragedy. When a group of boys, none older than thirteen and all from "good families," got into an argument, one boy drew a pistol and shot two of his companions, killing one of them. Such incidents controverted reports that abuse of firearms and acts of violence were entirely the work of Negroes. By June 1865 army units patrolled the city each night, arresting armed civilians and quelling disturbances, but even the combination of military protection and regular police patrols failed to stop the lawlessness.[7]

These disturbances were symptomatic of deep cleavages in Memphis society. During the flush times of the 1850s, an elite group of planters, professional men, and merchants had come to dominate a working class consisting of German and Irish immigrants and free Negroes. With the migration of blacks into the city after the war, the Irish in particular found jobs scarce. Fearing competition, Irishmen tried to drive all Negro draymen and hackmen out of the city; the result was an intense hatred that festered and infected both groups. The city's aristocracy viewed this struggle with apathy or disdain. As one witness testified before the congressional committee investigating the Memphis riot, "A great portion of the people were indifferent to the rioting . . . they did not care which whipped, whether the Irish killed off all the niggers, or the niggers killed off all the Irish."[8]

Antebellum Memphis politics had been luridly corrupt. After the war the Irish, with the aid of the state franchise laws, captured most county and municipal offices, including a majority on the city council. The tone of politics was low. The city's mayor, John Park, was often publicly intoxicated and once challenged a hostile newspaper editor to a duel for criticizing his administration. Later, during the riot, Major General George Stoneman reported the mayor "too drunk to talk." The city recorder, John C. Creighton, had been indicted for murdering a drunken man though it is not clear whether the case ever came to trial. With the Irish firmly ensconced in city hall, the freedmen obtained little justice from public officials.[9]

The confrontation between the Irish cop and the black citizen has become a set piece in the history of American race relations. Although the expansion of urban police forces before the war had helped reduce crime in most cities, the lack of professional training and blatant corruption certainly lessened police effectiveness. Police misconduct has been a common cause for racial unrest in American cities,[10] and Memphis was no exception.

The Irish held 180 of 186 positions on the police force and 40 of 46 jobs in the fire department. The chief of police complained that the mayor and police committee made removals and appointments without his knowledge; he candidly conceded his inability to control his men, many of whom were neither sober nor discreet. Even the rare policeman who was dismissed from the force for wrongdoing usually was reinstated by the police committee. The addition of 31 men in February 1866 strengthened the force but had no noticeable effect on either its efficiency or honesty. Memphis editors filled their local news columns with reports of drunken police and their outlandish behavior. Shortly before Christmas in 1865, the *Appeal* disclosed that four policemen had been arrested for mistreating or killing prisoners in their custody. The public showed little inclination to prosecute policemen, however, especially in cases of brutality against blacks. Evidence shows that the predominantly Irish police went out of their way to harass blacks; they often beat and sometimes shot black prisoners while hauling them off to jail or fired at drunken Negroes who fled from them or made even a token resistance to arrest.[11]

The federal troops and the Freedmen's Bureau agents were caught between the police and the freedmen. Some Memphians praised the good conduct of the Yankee soldiers. But drunken troops sometimes clashed with former Confederates, policemen, and the freedmen in fisticuffs and gun battles. The Freedmen's Bureau was almost universally unpopular among whites. The head of the bureau in Memphis, General Benjamin P. Runkle, discouraged vagrancy and forced idle freedmen to seek employment, but his agents and schoolteachers were viewed by many citizens as dangerous incendiaries. During the panic over a possible armed uprising by blacks in December 1865, Runkle never had enough soldiers at his disposal to handle all the complaints made by both races, but at Christmas time he dispatched some troops to patrol the city.[12]

Memphis might have escaped a major race riot had it not been for the final explosive element in the situation: the presence of Negro troops. Since 1863 the city had served as a collection depot for all black soldiers in the western theater of the war, and by the spring of 1866 some four thousand of them remained in the city. These soldiers spent their off-duty hours in the Negro settlement near Fort Pickering, where whiskey was available at almost any grocery store. Drunken men pushed whites off sidewalks, went carousing through the streets late at night, and discharged their weapons at all hours. Black soldiers regularly fought among themselves or attacked passing freedmen near local rum holes. The white officers conceded and the many court-martial orders testify that these men were hardly model soldiers. Whites, of course, exaggerated any untoward actions of uniformed blacks and readily blamed them for unsolved crimes in the city.[13]

The most common complaint against the black troops was petty larceny; grocery stores were their favorite targets. Negro soldiers swaggered into these establishments, grabbed whatever food or whiskey they wanted, brandished their guns at the owners and customers, threatened to shoot if anyone tried to stop them, and gunned down proprietors who resisted them. In one case, black troops set a store on fire after an argument with a grocer. Newspaper reports magnified the seriousness of these affairs, and later courts-martial sometimes exonerated the Negro soldiers. Whites became increasingly incensed over the large number of robberies.[14]

Black soldiers were accused of stabbing and shooting civilians and brutally mistreating citizens whom they had arrested. In January 1866 black troops seized two white men and hauled them before the local Freedmen's Bureau court on theft charges. When one tried to escape, his black guard shot him and then bayoneted him to death where he had fallen. When an angry crowd gathered, one soldier called them "sons of bitches" and defied them to arrest him.[15]

The animosity between the black troops and the Irish police increased during the spring. Negro soldiers tried to arrest policemen guilty of flagrant brutality; the police beat and abused Negro soldiers. When attempting to apprehend black troops or civilians, the police met stiff resistance from the soldiers, who rescued prisoners and sometimes fired at the arresting officers. If police tried to capture blacks during their forays into local shops, they might be overpowered by the troops. In February 1866 officer William Mower, while on foot patrol, met a group of Negro soldiers, one of whom accused Mower of following them. When Mower denied the charge, the soldier called him a "damned liar," pulled out a gun, and mortally wounded him.[16] Any of these clashes could easily have erupted into a serious riot.

The conservative press reflected the general white aversion to the Negro troops. In strident prose, editors denounced the black soldiers for their pernicious influence on the freedmen, their disorderly conduct, and their deliberate insults to respectable citizens. The rabidly unreconstructed *Avalanche* excoriated the Negro troops as the advance agents of radical oppression: "We are to have the black flesh of the negro crammed down our throats; we are to have the black soldier, the black magistrate, the black man's government, and if we cannot stomach it all, we are to be consigned to Hell, and exist within the black drapery of eternal damnation."[17]

In such a charged atmosphere, a tiny spark could set off an explosion. By April 29, 1866, the last regiment of black soldiers in Memphis had been mustered out of service, but many of these men remained in south Memphis waiting for their final pay. The following evening four policemen shoved a group of Negroes off a sidewalk into the street; one black stumbled, and a policeman fell over him. Another policeman struck a black over the head with a pistol but was then hit on the head by a stick wielded by another black. With oaths and threats to renew the fracas at another place and time, the two groups separated, but during the night drunken soldiers roamed the streets firing off their pistols.[18]

On May 1, nearly one hundred discharged soldiers and other blacks began drinking in south Memphis. By the middle of the afternoon, they had gathered along South Street, shouting and firing their guns into the air. About this time two teams of horses, one driven by a white man and the other by a Negro, collided; after exchanging angry words, the drivers came to blows. Some nearby policemen rushed to the scene but met a menacing crowd of black soldiers and freedmen, who started shooting at their Irish nemeses. One policeman died in the brief flurry of gunfire; his enraged comrades quickly ordered up reinforcements. The policemen arrested two black soldiers in the crowd and carried them away, followed by cursing blacks making threatening gestures and discharging weapons into the air. As they approached a bridge on Main Street, the police fired into the crowd, and the Negroes responded in kind. The police managed to drive the mob back but had to retreat again when they ran out of ammunition.[19]

Hearing of trouble in south Memphis and fearing for their families' safety, a few black soldiers left Fort Pickering that evening to aid their comrades in arms. Policemen chased and shot any Negro soldiers they discovered on the streets and, joined by angry civilians, swore to "kill the God damned nigger solders who were fighting here against their rights—the black sons of bitches." After the black troops retreated inside the fort, police began attacking any freedmen they saw. With no longer even a semblance of organization or discipline, the policemen singly and in groups prowled the streets beating and shooting Negroes. One officer urged the mob to kill all "god damned niggers," large and small alike; black prisoners were beaten on their way to the station house. White citizens joined the police in entering the Negro shanties to search for new victims, ransacking the humble dwellings and often shooting the occupants. Ignoring professions of innocence and pleas for mercy, the mob continued to assault helpless blacks well into the night.[20]

Rather than try to stop the mob, the civil officials encouraged them. The mayor as usual was too drunk to take control of the situation, and Recorder Creighton urged the whites to kill every black they could find from the cradle on up. County Sheriff P. M. Winters tried unsuccessfully to disperse the crowd with a posse and joined the mayor in an urgent plea to General Stoneman for soldiers to quell the rioting. Small detachments of troops finally restored order after several hours of mad slaughter.[21]

At dawn on May 2, large numbers of whites (there are no available estimates of the size of this throng) milled about near Fort Pickering, apparently eager to resume the battle. Who fired the first shot is uncertain, and witnesses disagree over whether the black troops fired from inside the fort. Although only a few Negro soldiers briefly left the fort to shoot at the whites, they were anxious to protect their families.

With great difficulty, their white officers prevented them from going out in force to attack. When Negro troops rushed the building where the arms were stored, white soldiers stopped them by firing over their heads. At nine in the morning, someone sounded an alarm, and the melee began anew as citizens ran to their homes for their guns. Since most businesses wisely closed for the day, rioters had to break into gun shops to obtain weapons and ammunition. The mob quickly became intoxicated, and several Irish policemen, swearing to kill all the Negroes, began assaulting blacks. Hearing news of the fighting, armed whites from the countryside poured into Memphis by train.[22]

Sheriff Winters again formed a posse to restrain the crowd, but it arrived long after the battle had gotten out of hand. General Stoneman at first refused to summon troops but finally ordered the posse disbanded and took personal command of the city. Soldiers with loaded rifles and fixed bayonets marched through the streets and dispersed the crowd by one o'clock in the afternoon.[23]

That evening police and civilians swarmed into the Negro quarter near the fort, knocking down doors and robbing and shooting the terrified freedmen. In cruel mockery of white racial ideology, some of these men brutally raped several Negro women. Setting fire to Negro homes, schools, and churches, drunken citizens and police howled like maniacs around the rising flames and shot at blacks trying to escape the burning buildings. Several blacks burned to death in their own homes. The few whites who tried to protect the blacks or dissuade the rioters were ignored or overpowered.[24]

The rioting to this point had followed a pattern remarkably similar to the racial disturbances of the first half of the twentieth century. Beginning with a series of seemingly minor (one might almost say "normal") confrontations between Irish police and blacks, the excitement escalated as a crowd gathered and grew increasingly excited. The crowd rapidly became a mob, lost its critical self-consciousness, and committed barbarities. Unlike the racial disorders of the 1960s, the Memphis riot was met with passivity by civil authorities, who allowed it to proceed until the military intervened.[25]

Sporadic burning and shooting continued on May 3 and 4, but the worst was over. The extent of the carnage was forty-six blacks and two whites killed, seventy to eighty persons wounded, five black women raped, four black churches, twelve black schools, and ninety-one black houses and cabins burned, and more than $130,000 in property damage. Whites continued to threaten the "nigger teachers" with fatal consequences if they did not leave Memphis, and many reluctantly decided to abandon their work.[26]

Following the riot, controversy centered on the role of the military.

On May 1, the first day of significant disturbances, General Stoneman alerted his men to assist the civil authorities. The mayor and other officials asked for troops to aid an armed citizens' patrol, but Stoneman instead sent out small detachments, both to disperse the mob and to keep the enraged black soldiers within the walls of Fort Pickering. When the violence subsided on May 3, Stoneman finally denied permission to form a civilian posse and ordered all armed bodies to disband. After reestablishing order, the general warned Mayor Park that if the civil authorities could not keep peace in Memphis, the military would. But Stoneman had only 150 men to use against the rioters, he had been in no hurry to put them into action, and Freedmen's Bureau agents advised frightened blacks that not enough troops were available to safeguard them. Stoneman deserves some criticism for dilatoriness, but, given the long history of minor outbreaks in the city, the general had no reason to believe that the clashes on April 30 or even the early fighting on May 1 would turn into a full-scale race riot.[27]

There was general agreement that inflammatory stories and editorials in the Memphis press had encouraged racial antagonism to become violence. Freedmen's Bureau investigators condemned the newspapers for instilling a belief in the community that northerners, Negroes, and schoolteachers could be murdered with impunity and blamed such outpourings for stirring up rowdy elements in the city. After the riot was over, local editors blasted the Yankees, and particularly the bureau, for arousing the passions of the freedmen and sustaining the black soldiers in their reign of terror. Adopting a practice that would become common during the Reconstruction period, the perpetrators of violence placed the blame squarely on the victims and their friends.[28]

Even the conservative press repudiated the rioters' most senseless acts: the burning of Negro schools and churches and the attacks on innocent freedmen. In classic paternalistic style, white leaders claimed to have only the kindliest feelings toward the Negroes and held the lower classes (and particularly the Irish) responsible for the terrorism. The editor of the *Argus* characterized these men as the "veriest scum of the community" and blamed the riot on criminal elements in the city. Despite protestations to the contrary, many of the "respectable" people, if not participating in the bloody work, encouraged and secretly applauded the atrocities committed by the police and the white mob.[29] Blaming outrages on the "lower orders" became a standard conservative response to northern bloody shirt waving.

These journalistic apologias provided a familiar explanation for the violence. The real cause of the riot, according to the editors, had been the incendiary behavior of the black soldiers that had fired the passions of turbulent men. The tragedy only intensified the belief in an "irrepressible conflict" between the races and reinforced the necessity for white rule.[30] This pessimistic world view and the justification of savagery as a defense of white civilization generally foreclosed the possibility of public opinion deterring bloodshed.

Such attitudes virtually ensured the rioters immunity from legal action. After the riot, Mayor Park promised General Stoneman that no guilty person would escape punishment. Park affirmed that local whites were best suited to keep the blacks in line because they lacked any "morbid, sickly sentimentalism" about the race and because Memphis was a "law-abiding and Christian community." But, although many of the rioters were well known, city officials made no effort to arrest them. As Memphis judge William Hunter admitted to the congressional investigating committee, no jury was likely to convict white men of crimes against blacks. The army took no action, instead referring the question of military trials to Washington. In the interim, many of the rioters fled the city for parts unknown. Attorney General James Speed advised President Johnson that the government had no jurisdiction to prosecute these individuals before a military tribunal because civil courts in Tennessee were operating. Plans for arresting certain ringleaders came to naught, and Union men claimed that they and their black allies were left at the mercy of the rebels.[31]

Investigations of the riot by the army, the Freedmen's Bureau, and a committee of the House of Representatives produced valuable evidence and testimony but no new or startling conclusions. Congressman Elihu Washburne of Illinois, chairman of the House committee, privately described Memphis Union men as "cowardly and pusillanimous." The committee's Republican majority depicted the riot as a massacre of blacks approved by the press and city officials. Local conservative leaders easily discounted the report as a radical propaganda pamphlet gotten up for the fall election campaign. After describing the findings as a pack of lies manufactured in Washington, the *Avalanche* dismissed the testimony of rape victim Frances Thompson as the tale of an "ugly old strumpet."[32]

Republican politicians intended to make political hay out of the Memphis riot, and the party majority in the House had a thousand copies of the report and testimony and ten thousand copies of the report alone printed for distribution to party stalwarts. The outbreak provided the northern public with fresh evidence of southern treason and the need for federal protection of the freedmen. Moderates and radicals alike agreed that the affair demonstrated the failure of President Johnson's lenient restoration policies and the necessity for black suffrage in the South.[33]

Nevertheless, the political impact of the riot was not nearly as significant as that of the later New Orleans riot. In part, this was a matter of timing; the New Orleans conflagration took place in July, conveniently (for the Republicans) on the eve of a critical congressional election campaign. Also, the Memphis outbreak had little ostensible connection with politics. Memphis exploded because of demography, economics, and deep social conflict rather than for political reasons. The substantial black migration into south Memphis had strained the economic and social resources of the city beyond their limits. The resulting overcrowding, disease, and particularly crime had inevitably produced clashes with civil authority and especially with police. An inflammatory public press, the ethnic and racial hostility between the blacks and the Irish, and the presence of Negro soldiers were the final ingredients in an all too familiar recipe for violence.[34] The origins and course of the Memphis riot had much more in common with twentieth-century urban racial disturbances than with the mostly rural night riding and terrorism of the Reconstruction South. In its own historical context, the Memphis riot reflected the upheaval and disorder of the postwar era. In the time of the Ku Klux Klan, the Knights of the White Camellia, and the White League, it stood out as a fascinating and horrible anachronism. In the age of Watts, Detroit, and Newark, it casts a long shadow across a century.

4. New Orleans and the Emergence of Political Violence

uperficially at least, the New Orleans race riot of July 1866 has some of the same modern characteristics as the Memphis one. In the latter city, however, political grievances contributed little to the outbreak of fighting, whereas in New Orleans, a struggle for political power in the state of Louisiana was the primary cause for the explosion.[1] The New Orleans riot resembles the disorders of the late 1860s and 1870s and is therefore a transitional event in the history of Reconstruction, marking a shift from social and economic disturbances to those based on politics.

By the end of the Civil War, Abraham Lincoln's attempt to restore Louisiana to the Union was floundering badly. His hopes for success had rested on a small group of Union men, who were deeply divided into a conservative planter faction and a more liberal "Free State" contingent, the latter itself split into moderate and radical wings over the question of black civil rights. Too often Union men of all stripes seemed more interested in federal patronage than in bringing their state back into the Union.[2]

Governor James Madison Wells had been a wealthy planter in Rapides Parish before the war, a Whig, and a Unionist during the secession crisis. In politics, Wells was above all a realist (his enemies would have said opportunist). He knew that he could not build a power base on the slender reed of the small, faction-ridden band of Louisiana Union men and therefore turned to the old Confederates to broaden his constituency. Wells prudently appointed conservative Union men as well as outright rebels to the offices at his disposal, steering a course carefully designed to ensure his own reelection but also guaranteed to arouse the ire of both wings of the old Free State coalition.[3]

In the 1865 state elections, Wells received the nominations of both the conservative Unionists and a large portion of the Democrats. He handily won reelection, and the Democrats gained control of the legislature. Both the Democrats and the conservative Unionists adopted platforms opposing Negro suffrage, and Democrats who supported Wells publicly proclaimed that white men must always govern the state.[4]

With many former Confederates back in power, Union men felt as persecuted and helpless as in the darkest days of the rebellion. Henry Clay Warmoth, a young Illinois carpetbagger, recalled the social ostracism and the suddenly cool treatment he received from the previously friendly southern belles. Cursed and reviled on the streets, Unionists claimed the rebels were plotting to drive them from the state, and many packed their bags and left for more hospitable climes. Loyal men in New Orleans were particularly alarmed about the election of former Confederates to city offices and the lengthy diatribes against "radicals" in the rebel-dominated newspapers.[5]

In addition to political ailments, Louisiana suffered from the same "diseases" of emancipation plaguing the rest of the South. Whites in the state were no less determined than their counterparts elsewhere to keep the Negroes in a carefully defined position of subordination, and they readily uttered maledictions against black freedom. Fragmentary reports from Unionist sources indicated that scattered outrages against the freedmen took place in the rural parishes throughout 1865, and white conservatives issued the usual denials, blaming the tragedies that did occur on northern men and assertive blacks.[6]

In New Orleans, racial tensions increased and the security of the freedmen declined as the Confederates returned to power. After an acrimonious controversy had alienated Governor Wells from his conservative supporters, the legislature, with the tacit approval of the Johnson administration, ordered city elections held in New Orleans in the spring of 1866. As a striking example of renewed conservative strength, former Confederate mayor John T. Monroe handily defeated incumbent and Wells ally Hugh Kennedy. A serious complication arose because Monroe had never received a presidential pardon, and since the city was still under military supervision, the local commander, General E.R.S. Canby, refused to allow him to take office until the president had pardoned him. Whether or not Monroe's election signaled, as Union men suspected, a renewal of the rebellion in New Orleans, the sudden appearance of armed bands naturally made embattled loyalists in the Crescent City uneasy.[7]

One of the new mayor's chief tasks was to reorganize and reform the New Orleans police department. He began by expanding the force to 550 men and appointing a new police chief, Thomas E. Adams, but Adams could neither persuade his men to wear uniforms nor root out corruption in the department. The police board suspended the chief for allowing citizens to go about the streets armed, but Monroe reinstated him. Despite personnel shuffling, New Orleans remained a dangerous city, and hopes for creation of an efficient and nonpartisan police force proved to be ephemeral. As one newspaper editor correctly noted, it was doubtful that many good officers could be hired at the starting salary of eighty dollars per month. Even conservative sources indicated that Monroe had been quick to dismiss Union men from the force and fill the department with Confederate veterans.[8]

Just as in Memphis, blacks could expect harsh treatment from the police. Officers frequently arrested them on flimsy vagrancy charges, sometimes hauling them from their homes, but ignored white derelicts on the streets. Freedmen's Bureau assistant commissioner Thomas W. Conway tersely summarized white attitudes: "A poor white man is deemed industrious till proved a vagrant; a poor black man is deemed a vagrant till proved industrious." Policemen attempting to enforce antebellum curfew laws broke up black religious meetings almost nightly in the summer of 1865. False arrests and the mistreatment of black prisoners completed the picture of chronic conflict between blacks and police.[9] Yet the New Orleans police never displayed (at least before the riot) the brutality of their Memphis counterparts, and clashes between blacks and police did not appear serious enough to explode into a race riot.

Nor did whites in New Orleans seem as fearful of black insurrection or crime as were other southerners, perhaps because the city had always had a substantial free Negro population with a well-established community life. The *New Orleans Times* expressed concern about the incidence of theft by the freedmen, but three conservative dailies reported only one case of violence involving a black soldier during 1865 and 1866. Shortly before the riot, however, the *Crescent* reported in some detail two apparent attempts by black men to rape white women.[10]

The inauguration of Monroe's administration and the growing social and racial tension in New Orleans unhappily coincided with a crisis in state politics. After battling with conservatives over patronage and the New Orleans mayoralty, by early 1866 Governor Wells had become disgusted with the "rebel" legislature and realized that his makeshift alliance of Union men and Democrats was unworkable. A clumsy attempt by a few conservatives to bribe the governor further catapulted him toward a complete break with his recent political allies. The critical question became how Wells and the tiny Union faction could take and hold power in the state. Under the constitution of 1864, the Democrats would easily control future elections barring any changes in the franchise. Although Wells had often publicly expressed his opposition to black suffrage, he now turned to it as the only available expedient and formed an alliance with the radical Unionists, who had long favored Negro voting as a matter of principle. Such a jerry-built coalition seemed preferable to kowtowing to rebels for the indefinite future.[11]

Radical Union men and black leaders had pressed for Negro suffrage immediately after the surrender of the Confederate armies, but the idea had always divided loyal men and won little support until it became the last hope of defeating the conservatives. Although the goal was clear, the means were not. Many Democrats in the legislature had favored scrapping the constitution of 1864 by summoning a new convention, but opposition from Governor Wells and President Johnson squelched the project. A few radicals had also hoped for a new constitutional convention, but they desired a document written by "loyal men" and inclusion of a provision for universal suffrage. Despite these obstacles, by the spring of 1866 both Wells supporters and radical Unionists began concentrating their efforts on a scheme to reconvene the adjourned constitutional convention of 1864.[12]

The idea of calling back into session a deliberative body that had not met in nearly two years seemed preposterous, but the radicals found a curious legal technicality. The 1864 convention had not adjourned sine die as was the usual practice but had disbanded "at the call of the president [of the convention], whose duty it shall be to reconvoke the convention for any cause, or in case the constitution should not be ratified, for the purpose of taking such measures as may be necessary for the formation of a civil government for the State of Louisiana." A reassembling of the convention would have been necessary had ratification failed, but it is not clear why the delegates adopted such a peculiar adjournment resolution. This loophole gave the radicals an opportunity to bypass the conservative legislature in changing the organic law of the state. Beginning in March 1866, Union men held private meetings in New Orleans to discuss the status of the convention. According to Warmoth, Governor Wells, using Andrew Jackson's favorite oath, swore: "By the Eternal, he intended to beat the rebels and keep them out of power, if in doing so he destroyed the state government and produced anarchy for twenty years." Admitting his former opposition to universal Negro suffrage, Wells nevertheless gave his support to reassembling the 1864 convention. The state's Union men were still far from united on this scheme, and heated arguments about it continued well into June. Some radicals, including several black leaders, believed the convention of 1864 was dead forever and could not be revived on such a shallow pretext.[13]

In addition to the convention's shadowy legal existence and uncertain Unionist support, there were other barriers to the proposal. The convention of 1864 had represented only the areas of the state then under federal occupation, so its reassembly would necessitate new elections in the unrepresented parishes as well as filling vacancies from others. When forty-three delegates (out of an original membership of ninety-eight) met at the Mechanics' Institute in New Orleans on June 26, 1866, a second difficulty arose. Fearing bloodshed and probably distrusting any project supported by the wily governor, several members, including the president of the 1864 convention, Judge Edmund H. Durell, refused to participate. Although the convention could reconvene only at the call of the president, the determined delegates elected an associate justice of the state supreme court, Rufus K. Howell, president pro tem. Howell issued a proclamation on July 7 calling for the delegates to assemble at the Mechanics' Institute on July 30, and Wells set September 3 as the day for elections to fill the vacancies. Minority control of the body was critically important because the Union men did not unanimously support the convention.[14]

Conservatives later charged that the convention was engineered by radical Republicans in Washington or at least had their explicit approval. Leading northern radicals later admitted to consulting with Judge Howell in Washington, but their recollections of these conversations were vague at best. Evidently several Republicans gave Howell general assurances that they would "recognize" the convention. On July 16 Representative George S. Boutwell of Massachusetts notified the Republican caucus that the Louisiana convention was to convene on July 30 and that if Congress was still in session at that time, it could accept a new constitution drafted by the delegates as the true organic law of the state. But with a heated congressional election campaign rapidly approaching, no one wanted to prolong the session, and Congress adjourned on July 26. Undoubtedly, the Louisiana politicos received some advice from their friends in Washington, but there is little evidence of a "radical" conspiracy.[15]

Revisionist efforts to discount the idea of a Washington-based plot fail to provide insight into the contemporary perspective. New Orleans conservatives saw the attempt to reconvene the 1864 constitutional convention as a radical device to deprive Louisiana of her liberty by forcing Negro suffrage on the state. Since most whites questioned the legitimacy of the 1864 convention, they naturally denied the right of a small part of that body (or "rump" as many commentators contemptuously dubbed it) to meet for the purpose of rewriting the state's constitution. These "slippery characters," conservatives maintained, were mostly treacherous former Confederates seeking power and position for their own ignoble purposes. Some conservative leaders disregarded the assembly and professed to take no notice of its proceedings. As Lieutenant

Governor Albert Voorhies pointed out, however, although such a conclave could be ignored in "ordinary times," these were not ordinary times. Voorhies and other anticonvention politicians knew that native radicals had the full support of their fanatical friends in Washington, a fact that lent wider and certainly deadly significance to an ostensibly local affair. Louisiana radicals, claimed the *New Orleans Times*, had visited the nation's capital, had "divided their time when there between rum shops and brothels," and had poured their tales of suffering and woe into the receptive ears of unscrupulous politicians. These political wire-pullers would be more likely to succeed, some editors cautioned, if they could provoke a violent outbreak in New Orleans and thus win national support with their cries of persecution and resurgent rebellion. Although many conservatives urged citizens to restrain themselves while the convention met, the mere assembling of such a revolutionary body seemed to justify any measures, including violence, to suppress it.[16]

The convention alone could hardly generate enough attention to provoke violence; the object was more important than the means. The mere mention of black suffrage sent many whites into a sustained frenzy. Although the sophisticated editor of the *Picayune* might satirize the actions of "darkey politicians," whose oratorical malapropisms were directed toward reducing the working day from eight hours to four, most Louisianians failed to see any humor in the issue. Black enfranchisement would mean the Africanization of the South with all its attendant evils—white degradation, miscegenation, and social anarchy. Conservatives nervously forecast that the adoption of such a measure would produce bloodshed on election day and continuing racial strife.[17] In the language of social psychology, black suffrage was the "cue" in the environment that could stimulate aggression once the populace had been sufficiently "aroused."[18] Conservative editors and politicians through their hyperbolic statements had already done much to stir popular passions and break down the social and moral restraints on violent behavior. Their rhetorical excesses foreshadowed the brutality of the New Orleans mob. Whether these reactions were realistic is irrelevant to understanding white thinking; aggression occurred because whites exaggerated the dangers and geared their actions to their fears.

With the exception of Governor Wells, most high state officials strongly opposed the convention. District Judge Edmund Abell, who had been a delegate in 1864, charged a New Orleans grand jury that the attempt to reassemble the convention was "subversive to good order and dangerous to the peace of the State." Conservative leaders accused Wells of being in league with the radicals but saw no way to thwart the governor's "illegal" course. Since the state remained under military supervision, they hoped to convince President Johnson to order federal troops to break up the "revolutionary" assembly.[19]

After joining the meetings of the anticonvention forces, on July 25 Mayor Monroe informed the federal commander in New Orleans, General Absalom Baird, that "a body of men claiming to belong to the convention of 1864, and whose object is to subvert the present municipal and State government [sic]," would assemble in the city on July 30. Terming the convention an "unlawful" meeting and citing his duty as mayor to disperse such gatherings, Monroe revealed his intention to arrest the delegates for violating unspecified municipal ordinances. Baird, who showed a great deal of naiveté, if not blissful ignorance, in the midst of the growing crisis, replied that the proposed convention had received no sanction from the army and falsely claimed that the military authorities had "held themselves strictly aloof from all interference with the political movements of the citizens of Louisiana." Baird then gave the mayor a supercilious lecture on the right of citizens to assemble peaceably to discuss political issues. The general discounted Monroe's fears of revolution because if the meeting had no legal authority to modify the government of the state, it would be nothing but a "harmless pleasantry." Obviously, the general concluded, it was not the duty of either the mayor or himself to determine the legality of the convention or forcibly disperse it. If violence occurred, troops would be available, but Baird should have recognized the uselessness of legalisms in such an explosive situation. As plans for the convention progressed, Union men in New Orleans received "suggestions" to leave the city and threats against their lives. At this point Baird should have watched state and local officials closely and held his troops in readiness to take command of the city in the event of trouble.[20]

Though more attuned than Baird to the possibility of violence, the radicals nonetheless held a mass meeting attended by an estimated fifteen hundred blacks and addressed by several fiery speakers. What was said on this occasion remains cloaked in controversy, and eyewitnesses gave widely conflicting accounts. Although most persons present agreed that the speakers strongly advocated Negro suffrage and urged blacks to attend the convention on July 30, conservative newspapers and witnesses charged after the riot that the radical dentist and former state auditor, A. P. Dostie, had exhorted blacks to arm themselves and kill whites. More credible witnesses reported that Dostie advised blacks to return to their homes but to kill anyone who attacked them. Ascertaining Dostie's exact words would contribute little to understanding the causes of the riot. Even if the less damning testimony is correct, the admonition for the Negroes to use their weapons, even in self-defense, was bound to alarm whites. The attacks on the "rump" convention as a revolutionary body and conservative racial fears certainly affected white reactions, and the inflammatory and often inaccurate reports of this meeting in several newspapers did nothing to ease their anxiety. The events of July 27 further convinced the conservatives of the absolute necessity for stopping the convention.[21]

The various parties spent a busy Saturday (July 28) in private conferences and at the telegraph office. At a meeting of state and local officials, Andrew J. Herron, the attorney general of the state, presented a three-part proposal: the convention should be allowed to meet with police protection, the grand jury should indict the individual delegates, and, if General Baird prevented their arrest, an appeal should be sent to Washington. Herron left thinking his plan had been agreed to and joined Voorhies in telegraphing the information to Andrew Johnson. They asked the president if the military would interfere with the arrest of the convention members. Johnson had wired Governor Wells earlier in the day questioning his authority to issue a proclamation calling for a meeting of the convention,[22] and his position became more clear in his reply to Voorhies: "The military will be expected to sustain, and not to obstruct or interfere with, the proceedings of the courts." Johnson thus lent both his prestige and the power of his office to the conservatives and at the same time foolishly gave them far too much discretion.[23]

General Baird had at his disposal approximately 860 men in barracks three miles south of New Orleans but had made no arrangements to deploy them. Sharing in the reluctance of his immediate superior, General Philip Sheridan, to become enmeshed in the quagmire of Louisiana politics, Baird hoped to preserve the peace while maintaining the army's political neutrality. Therefore, on July 28 the general telegraphed Secretary of War Edwin Stanton the details on the developing crisis. Pointing out that he could not allow the civil authorities to arrest the delegates to the convention without orders from Washington, he asked for instructions. Unfortunately, Baird never received a reply to his urgent wire.[24]

Sunday, July 29, the day before the convention, was uneventful. General Baird instructed the soldiers south of the city to be ready to march in the event of disturbances, but the languid stillness of a hot and humid Sabbath was unbroken.[25] Radicals, conservatives, civil officials, police, and the military all rested in the assurance that the situation was well under control.

Monday was another steamy day. Conservative editors again advised citizens to curb their anger and avoid an outbreak that could only benefit the radicals. Mayor Monroe issued a proclamation calling on the people of the city to avoid a collision with the illegal convention by staying away from the Mechanics' Institute. Monroe and Chief of Police Adams later testified that they had placed the police force on alert to keep the peace, but both men were bitter opponents of the convention and hardly maintained political neutrality during the riot. Several policemen boasted that morning that they were going to break up the assembly and murder blacks and Union men.[26]

After conferring with Monroe and Voorhies in the morning, Baird decided to send soldiers to the Mechanics' Institute as a precautionary measure. There was only one problem: the convention was to meet at noon, but Baird thought it would not assemble until six o'clock in the evening. Although the general later charged Monroe and Voorhies with deceiving him about the correct time, he should have known this vital piece of information and cannot be exculpated for his ignorance. This final blunder, committed by a man who was unsuited for such a responsible command, guaranteed the mayor and the police a momentarily free hand in dealing with the Unionists.[27]

As Monroe massed his forces in the morning, rumors spread through the city of an impending move to break up the convention by force. Conservatives warned Unionist friends to stay away from the Mechanics' Institute to save their lives. Yet few people expected a serious outbreak of violence, and the delegates neither heeded the warnings nor armed themselves in self-defense. When the convention assembled at noon, twenty-six members were present for the opening prayer. Judge Howell adjourned the proceedings until 1:30 so that the sergeants-at-arms could round up enough members for a quorum. Spectators, including a large number of blacks, milled around in the hall, and the convention seemed to be a great fizzle.[28]

About noon, a procession of between one hundred and two hundred blacks marched in support of the convention carrying an American flag. They paraded along Burgundy Street, crossed Canal Street, and headed toward the Mechanics' Institute on Dryades Street. Hostile witnesses testified that they were heavily armed with sticks, clubs, and revolvers, but few of the marchers probably carried weapons. As they crossed Canal Street, the incident took place that precipitated the New Orleans riot. A young white man either insulted the Negroes or blocked the street, and a black man in the procession knocked him to the ground. Depending on which witnesses one believes, either one of the blacks fired at the fallen white youth or the first shot came from the crowd of policemen and citizens who lined both sides of the street. In any event, the blacks in the procession fired several shots, and some policemen tried to arrest one of the marchers. The mob of whites and police along the street began to hurl brickbats and to fire at the blacks.

The well-armed citizens at first scattered but then regrouped and chased the Negroes. The marchers, many of whom were unarmed and certainly not prepared for a street battle, fled before their white pursuers in the general direction of the Mechanics' Institute.[29]

The police, who had braced themselves all day for just such an occurrence, swarmed into the area of the fighting. Instead of restoring order, officers joined their colleagues and the white mob in assaulting blacks.[30] Some Negroes threw brickbats at the surging crowd, and a few fired their guns to ward off the attackers. Despite the belief of many whites in a black conspiracy to incite a riot, most of the blacks retreated in disarray before the onslaught. Rather, the coordinated actions of the police and mob lent some credence to the charge that the New Orleans riot was a preconcerted plot to massacre Union men and blacks.[31]

By his own account, Mayor Monroe ordered the police to stop the bloodshed and summoned all citizens to be sworn in as special deputies at City Hall. By this time, however, the police had become an indistinguishable part of the mob, if not the actual phalanx of the rioters. Losing all sense of discipline and rational control, they chased, beat, and shot any black in sight. Freedmen pleading for mercy were brutally kicked, and police shot down several of them and then stood by while citizens beat the wounded men. Firemen joined the fray and savagely attacked blacks with heavy wrenches. Some policemen bragged of the number of blacks they had murdered during the day and swore they would shoot any others they could find. As one officer remarked to one of his colleagues, it was "no sin to kill a nigger."[32]

The composition of the mob presents a striking contrast to that of the anticonvention forces. The conservative politicians and editors watched the riot with approval, but few participated in the fighting. Instead, the mob consisted largely of poorer whites, particularly young boys, with a sprinkling of Confederate veterans. Ten-year-old lads roamed the streets brandishing revolvers stolen from gun shops. Former Confederate General Richard Taylor described vividly how a "crowd of roughs, Arabs, and Negroes" ran down Canal Street toward the Mechanics' Institute to join the melee. Prostitutes stabbed some blacks who had fallen to the ground wounded.[33] The blacks probably faced superior numbers (there are no estimates available on the size of the mob), and the close cooperation of white citizens and police left them to the mercy of their bitterest enemies. When the fighting spread and intensified, many blacks retreated toward the Mechanics' Institute in the hope of finding safety with the white radicals.[34]

As the crowd swept toward the convention hall, some blacks huddled near the building, and many moved inside. The police later claimed they had received heavy fire from within the building, but the men in the Mechanics' Institute told a different story. The members of the convention and spectators (perhaps as many as 150 black people of all ages and sexes) denied firing and insisted the police and citizens had shot at them and had thrown brickbats through the windows. Still other witnesses said shots were fired by both sides. In all probability, the white mob did most of the shooting because relatively few persons in the Mechanics' Institute were armed.[35]

During the attack, confusion reigned among the delegates and on-lookers. The police rushed the entrance on Dryades Street, firing through the doors. Pushing inside, they shot wildly into the frightened group of delegates and blacks. A Confederate veteran, who had lost both his arms in the war, harangued the mob to "kill every damned son of a bitch in the building, and not let any escape." The police came up in waves to fire into the doorway, particularly searching out convention delegates.[36] Firemen and citizens joined them, entering the hall, smashing windows, chairs, and most of the furnishings, and shooting at the panic-stricken delegates. Shouting that the American flag, which the black procession had brought into the building, was a "dirty rag," police refused quarter to either white or black. In the confusion, delegates and blacks retreated behind a railing that divided the hall in half and hid near the speaker's platform. Two leading members of the convention, Judge Howell and R. King Cutler, urged them to remain quiet and peaceable as the enraged mob rushed into the building. Some terrified persons lay on the floor to protect themselves; others tried to barricade the doors and fight off the charging police with chairs and a few small arms. The defenders amazingly managed to repulse the invaders four or five times before being overcome by numbers and fire-power. Several white Unionists waved handkerchiefs as white flags of surrender, but the police ignored them and pummeled and shot those crowded into the rear of the building; several blacks who had fallen to their knees pleading for their lives were killed. Attempts to escape the onslaught grew desperate; blacks fled to the second floor with their relentless enemies at their heels. They jumped from windows to the street below only to be seized by the mob outside and shot.[37]

Those persons lucky enough to escape the carnage inside the building had to run an additional gauntlet outside. The mob beat and shot fleeing blacks, chasing the wounded through the streets. Citizens and police dragged injured and dying men from the building and savagely made sure that the wounded would not live. The police rapidly hauled prisoners away but allowed the white mob to knock these helpless victims about as they were carried along, singling out leading members of the convention for the hardest blows. Former Governor Michael

Hahn, his body covered with blood, had his clothes ripped to shreds as the police pulled him through the streets; several citizens screamed for the officers to kill him. When the mob spotted A. P. Dostie in police custody, five or six whites came out of the crowd and fired their revolvers at the hated radical. Trampled, beaten, and at one point left for dead, Dostie's nearly lifeless body was thrown into a filthy cart and taken off. He died a few days later.[38]

The police carelessly threw wounded and dead blacks into the same jail cells. A physician told military investigators that overcrowding in the "prison surpassed the Black Hole of Calcutta." He estimated the temperature at between 100 and 130 degrees, and he was sick for two days from the stench. The police abused the wounded as they lay. Because of the large number of prisoners, wounded and dying men covered the prison yard, and little effort was made to alleviate the suffering. An aide to General Sheridan described the scene as "more like a slaughter-pen for animals than a receptacle for human beings."[39]

Some rioters left the area of the Mechanics' Institute and roamed the streets, beating any blacks they could find, much as their counterparts in Memphis had done. Late into the night, drunken whites hauled blacks from their houses and ferociously assaulted them. White newspaper boys burst into the home of a black woman, grabbed a black man, and shot him in the head; they killed several other blacks in her yard by splitting their heads open with an ax. According to a *New York Times* correspondent, Chief of Police Adams sincerely regretted the atrocities committed by his men and promised that the guilty parties would be punished. This pledge was never kept.[40]

After the riot had raged for nearly two hours, federal troops finally arrived to restore order. General Baird placed New Orleans under martial law, but his failure to act more promptly had cost many innocent lives. Union men were convinced the rebels and civil officials had carefully coordinated the attacks on the blacks and convention delegates. Although some whites feared retaliation, military control brought a return of peace.[41]

The casualty figures made the riot as severe as any twentieth-century disturbance.[42] Although Monroe and Voorhies reported that 42 policemen and several citizens had been killed or wounded in the fighting, army surgeon Albert Hartsuff found that only 22 policemen had been injured, and 10 of those were back on duty the following day. On the other hand, 34 blacks and 3 white Unionists had died, and 119 and 17 respectively, were wounded. Only one "rebel" perished in the fighting. These statistics are eloquent testimony to the one-sided nature of the battle.[43]

On hearing news of the outbreak, General Sheridan returned from

Texas on July 31 to resume command. He found New Orleans still in a state of high excitement and heard idle threats about driving the military from the city. On orders from General Ulysses S. Grant, Sheridan kept a wary eye on the municipal officials and the police. His inquiries into the origins and course of the violence produced some startling conclusions. In a telegram to Grant, he described the convention supporters as "political agitators and revolutionary men." Before his departure to Texas to investigate troubles with Mexico, he had decided to arrest the delegates at the first sign of trouble. Charging Monroe and the police with "premeditated" murder, the general characterized the riot as an "absolute massacre by the police, which was not excelled in murderous cruelty by that of Fort Pillow." A garbled version of Sheridan's dispatch appeared in several northern newspapers without the significant paragraph condemning the actions of the police and the mayor. Outraged at this apparently deliberate distortion of his views, the general immediately wired Grant for an explanation. Grant and Stanton decided, with the authorization of President Johnson, to publish in full all telegrams concerning the riot. Evidently either Johnson or one of his friends had sent incomplete copies of Sheridan's dispatches to the papers in order to protect the administration from Republican attacks over the handling of the affair.[44]

Voorhies and other conservative leaders were quick to condemn the military and defend the actions of the civil authorities and police. Arguing that local officials could have controlled the violence, editors castigated General Baird for sending troops to prevent the police from finishing their job. As the attacks on Baird's performance became more strident from all directions, both the army and the Freedmen's Bureau vainly tried to defend him.[45]

Mayor Monroe, Lieutenant Governor Voorhies, and Attorney General Herron naturally hoped to persuade Washington officials to accept their version. In a long letter to President Johnson, they reiterated their belief in a radical plot to overthrow the state government and blamed the bloodshed on the "armed mob" supporting the convention. They also censured the military for failing to cooperate with the civil authorities in arresting the delegates. President Johnson evidently agreed with many of these contentions, and he closely questioned General Sheridan about the causes and course of the riot. In his charge to a New Orleans grand jury, Judge Abell asserted that the riot had originated from a conspiracy to subvert the government in Louisiana. The grand jury blamed the riot on the radicals and cited Dostie's "incendiary" speech of July 27 as the spark that ignited the conflagration.[46]

The New Orleans press, which must bear some responsibility for inciting the riot, echoed the conservative consensus. Violence had occurred because revolutionaries, both in Louisiana and in Washington, had attempted to reassemble a convention of "political adventurers," who sought only the spoils of office. The fighting began, according to these spokesmen, because the deluded Negroes listened to unprincipled fanatics and planned to kill white people. Asserting that only those blacks in league with the radical conspirators had suffered during the disorders, several editors praised the police and citizens for behaving with "restraint" under extreme provocation. They accused white Unionists of manufacturing false atrocity stories for political consumption in the North.[47]

The New Orleans riot temporarily accomplished one important conservative objective: it left the Republicans in disarray. Fearing for their lives, several leading radicals left the state; other Unionists blamed President Johnson's policies for their peril and dreaded the end of martial law in New Orleans. Frightened men predicted a resurgence of the rebellion and the restoration of slavery within five years. Governor Wells wrote his own apologia in the form of an address to the "loyal people of Louisiana" defending his policies. The governor recounted the failure of conciliatory gestures toward the former rebels and charged the mayor and the police with conspiring to murder loyal men. Wells thought Union men would be safe only if federal troops remained in the state and the Fourteenth Amendment was ratified.[48]

Thorough investigations of the riot by a board of army officers and a congressional committee produced pages of documents and testimony but no end to the disputes over the origins and meaning of the event. The military report whitewashed General Baird's mistakes and charged Monroe and the police with premeditated violence against the convention. The Republican-controlled Thirty-Ninth Congress established a select committee of two Republicans and one Democrat to probe the affair. When the congressmen arrived in New Orleans in December 1866, both Republicans and conservatives courted their favor. Radicals worried that the rebels would flatter the committee into believing their version of the story, and conservatives did warmly greet the committee members. Editors cautioned the congressmen to listen to radical witnesses with critical minds and write an "objective" report, but the conclusions of the Republican majority dashed their hopes. Thomas D. Eliot of Massachusetts and Samuel Shellabarger of Ohio sustained the legality of the reassembled convention of 1864, charged city and state authorities with incitement, and accused President Johnson of encouraging the bloodshed. The minority report, drafted by Democrat Benjamin M. Boyer of Pennsylvania, assailed the legitimacy of the convention and denounced the radicals and the Negroes for infuriating the police and white mob. The *New Orleans Times* spoke for many white citizens when it dismissed the congressional report as the "jaundiced decree of partisan animosity."[49]

Long before the congressional committee issued its report, many northerners had drawn their own conclusions about the riot because the issue was extensively debated during the 1866 congressional election campaign. Republicans promptly charged President Johnson with complicity in and approval of the brutal acts of the New Orleans mob. The president's conservative restoration policies had encouraged Confederates in New Orleans to slaughter loyal men; in the words of the *Chicago Tribune,* "Blood is upon his hands, the blood of innocent, loyal citizens, who had committed no crime but that of seeking to protect themselves against rebel misrule, which he, Andrew Johnson, had foisted upon them." Even if Johnson was not personally responsible, the tragedy was clearly the inevitable result of his leniency toward traitors. Searching for words to describe their outrage, Republican editors compared the New Orleans riot to the St. Bartholomew's Day massacre and, mixing their historical analogies, cast Andrew Johnson in the role of Oliver Cromwell and Napoleon. Theodore Tilton, in his influential religious weekly the *Independent,* likened Dostie to the early martyrs of the Christian church.[50] The political lesson was painfully obvious: the voters of the North had but one choice—to repudiate the president's treasonous policies by electing a large Republican majority to the next Congress.

As usual, the comments of southern editors aided the Republican polemicists. Attributing the violence to the teachings of radical incendiaries who had infested the South since the end of the war, they accused these fanatics of inciting Negroes to acts of barbarism in order to make political capital. These editorials displayed little sympathy for the dead and wounded of New Orleans, and the editor of the *Mobile Tribune* harshly satirized the emergence of A. P. Dostie as the latest abolition cause célèbre: "Let Dostie's skin be forthwith stripped and sold to [P. T.] Barnum—the proceeds to go to the Freedmen's Bureau and negro newspapers, to be sold by them for the benefit of Negroes who have no taste for work. Dostie's body will make good soap. Let him be boiled down, preparatory to being distributed in bars to Yankee school marms. Delicious will be the kisses sipped, by those angular females from ebony cheeks, late lathered with sweet scented Dostie."[51] The comments in the New Orleans press and other conservative papers were similar to editorials appearing after the Memphis riot and set a pattern for later defenses of white terrorism.

Hindered more than helped by his would-be southern allies, President Johnson responded to Republican attacks by repeating the stock arguments about radical conspiracies.[52] The combative Tennessean could never win a debate over southern outrages, and his opponents effectively waved the bloody shirt against him. To Republicans of various stripes, the New Orleans riot seemed to portend not only the collapse of Johnson's program but resurgent rebellion in the South and the sacrifice of the fruits of northern victory in the war. Despite impending disaster, the nation still had the opportunity for a genuine reconstruction based on the absolute necessity for protecting the lives of the loyal men in the South through the imposition of black suffrage.[53]

These arguments were not wholly campaign bluster or empty speculation. Whatever the political advantages to be gained, the bloodshed in New Orleans had rekindled wartime passions. Cyrus Hamlin, son of the former vice-president, best expressed these emotions in his eyewitness account of the fighting: "I have seen death on the battle field but time will erase the effects of that, the wholesale slaughter and the little regard paid to human life I witnessed here on the 30 of July I shall never forget."[54] More than any previous episodes of Reconstruction violence, the New Orleans riot marked the emergence of disorders directly related to the central political issues of the day: the restoration of state governments, the dangers of returning Confederate influence, the means of building a southern Republican party, and the complex and multiplying questions centering on the black man's position in postwar America. If northern politicians used the lessons of New Orleans to justify and frame a harsher policy toward the southern states, conservative leaders and their white followers would prove equally ingenious in discovering new forms of resistance.

5. Military Reconstruction: The Triumph of Jacobinism

y the fall of 1866, attitudes in both the North and South had hardened. During the congressional election campaign, the Republican press effectively publicized southern outrages—an issue that, according to the editor of *Harper's Weekly,* "has done more than the abstract arguments of a year to impress the country with the conviction that we can not wisely hope for peace at the South so long as inequality of guarantees of personal and political liberty endure." There were not many men, Horace Greeley averred, who would "go to the polls to vote for murder, arson, robbery, torture, cruelty, oppression, systematic swindling and lynch law."[1] Thoughtful southerners were alarmed because idealistic radicals such as Thaddeus Stevens and Charles Sumner had been joined by Roscoe Conkling of New York and John A. Logan of Illinois, two wily and unprincipled state bosses, in waving the bloody shirt.[2] Outbreaks of violence in Memphis, New Orleans, and elsewhere had created a unity among Republicans that had not existed even during the war.

At the beginning of 1867, a northern majority stood solidly against further truckling with defiant Confederates. The great desideratum became the security of loyal men and the establishment of new governments in the South; these ends might require military rule for a time because justice and necessity precluded other options.[3] This consensus for immediate action was apparent as the members of the lame duck Thirty-Ninth Congress resumed debate on reconstruction. Seizing the opportunity, Stevens sought to push the House toward accepting more radical measures. Lashing his colleagues for sitting quietly while Union men and blacks were slaughtered by southern barbarians, the cadaverous Pennsylvanian poured his still substantial energies into preventing any delay in a comprehensive reconstruction of the former Confederate states, but his harsh invective was no longer necessary. Despite significant differences among Republicans about the final shape of the Reconstruction acts (reflected in their slipshod drafting), moderates and radicals were at last ready to place the South under military control for the immediate future. In the Senate, cautious and conservative leaders, such as John Sherman of Ohio and Lyman Trumbull of Illinois, asserted that the first duty of government was to protect loyal citizens. Going further, Republicans of various ideological stripes supported black suffrage in the South as the only practical safeguard for the freedmen against the cruelty of former slaveholders.[4] As most historians have recognized, for the white South military Reconstruction was a self-inflicted wound.

When Congress approved the first of the Reconstruction acts in March 1867, a deep gloom spread over the white South. The dismay, consternation, and confusion rekindled memories of the end of the war. The enormous uncertainty about the future made southern politics increasingly complex and disorganized. Conservative leaders saw their region in the grip of a revolution whose final direction they could only guess. Republican government had passed away with the war, a South Carolina editor lamented, and Washington was rapidly becoming the new Rome. Alexander H. Stephens saw the nation "in the death throes of Constitutional liberty on this continent," and one of his Crawfordville, Georgia, neighbors agreed that "madness rules the hour." Southerners had become the victims of a cruel despotism that sought to uproot their most deeply held convictions; the experience of generations and the white legacy of republican government were being cast aside in a careless moment. Novelist Augusta Evans questioned how the destiny of the American nation could be placed in the "hands of insensate Jacobins." She described the bleak condition of the South and its probable future: "More pitiable than Poland or Hungary, and quite as helpless as were the Asia Minor provinces when governed by Persian Satraps, we of the pseudo 'Territories' sit like Israel in the captivity, biding the day of retribution . . . that must surely dawn in blood upon the nation which oppresses us."[5]

The hyperbole and paranoia of these statements were indicative of the psychological jolt suffered by the white South. Having for some time clung to the illusion that President Johnson and his conservative policies would prevail, many of the region's traditional leaders faced political reality for the first time. Having had their hopes for the future raised considerably during presidential Reconstruction, they suddenly found them dashed by the "arbitrary" actions of vengeful politicians. Because the restoration of their rightful place in the Union had seemed so close, their frustration after Congress blocked this reunion was especially intense.[6]

Many stalwarts of the old order suffered from what social scientists have called "relative deprivation." By any absolute standards, white planters and merchants normally dominated politics, the economy, and social life, but during Reconstruction their expectations greatly exceeded their capabilities.[7] Power was slipping out of their hands into those of outsiders ("carpetbaggers"), native traitors ("scalawags"), and an inferior caste (the blacks). The collapse of presidential Reconstruction and the imposition by Congress of stiffer conditions for readmission further widened the gap between southern perceptions of their legitimate status and their actual prospects. As a result, passage of the Reconstruction acts markedly increased the potential for civil strife.

Ironically, southern Republicans exacerbated white fears of a world turned upside down through their apparent determination to remake southern society from the bottom up. Carpetbaggers and some native Republicans openly proclaimed their intention to reshape the South into the image of radical New England. Scalawag governor James Lusk Alcorn attacked the sacred memory of John C. Calhoun and bluntly lectured his fellow Mississippians that following the doctrines of the great South Carolinian had retarded their economy. This purblind adherence to outmoded ideas had made the surrender at Appomattox inevitable, and Alcorn called for the South to become a part of northern industrial civilization. North Carolina Republican Thomas Settle rejoiced that free labor would create a new agricultural prosperity and advised that "Yankees and Yankee notions are just what we want in this country." The love of money, Settle concluded, was not evil but natural, and northern capital and expertise would make the South into a paradise for both races.[8]

Conservatives feared otherwise. Robert M. T. Hunter argued that the Reconstruction policies of the radical Republicans would "Africanize" the South, drive the whites away, and extinguish Christian civilization. Alarmed whites believed that Negro enfranchisement would lead to "social equality" and eventually to racial amalgamation. With the barbarians at the gates, the darkest nightmares of the proslavery apologists had become all too real. The days of the "white man's government" were numbered, Governor Benjamin G. Humphreys of Mississippi wrote to a political friend: "You and I will have to take back seats or be elevated at the end of a rope. Such is the civilization of the age."[9]

The rejection of black political power, much less "Negro rule," as many editors termed radical Reconstruction, was axiomatic. Yet a number of southern leaders found themselves disfranchised and barred from holding public office; their feeling of frustration was compounded because their political status had fallen below their social and economic position. This challenge to white political supremacy threatened one of the region's most salient values and further intensified the sense of relative deprivation.[10] Although modern scholarship has clearly shown that comparatively few blacks held public office in the Reconstruction South, this fact does not help explain white attitudes. Even small numbers of black officeholders enraged many conservatives; having to conduct business with these Negro politicians seemed not only an added humiliation but another evil result of emancipation. As legislators, former slaves possessed more political influence than the "best men" of the old regime. The *Raleigh Daily Sentinel* sadly reported a dinner attended by three former governors, a former justice of the state supreme court, one or two former members of Congress, and several other distinguished men. The only person in this august gathering who could vote was the black man waiting on the tables. With Negroes holding the positions once occupied by a Cheeves or a Calhoun, Alfred Huger wondered why "cruelty and oppression have not doomed us to madness or driven us to suicide."[11]

For some former rebels, the only solace lay in the past because it was far easier to relive bygone glories than to deal with present realities. History also comforted white southerners by showing that their present suffering was far from unique. Many conservatives became obsessed with the search for historical parallels to the current situation. Some southerners found the Norman conquest of Britain or the English subjugation of Ireland to be apt analogies. But no comparison seemed so persuasive as the notion that the French Revolution was being reenacted in the South. Alexander Stephens declared Congress's Joint Committee on Reconstruction to be a "Jacobin junto," and his newspaper organ labeled Congress a "Central Directory." Republicans loudly proclaimed the principles of liberty, equality, and fraternity, but in fact this slogan was a mask for despotism. In setting up their reign of terror, the fire-eating *Charleston Mercury* warned that the radicals risked sharing the fate of Robespierre and Marat, who were eventually consumed in their own revolution. Carrying this line of reasoning one step further, former Confederate diplomat James Mason predicted from London that the Yankees might soon find their own Napoleon.[12] These statements were more than idle bombast; they reflected the unwavering conviction of many white southerners who envisioned themselves in the midst of a cataclysmic upheaval.

As northern and southern Republicans set up their "revolutionary" regimes in the South, they unintentionally handed angry whites a powerful rationale for counterrevolution. By denying the legitimacy of the state governments established under the Reconstruction acts, southerners could readily justify counterrevolutionary terrorism.[13] The real constitutional debate therefore took place, not in Congress, but in the southern press and the private discussions and letters of conservative politicians. Refusing to recognize the authority, much less the sovereignty, of the new state administrations seemed to reduce southern society to a Hobbesian state of nature.

White leaders, however, much preferred John Locke to Thomas Hobbes and chose to base their continued defiance of national power on an appeal to the Anglo-Saxon tradition of resistance to tyranny, particularly the spirit of 1776. Such a noble-sounding rationale could palliate enormous brutalities and cast bloody-handed night riders in the roles of George Washington or Paul Revere. Yankee oppression purified the Confederate cause and made it appear more genuinely American; war against radicalism thereby became for many southerners a sacred duty performed to vindicate the memory of the founding fathers.[14]

According to former Confederates, this noble heritage had been corrupted. The Yankees had appropriated all the symbols of American nationalism. Although southerners considered themselves the nation's genuine republicans, they no longer flew the stars and stripes. Patriotic holidays such as the Fourth of July became days of somber reflection rather than of celebration. Indeed, claimed the editor of the *Charleston Mercury,* the appetite of the radical "Moloch" was insatiable, and the final goal of northern fanaticism was to crush the South under the banner "Carthago delenda est."[15]

Tragically for southern whites, Reconstruction meant not only political chaos but social anarchy as well. Since the end of the war, blacks had become increasingly assertive about gaining equal access to public transportation facilities on railroads and streetcars in some southern cities. Despite the lack of statutory requirements, segregation was probably the unwritten rule and nearly universal practice in most areas of the South because whites were much more sensitive about social intercourse than political rights. Jubal Early, for example, strenuously objected to attending a ceremony in Richmond for the unveiling of a statue of Stonewall Jackson after several companies of Negro soldiers had been invited. Governor James Kemper sharply informed the irascible Early that the blacks had asked to participate in order to improve race relations and that the program would go ahead as originally planned. Apparently, "Old Jube" stayed home.[16]

The southern horror of racial egalitarianism was no mere irrational anxiety about social mixing but rested on a deep-seated fear of miscegenation. Scattered reports of such practices confirmed the worst suspicions. A Mobile, Alabama, editor fumed: "Whenever you determine that your ignorant, brutal, filthy and licentious negro, has a right to obtrude into white people's houses, in their church pews, theatre boxes, &c., you make an issue of instant life or death."[17] These speculations acquired substance when in 1875 Congress enacted a comprehensive Civil Rights Act that guaranteed blacks equal access to public accommodations and transportation facilities. Representative William S. Herndon of Texas lambasted the measure as a frontal assault on the South's social system and a sure road to anarchy. A Mississippian described several outrageous responses to this explosive piece of legislation: a black woman had demanded a seat in church beside a white man, a black man had sat next to a white woman at a funeral, men and women riding in railroad cars had to drink from the same water cup as a "greasy strapping negro," and worst of all, a carpetbagger and his black wife had attempted to register at a local hotel.[18]

Changes in the pattern of racial accommodation and behavior in the Reconstruction South violated the basic tenets of white democracy. Louis Hartz, C. Vann Woodward, and George Fredrickson have all demonstrated that antebellum ideologues had constructed a theory of "herrenvolk democracy" in which the equality of all white men depended on the subjugation of black men.[19] The end of slavery made the preservation of political and social distinctions based on race even more important to white southerners because they were convinced blacks could not be elevated socially or politically without a consequent degradation of whites. One race or the other had to dominate; egalitarianism was impossible and could lead only to black supremacy. Clearly, when white leaders harped on the danger of "Africanization," they meant exactly that—a monstrous evil that would negate the accepted values and practices of Western civilization and allow an inferior race to rule over a superior one. The firm conviction that raising the status of one group automatically lowered the status of another naturally made southerners interpret Reconstruction and Negro suffrage in apocalyptic terms.[20]

This tortured logic rekindled fears of racial warfare. Although by 1867 the annual insurrection panics had subsided, a conflagration like the one in Saint-Domingue in 1791 still seemed possible in states where blacks outnumbered whites. Ignoring the inherent contradictions in their argument, conservatives asserted that the southern people would soon rise up and could easily crush their black rulers.[21]

A restoration of antebellum race relations seemed impossible as long as blacks served on juries, voted, and occupied political offices. As late as the 1870s, some whites still advocated Negro colonization as a final solution to the region's racial problems, and a few predicted the eventual extinction of the blacks.[22] Such doomsday prophecies pointed up the vitality of proslavery ideology even after slavery was gone. The scriptural and pseudo-scientific theories of black inferiority retained their support; biology still decreed the course of history. Had not black people, conservatives asked, always been barbarians? Had they ever established any great civilizations? Though largely ignorant of African history, white commentators baldly asserted that the black race had made no progress since the time of the Egyptian pyramids and would soon relapse into savagery.[23]

Although most white southerners were horrified by military Reconstruction and the threat of Negro rule, they responded in different ways. Since the days of Calhoun, conservative leaders had seen divisions in their ranks as a wedge for Yankee doctrines and practices to penetrate the South, and the passage of the Reconstruction acts inaugurated a furious debate over the relative merits of submission, cooperation, defiance, and a host of other political stratagems. In the back of many minds lurked the fear that indecisiveness might result in Republican control of the new governments by default.

But southerners vigorously aired their differences. Moderates criticized conservative leaders for having consistently misled the South during presidential Reconstruction by encouraging defiance and ignoring the drift of northern public opinion. When the Reconstuction acts were being debated and passed in Congress, even some of the South's traditional leaders had advised submission.[24] The only way to prevent further revolution and upheaval, James Longstreet wrote to Robert E. Lee, was for "our best people" to take control of the Reconstruction process. Although such men as Joseph E. Brown of Georgia would always face charges of political opportunism for temporarily allying themselves with the Republicans, some moderates saw no other choice. Franklin J. Moses, Jr., of South Carolina urged former Confederates to be "alive to the necessities of the hour" and thereby redeem the southland from imminent peril. Such redemption, however, did not mean an end to antebellum political differences. Historians have stressed the survival of Whiggery in the southern Republican party, but there were elements of Jacksonian Democracy as well. If James L. Alcorn hoped to get Mississippi Republicans to adopt Whiggish economic policies, James L. Orr of South Carolina was equally insistent on securing two great Democratic measures: a homestead law and a debtor relief law.[25]

The impact of this fragmentation of the southern elite at first seemed enormous. Did the emergence of these moderate voices demonstrate that congressional policy could not only tame white intransigence but also build a genuinely biracial Republican party in the South? In 1867 and 1868, the prospects for political reform, and perhaps economic and social improvements, appeared bright. The shallowness of this supposed change in attitudes and the weaknesses of many of the new converts to reason was not yet apparent.

Voices of moderation elicited a chorus of conservative protest that exploited the old issue of southern honor. In a brilliant series of news-paper essays entitled "Notes on the Situation," Ben Hill of Georgia denied that the South had failed to meet any of the conditions of sur-render, ridiculed the notion that further resistance would produce harsher legislation in Congress, and expressed no hope for a people who would sacrifice their birthright as southerners for a sorry mess of radical pottage. The prewar South's greatest novelist, William Gil-more Simms, likewise demurred from taking the path of conciliation: "We may submit, as a conquered people to the chain, but we shall not hug, nor embrace the knees of our conquerors. We shall only loathe them the more, and feel ourselves at all times free of all obligations." The route of expediency, then, inevitably led to greater evils and new disgrace; it was far better to suffer degradation out of necessity than to assist one's enemies in fastening new shackles. The distinction was, in the words of Alexander Stephens, between "martyrdom and suicide," or as his friend Herschel Johnson put it: "I will not attend the funeral [of constitutional liberty], much less serve as a pall-bearer."[26] To ac-knowledge the sincerity of such sentiments does not mean taking them too seriously as prescriptions for or indications of future action.

The southern dilemma was that the time for rhetoric had passed, and hard decisions had to be made. Despite fundamental agreement on the nature of the political crisis, white leaders in the early phases of "radi-cal" Reconstruction arrived at no workable consensus on strategy.[27] Because careless drafting of the Reconstruction acts allowed south-erners to avoid reconstruction and remain under military rule by sim-ply registering and then refusing to vote in the ratification elections for the new state constitutions, the old policy of "masterly inactivity" revived. By the summer and fall of 1867 cooperationists came under sharp attack from conservatives, who called for renewed resistance to northern demands. When, in a fourth Reconstruction Act in March 1868, Congress closed off the escape route, all the states of the former Confederacy (except Tennessee, which had been readmitted after rati-fying the Fourteenth Amendment) would have to undergo the recon-struction process. This new situation, of course, forced a drastic revi-sion of conservative strategy.

Fanatics might continue to bluster and pontificate about the uncon-stitutional, oppressive, and revolutionary nature of the Reconstruction Acts, but speechmaking could not end their subjugation. The question for experienced politicians became whether to sit back and wait for the new state governments to collapse or to enter the political lists and joust with white and black Republicans for control of state and local governments. There was no simple answer. A tactic that succeeded in one place might fail miserably in another. Some reactionaries favored a boycott of all political activity,[28] but as early as the spring and summer of 1867, prominent editors were advising their readers that to register and vote was the only way to defeat the Republicans and prevent the imposition of Negro rule.[29]

Conservatives generated some enthusiasm by holding conventions to counter radical proselytizing efforts. These assemblies drafted platforms proclaiming the unconstitutionality of the Reconstruction acts and supporting a program of white supremacy in opposition to black suffrage. Herschel Johnson encouraged white Georgians to unite and thereby dominate state politics. He cautioned his fellow citizens not to acquiesce in the destruction of republican government but rather to cling to the Constitution as an ark of safety in a "storm tossed sea." The South's traditional leaders began to throw off their torpor and reenter political life.[30] Conservative hopes seemed bright in the states where whites made up a majority of the electorate, but even there the "scalawag" element might hold the balance of power. In states with black majorities, the future appeared much more forbidding.

Such grim prospects forced reluctant white leaders to solicit black votes. This tactic did not signify acceptance of Negro suffrage as a wise and necessary reform. On the contrary, conservative speakers, even when addressing black audiences, denounced it. Vainly attempting to discover virtue in necessity, some politicians pragmatically sought to lead black voters in the "proper" direction and, above all else, avoid any permanent alienation between the races. Paternalists carefully cultivated black voters; less idealistic office seekers considered that voters were voters, no matter what their color.[31] The strange sight of planters soliciting the votes of their former slaves spoke more eloquently than a thousand editorials about the revolutionary impact of congressional Reconstruction.

Conservative expectations for winning black votes partook more of wishful thinking than of realism. The constant refrain was that the Negroes had been tricked by wily carpetbaggers for the last time, had learned their lesson, and would join with whites in routing radicalism. Even when blacks had supported the Republican ticket in several elections, some optimists persisted in hoping for their assistance in throwing off the yoke of radical thralldom. In their view, blacks could be free and independent only when they voted according to the dictates of their white friends and neighbors.[32] Only Republicans apparently noticed the paradox in this assertion.

Wooing the black electorate became a complicated and costly process for southern politicians. They lit bonfires, held mass meetings, and hosted large barbecues to bring blacks together for campaign speeches; they organized black Democratic campaign clubs with great fanfare

and publicity. Yet most blacks naturally distrusted men who had opposed their enfranchisement and who now forced them to eat at separate tables at the political picnics. In sum, plaintive harangues, free
meals, and outright bribes were ineffective. Blacks listened to the
Democratic speakers, feasted on the bounteous viands, and then voted
Republican. A common expression held that the Negro would follow
his old master in everything but politics.[33]

The failure of these stratagems made a search for outside assistance
imperative. In effect confessing their political impotence, white leaders
came to see the northern Democrats as their only hope. Assuming that
a Democratic president would refuse to enforce the Reconstruction acts
and would allow the restoration of home rule, they attached special
importance to the 1868 presidential election. Faith in the Democracy,
however, was far from universal. Beginning with the disputes between
Calhoun and prominent party leaders in the antebellum period, southerners had long debated the advantages of a national political party
versus a strictly southern one. As Ben Hill, Wade Hampton, and other
skeptics noted, the northern Democracy had proved unreliable in 1861,
and there was no reason to expect it to do better now.[34] Most southern
whites nevertheless buried such doubts and entered the campaign with
determination and enthusiasm.

Southern Democrats insisted that the party condemn the usurpa-
tions of the radical Republicans in unequivocal language. Specifically,
the Reconstruction acts and radical southern policies must be repudiated. When the party adopted a platform declaring the Reconstruction
acts unconstitutional and void, southerners had achieved all they
could have hoped for. During the canvass, stump speakers spent more
time praising the platform than extolling the virtues of the party's
nominees.

This ultraconservative platform combined with the injudicious
speeches of several prominent old Confederates gave the Republicans a
ready-made campaign theme. Southern Republicans set the tone for
the canvass by defining the voters' choice as one between the Republicans and peace and the Democrats and war. Frightened radicals
claimed that a Republican defeat would mean death for the party's
southern wing. The *Tallahassee Sentinel,* which had recently changed
its political stance from conservative to radical, predicted the destruction of the public schools and the renewed persecution of loyal men if
the Democracy should triumph.[35]

The image of white Unionists and blacks being assassinated along
lonely country roads effectively aroused the northern electorate and
infuriated southern conservatives. There was little doubt that the
question of a rekindled rebellion could prove decisive. Strenuous ef-

forts by Democratic leaders to defuse this explosive issue failed, but to a great extent they had only themselves to blame. According to William Hidell, a southern journalist of moderate views, the people were "more rampant and crazy" in South Carolina than anywhere else and were talking war just as they had done in 1860. Hidell had heard a drunken Robert Toombs urge a cheering audience to clean their muskets, rifles, and shotguns and prepare to kill Yankees and Negroes. Some of the people, Hidell sadly concluded, "are just big enough fools to imagine they can of themselves be an army and wage successful war."[36]

In an atmosphere rent by a rhetoric of desperation, many southern whites found it difficult to control their emotions. Although Democratic speakers repeated the usual charges about radical agitators fomenting black insurrections, conservatives were the real incendiaries. The editor of the *Atlanta Constitution* suggested that white radicals "be made to feel the cold steel" whenever racial disturbances occurred. The inauguration of a Democratic president, the fanatical Ryland Randolph crowed to his fellow Alabamians, would be the signal for hanging the scalawags and carpetbaggers.[37] Such extreme statements were not typical of southern editorial comment during the campaign, but they are significant because individuals and groups put this advice into practice.

The violence of the 1868 canvass marked a clear departure from the earlier pattern of Reconstruction disturbances. Outbreaks with a primarily political purpose occurred in nearly every state. If enough potential Republican voters could be convinced that casting their ballots would be dangerous, the Democrats might well carry the southern states. Although the New Orleans riot of 1866 was political in origin, the first widespread political disorders in the postwar South occurred in 1868. From this point on, Reconstruction violence became increasingly organized (at least at the local and state levels) and less random and individualistic.

The first manifestation of this change was the geographical expansion and stepped-up activity of the Ku Klux Klan. Organized in 1866 in Pulaski, Tennessee, by several young Confederate veterans, the Klan was always shrouded in secrecy and mythology. The Klan, with its mysterious name and elaborate rituals, initially was a social club for the amusement of its members. By early 1867, however, the group had become a band of regulators whose ostensible purpose was to stop a black crime wave. Initially, Klan activities were confined to pranks and verbal intimidation. Its aims became more serious as it spread through Middle and West Tennessee, proclaiming itself the chief defender of white civilization against the oppressive regime of Governor

William G. "Parson" Brownlow. Although the Klan's prescript established an elaborate hierarchy, in practice local dens operated autono-
mously with very little central direction. It is doubtful whether in this
early period the Klan extended much beyond Tennessee and a few
counties in northern Alabama. Klansmen apparently engaged in some
night riding during the 1867 election campaign in Tennessee but did
not conduct the systematic and widespread terrorism that would become synonymous with the organization's name.[38]

Allen Trelease has argued that Klan violence first became evident in
the spring of 1868, when the original leaders lost control of the organization, but the relationship between the officers and the rank and
file is complex and raises important questions about the nature of and
support for violence in the Reconstruction South. Because the formal
chain of command probably never functioned according to the regula-
tions in the prescript, Klan members often acted without instructions
from their superiors. But the leaders' denials of responsibility could
also have been a convenient excuse for prominent citizens who secretly
welcomed vigilantism and bloodshed. Conservative leaders commonly
condemned certain "excesses" while denying their own involvement.

Ironically, Brownlow could have used the same logic in disclaiming
any connection with the occasional outrages committed by his state
militiamen. Indeed, the contest between the militia and the Klan was
at first very even. White Tennesseans denounced Brownlow's Negro
militia for committing numerous depredations in the state but apparently were more alarmed by its effectiveness in suppressing night riding than by its crimes. Unionists regularly complained to the governor
of rebel attacks and requested state arms to defend themselves. Before
the beginning of extensive Klan disorders, the Tennessee militia performed its extremely difficult task creditably.[39]

Many of the troubles in Tennessee were unconnected with politics;
they involved meting out extralegal justice to Negro criminals and
settling private quarrels with a deadly finality. The conservative press
often criticized such abuses but lamely contended they had not been
committed by "genuine" Ku Klux, whatever that meant. By the summer of 1868, the raids in Tennessee had nearly ceased, but Republicans
still demanded a more effective state militia to protect black citizens
who had been driven from their homes, and conservatives countered
with charges of misconduct against Brownlow's men.[40]

Even as the violence abated in Tennessee, the Klan moved into other
states. In most areas, the Klan sprang up simultaneously with the
formation of Republican state governments in the spring of 1868 as a
response to the supposed evils of radical and black domination. The
dens remained largely independent of one another; a group of young

men generally formed a den after hearing news of the organization elsewhere. The Klan was active in all the former Confederate states and Kentucky, but it grew less rapidly in the black-belt areas and in counties with a large number of white Republicans.[41] The Klan entered Virginia, North Carolina, and Florida in the early spring but confined its activities to organizing and occasionally publishing bizarre notices in the newspapers. In South Carolina, Ku Klux conducted raids and whipped some blacks; in Georgia, Klansmen assassinated prominent white Republican leader George W. Ashburn; and in Alabama, they engaged in scattered acts of terrorism. Ku Klux appeared in a few Mississippi counties, but cautious planters opposed any organization that might stimulate black resistance. Violence against blacks would supply Republicans with political ammunition and upset relations between capital and labor.[42]

In the trans-Mississippi South, where frontier conditions still prevailed, the Klan had a more violent career. It apparently existed only briefly in the Florida parishes of Louisiana, but similar organizations, primarily the Knights of the White Camellia, operated throughout the state. In the northern parishes men in disguise whipped blacks, assassinated Republican leaders, and destroyed the press of a Republican newspaper. Ku Klux in the southern counties of Arkansas rode as masked vigilantes, chased Union men from the area, and fired into houses at night. With crime already rampant and murder nearly an everyday occurrence, Texas hardly needed another band of bloodthirsty vigilantes. Bandits and desperadoes, often without disguise and in the daytime, roamed about the state committing depredations. But even in the wilds of Texas, the Ku Klux did not operate entirely unopposed. Blacks shot at Klansmen who rode into Millican in Brazos County, but several were killed in the ensuing exchange of gunfire. Conservative newspapers commonly labeled such affrays "Negro riots" and blamed them on the inflammatory teachings of white radicals.[43]

Manufactured tales of black insurrection circulated through the South during every Reconstruction election campaign. Peaceful political meetings were interpreted by nervous whites as the prelude to race war. After a group of Negroes in Conway County, Arkansas, had reportedly resolved to exterminate the white people, one hundred armed men gathered in the town of Lewisburg; a small group of whites then exchanged fire with blacks in the countryside. Sensing the beginning of a pogrom, the blacks gave up their arms and went home. In St. Martinville, Louisiana, the mayor dispersed a Republican parade. Although some blacks threatened to burn the town, they left without incident.[44]

White fears were most intense in South Carolina. Reports that armed Negroes were drilling at night spread throughout the state. Frightened citizens abandoned their political scruples and begged Republican Governor Robert K. Scott for assistance, but conservative leaders conceded that many of the freedmen genuinely feared reenslavement if a Democratic president were elected. The existence of black political organizations not only increased white paranoia but served as a convenient pretext for whites to form vigilante groups.[45]

The work of Democratic clubs alarmed Republicans, who raised a hue and cry about large weapons shipments coming into the South. Repeating rifles became a standard accouterment for men attending campaign rallies; Union men feared that bullets rather than ballots would determine the election results. Democrats agreed, but from their viewpoint the danger came not from Ku Klux but from state militias. Livid editors attacked a Republican plan for Congress to supply state forces with arms; such appropriations were not made until after the election. Republican Governor Harrison Reed of Florida purchased guns and ammunition in New York, but Klansmen intercepted the shipment between Jacksonville and Tallahassee, scattering the weapons along the railroad tracks. Ironically, men who recognized the danger, such as Governor Scott of South Carolina, still defended the "constitutional right" of citizens to carry arms, even if the exercise of this privilege meant brandishing shotguns and rifles at political rallies.[46]

Acts of intimidation against Republican voters occurred in nearly all the southern states. Arkansas Klansmen forcibly prevented blacks from registering and insisted on enrolling Confederates who had been disfranchised by the state's new constitution; armed bands in Alabama made Negroes sign pledges to vote the Democratic ticket; local officials in Tennessee arrested freedmen who attended Republican meetings.[47] In most states, such coercion was scattered and sporadic, and its effect on the outcome of the election is uncertain. Radicals may have exaggerated the extent of the problem, but such tactics created an aura of fear even if they did not prevent significant numbers of voters from going to the polls.

Accounts of night riding regularly appeared in Republican newspapers, letters written by southern Republicans to their northern political allies contained moving appeals for protection, and Republican governors received numerous requests for military assistance. Disguised men visited freedmen's homes at night, confiscated weapons, whipped black men, and terrified families. Shootings became common as election day approached.[48] Many of the attacks seem random and capricious—a tactic that served, whether intentionally or not, to heighten the terror.

At other times the armed bands were calculating in choosing their victims. In the tradition of European and American mobs, they acted with restraint, carefully selecting "real enemies" as targets.[49] The most prominent Republican to be assassinated was Congressman James M. Hinds of Arkansas, who was shot from ambush in October on his way to deliver a public speech. In the upcountry of South Carolina, three whites killed Benjamin Franklin Randolph, a black member of the legislature from Orangeburg County. Conservatives attempted to discredit Randolph and thereby divert attention from the crime by charging him with misleading Negroes, alienating the two races, and advocating social equality. Republican sources claimed that three members of the South Carolina legislature and one delegate to the constitutional convention had been murdered since the beginning of the canvass.[50]

To Republican leaders, these incidents proved the existence of a conservative conspiracy to drive loyal men out of the South. The lives of state and local officials in Alabama and South Carolina were threatened, and Charleston black leader Richard Cain believed Democratic clubs had marked him for assassination. To ferret out the truth in these incidents is impossible, but even accounting for some exaggeration, a pattern of persistent if not systematic intimidation emerges. To the Republicans and their families on the firing line, the terror was all too real. A frightened woman in Anderson, South Carolina, recounted how the Ku Klux Klan had abused local Republicans and were attempting to drive her husband from the country. "I never lie down to sleep," she sadly noted, "with that sense of safety which I could feel, if my husband's principles were democratic."[51]

Although Republicans' fears mounted as the campaign progressed, most of them cast their ballots for Grant. The party carried all the southern states except Georgia and Louisiana, where by November night riding and other forms of violence had turned the Republican majorities of the spring elections into Democratic ones.

Early in the Georgia campaign, Republicans accused their opponents of plotting to deprive blacks of their right to vote. That recent convert to the party, Joe Brown, predicted more bloodshed if Democrats attempted to terrorize black citizens. Appealing to northern friends for assistance, Republicans insisted the Georgia Democracy was gaining black support through coercion.[52]

Intimidation focused on a single community could be remarkably effective. In September political tensions became so inflamed that Democrats in Camilla decided to crush black political activity with overwhelming force. A small town located in Mitchell County in the extreme southwestern corner of Georgia, Camilla was the scheduled site for a Republican meeting on September 19. When two to three hundred blacks, some armed, assembled on the appointed day, Sheriff M. S. Poore and a handful of white citizens met them a few miles from town. The Republicans could hold a meeting, the sheriff told them, so long as they did not bring in any weapons. Two white Republicans then led the procession into Camilla, where waiting townspeople opened fire. Despite attempts by the scalawags to rally them, the blacks fled into a nearby woods. Nine blacks died, and twenty-five to thirty were wounded. No whites were killed, and only six were wounded. As in most such affrays, the evidence of prior planning is circumstantial, but the hand of the Young Men's Democratic Club was plainly visible. Conservative editors blamed radical leaders for secretly ordering blacks to provoke outbreaks in the South during the campaign. If this charge was true, conservative whites had certainly cooperated. The people of Georgia, the normally temperate editor of the *Augusta Constitutionalist* warned, "are not obliged to meekly submit to armed invasions of our cities and villages." Many whites believed Republican Governor Rufus Bullock and other knavish scalawags and carpetbaggers would risk racial warfare to obtain political advantages. Yet the fact that armed whites had chased, shot, and killed blacks in the woods near Camilla gave pause to some conservatives. As Linton Stephens noted in a letter to his brother, "From all I have seen about the Camilla riot, I am afraid our people cannot stand wholly justified."[53] But if men such as Stephens were concerned, they did nothing to stop the terrorism.

The Klan was active in many parts of Georgia during the campaign, threatening Republicans, searching for weapons, whipping men of both races, and committing an unknown number of murders. Ku Klux also acted as vigilantes in affairs unrelated to the election. A mob in Jefferson County near Augusta seized a black man for allegedly raping a white woman, bound him to a stake, and burned him alive. In other areas of the state, "radical Negroes" had to sleep in the woods to avoid the roving white bands. On election day, whites surrounded the polls in Savannah to prevent blacks from voting and drove insistent freedmen away with guns.[54] The effect was striking: Republican majorities in many counties evaporated, and the Democrats easily captured the state's electoral votes. The lesson to be drawn by the conservative victors was equally simple: force works.

But Georgia was tranquil compared to Louisiana. Governor Henry Clay Warmoth may have exaggerated the danger in claiming that 150 men had been murdered in that state in a month and a half,[55] but armed companies, especially the Knights of the White Camellia, were at work throughout the campaign. The raison d'être for the Knights was to maintain white supremacy and protect the country from political equality and miscegenation. Alcibiades DeBlanc of St. Martin Parish, the founder of the order, accused radicals of attempting to turn the southern states into "African provinces" and of inciting their black dupes to acts of barbarism. As usual at the beginning of a campaign, white Louisianians claimed armed blacks were terrorizing the state.[56]

For the most part, these incendiaries were products of fevered imaginations, in contrast to the all too tangible Democratic night riders. The Knights of the White Camellia and other such groups broke up Republican meetings and destroyed Republican ballots, thus paralyzing the party in many sections of the state. Voter intimidation consisted of warning blacks not to vote Republican, their "voluntary" enlistment in Democratic clubs, and forcing them to sign pledges to vote Democratic. Beatings and death threats brought reluctant converts into line.[57] Although these outrages were concentrated in the Florida parishes of southeastern Louisiana and in the extreme northern part of the state, no area escaped unscathed.

Freedmen's Bureau officers, parish officials, and black politicians received anonymous threats and not so anonymous mention in Klan or Knights newspaper notices. Registration officials enrolled black voters at some peril to themselves. As in Georgia, the murder of selected Republicans served as an object lesson to the rank and file. When black leader John Kemp of St. Helena Parish was assassinated in late October, Negro Republicans abandoned their efforts to resist Democratic regulators. Although the Republicans saw evidence of a massive conspiracy in these outrages, in Louisiana as elsewhere, white terrorists were not organized beyond the local level. The *New Orleans Picayune* was perhaps correct in asserting that many of the murders were for personal rather than political reasons, but the line between partisan intimidation and private vendetta was often thin.[58] Persecution in any form could have the same political result.

Besides scattered acts of violence, there were also full-scale race riots. In Bossier Parish in the far northwestern corner of the state, armed and drunken Negroes tied up and beat an Arkansas cotton salesman who had snapped his pistol at one of them. After the blacks killed two other men on September 30, a body of armed whites, many from Arkansas, surrounded the Negroes on a plantation and murdered at least one hundred of them. Conservatives blamed white radicals for inciting the blacks, but the resulting slaughter, even by Levitical standards of punishment, hardly fit the crime.[59] This mob apparently acted with no obvious partisan purpose but massacred blacks indiscriminately.

In St. Landry Parish mob violence was more overtly political but equally deadly. Located in south-central Louisiana, St. Landry had a large black population, few native Republicans, and two prominent carpetbaggers, Emerson Bentley and Michael Vidal, the publishers of the radical *St. Landry Progress*. Although the Democrats had easily carried the parish in the April state elections, by summer the Republicans were better organized and held meetings with black sentinels standing guard. Whites suspected the carpetbag leaders of making incendiary speeches at these gatherings, and a rumor circulated that the blacks intended to burn down the small town of Washington. Conservative sources alleged that Bentley had advised the blacks to use matches during the campaign and had prevented them from attending Democratic rallies. On September 28, two whites visited Bentley at a school he had set up for the black children in the parish and severely caned him for an article he had written attacking the terrorism of the Democratic clubs. The schoolchildren ran from the building screaming that their teacher had been murdered.

Excited Republicans of both races converged on Opelousas, the parish's largest town. After blacks and whites exchanged gunfire near the outskirts of town, white bands fanned out along the country roads, captured twenty-nine black men, and hauled them back to the jail in Opelousas. The next day a mob seized all but two of the prisoners and shot them to death. Night riders again moved into the countryside, brutally murdering any blacks they could find. Republicans later estimated that Democratic clubs had slain some two hundred, and the Democrats conceded that twenty-five to thirty had been killed. The Democrats had assured their victory in the election. One witness told a congressional investigating committee that "the Republican party had ceased to exist in St. Landry."[60]

With its long tradition of political warfare from the days of the Know Nothings through the riot of 1866, New Orleans could hardly have escaped bloodshed during the 1868 campaign. Warmoth later described the city at that time as "dirty, impoverished . . . with a mixed, ignorant, corrupt, and bloodthirsty gang in control. It was flooded with lotteries, gambling dens, and licensed brothels. Many of the city officials, as well as the police force, were thugs and murderers." By September, partisan excitement had made New Orleans a powder keg. The Democrats raised their perennial cries of Negro insurrection and complained of blacks parading in the streets committing untold outrages and terrifying white citizens.[61]

Taking advantage of police inefficiency, New Orleans conservatives formed quasi-military organizations such as the Crescent City Democratic Club and the Seymour Legion. These groups patrolled the streets, ostensibly to control black crime, but their opponents saw their real purpose as assaulting Republicans. United States Marshal Stephen B. Packard complained that Democrats regularly stole weapons from local gun shops. One anxious radical reported that Democrats planned to sound the fire alarm as a signal to begin a massacre of the Republicans in the city.[62]

Federal troops nervously watched the growing disorder under War Department instructions to remain alert for signs of trouble. Conservative General Lovell H. Rousseau, commander of the soldiers in the state, feared the growing mob spirit and realistically concluded that the partisan police force would be useless should disturbances arise.[63] Neither the Johnson administration nor Rousseau was willing to use the available forces to protect Republicans, thereby allowing the Democrats to act with impunity.

The first significant outbreak occurred on the evening of September 22, when black and white political processions clashed. As the black Grant and Constitution clubs marched along Canal Street, a white man on a balcony let out a yell for Horatio Seymour and Francis P. Blair, Jr., the Democratic presidential and vice-presidential nominees. The blacks charged the building, broke through the doors and windows of a restaurant, and fired. Members of a Democratic club rushed into the melee, hurling rocks and using their knives and pistols against the blacks. One black man died in the fighting, and several persons on both sides were injured before the military and the police finally restored order. Crediting white incendiaries with stirring blacks to commit aggressive acts, the editor of the *Picayune* warned that the carpetbaggers and scalawags would be held personally answerable for future racial disturbances.[64]

During October, the Democratic clubs became more brazen, breaking up Republican meetings, burning schools and churches, and murdering Negroes. The predominantly black Metropolitan Police could not make arrests because white bands patrolled much of the city and threatened to attack them if they tried to curb the bands. On October 25, members of the Democratic Workingmen's Club disrupted a Republican procession and killed several blacks. After initially fleeing from their assailants, the Negroes grabbed their weapons and shot at white men on the streets until soldiers arrived to restore order. Despite the strength of the Republican clubs and the apparent willingness of the blacks to match their enemies blow for blow and shot for shot, white Republicans in letters to their northern political supporters painted a picture of cowering Negroes intimidated by armed whites.[65]

Besides revealing some of the racial preconceptions of white Republican leaders, their reports of black cowardice show that paternalism could exist on both ends of the political spectrum. Did the carpetbaggers and scalawags fear race war as much as the Democrats, or were they more concerned about black assertiveness within the Republican party and their own positions of power? Scalawags in particular were sensitive about the costs of unleashing their black supporters against white terrorists, and their hesitation often proved fatal because it allowed Democrats to take the offensive.

Ignoring Governor Warmoth's proclamation requesting that neither party hold any more political demonstrations before election day, the Democratic clubs continued to rampage through the streets. On the evening of October 26, the Innocents, a misnamed polyglot group of Sicilians, Italians, Spanish, Portuguese, Maltese, Latin Americans, and Creoles, emptied their guns into Republican clubrooms. When one of their members was slain in the return fire, the Innocents ransacked Negro homes and Republican headquarters. The Metropolitans were powerless and greatly feared for their own lives. Casualty estimates ranged from a score to well over a hundred.[66] These pitched battles in the streets of New Orleans pointed up the inability of the state government to protect its citizens in its own capital.

In the midst of burgeoning disorders in Georgia, Louisiana, and other southern states, the army remained uncertain about its role. Southern governors sent numerous requests to Washington for additional soldiers in the hope that more troops would deter Democratic outrages and ensure a peaceful election. Soldiers were already stationed in the South, and southern Republican leaders sometimes dictated their distribution within the states. The Johnson administration nevertheless informed state officials that they were responsible for keeping the peace and should call for federal help only if faced with overwhelming resistance. General George G. Meade, the commander of the Department of the South (which then included the states of North Carolina, South Carolina, Georgia, Florida, and Alabama), did not have enough men to meet all the pleas for assistance. The shortage of troops and limitations on their employment placed the generals in an uncomfortable position. An example is the vague instructions of Secretary of War John M. Schofield and President Johnson to General Rousseau in Louisiana to prevent bloodshed without interfering with the functions of civil government. The bewildered general was left to stumble about on his own in the quicksands of Louisiana politics. The army therefore assumed a largely passive role during the canvass, intervening only to suppress some of the more sanguinary disturbances and providing the beleaguered Republicans with virtually no protection.[67]

Early in the campaign, some Republican leaders had realized that conservative intimidation would result in a Democratic victory. By October, the situation seemed hopeless, at least in Georgia and Louisiana. Night riding had cowed Republican voters, and Democrats threatened to take control of the election machinery.[68] Although there were no major disturbances on election day, radicals in Georgia and South Carolina complained that armed (and sometimes disguised) Klansmen prevented blacks from voting. Democratic election officials challenged Negro voters at the polls, and whites crowded around the ballot boxes to stop Republicans from depositing their tickets. The police in several towns and cities chased blacks from the polls and shot some voters.[69]

Aided by intimidation and terrorism, the Democrats carried two southern states. Some black voters in Georgia, justifiably frightened by threats from the Ku Klux Klan, either did not go to the polls or voted Democratic. In Louisiana, Republicans advised their followers not to vote if to do so would risk their lives. As a result, the party received but a handful of votes in several parishes that had gone strongly Republican in the April state elections. The outcome of the voting unmistakably demonstrated that even a crudely conceived and badly organized campaign of coercion and violence could significantly reduce Republican strength in the South.[70]

The election also reveals two important generalizations about the role and efficacy of threats and bullets in a national political contest. The bloodshed in 1868 was spread, albeit unevenly, across much of the South, hampering the federal government's use of the army to quell, much less prevent, disturbances. But only in Georgia and Louisiana were the whites sufficiently organized to employ violent methods that would affect the outcome of the balloting. Disorders in a national campaign might be difficult to suppress, but their effect is also easy to negate. Had the result been close, the Republicans either would have refused to count the electoral votes from Georgia and Louisiana or would have investigated the outrages and awarded the states' electoral votes to Grant. As it happened, the House and Senate were unable to agree on whether Georgia's electoral vote should be counted. In a state election, it would have been much harder for the federal government to remedy the effects of irregularities because federal intervention would have fewer constitutional buttresses and much less public support. By 1876 the Republicans found it much more acceptable to "count in" their presidential candidate than to aid southern Republicans in bitterly contested state races.

This lesson was not lost on conservative southerners. Although many politicians would flirt with Liberal Republicanism, support Horace Greeley in 1872, and stump for Samuel Tilden in 1876, they never again considered national elections or national party leaders the keys to salvation. After Grant's inauguration, the attention of the white South turned inward toward the operation of the Republican state and local governments. Thereafter, the revolt against Reconstruction took place on these levels, steadily eroding Republican and black power and eventually restoring white Democratic hegemony.

Conservative southerners' attention to state and local governments added considerable depth to conservative perceptions about revolution and counterrevolution. Many whites perceived the Reconstruction regimes as petty tyrannies. To them the illegitimate nature of Republican rule justified revolutionary action. The rhetoric and depth of emotion in many public and private statements on these issues precluded moderation or gradualism. Since peaceful methods had failed to achieve the liberation of the southern homeland, perhaps only the knife, the rope, and the gun could drive the Republicans from power. Few southerners probably were as rabid in such convictions as Ryland Randolph, editor of the *Tuscaloosa Independent Monitor,* who called for a general massacre of radical leaders whenever a racial disturbance took place. Yet neither would many whites actively oppose terrorism. E. John Ellis of Louisiana, a respectable lawyer, businessman, and conservative politician, wrote almost whimsically, "If there was one hope of successful armed revolution I would be willing to enlist for life."[71] The path of resistance to Reconstruction in several states would therefore be strewn with dead bodies, both black and white.

6. The Origins of the Counterrevolution

The reality of Republican rule seemed nearly to match conservative southerners' worst prophecies. Not only did the new regime lack legitimacy and constitutional authority, but it was also an engine of oppression. Excluded from the inner circles of power, former Confederates stood outside the political process and lacked not only control but nonviolent channels through which to express their hostility.[1] Because they were shut out of the governing process, they saw themselves as impotent. Such a situation in which rulers are or seem to be unresponsive to the aspirations of a large group encourages civil violence.[2] The peculiarity, if the not the perverseness, of lumping southern conservatives with third-world revolutionaries or twentieth-century black power advocates is obvious, but clearly their perceptions of the established order are remarkably similar. The sense of deprivation and frustration must have been more intense for southern leaders because they had long been accustomed to wielding substantial influence.

Their feelings of powerlessness and natural antipathy toward those in power led many southerners to exaggerate the defects of the new governments. Revisionist scholars have corrected many hyperbolic statements about oppressive taxation, extravagant public expenditures, and official peculation, but reality does not account for the intensity of the opposition or the ferocity of the resistance. Whatever their basis in fact, vigorous condemnations of corruption became a rallying cry for the crusade against Republican Reconstruction.[3] The central issue, however, was not the fiscal irresponsibility of the carpetbaggers, scalawags, and blacks but their base purpose and unscrupulous means.

In the first heated response to the Reconstruction acts, conservatives stressed their unprecedented and revolutionary nature, but the persistence of this line of attack demonstrates both the political usefulness of the critique and the sincerity of those making the charges. Even as the southern governments began operation, their opponents saw the radicals as zealots whose goal was the complete centralization of government. Although the more strident critics were fanatics with limited influence, many men of normally moderate views held forth in eloquent perorations against the Republican governments. Linton Stephens of Georgia, a temperate man who opposed extremism, presented a searing analysis of a world turned upside down:

> These revolutionary governments are in the hands of carpet-baggers and scalawags, who treat the laws of their own organization with disgraceful contempt; and, under the forms of official authority, heap upon our people injuries and insults which never before were borne by men born and bred and educated in the principles of Liberty. Shameless plunder, malignant slander, corrupt favoritism, impunity for crimes committed by the partisans of the Government, gigantic extension of the credit of the States to penniless adventurers who come among us under the false and fraudulent plea of "developing our resources," robbery of the very negroes who are sought to be used as the chief instrument of upholding this gigantic system of revolutionary fraud and force—these are the fruits of these revolutionary governments. These are the products of reconstruction.[4]

This comprehensive list of Republican crimes, however, lacked one essential item. "The history of the Radical party proves," Mississippi Democrats resolved in 1868, "that they are even now engaged in the work of Africanizing the Southern States by establishing negro rule and negro supremacy." This statement ignored the fact that blacks held relatively few public offices and never "ruled" any state. Southern whites believed they were dominated by their former slaves, and this belief was a primary cause for the eruption of violence. The veteran politicians' personal revulsion against sitting with Negroes in legislative assemblies only intensified alarms about "Africanization."[5]

The program of black supremacy seemed even more outrageous because the radicals were unblushing hypocrites. Before the passage of the Fifteenth Amendment, southern conservatives, with some justification, pointed out that Republicans were willing to impose black suffrage on the South but feared to broach the subject among their own constituents. Editors emphasized racial prejudice in the North to illustrate radical duplicity; as one North Carolina newspaper put it, "Our Northern friends do not like the taste of the cup they prepared for their Southern brethren." This bitterness led to the half-facetious suggestion that southerners elect only blacks to Congress and see how advocates of Negro supremacy would respond.[6] Such idle speculation perhaps served as an outlet for angry men, but it also demonstrated enormous self-delusion.

To expose the inaccuracy of the myth of "radical Reconstruction" is not, however, to exorcise its influence. By writing their own version of Reconstruction history, conservative southerners had a ready-made defense of white supremacy. They had only to conjure up the horrors of black rule and all dissent disappeared. Such potent social myths have often generated popular unrest, and in this case they served as formidable justification for violent resistance to Reconstruction.[7]

Southern outrage over military Reconstruction guaranteed open defiance of the newly established authorities. "How long can these things be," the editor of the *Atlanta Constitution* asked, "and retributive justice not overtake their [the radicals'] crimes?" Less discreet editors asserted that only federal bayonets could enforce Negro rule in the southern states and warned that Yankee oppressors would eventually meet the fate of all tyrants. North Carolina Bourbon spokesman Josiah Turner explained the eruption of racial violence in Mississippi as "the direct, natural, logical consequence of negro supremacy. White men will not, they ought not, to submit to the control of an inferior race of people. We should despise our own blood, our own people, if peacefully and tamely submitted to the dominance of the African."[8] Resistance to tyranny, in this schema, became a sacred duty to past, present, and future generations.

Particular enemies of the commonweal were easily identified. The popular stereotypes of the carpetbagger and scalawag developed early in the Reconstruction period, when their very names became symbols of unalloyed evil. The mere mention of a prominent white Republican by an editor or stump speaker produced a heated response among the white masses.[9] "The day will come," Josiah Turner warned, "when all or many of such crimes will be mercilessly exposed. And such perpetrators of crime will henceforth be a stench in the nostrils of all decent men, white and black. Everybody will hate them, mock and hiss at them as they pass by."[10] To say that a carpetbagger was more despised than a scalawag would be similar to saying that one skunk emitted a stronger odor than another. In the pantheon of southern villains, the carpetbagger and the scalawag occupied positions of equal ignominy.

Carpetbaggers easily aroused conservative wrath for causing racial disturbances; editors suggested that they be "dispatched" whenever racial violence erupted. As Faulkner's Drusilla Sartoris pointed out in explaining the political terrorism practiced by her ancestors, killing carpetbaggers was justified because "they were northerners, foreigners who had no business here. They were pirates."[11]

Southern conservatives might dream of a mass auto-da-fe of radicals, but they could not heedlessly execute their enemies. The murder of a white person, even a carpetbagger or scalawag, was a serious matter that might provoke federal intervention. If an attack against a "real" enemy is too dangerous, aggrieved individuals commonly displace their hostility onto a person or group that is unlikely or unable to retaliate. Because southerners could not avenge themselves directly on the hated Yankees, they took out their frustrations in brutal attacks on Negroes.[12] Though conservative spokesmen never admitted the logical connection between the risk of assaulting white Republicans and the freedom to commit violence against blacks, the action of white mobs illustrated this rationale at work.

In the scattered acts of violence against white Republicans that did occur, Democrats placed more blame on the victim than on the perpetrator. The Republicans' greatest crime was seen as their control over the loyalty and especially the votes of black men. According to conservatives, the designing radicals filled the heads of Negroes with false notions of their own importance and lies about their white neighbors. If the carpetbaggers and scalawags would leave, a natural harmony would return to race relations. As a disgruntled North Carolinian put it, "The people are disquieted by the travelling political tricksters and intriguers. . . . It [the South] is filled with rogues, thieves, liars, drunkards and political mountebanks."[13] Republican machinations were insidious, mysterious, exasperating, but above all dangerous.

When conservative newspapers spoke of "radical incendiaries," they meant precisely that. Men who advised patience and peaceful protest often did so not because of moral objection to the use of force but because it would only help the Republicans. Indeed, many conservative editors argued that their enemies wanted to provoke outbreaks in the South simply to win votes in the North. This vast intersectional conspiracy to foment race war for political gain made each riot part of a larger design. The editor of the *Atlanta Constitution* even charged that "loyal men" would deliberately murder each other to ensure the ascendancy of the radical party by placing the southern states back under military rule. These conscienceless manipulators, trumpeted the *Augusta Chronicle and Sentinel,* would "prefer to see the black race exterminated or driven from our borders—to witness the smoking ruins of desolated homes—to hear the cries of widows and the wails of orphans over the stiffened corpse of the assassinated husband and father—to see this fair land drenched in blood from the Potomac to the Rio Grande—rather than lose their power."[14]

Republican organizing efforts, black political activity, and white paranoia caused rumors of Negro insurrections in southern communities long after the initial period of labor unrest during presidential Reconstruction. Local panics commonly began with tales of arson plots and arms caches and ended with the arrest of several blacks. Although often connected with political excitement, these alarms were not confined to election campaigns or to states where Republicans still held power.[15]

The Union League was to white conservatives by far the most dangerous Republican organization. Founded in the North during the war, the Union League of America established chapters in the South early in the Reconstruction period. The southern branch, commonly called the Loyal League and consisting primarily of blacks enrolled by white radicals, was both a social and a political organization designed to mobilize Republican electoral strength. White southerners believed that the clandestine meetings, the rituals, and the elaborate regalia attracted superstitious blacks. Although this may have been true for some Negroes, many more were motivated by the League's association with the party of emancipation. Because members allegedly had to sign an oath swearing they would vote Republican, Democrats believed them to be radical thralls. The obvious irony is that conservatives often sought to coerce blacks into supporting the Democrats. Their real objection to the League was its political effectiveness.[16]

Information on the operations of the Loyal League is sketchy. There were occasional reports in some states of armed blacks marching and drilling at night. Although conservatives charged League members with herding Negroes to the polls and forcing them to vote Republican, the evidence is vague, particularly about dates and places. The only serious incidence of violence occurred in Franklin, Tennessee, in 1867, when League members and conservatives shot at each other in the center of town for about an hour. Newspaper stories often lack specific information; as a North Carolina Republican editor noted, whites denounced the League in Wake County as incendiary because members marched to drum music and carried an American flag.[17]

Given the conspiratorial mind set of many southerners, it is not surprising that they saw the Loyal League as part of a plot to alienate blacks from their white employers, encourage arson against private property, and inaugurate a racial Armageddon in the South. A careful reading of editorial comments on League activity shows that whites were awed by if not envious of the ability of the radicals to control their black supporters. Yet this supposedly solid Negro phalanx did not cow conservatives. As the editor of the *Augusta Constitutionalist* grimly noted, if the League forced a violent collision upon the whites, "they will not shrink from it, but rather with all the manhood of a proud and still powerful people make the issue so complete that another shall be impossible."[18]

The Loyal League provided an excuse for Ku Klux Klan raids. Areas of the greatest League activity also witnessed the most outrages committed against blacks by white vigilante groups.[19] A standard conservative response to stories of Klan terrorism was the counterclaim that radicals engaged in similar activities through the Loyal League, but such reports were vague and are difficult to substantiate. The obvious political motivation of the conservative sources makes such accounts as suspect as similar Republican tales presented before congressional committees.[20]

Republican sources do indicate that conservative blacks were sometimes bulldozed by their Republican brethren. During the excitement of a political canvass, Republican blacks jeered Democratic blacks who addressed public meetings and threatened the lives of these men, whom they considered traitors to the race.[21] Conservative intimidation of blacks makes any estimate of the numbers of voluntary black Democrats meaningless and the extent of Republican coercion impossible to determine.

How many outrages took place in the South after the passage of the Reconstruction acts is unknown. The nature and scope of the violence varied with the political climate of each state or locality. In North Carolina, according to Freedmen's Bureau compilations, whites attacked blacks several times each month during 1867 and 1868. If by Reconstruction standards North Carolina was relatively peaceful, Texas literally ran with blood. A committee of the Texas constitutional convention of 1868 reported some 939 homicides since the end of the war. This total included 372 blacks murdered by whites but only 10 whites killed by blacks. In 1872 the United States attorney in western Texas estimated that 2,000 murders had occurred in the state since 1865, but how many were racially or politically motivated is unclear. Democrats downplayed the significance of these figures; Republicans were sure that the "rebel Democracy" was responsible for most of these crimes.[22]

The complexity of this violence generally escaped the notice of partisan commentators. The commissioner of the Freedmen's Bureau, General O. O. Howard, who was not inclined to underestimate the racial animus of southern whites, reported in 1869 that many of the attacks on blacks were committed by "bands of lawless men, organized under various names, whose principal objects were robbery and plunder." Southern conservatives asserted that most of the region's murders had no political overtones, and they denied that Union men and blacks were special targets of attack. Despite differences on the origins of the bloodshed, the parties often agreed about the seriousness of the disorders. The *New Orleans Republican* described the violence as a "Moral ulcer" on the body politic. Because the community failed to take action against the disease, it was "spreading and inflaming healthy members."[23]

Although historians have not given the southern court system the detailed study it deserves, contemporary observers had little good to say about the judicial process, particularly in the frontier regions. Civil officials in Louisiana and Texas often failed to arrest, indict, or try criminals: General Abner Doubleday claimed that no white man in Texas had been punished for murder since the revolt against Mexico.[24] When a black was the victim, there was even less chance of bringing the guilty party to justice. Some whites still believed it was not a crime against God or man to kill a Negro, and in the rare instance when such a case came to court, the jury usually brought in a verdict of justifiable homicide. Public indifference was even greater when one black person murdered another.[25]

The new state governments set up under the Reconstruction acts did little to improve the quality of southern justice. A South Carolina Republican editor wrote that if a white man committed an offense against a black man, his chance for conviction was one in one hundred. To be sure, prejudiced and incompetent local officials hamstrung the legal process, but the real difficulty lay outside the courtroom. Peaceful citizens protected the guilty parties and either out of sympathy for or fear of them refused to support attempts to suppress disorder.[26]

Conservatives recognized the political ramifications of violence. Several editors charged that radicals in Washington subsidized Republican newspapers in the South whose chief task was to manufacture fresh tales of white barbarism. Such false reports misled northern citizens by perpetuating the myth of an unreconstructed South.[27] Indeed, in comparison to the northern states, southerners described their society as the embodiment of law and order—at least in areas under Democratic control. Northern crime rates, conservative spokesmen claimed, far exceeded those of the southern states, and therefore the public outcry about southern outrages was sheer hypocrisy and political flimflam. Editorial writers eagerly seized on accounts of northern violence, particularly the lynching of blacks, to show that the region was infested by bloodthirsty mobs.[28] This effort to wave the bloody shirt in the opposite direction failed. The crime and violence in the North could not obliterate the record of southern night riding.

The preponderance of violence during election campaigns makes its partisan purpose unquestionable. Rioting became a familiar part of the political process. Intimidation was particularly effective against local officials who were far from military protection. Republican registrars of voters faced threats and occasional assaults from whites who swore they would never allow blacks to vote.[29]

Union men had long felt the fury of rebel wrath, but their northern political allies soon got a firsthand taste of Confederate hospitality.

During the spring and summer of 1867, several northern Republicans, including Congressman William D. "Pig Iron" Kelley of Pennsylvania, toured the South on a proselytizing mission. Most communities greeted these radical emissaries with coolness or disdain. In Mobile, Alabama, on May 14, Kelley spoke to a crowd of some four thousand persons, most of whom were black. The Pennsylvanian delivered a rousing stump speech in which he blamed the South for the war and defended the right of Republicans to campaign freely in the rebel states. When a few white men in the audience became unruly, Kelley boldly stated that he had federal troops at his side. A gang of rowdies on the edge of the crowd shouted such pleasantries as: "Put him down!" "Give that dog a bone." "How many Negroes and pianos did you steal?" When the chief of police tried to arrest the principal heckler, a scuffle ensued. This activity spooked a team of horses pulling an army ambulance, and they careened dangerously toward the crowd. Shots rang out from the rear of the mob, blacks fired their guns into the air, and many persons took to their heels. When the shooting began, Kelley had ducked under a table, and some friends spirited him away to his hotel, where a military guard protected him until he left the city.[30]

Their brief encounter with political violence probably did not permanently impress these northern politicians because they could go home. Their southern brethren could not escape and often received threats against their lives during hotly contested election campaigns. Attacks on state and minor federal officials occurred sporadically but frequently enough to make it plain that being a southern Republican could be hazardous to life and limb. Carpetbaggers and scalawags sent impassioned letters to their friends in Washington pleading for protection. Although some of these bloodcurdling accounts may be dismissed as self-serving and partisan, they present a frightening picture of persecution and terrorism.[31]

The irregularities and disruption on election day make any detailed analysis of voting behavior meaningless. During the ratification election for Mississippi's new state constitution in the spring of 1868, whites crowded the polls in several counties and assaulted black voters. More dispassionate men quietly but openly took down the names of blacks who voted for the constitution. The use to which this list was put is not known, but its compilation must have had a chilling effect on the newly enfranchised blacks. Such practices became increasingly common in southern elections for the rest of the century.[32] Although scalawags and carpetbaggers were sometimes threatened and attacked, armed whites directed most of their attention to the blacks. If they could either be "persuaded" not to vote or to vote Democratic, the strength of the Republican party would disappear.

Clever conservatives wooed blacks by bribery, trickery, and legal technicalities. Blacks were plied with liquor to prevent them from going to the polls or to win besotted converts to the Democracy. Ardent party workers stuffed ballot boxes or paid off Republican election officials for a favorable count. Since most blacks were illiterate, unscrupulous men substituted printed advertisements and other worthless pieces of paper for Republican tickets. Conservatives upbraided radicals for herding underage blacks to the polls and encouraging their supporters to vote several times, but they were not averse to using repeaters on their own side.[33]

Even during relatively peaceful canvasses, wild rumors and inflamed passions could lead to bloodshed. In Donaldsonville, Louisiana, a small town on the west side of the Mississippi River below Baton Rouge, United States troops watching over the polls on election day in 1870 started fires to keep warm, and panicky whites suspected the Negroes were burning down the town. The Democrats, who had lost the election, planned to seize the ballot boxes in town and prevent the commissioners of election from collecting the boxes on the east side of the river. Hearing of this scheme, black militiamen marched into Donaldsonville to stop the Democrats but instead clashed with white Republican leaders. This quarrel of hazy origins led to the murder of the mayor and a local judge, both Republicans apparently killed by their partisans. The disturbance thwarted the Democrats, and the Republican candidates eventually took office. A similar attempt by Democrats to steal the ballots in Baton Rouge caused a riot in which several black men were killed or wounded and United States troops finally had to restore order.[34]

Fraud and coercion took many forms, including the exploitation of black poverty. Conservatives maintained that planters and other employers should not hire Negroes who voted Republican or were active in the Union League. They likewise withdrew their patronage from "radical" draymen, barbers, and porters. White leaders confidently expected to show the blacks where their true interests lay and thereby win their votes.[35]

Under attack from northern politicians for intimidating blacks, southerners responded that to reward friends and punish enemies was natural. Employers cited the traditions of the common law and liberty of contract in defending their right to dismiss laborers who were politically hostile. Democrats asserted that they coerced voters less effectively than the radical Loyal Leagues and added, with some truth, that northern employers of both parties had long dictated the votes of their workers.[36]

A variety of economic weapons were applied against blacks. Planters warned their field hands that if they voted Republican they would have to leave both their jobs and their homes. Farmers made informal agreements not to hire Republican blacks or those discharged by other employers; physicians threatened to withhold medical services. During election campaigns, whites organized Negro Democratic clubs by promising employment and protection for the members. When attempts to keep the freedmen ignorant of voter registration and elections failed, a more direct approach was taken. A Tennessean later recalled: "I had fully made up my mind that to be governed by my former slaves was an ignominy which I should not and would not endure." On election day he gathered up his black laborers, handed them all conservative tickets, marched them to the polls, and watched them cast their ballots.[37]

Throughout the South, employers carried out their threats by dismissing or refusing to make new contracts with Republican blacks. In some areas, planters drove the Negroes from their homes.[38] Although it is not possible to measure precisely the impact of this economic intimidation, it was probably not nearly so effective as contemporary observers or later historians have contended. A persistent labor shortage in the postwar South made it impractical to hire only Negroes who either did not vote or supported the conservatives. Some employers who tried to control the political activities of their workers found themselves without hands and forced to hire white men and black women, who were unsatisfactory. Shrewd blacks joined the Democratic clubs and made fulsome promises to support the Democratic ticket but quietly cast their Republican ballots on election day. Blinded by a determination to end Reconstruction in their states, some southerners made a substantial monetary sacrifice by refusing to employ men of unsound political principles.[39]

Whatever limited success economic coercion produced came about because the region's economy failed to grow after Appomattox. The South remained predominantly agricultural, and farmers and planters were more dependent on cotton than ever. Food production fell sharply, so both large and small operators ceased to be self-sufficient. White and black farmers became enmeshed in the crop lien system—an arrangement that bound them to the soil almost as effectively as the laws and customs of feudal Europe. The self-destructive cycle of overproduction, declining crop prices, and burgeoning debt made the South the nation's poor relation for the next century. The signs of decay were all about: precipitous drops in land values, frequent tax forfeiture sales, and general discontent with sharecropping by both races. The panic of 1873 merely added to the economic weaknesses of the southern economy and plunged the region into a depression whose effects would linger for the rest of the century.[40]

Postwar southerners suffered economically, from what Ted Gurr has called "decremental deprivation." Their expectations reflected the flush times of the 1850s, but their means declined so precipitously that the gap between goals and capabilities widened. Attempts to correlate lynchings with various economic indexes have produced inconsistent results; to argue that hard times cause violence oversimplifies a complex relationship. Yet financial distress and Reconstruction violence clearly were related. When black workers were brought into Orange County, Florida, to clear land for orange groves, for example, local "crackers" attacked their camp and attempted to drive them off. In an era of decreasing opportunity, unemployed or marginally employed whites readily blamed Negroes for their plight.[41]

In the late 1860s and early 1870s the South was in the throes of a social and economic revolution. The transition from slave to free labor came slowly, and the place of blacks in southern society remained undetermined. After initial hesitation and resistance, planters haltingly began to accept free labor and adjust their attitudes accordingly. Travelers reported blacks working well and white farmers generally satisfied, but most of this evidence predates the collapse of cotton prices in the 1870s.[42] The planters' commitment to paternalism somehow survived in an unstable economic environment. Picturing themselves as the true friends of the Negro and the all-knowing providers of employment and sustenance for a benighted people, they glowingly described a mutuality of interest between the races that should keep them working together on the land for generations. Explicit in this belief was the idea that blacks should also vote with their white friends. But paternalism clearly failed at the ballot box.[43]

Because black aspirations and ideas about the new economic order did not match those of most whites, the old paternalism and submissiveness existed only on the surface. Northern and foreign travelers found Negroes working contentedly for the former slaveholders, but farmers and planters knew better. During the long, languid summer afternoons, many white farmers sat around complaining about black labor and even blamed the freedmen for crop failures. One disgusted Tennessean bitterly remarked that he would lose his religion if it depended on "keeping my temper with free Negroes, when work should be done." A Mississippi planter, reflecting the prevailing white assessment of the black character, wrote in his journal: "The leopard cannot change its spots and the nigger will continue to remain as he is until the Angel Gabriel blows his horn."[44]

Postwar labor difficulties led some southern whites to the uncomfortable conclusion that slavery and not the Yankees had made the South economically backward. Supervising black labor, these men asserted, had drained the region's physical and intellectual resources. The sooner the South was freed from this curse the better, and promoters dreamed of importing white or even Chinese workers to replace the Negroes. At the other extreme were whites who continued to curse emancipation and long for the restoration of slavery. As one angry North Carolinian put it, "The nigger, sir, is a savage whom the Almighty maker appointed to be a slave. . . . With him free the South is ruined, sir, ruined."[45] Attempts to encourage immigration failed miserably; the underdeveloped South could not attract men seeking to improve their fortunes.

Dissatisfaction with labor arrangements was widespread and chronic. Planters complained that the blacks grumbled about their wages and hours and shirked their duties during political campaigns. At the end of each growing season laborers left their employers, who were forced to look for replacements. Blacks were no happier than their white bosses. Planters took advantage of their illiteracy to cheat them at the plantation store and in drawing up contracts. Whites resented blacks who purchased their own land, and posses sometimes drove them off newly acquired homesteads.[46] As always, the keynote was race control; white landowners could not tolerate any labor system that jeopardized their dominance over black people.

On rare occasions, blacks who could no longer abide harsh treatment struck back at their tormentors. Planters who whipped black workers might be arrested by the military or in extreme cases assaulted by their employees.[47] It is impossible to determine how many of these conflicts became violent, but they were frequent enough to remind both races of the new order's fragility and instability.

Economic problems merely added to the South's political, social, and psychological tensions and fostered the expansion of the Ku Klux Klan. Although historians have stressed the political nature of Klan activities, the organization was concerned with race control in the broadest meaning of that term and was especially sensitive to economic and social challenges to white hegemony.[48] The nature of its membership changed, more violent men became dominant, and Klan groups behaved like ordinary criminal bands.

The Klan developed as part of an American vigilante tradition. Men willing to take the law into their own hands have commonly rationalized their actions by pointing to the corruption and ineffectiveness of state and local governments. Extralegal action therefore became not a matter of personal whim or individual desire but of public necessity.[49] Southerners willing to acknowledge the existence of the Ku Klux argued that it was born to answer the evils of Republican rule. "Oppression will ever produce resistance," cried the editor of the *Charles-*

ton Courier, "and the real cause of these difficulties. . . . [can] be attributed to an arbitrary and personally irresponsible constabulary, to an armed and defiant colored militia, and to a constant and petty tyranny under the forms of law, at once at variance with the public peace and welfare, and in violation of every element of freedom." Even after serving time in prison for night riding, Randolph Shotwell defended Klan terrorism by citing the example of secret organizations formed in England, Ireland, and France to defy oppressive governments.[50]

Klan sympathizers attempted to explain away their most brutal acts by exaggerating the evils of Republican rule and multiplying the horrors of black suffrage and equality. On a cruder level, Klansmen talked of personal vengeance against radicals and the need to suppress the Loyal Leagues. The editor of the *Arkansas Gazette* charged that the true Ku Klux were the "radical carpet-bag vultures—the leeches who are sucking the life-blood out of the south." Yet as Republicans were quick to point out, the mere theft of public money paled before murders committed by men in disguise on behalf of the Democratic party.[51]

Conservatives defended vigilantism with the argument that the former Confederate states were in a condition of anarchy. For opposite reasons, Republicans had drawn this conclusion all along. Intemperate conservatives wrote in lurid terms of a black crime wave and argued that Negro burglars, rustlers, and murderers were either protected or aided by Republican officials and if convicted were pardoned by Republican governors.[52] An inefficient or corruptible legal process is likely to produce vigilantism; the formation of extralegal patrols generally has followed a series of public complaints about unchecked lawlessness. This obvious rationalization raises the problem of excusing "the people" taking the administration of justice into their own hands. Richard Maxwell Brown has perceptively shown how the idea of popular sovereignty, dating back to the American Revolution, has buttressed the private use of force to stop crime.[53]

White southerners believed the threat to society extended far beyond random criminal acts. Former Confederate General John B. Gordon of Georgia testified before the congressional committee investigating the Ku Klux outrages that the Klan was organized in Georgia to prevent Negro insurrections. Josiah Turner charged that radicals had long conspired to foment a race war in the South patterned after the Nat Turner slave revolt. Southern Republicans recognized that such alarms provided a ready excuse to break up Republican meetings and intimidate black voters.[54] This perception of attack, however unrealistic, tended to stimulate aggression among whites and also allowed them to palliate the most barbarous assaults.[55]

The events in Laurens County, South Carolina, in the fall of 1870 illustrated this concept of attack and self-defense in practice. White Republican Joe Crews organized a black militia unit in the county. Anxious whites claimed that the company's drilling made it unsafe for respectable people to walk the streets, and rumors spread of a Negro plot to burn down the town of Laurensville. A false alarm in September placed the whites on their guard, but their feverish precautions apparently prevented Crews and his armed men from carrying out any incendiarism. On October 20 a street fight between a white conservative and a constable resulted in several members of each race exchanging shots. The better organized whites then rushed to the houses where the militia arms were stored, grabbed the weapons, and began a general assault on the Negroes that sent them scurrying out of town. Posses roamed the countryside and killed an unknown number of blacks.[56]

As a response to Republican "misrule," unchecked criminal activity, black "insurrections," and the arming of the state militias, the Klan sought to preserve the racial status quo, albeit to alter the prevailing political balance. This conservative purpose does not mean, however, that the Klan was dominated by the white aristocracy; as recent scholarship has demonstrated, members came from all social and economic strata. In its early phases prominent citizens led the organization, and Klan apologists have stressed the respectability of the members. Raids were generally conducted by the younger men, often the sons of planters and merchants. Klan leaders played on the racial phobias of the yeoman and poor whites to recruit members, and some dens did not scruple about admitting men with criminal records.[57]

The breadth of Klan membership resembles that of other American vigilante groups, which were at first controlled by elite citizens of the community and won strong support among businessmen. Even those who participated in the violence were not the dregs of local society; studies of revolutionary crowds in Europe have shown that mobs usually consisted of artisans and tradesmen rather than street criminals.[58]

The prominence of some Klan leaders strengthened the organization and helped it win wide community approval. Governor Rufus Bullock of Georgia charged that prominent conservatives such as Robert Toombs and Benjamin Hill encouraged violence by their constant attacks on black suffrage and Republican officeholders. Certainly the endorsement of the Klan by a Nathan Bedford Forrest or a John B. Gordon helped increase membership. More important, the presence of these men sanctified night riding because they served as models for more humble Klansmen.[59]

Klan activity built racial solidarity by bringing diverse individuals together for a common purpose. Rioting and raiding became an expression of collective values and a means to unify the white community. The southern aristocracy had long used the race question to avoid class conflict in the South, and during Reconstruction racial concerns continued to transcend social and economic divisions.[60]

This is not to say that there were no differences between leaders and ordinary members in the various dens. Around 1867 the founders began to lose control of the organization. Many of the Klan's more notorious raids apparently took place without the knowledge or approval of the men nominally in charge. The lack of central direction made each den a law unto itself and encouraged what might be called free-lance terrorism. Sketchy evidence indicates that the Klan briefly disbanded in 1869 but soon reemerged as an even more violent body. Ironically, the breakdown of leadership allowed some Klansmen to dismiss the most bloody outrages by blaming them on irregular night riding by young men who were not members of the Klan. Yet this distinction between "genuine Ku Klux" and other armed bands is spurious; under whatever name they operated, the results were the same. Indeed, if the purpose of vigilantism, as Richard Maxwell Brown has argued, is to prevent the lower classes from destroying the structure of the community, the Klan in many areas acted in such a way as to undermine the values its leaders claimed to be preserving.[61]

The nature of the Klan appeal made these developments inevitable. The Klan overtly recruited frustrated individuals and in effect encouraged them to transfer blame for their own personal failings from themselves to treacherous scalawags, wily carpetbaggers, or corrupt blacks. The offensive against Reconstruction rested on the assumption that the South's suffering arose from external forces and internal treason. Angry young men gained personal satisfaction and reaffirmed their dedication to the ideals of their fathers as part of a mass social movement. As the carpetbagger Charles Stearns observed after his experiences in Georgia, violence was part of the southern character, and no one should wonder at the hostility of the old Confederates: "The Southern people are none of your patient Jobs, but almost universally fiery Hotspurs; with whom a blow is sure to follow a word, and quite as often to come first. They are irascible by nature, and impetuous beyond conception. No southern man dare call another a liar, without being prepared for the use of powder and ball."[62]

Despite a lack of organization and a tendency toward random terrorism, the Ku Klux Klan had an overriding purpose—the destruction of the Republican party in the South. The Klan became, in effect, the military arm of the Democratic party. Although it is commonplace to speak of "senseless violence," violence seldom occurs without a cause. Klan raids sought to achieve a particular goal—the restoration of home rule in the southern states. For the Klansmen themselves, night riding was a rational attempt to resolve political conflict; if terrorism increased white solidarity, it also gave young men excluded from political power a sense of achievement denied them by the established political structure. Working toward a specific goal may well have intensified Klan aggressiveness and probably increased the brutality of the raids.[63]

Ku Klux engaged in terrorism against Republican leaders across the South. Klansmen in several north Florida counties forced Republican officials to resign during 1871. Night riders in Warren County, Georgia, assassinated local and state officials of both races. The message was as unmistakable as the medium. Republican leaders suddenly faced an apparent conspiracy to drive them out of the southern states.[64]

Night raids against black's homes, often including threats and whippings, struck at the heart of the Republican electorate. Although a frightened justice of the peace in Alamance County, North Carolina, claimed there was no excuse for this violence, the perpetrators always had an excuse. If several blacks were murdered in one county, the price of being a Republican became terrifyingly apparent. Likewise, the assassination of black officeholders starkly revealed the consequences of political activism.[65]

This violence was squarely within the tradition of American mob behavior. There was no general slaughter of black men, as excited southern Republicans sometimes claimed. Although many assaults were capricious, selective attacks on influential Republicans made the desired impression on the masses.[66] More effective than random terrorism, carefully executed raids against blacks naturally resulted in fear.

The diffuse and disorganized nature of the Klan limited its success in ending Republican rule in the southern states, but individual dens could be frighteningly efficient. Most of the white males in York County, South Carolina, were Klansmen. Night riders systematically disarmed black militiamen, whipped several hundred blacks, and murdered eleven men. Perhaps as many as 150 people died in racial and political violence in Jackson County, Florida, between 1868 and 1871. Several political assassinations in any one county could end Republican activities there.[67]

More than a military adjunct of the Democratic party, the Klan sought to preserve white economic and social power. Like the mobs of seventeenth-century England, Klan dens often had very specific local goals. This fact explains, for example, why night riding continued in Georgia and Alabama after conservative election victories.[68] If the Klan was a counterrevolutionary force in politics, it was a reactionary influence in society.

Black economic advancement and especially landownership directly challenged many cherished notions of white supremacists. In areas with large Negro populations, the Klan acted on behalf of planters who sought to maintain a docile labor force. Elsewhere, white yeomen who feared competition from black farmers joined the Klan to drive them off the land. Alabama posses crossed the border into eastern Mississippi to apprehend blacks who had violated labor contracts. In response, armed Negroes in Meridian paraded against night riders during the spring of 1871. On March 4, a fire broke out in the business district; as quickly as the flames, rumors spread that blacks were planning to burn down the town. Three prominent Negro leaders were arrested on charges of inciting to riot and on March 6 appeared in a courtroom filled with grim-visaged whites. During a dispute over the testimony of a witness, shots rang out, and a general melee ensued. The white Republican judge and two blacks fell dead instantly. Armed whites then searched the town and killed perhaps as many as thirty Negroes.[69] For dens such as those of Meridian, the preservation of economic supremacy was a deadly serious matter.

Equally essential for most white citizens was the maintenance of southern racial customs. The *Wilmington Journal* claimed that Klansmen appeared in Alamance County, North Carolina, only after a black man had attempted to hug the daughter of a white planter. Savage night riders became, *mutatis mutandis,* the protectors of southern womanhood. In Marshall County, Mississippi, for example, Klansmen visited a Freedmen's Bureau agent who had had the temerity to summon white women to his court on the complaints of Negroes. Apologists for terrorism argued that the Klan protected white women from being raped by black men, but there is little contemporary evidence for this assertion. Mere suspicion was usually enough, as in Wilkinson County, Georgia, where Klansmen castrated three black men accused of connection with white women. Blacks who sent their children to school or dressed too fancily received visits from white men eager to reinforce the nuances of the established racial order.[70]

In southern theory and law, education for blacks was both unnecessary and dangerous; educated blacks would give the lie to ancient racial dogmas. Even whites who supported Negro schools bitterly opposed Yankee teachers, whom they suspected of giving more instruction in politics than in arithmetic. Schoolhouses where Loyal League meetings were held became frequent targets for arson. Klansmen visited northern schoolteachers at night, warned them to leave the area, and occasionally whipped them. Defenders of these methods accused the teachers of dishonestly pocketing school funds and being too politically active. Physical assault and arson were sporadic but frequent enough to show a general hostility to any education for blacks that was not controlled by white conservatives.[71]

Klan attacks on schools and teachers were a part of a general assault on local authority. The lack of public faith in the court system produced a growing reliance on "popular justice." The Klan in Alamance County, North Carolina, whipped and murdered Negroes suspected of being thieves, barnburners, and rapists. These "regulators" claimed to be the only effective force against black crime. Hard times certainly increased the problems of theft, but many whites thought most Negroes were thieves anyway. Vigilantes in Sumter County, South Carolina, raided the businesses of several white Democrats who had been lucratively buying stolen seed cotton from blacks at night. A white Alabamian lamented: "A hog has no more chance to live among these thieving negro farmers than a juney bug in a gang of paddle ducks."[72] Since Republican sheriffs supposedly winked at petty larceny, the hard-pressed farmers saw no choice but to exact their own punishment.

The main advantage of vigilante justice over established legal processes is its swiftness. In regions such as the West and the South that lacked adequate jails and prisons, banishment, flogging, or hanging were common penalties, and armed bands made sure the sentence was carried out promptly.[73]

When freedmen lost their economic value as slaves, they also lost their immunity from vigilante action. There are no statistics available on the number of lynchings during Reconstruction, but the practice was widespread. The usual procedure was for disguised men to remove a prisoner from jail during the night, take him into the countryside, and hang him. Apologists for these extralegal executions have always claimed that they occurred only in extreme cases such as the rape of a white woman, but a black person could be lynched for many minor offenses ranging from insulting a white person to general "insolence." Whites faced the wrath of the lynch mob, but more often the victim was black. Vigilante hangings occurred because peaceful citizens welcomed or at least did not oppose them; even a man of moderate and humane views such as South Carolina's Wade Hampton believed that "there are crimes which militate [sic] if they do not justify such swift retribution."[74]

A danger inherent in any vigilante movement is that members will use their power and anonymity for private gain. Some Klan dens appeared much more interested in robbing blacks than intimidating voters. Drunken regulators in bizarre disguises avenged private quarrels. Night riders in parts of North Carolina and Georgia protected bootleggers and horse thieves from arrest. The infamous Baker gang in Texas would reportedly kill any Negro for a few dollars.[75] The line between political and personal purpose was not always distinct, and many attacks on blacks were not racially or politically motivated.

At first, prominent white leaders ignored the existence of terrorism, and one can learn very little about the Ku Klux from reading conservative newspapers. Southern humorists not only skewered carpetbaggers, scalawags, and black politicians with bitter satire but wrote of Klan raids in tones that made them sound more like innocent frolics than deadly affairs. Some editors dismissed the question of violence as a phony issue gotten up by Republicans to secure Grant's reelection in 1872 and cover up administration corruption. Governor Gilbert C. Walker of Virginia welcomed a group of northern newspapermen to Richmond in 1871 by congratulating them on the safe journey through the land of Ku Klux. The editors playfully responded that they had seen none of these ghostly figures en route.[76]

"The 'Republican' party must have an issue," cried one Georgia editor, "what would the 'Republican' party be without the 'skinned nigger' and 'bloody Ku Klux?' " Conservatives believed that the Republicans were no more concerned about their black brethren in the South than they were about aborigines in Australia. Skeptical of any federal investigation of the Klan, Democrats accused southern radicals of paying men to commit outrages so they could wave the bloody shirt in election years. Denigrating the character of any witnesses who might testify about disorder in the South, the editor of the *Augusta Chronicle and Sentinel* let forth a mighty blast at the so-called radical outrage mill: "Every strolling vagabond who will assume the slightest pretension of loyalty can gain the ear and the willing sympathies of the powers that be at Washington, no matter what frauds he may have perpetrated, or thefts he may have committed. . . . He can create a sensation which will fill the eye and ear of the Northern public."[77] Such blustering denials failed to account for the dead bodies strewn across the southern countryside.

As the terrorism spread, a few prominent conservatives denounced the violence. Some men were morally revolted by the Klan's bloody deeds; others had practical doubts about the efficacy of vigilante justice. Could men bound by secret oaths be trusted? How many innocent men died at the hands of regulators? After witnessing a Klan march through his own town of Crawfordville, Alexander H. Stephens warned that mob law only worsened social tensions. Yet significantly, most of these criticisms of night riding were in private letters; public denunciations were not only rare but couched in narrow, pragmatic terms. Klan terrorism was inappropriate, some conservatives argued, because it would provoke federal intervention in the southern states. One

Mississippian, in a letter to a northern correspondent, welcomed the suppression of the Ku Klux but denied that any such organization operated in his state. He reserved his sharpest invective for the Republican state government.[78]

As would be the case throughout Reconstruction, men of goodwill refused to take action to stop the bloodshed. Conservative leaders winked at the means used to achieve the overthrow of the Republican regimes. The crusade against Reconstruction demanded that individuals set aside personal scruples and march under the triumphant banner of home rule and white supremacy. Whether southern Republicans or the federal government could or would halt the tide of counterrevolution remained the unanswered question.

7. The Search for a Strategy

The Ku Klux Klan was not the instrument of "redemption" for the southern states. The organization's career, though occasionally spectacular, was brief. The Klan declined in strength in part because of internal weaknesses: its lack of central organization and the failure of its leaders to control criminal elements and sadists. More fundamentally, it declined because it failed to achieve its central objective—the overthrow of Republican state governments in the South.

Ku Klux operated most effectively in areas where the Negro and white populations were about equal in size. Although planters sometimes formed dens in the black belt, the danger of reprisals there was great.[1] Southern whites recognized the possibility of retaliatory violence by blacks, especially when there were rumors of insurrection. To be sure, black leaders have generally been realistic and have refused to launch revolts that had little chance for success. Yet as the carpetbagger Charles Stearns observed, the longer the black man was oppressed and the more his resentment smoldered, the greater the chances for the outbreak of race war.[2]

Blacks who fought back against the Klan occupy a place of honor in Negro folklore. Black men in several North Carolina counties organized patrols to deter Ku Klux from attacking their homes. Against overwhelming odds and at great personal risk, courageous individuals defied the night riders. When Klansmen visited a Negro in Graham, North Carolina, a scuffle broke out inside the house. The black man's wife let an ax head fall on one of the white men, splitting his head open. Regulators in Danville, Kentucky, visited the home of George Bland, a powerful and belligerent former slave. They strung Bland's wife up to a nearby tree and then hacked her to death with knives. After they dragged Bland out of the house to look at their handiwork, he asked to go back inside to get something to wrap around his wife's body. Instead, he grabbed his Winchester rifle and opened fire, killing several of the Klansmen. Such retaliation, however, often came at a fearful price. A Georgia black who attempted to defend his wife from a beating was shot. He fled but was captured, and both he and his wife were taken to jail. A band of whites dragged them from the jail that night and lynched them; later reports claimed that the man's heart had been cut out and fed to the dogs.[3]

The brave but ineffectual black resistance to Klan outrages meant that the primary responsibility for stopping the bloodshed rested on the Republican state and local governments. But from its beginnings, the southern Republican party had displayed grave internal weaknesses that made it unequal to the task.

The party's early efforts to split the white vote in the South came to naught. In spite of initial success in recruiting some well-known old Whigs, Republicans never won over enough white voters to make their party genuinely biracial. Scalawag leaders such as Joe Brown in Georgia and James Longstreet in Louisiana pleaded with President Grant to use the federal patronage to divide the Democrats, but this hope of winning over moderates from the enemy camp vanished as quickly as it had appeared.[4]

Not only did southern Republicans fail to gain many white converts, but they could not maintain unity in their own ranks. Factionalism became chronic and often disastrous. The most significant cleavage in the party was between scalawags and carpetbaggers. Although the two groups quarreled over political strategy, white disfranchisement, economic questions, and black rights, their most bitter disputes erupted over distributing the spoils of victory. Scalawags complained that carpetbaggers had received the bulk of the federal patronage, and each faction chafed over seeing its rivals ensconced in positions of power and profit.[5]

In the end, racial differences did as much as anything to divide southern Republicans and sap their limited strength. Blacks were the mainstay of Republican power in most states, yet the party also had to win a certain number of white votes. Such a careful balancing of personality, ideology, and interest proved difficult and finally impossible. Some scalawags opposed appointing blacks to public office because they doubted the ability of the freedmen to handle such duties responsibly. Negro Republicans had legitimate grievances on this score because they never held offices in the South in proportion to their numerical strength in the party. Conservatives mischievously played on these disputes and chided white radicals for not being more generous in sharing power with their black friends.[6]

Taken together, these divisions and infirmities meant that the Republicans would not only fail to suppress violence but could not protect their state governments from being overthrown by hostile whites. Conservatives recognized this impotency and came to believe that any weakness in the regime was an invitation to revolt; not only did they distrust their Republican rulers but they believed that the use of violence would topple these governments.[7]

The issue of terrorism itself contributed to and exposed new fissures in Republican ranks. Scalawag Governor William H. Smith downplayed vigilantism in Alabama while carpetbag Senator George E. Spencer exploited the issue of Klan violence in attacking his native rivals in the party. Governor James Lusk Alcorn of Mississippi, a former Whig and substantial planter, favored state action against disguised bands, but his political enemy, Maine carpetbagger Adelbert Ames, pressed for federal intervention.[8]

Even where Republicans agreed on the need to suppress the Ku Klux, there remained the question of means. Governor William W. Holden of North Carolina conceded that armed desperadoes infested his state but admitted uncertainty about how to proceed against them. General Alfred H. Terry reported that civil authorities in Warren County, Georgia, long a center of Klan activity, had done nothing to bring the perpetrators of outrages to justice because the county sheriff was in hiding for fear of his life. Witnesses refused to testify against night riders unless they had protection, which was nearly impossible to provide. Judge Albion Tourgée of North Carolina wanted to crush the Klan bushwackers with an "iron heel" but faced strong local opposition. When a grand jury issued indictments, witnesses were difficult to track down, and the accused parties produced a multitude of alibis. To arrest suspects was not easy, and many fled prosecution. Tourgée became disgusted with jurors who refused to convict men whose guilt had been overwhelmingly established and sadly told his wife, "It is no crime for a white man to cut a colored man open in Alamance [County]."[9]

In the absence of effective civil remedies, several Republican governors strengthened state militias to check the spread of lawlessness. After much lobbying in Washington, southern Republicans convinced the federal government to furnish a few arms for these state forces. But it was race, not weapons, that aroused opposition. Although some whites enlisted, particularly in Tennessee, Louisiana, and North Carolina, blacks dominated the companies in Arkansas, South Carolina, Mississippi, and Texas.[10]

The conservative protest came swiftly and predictably. There was no need for state troops, white leaders claimed, because the southern states were peaceful. Immediately raising the cry of "militia outrages," Democratic editors accused Republicans of using state troops solely for their own political advantage. The idea of armed blacks drilling and harassing peaceful citizens threw some whites into a frenzy.[11] In South Carolina, conservatives charged that Governor Robert K. Scott would use the militia to intimidate Democratic voters. In counties where the militia drilled, the Klan was most active.[12] Given white paranoia about armed blacks, it is not surprising that these units stirred up deep fears in the South.

Shortly before the 1868 presidential election, Klan raids against Republicans in Tennessee became more frequent, and they continued after the election. Prominent conservatives condemned vigilantism out of fear that it might induce Governor Brownlow to declare martial law and send the greatly despised Negro militia into the field. After a brief period of martial law in early 1869, both the Klan and the militia faded from the scene. Because of factional wrangling among the Republicans, Tennessee by 1869 had quietly returned to conservative control.[13]

North Carolina Union men complained that they were threatened, beaten, and driven from their homes by the Ku Klux. Governor Holden and other leading Republicans decided that this terrorism made the organization of a state militia imperative during the 1868 election campaign. Accusing the governor of conspiring to cow the voters with military force, conservatives raised the shopworn cry against standing armies in time of peace. Josiah Turner screamed that no white man would allow any "drunken or ignorant worthless negro to arrest him" and that the mustering of a "loil militia" meant war.[14] Fortunately, this heated invective marked the extent of the hostilities.

To meet Klan raids in 1869 and 1870, Holden attempted through persuasion, proclamations, and promises of pardons for past crimes to convince the group to disband. But the murder of state senator John W. Stephens in Yanceyville and disturbances in several counties during the first half of 1870 inspired Holden and other Republican leaders to hold a secret meeting in Raleigh at which they resolved to raise a force of volunteers to arrest the guilty parties. The governor authorized George W. Kirk, a United States Army veteran who had served in Brownlow's Tennessee militia, to organize this predominantly white force, which was sent immediately to Alamance and Caswell counties. Conservatives howled in protest, particularly after their mouthpiece Josiah Turner was incarcerated, but Kirk's men committed few depredations though they may have tortured prisoners to extract confessions. Some Republicans questioned the expediency of military force and advised the governor to disband Kirk's men. Constitutional questions about the legality of the arrests as well as confusion on the part of Holden and Kirk eventually led to the release of all the prisoners. Although Klan activity subsided, the governor paid a high price for his bold course. After the Democrats gained control of the legislature in 1870, they impeached Holden and removed him from office.[15]

The establishment of a militia in Arkansas produced political acrimony but favorable results for the Republicans. In July 1868 Governor Powell Clayton urged the legislature to authorize a militia and threatened to send it out into the countryside if Klan violence continued. During the fall, Clayton purchased four thousand rifles and ammunition in New York, but Klansmen captured the steamboat carrying the weapons and dumped them in the Mississippi River. Clayton's appeal for federal troops met a cold rebuff from the Johnson administration, which looked askance at such requests from carpetbag regimes. Although some two hundred murders had been committed in Arkansas between July and October 1868, Clayton hesitated to call out the militia for fear of the political consequences. Certainly the Democrats would have protested; they were already complaining that Loyal League meetings were inciting the blacks. On November 4, the day after the presidential election, Clayton declared martial law in ten counties where Klan night riding had been most serious and divided the state into four militia districts. Both white Unionists and Negroes responded to the governor's call for volunteers but served in separate companies.[16]

The state troops entered several counties, making arrests and seizing weapons and provisions. Although conservative newspapers filled their columns with reports of outrages by the Negro militia, the troops behaved in a reasonably disciplined manner. When four black militiamen raped two white women in Crittenden County, they were immediately tried by court-martial, sentenced to death, and shot by an all-black firing squad. Arrests of night riders did not necessarily lead to either trials or convictions. Few Klansmen ever faced a judge, but a handful evidently were executed without trials. Refusing to retreat from assassination threats, Clayton's courageous declaration of martial law had succeeded in crushing the Klan in Arkansas and setting an example of firmness for other southern governors.[17]

Texas Republicans established a state police force that could well have served as a model for other southern states. Its vast untamed and unsettled areas populated by hostile Indians, postwar Texas was a haven for highwaymen and murderers. The state government organized militia (officially called the state police) to cope with the prevailing lawlessness. Few whites chose to join, and conservatives accused Negro state policemen of being the vanguard of a black insurrection. Local defiance of the state police forced Governor Edmund J. Davis to declare martial law in several counties, and violence broke out when black officers tried to arrest white civilians. Republicans sometimes used the police for electioneering purposes, but even its opponents conceded its success in reducing crime. When the Democrats disbanded the state police after winning control of the legislature in 1873, brigands and assassins roamed freely once again.[18]

The record of the southern militias was mixed; successes in Arkansas and Texas were not matched elsewhere. Few Republicans were willing to apply forceful measures against the Ku Klux. Conservative Republican governors such as Harrison Reed in Florida and William H. Smith in Alabama downplayed the violence and believed the declaration of martial law or the suspension of the writ of habeas corpus unnecessary and dangerous to constitutional liberty (arguments that must have sounded persuasive to the most rabid Democrats). Some Republicans hesitated to send armed blacks into already disturbed counties because they feared race war as much as white conservatives did. The development of Negro militia companies in the deep South would have created a panic among the white population and might well have provoked a war of extermination. Republican governors therefore found themselves in an impossible situation: they could either allow the Klan to continue its terror campaign or they could risk all-out war by attempting to meet the Klan on its own bloody terms.[19]

The failure of the state governments to control violence forced Republicans to push for congressional legislation against voter intimidation and night riding. Radical congressmen argued that if the states could not maintain order, the federal government had the responsibility to do so to preserve its Reconstruction policies. Black representatives movingly demanded protection for black voters, asserting that Klan violence was an attack on the federal government and a symptom of renewed rebellion.[20] Congress eventually passed three Enforcement Acts in 1870 and 1871 providing for federal prosecution of persons who through intimidation or physical force prevented citizens from exercising their rights under the Fourteenth and Fifteenth amendments. These laws prohibited a host of activities associated with the Ku Klux Klan (such as riding about in disguise) and authorized the president to suspend the writ of habeas corpus in states where the resistance to legal authority had become overwhelming.

Southern conservatives raised the expected objections to the "tyranny" of what they labeled "force bills." Linton Stephens declared the Enforcement Acts null and void because the Fourteenth and Fifteenth amendments had never been constitutionally ratified. Excited editors claimed these laws struck the death knell of liberty in America and clothed Grant with the powers of a Roman emperor or an Asian despot; such partisan legislation allowed the Republican party to persecute Democrats legally. The imprisonment of accused Ku Kluxers served no other purpose than to secure Grant's reelection.[21]

Whatever the constitutional and partisan ramifications of this legislation, it ran head-on into a long tradition of southern lawlessness. Southerners may have believed that laws protected society from outbursts of passion and violence, but they had never had much faith in legal procedure. To the average citizen the defects in the system seemed glaring: criminals easily escaped justice; crafty lawyers got their guilty clients acquitted; judges and jurymen accepted bribes. Such imperfections explain occasional resort to extralegal justice and even lynch law. If southerners often refused to respect laws of their own making, how could they be expected to obey acts passed by a Congress for which many of them had only contempt and loathing? Conservatives pictured themselves as the true upholders of the Constitution and saw the radicals as usurpers, who brought the law into contempt by foisting upon the people oppressive, unqualified, and corrupt officeholders. An outraged Alabamian added the final element to this syllogism by blaming vigilantism on a lack of confidence in Republican judges.[22]

Conservatives loudly protested the dragging of white citizens from their homes in the dead of the night on the word of an unreliable Negro or carpetbag knave. They accused federal judges of sending men to prison for no other crime than the exercise of their political rights under the Constitution. Southern Democrats believed indictments stemmed from personal and political vengeance rather than actual wrongdoing and that perjured witnesses and packed juries ensured convictions. This overblown rhetoric turned federal prisons into Bastilles and Justice Department officials and army officers into Persian satraps.[23]

The impassioned denunciations of the Enforcement Acts did not reflect their actual operation. United States district attorneys and marshals confronted the same problems faced by state and local officials. Arresting Klansmen at first provided Republicans with some security, but many of the leaders successfully evaded capture. Bands of desperadoes intimidated deputy marshals and even assassinated witnesses. The Klan's victims were generally poor and illiterate men unlikely to bring their plight to the attention of federal officials, and many rightly feared the consequences of doing so. Congress never appropriated enough money to hire detectives for thorough investigations or to carry through lengthy prosecutions. The burden of enforcement fell on the shoulders of district attorneys and marshals, whose ability and willingness to bring the guilty to justice varied widely. Federal judges in the South were also of uneven quality, and court decisions significantly circumscribed the reach of their authority.[24]

Statistics compiled by the Justice Department show that government prosecutors obtained convictions in a high proportion of Enforcement

Act cases, but, as time went on, many indictments were dropped or declared to be *nolle prosequi*. This trend indicated not only the demise of the Klan but also the limitations of federal law enforcement in the South. Because of the heavy case load, Attorney General Amos T. Akerman instructed a United States district attorney in Yorkville, South Carolina, to bring Klan leaders to trial but to release lesser offenders on light bail or not prosecute them. Akerman and other federal officials realized that the federal government was reluctant to punish persons guilty of crimes normally falling under state or local jurisdiction, especially when most citizens sympathized with the defendants. The combination of waning northern support for Reconstruction, unfavorable court decisions, and the lack of sufficient funds to prosecute those persons already indicted ended the federal enforcement program and later allowed groups such as the Louisiana White League to carry on its operations with little fear of federal interference.[25]

The ultimate weapon in the federal arsenal against southern lawlessness was the army. Between 1867 and 1871, withdrawal of troops made keeping the peace increasingly difficult. Moreover, the soldiers generally could be deployed only on the request of civil authorities. Hamstrung by legal technicalities, conflicting instructions from their superiors, and meager appropriations, the army in the South confronted an impossible situation with less and less enthusiasm.

The most onerous duty for the troops came at election time, when they tried to prevent the outcome from being decided by shotguns. Although most commanders preferred to leave peacekeeping to local authorities, they frequently had to interfere when these men either could not or would not preserve order. The task was both thankless and herculean. Conservatives denounced the presence of uniformed soldiers near a polling place as an attempt to control the election. To preserve political neutrality and maintain order at the same time was a difficult job, but one that the army usually accomplished. Commanders might station troops within a state according to the wishes of leading Republicans, but they turned down requests they suspected of originating in a desire to intimidate Democrats.[26]

However fair the army was in carrying out its mission, it could not escape criticism. After the Reconstruction acts had been in effect for several months, Governor Jonathan Worth of North Carolina wrote a forty-one-page letter to President Johnson complaining of the arbitrary actions of military authorities and their circumvention of civil procedures. Conservatives pointed out to penurious northerners that keeping troops in the South was an enormous drain on the federal treasury. These regiments were portrayed as dangerous to liberty and partisan tools of the Grant administration. Local officials harassed soldiers performing their duties by arresting them on petty charges. The attorney general suggested that such nuisance prosecutions be transferred to federal courts if possible, but that in any event, United States attorneys should conduct the soldiers' defense.[27] Although violent clashes between troops and civilians were rare, the army's presence was a constant reminder of Yankee oppression.

Protests against "military despotism," however, did not constitute the essence of civilian-military relations. Many whites got along reasonably well with the soldiers and claimed to prefer military rule to government by Republican scoundrels. Conservative editors praised the conduct of the federal troops, stating that most of the officers were "gentlemen" who sympathized with the region's suffering. Since many soldiers were Democrats or conservative Republicans, southern radicals rightly suspected that the troops helped the opposition more than they did the party of Reconstruction. A Georgia Republican grumbled that the soldiers of one garrison hobnobbed only with Confederate cutthroats.[28]

Most officers detested service below the Mason-Dixon line. Conservative generals such as George G. Meade, Winfield Scott Hancock, and John M. Schofield disliked interfering with civil government and abhorred their inevitable entanglement in southern politics. The incessant requests by Republicans for assistance drove many soldiers into the Democratic camp. The army's effectiveness was further limited because its superiors in Washington discounted reports of southern outrages and favored a restrained use of military force. After struggling with the maddening complexities of Georgia politics, General Alfred Terry informed General William T. Sherman: "I would not again go through with a job of this kind even if it would make me a Marshal of France." The common soldiers shared many of their commanders' prejudices, were often hostile to the government's Reconstruction policies, and were seldom racial egalitarians.[29]

When the War Department became preoccupied with the Indian wars on the Great Plains, the army's position in the South grew more precarious. In 1867 there had been one soldier in the former Confederate states for each 708 civilians; by 1876 the ratio would be one for 3,160. Division and department commanders moved slowly against the Klan and opposed military trials for these outlaws. Mounted southerners easily evaded pursuit by infantry detachments. As General Philip Sheridan, an advocate of vigorous federal action in the South, had lamented in 1867, many crimes and outrages were beyond the reach of military power.[30]

The weakness of federal policy and will certainly stimulated disorder. With neither swift nor certain threat of punishment, southerners could vent their aggression with little fear of retribution. Indeed, moderate force, such as that applied by the army in the South, is more likely to produce a violent response than more draconian measures or a laissez-faire policy.[31] By draining the North's moral, psychological, economic, and political commitment to suppressing terrorism, the Ku Klux Klan, the Knights of the White Camellia, and other such organizations had been partially successful even though they disappeared as a result of the federal enforcement program. When new paramilitary groups sprang up in the mid-1870s, there was no longer even a minimal federal deterrent in place.

The Ku Klux Klan, then, is not the key to understanding the southern counterrevolution because its legendary stature far exceeded its actual accomplishments. Allen Trelease, the leading student of the Klan, has concluded that it achieved very few of its goals during its brief career. In states such as Alabama and South Carolina, Ku Klux raids constituted but a small part of the political violence that continued long after the ghostly night riders had vanished.[32] The Klan contributed to conservative election victories but failed to overthrow a single Republican state government. Following a series of outrages and murders in several north Florida counties during 1869 and 1870, the Democrats won a partial victory in the 1870 state elections.[33] Sustained terrorism in more than a dozen North Carolina counties reduced the Republican vote and helped the Democrats win a legislative majority in the same year. But the Klan may not have been the decisive factor. A long-simmering railroad scandal had divided the Republicans and severely diminished their popularity.[34]

Relatively little violence and intimidation (by Reconstruction standards) took place during the 1870 elections in Alabama, but earlier Klan raids had established an aura of fear. Republicans pleaded with Governor Smith for federal troops to prevent Democrats from disrupting their meetings and threatening black voters. Armed Democrats broke up a Republican meeting in Eutaw, where the despised Congressman Charles Hays was addressing a biracial audience. On election day, whites crowded the polls in some precincts, but in several counties federal soldiers stood within sight of the ballot boxes.[35] The result was a narrow, albeit disputed, Democratic triumph, in part attributable to the work of Klansmen but also to the feuding between the scalawag and carpetbagger wings of the Republican party.

The conservative conquest of Georgia was more complete. Historians disagree over the extent to which night riding contributed to the Democrats' capture of a legislative majority, and there may have been less violence in 1870 than in 1868. Klan raids probably reduced the black vote in several counties, but Georgia Republicans brought on their own defeat by failing to settle their internal quarrels in the face of a resurgent Democracy.[36]

The Ku Klux Klan brought the southern states only a short distance down the road to "redemption." To be sure, Ku Klux destroyed the Loyal League and shattered Republican voting strength in many counties. Yet the Klan's lack of organization beyond the local level made it a weak instrument to attack Republican state governments. This absence of well-defined goals and effective leadership made it vulnerable to federal suppression; indeed, the hooded riders seemed to dissolve into the night once federal marshals and soldiers moved against them. The Klan experience unquestionably taught conservative leaders some valuable strategic lessons. In the future, they organized powerful extralegal bodies, which through a combination of political agitation, intimidation, and the calculated use of force undermined and eventually overthrew Republican state governments. These white supremacy groups had little contact with their counterparts in other states but had the significant advantage of operating in a changed political atmosphere. The willingness of the federal government to intervene on behalf of beleaguered blacks and Republicans in the South sharply declined after the breakup of the Klan, and the growing internal weaknesses of southern Republicanism opened the way for "redemption."

As Tennessee, Virginia, Georgia, and North Carolina fell back into conservative hands, the tide of counterrevolution gained momentum. The Grant administration had tried in a variety of ways to build a strong and self-sufficient Republican party in these states but had failed. Violence had not played a decisive role in these conservative victories, though the Klan had been active in all these states except Virginia. Factionalism, whether based on race, nativity, or a scramble for patronage had been more decisive than force in sapping Republican strength in the South. The Democrats had achieved success with relative ease, greatly aided by their opponents' folly; after 1870, redemption became both more difficult and more sanguinary.

By 1873 the Republican party in Texas lay in shambles. The administration of Governor Edmund J. Davis had used declarations of martial law and the state police to control endemic lawlessness but in the process had alienated many conservative Republicans and allowed the Democrats to gain control of the legislature in 1872. After losing a bid for reelection in 1873, Davis attempted one last stand against his opponents. Seizing on a legal technicality, he refused to abide by the election results and announced that he would remain in the governor's chair to protect the state from the Ku Klux Democracy. The governor appealed to Grant for troops to support his claim to office, but the president icily refused, giving Davis a brief lecture on "yielding to the will of the people as expressed by their ballots." The Democrats were determined to inaugurate their winning candidate, Richard Coke, but were equally bent on avoiding a violent clash with the Republicans that might provoke Grant into declaring martial law. On January 16, 1874, conservative forces seized the arsenal in Austin. Davis fortified the lower floors of the capitol with militia, but Democrats occupied the upper stories. When it became clear that the federal government would not intervene, Davis surrendered on January 17.[37] Like most Reconstruction statehouse confrontations, there had been a good deal of posturing, no shortage of bloodcurdling threats, but a reluctance by both parties to start shooting.

The political situation in neighboring Arkansas was more confusing and potentially more explosive. In 1872 a group of "Liberal Republicans," in revolt against Powell Clayton's machinations, nominated Joseph Brooks for governor; the party regulars chose Clayton's man, Elisha Baxter. After a campaign replete with fraud and the appearance of armed men at the polls, Clayton's election officials counted in Baxter. No sooner was he in the governor's chair than Baxter abandoned his political friends. Much to the disgust of Clayton and his henchmen, the new governor appointed Democrats to offices, vetoed a Republican railroad scheme, and urged an end to the disfranchisement of former Confederates.[38] Clayton's faction, in a neat bit of political legerdemain, repudiated Baxter and announced their support for Brooks's claims to the governorship.

This swirling sea of shifting allegiances, broken promises, and fratricidal strife became more storm-tossed early in 1874. On April 15, a circuit court in Pulaski County, whose jurisdiction was questionable, ruled that Brooks was the legal governor of the state. The Brooks forces immediately seized state buildings, broke into the armory, and demanded that Baxter vacate his office. When black militiamen began carrying weapons through the halls, Baxter wisely abandoned the statehouse. Both "governors" fired off hasty telegrams to Grant explaining their positions; Attorney General George H. Williams telegraphed the United States marshal in Little Rock to hold federal troops ready to quell any disturbances. The administration did not respond to either of the "governors" and instructed the commander of federal troops in Little Rock, Captain Thomas E. Rose, to maintain strict neutrality, in effect accepting Brooks's fait accompli and granting him de facto recognition. Brooks's armed supporters filled the statehouse, bringing with them two twelve-pound artillery pieces. Baxter raised a volunteer force that ringed the statehouse. After Baxter declared martial law in Little Rock, Brooks frantically wired Washington that he was about to be attacked. Captain Rose pleaded with both sides to disarm.[39]

With the two parties only three hundred yards apart, an armed clash seemed inevitable. Black militiamen loyal to Baxter marched into Little Rock, and on April 20 one of them shot at Captain Rose as he rode between the lines. During several minutes of general firing, one man was killed and another wounded. The Baxter forces moved up their artillery pieces in apparent preparation for an assault on the statehouse. The militiamen, commanded by King White, were eager to attack the Brooks forces and periodically paraded before their enemies cheering for Baxter. On April 30, after both sides withdrew, armed blacks from Little Rock clashed with Brooks forces near Pine Bluff. Nine Brooks partisans were killed and twenty wounded, but only nine Baxter supporters suffered injury. Rumors spread of large arms shipments, but White's men appeared to command the countryside. By the time the Baxter forces kidnapped two supreme court justices, many Arkansans no longer cared which faction prevailed.[40]

Both sides appeared to be arming for a final battle, and civil war seemed likely. On the night of May 7, Brooks's men seized the steamship *Hallie,* which was carrying arms for the Baxter militia. Although Baxter supporters feared the boat would then be used to attack them, this setback was only temporary. Sporadic street fighting continued in Little Rock, and the Baxter militia moved two more brass artillery pieces into position near the statehouse. The balance of power was shifting; Brooks was losing followers and Baxter gaining them. Grant finally issued a proclamation recognizing Baxter as the state's legal governor.[41]

The president's action calmed the situation but left Arkansas Republicans in a precarious position. The Clayton contingent was furious but powerless; jubilant Democrats moved quickly to consolidate their gains. Abandoning Baxter, they elected Augustus H. Garland governor and solidified their hold on the state government in the 1874 elections. Reversing his earlier course, Grant suddenly proposed intervening to reinstate Brooks, but moderate Republicans in Congress demurred, and Arkansas passed quietly into Democratic hands.[42]

Elsewhere as the 1870s began, political and racial lines were hardening. Although extremists had early agitated for the formation of a white man's party,[43] some conservatives had attempted to accommodate themselves to the new order and had courted black voters. The results were disappointing. Few Negroes voluntarily deserted the Republican party, so there seemed to be no alternative but to draw the color line. Racism reasserted itself to sanctify the total exclusion of the Negro from southern political life.[44] This strategic shift failed to consider demographic reality. In all the states still in Republican hands except Florida, blacks constituted a majority of the voting age population. White unification, as in Georgia and North Carolina, was not enough to defeat the radical regimes. Since persuasion had failed, white conservatives turned to more forceful methods either to win black support or to prevent the race's participation in politics.

Alabama became the first testing ground for a new Democratic strategy of white solidarity and the calculated use of violence. By 1874 Alabama Republicans, long divided into carpetbag and scalawag factions, were in desperate disarray. Native whites deserted the party in droves over the issue of Senator Charles Sumner's proposed Civil Rights bill and growing black demands for a larger share of the political loaves and fishes. The state's Republicans desperately tried to retain white voters by straddling the civil rights question and denying any support for "social equality" between the races. By way of contrast, the Democrats patched up their personal and political quarrels to unite on the single issue of race. Castigating the radicals for first drawing the color line, Democratic politicians gave up trying to woo black voters and openly declared themselves to be a white man's party. By nominating the conservative and colorless George Smith Houston for governor and by publicly repudiating violence, the Democrats sought to appear responsible and restrained.[45]

In this new spirit of harmony, the Democrats saw a great opportunity to capture the governorship and control of the legislature. Warning Republicans that they would carry the contest at all costs, conservatives stepped up social ostracism of the men they termed "Judases" to their race and "discouraged" black orators from addressing black audiences. In September, Congressman Hays wrote a public letter denouncing the Democrats for engaging in a campaign of intimidation, terror, and murder against black and white radicals. Hays and other leaders provided detailed accounts of murderous attacks by night riders during the canvass. The Democrats heatedly denied harassing anyone and attributed most of the disturbances to factional disputes in their opponents' ranks. Party spokesmen refuted the specific charges in the Hays letter and lambasted the Republicans for waving the "bloody shirt." The "peaceful" Democrats, however, attended Republican meetings in force, pelted speakers with rotten eggs, and in several counties took more serious steps to carry their political point.[46]

Democratic editors countered Hays's letter by accusing Republicans of arming and drilling their Negro supporters. Racial disturbances were blamed on a conspiracy by the national Republican party to retain power against the will of an angry white majority. Reports of black military companies marching at night poured into the office of the Republican governor, David P. Lewis, but few of these tales had any factual basis.[47]

Unlike the Ku Klux Klan terrorism and indicative of weakened Republican resistance to violence, most of the campaign disturbances took place in the Alabama black belt, an area running from east to west across the south-central part of the state. In Choctaw County, on the western edge of this region, influential black leader Jack Turner held several secret meetings. His followers whipped a Negro named Huff Chaney for passing information on these gatherings to whites. Knowing Turner to be a formidable foe, on August 13 Democrats sent out a posse to intercept him and his men as they were walking toward the small town of Mount Sterling. When the whites threatened to jail him for involvement in the Chaney beating, Turner agreed to sign an appearance bond. He then summoned his followers to a nearby school-house, which led whites to expect an armed invasion of Butler, the county seat. Again a posse rode out to stop the blacks; Turner agreed to appear in court but refused to give up any arms. As Turner and his men moved toward Butler, nine men from Mount Sterling ambushed them from the rear. Caught in a crossfire between the white parties, the blacks fled into the woods. Conservatives accused Turner and other blacks of insolently asserting their rights under the proposed federal Civil Rights bill, of plotting an insurrection, and of threatening to kill any black who supported the Democrats. An overzealous Republican apparently started a rumor that ten of Turner's men had been killed by the whites, and this groundless tale appeared in Hays's letter. The Democrats ended any further Republican activity in the county by chasing several black leaders into the swamps for the duration of the canvass.[48] Federal troops were sent to Butler, but election day passed quietly, and the Democrats carried the county.

Whites in neighboring Greene County heckled Republican speakers and threatened candidates with assassination if they held any more meetings. Two hundred armed Democrats prevented Republicans from assembling at Eutaw. When Negroes reportedly threatened to burn the tiny village of Forkland, whites pursued them into the countryside and evidently killed and wounded several of them. United States soldiers arrived to arrest the perpetrators, and the Republicans won the election.[49]

Democrats in Sumter County, on the northwest corner of the black belt, were more discriminating in their selection of victims. Walter P. Billings, a northern lawyer and prominent local Republican, traveled through the county during July speaking to large black audiences. Returning from a meeting on August 2, he was ambushed within sight of his home; five shots killed both Billings and his horse. Tom Ivey was a railroad mail agent and black Republican speaker who had received many threats against his life because of his political activities. On

August 29, white men flagged down a train on which he was riding and, when the unfortunate Ivey looked out a window, nearly blew his head off with shotgun blasts. There was little doubt that the assassins of Billings and Ivey intended to rid the county of two important Republicans, but eyewitnesses feared to tell their story to deputy federal marshals. Some angry black leaders called on their followers to arm themselves and kill one Democrat for each Negro who was murdered. Such incendiary, if understandable, advice led whites to raise the old cry of black insurrection and arrest the ringleaders, accusing them of planning to burn down some small settlements. Night riding forced several blacks to hide in the swamp near Belmont for the duration of the canvass. Democrats denied intimidating Negroes at the same time they apparently discussed killing Robert Reed, a black member of the legislature. After two Justice Department undercover agents investigated the deaths of Billings and Ivey, troops arrived to arrest whites accused of these crimes. Conservatives charged that the government was using the "mailed fist" to prevent a Democratic victory in the election. Editorial writers denounced the "cruel" treatment of the Sumter County prisoners and accused federal officials of inaugurating a "reign of terror" and allowing vengeful Negroes to prey on innocent citizens. Once again a timely application of military force proved decisive; Sumter County stayed in the Republican column.[50]

Elias Kiels was a scalawag judge and the most influential Republican in Barbour County on the extreme southeastern corner of the black belt. Whites disliked Kiels not only for his politics but for his alleged shielding of black criminals. Some Negroes also chafed under Kiels's nearly absolute control of county Republicans. Claiming they had been too long cheated by radical scoundrels, Democrats organized a White Man's Club to rally the voters for the November election. Republicans maintained that the conservatives had attempted to break up the county Republican convention, threatened Republican Negroes with the loss of their jobs, and forced them to sign pledges to vote the Democratic ticket. Kiels joined with United States Marshal Robert W. Healy in asking that troops be sent to the county seat of Eufaula, but Governor Lewis, who considered Kiels either a scoundrel or a fool, denied this request and declined to declare martial law in the county. Although a handful of soldiers eventually arrived, they could do little to stop the determined Democrat.[51]

On election day, several hundred blacks marched into Eufaula to vote; Kiels had advised them to come unarmed, and most did. Whites and blacks filled the street near the town's three polling places. Around noon, a dispute broke out between a white druggist, Charles Goodwin, and a black Republican, Milas Lawrence. Goodwin claimed to be protecting a black Democrat from intimidation by his Republican brethren, but apparently the whites had forced the young man to support their ticket. When Lawrence objected that the man was underage, he and Goodwin exchanged words regarding each other's paternity. Someone (probably Goodwin) pulled a gun, and whites in the buildings on both sides of the main street fired into the crowd of Negroes with a rapidity that suggested prior planning. The blacks fled in disarray, and exultant whites bragged about being ready to fight federal troops.[52]

Captain A. S. Daggett had stationed his detachment of ten enlisted men within sight of the polls but kept them under strict orders not to interfere with the voting. Daggett's soldiers had the authority to serve writs issued by federal courts, but the captain denied a request from a deputy United States marshal to use the soldiers to quell the rioting. In nearby Spring Hill, when a mob killed Judge Kiels's teenage son and burned the ballot box, the soldiers did nothing. "The company at Eufaula," an outraged Marshal Healy complained, "stood idly by while human life was being fearfully sacrificed." The following day, Daggett tabulated the casualties: one white man killed, twelve wounded, six or seven black men killed, and about seventy wounded.[53] The Democrats carried the county because many blacks had not been able to vote before the fighting broke out. Kiels left Eufaula for fear of his life—another victim of white supremacy and a grim warning for native Republicans.

On election day in Mobile, a turbulent and racially mixed mob crowded around the polls. Democratic leaders instructed their followers to watch for black repeaters, and some whites tried to dissuade Negroes from voting Republican even once. As sheriff's deputies arrested blacks on trumped-up charges of election law violations and carried them off to jail, a few whites shot at the prisoners. Democrats accused prominent black leader Allen Alexander of inciting a riot and placed him under arrest. Correctly fearing that Alexander might be killed, angry blacks demanded his release. After sporadic firing, they rescued Alexander, and the disturbances ended. But the Democrats had forced many blacks to leave the polls without voting.[54]

With the notable exceptions of Eufaula and Mobile, the election had been reasonably peaceful in most of Alabama. Many blacks, by Republican accounts, had decided it was not worth risking their lives to cast a ballot. White Georgians apparently crossed the state line to vote, a not uncommon practice in southern elections during this period. Most of the troops stationed around the state stayed quietly in their barracks. Although there were only 679 soldiers in Alabama on election day, conservatives ritualistically complained of intimidation. Troops did assist deputy marshals in making arrests of persons charged with violating the Enforcement Acts, but the military presence had little influence on the outcome of the election.[55]

What might be appropriately termed the "Alabama plan" had achieved a striking success. By reducing Republican strength in the black belt and in Unionist counties in the northern part of the state, the Democrats elected Houston and won a solid majority of the seats in both houses of the legislature. Alabama Republicans petitioned Congress to overturn the results of the election because of Democratic fraud and violence. If the "rebel party" was allowed to take over the state government, they warned, it would nullify the postwar constitutional amendments, return blacks to slavery, and drive loyal men from the state. In counties carried by the Republicans, Democrats prevented elected officials such as tax collectors and sheriffs from raising the required bonds; defeated Democrats thereby took office by default. After a congressional committee investigated the election of 1874 in Alabama, its Republican members agreed that the Democrats had used force to overturn the state's Republican majority, but Congress was unwilling to act on these findings. Attorney General George H. Williams refused to provide troops to arrest persons accused of political intimidation, thereby eliminating the final obstacle to Democratic ascendancy.[56]

For conservative southerners, the redemption of Alabama happily coincided with the Democrats' first real chance since the 1850s to win control of the national House of Representatives. Because of corruption, rumors that Grant was seeking a third term, the depressed economy, the controversial federal Civil Rights bill, and serious internal divisions over southern policy, Republicans were on the defensive everywhere.[57] Recognizing their enormous opportunity, southern conservatives sought to convince skeptical northerners that they could abandon coercive southern policies with perfect safety. Veteran North Carolina politico Zebulon Vance predicted racial peace after the withdrawal of federal troops and even speculated about political cooperation between whites and blacks. Conservative editorialists cautioned their readers to be discreet in both word and deed because the radicals would seize on the slightest pretext to conduct a bloody shirt campaign.[58] As usual, impetuous Democrats were their own worst enemies. Blaming all political and racial disturbances on the Republicans and aggressive blacks, fire-eaters expressed all too much enthusiasm about fighting for white supremacy. A candid Georgia editor described the redemption of his state: "Had our people failed to repel force by force—had they failed to meet the carpet-baggers, the scalawags and the deluded negroes upon ground of their own selection, with weapons in their hands to defend their birthright and their manhood. . . . The State government would still be in the hands of adventurers and thieves."[59]

Southern Republicans knew these hotspurs could not restrain their tongues and feared they could not control their itchy trigger fingers. In several states, Democrats forced blacks to sign protection papers pledging to vote conservative. In letters written to their northern political allies, southern Republicans painted a gruesome picture of large arms shipments coming into the South and of Negroes being slaughtered like cattle. A triumphant Democratic party, a South Carolina Republican editor warned, would give no quarter to Union men or blacks.[60] The plaintiveness of these pleas reflected the desperation of southern Republicans. The halfhearted support of national party leaders coupled with the mounting tide of counterrevolution in the southern states darkened the political future.

With their enemies in disarray, southern conservatives expected the radicals to resort to an old-fashioned sectional campaign as a final ploy to retain their power. Southern editors charged that Senator Oliver P. Morton of Indiana and Attorney General Williams had sent out instructions to their stooges in the South to manufacture outrage tales for northern consumption. When Powell Clayton issued a pamphlet on violence in Arkansas, the leading Democratic newspaper in the state caustically commented: "Nothing would suit Senator Clayton's views more than to see a hundred or two colored men killed. It would be a sweet morsel, with which he would appeal to a partisan Congress to reinstate him in power."[61]

Although the bloodshed in Dixie was all too real, southern conservatives were correct in charging certain northern Republicans with an eagerness to exploit the issue and avoid more politically dangerous questions. As the Democrats appeared to be gaining strength in the early fall balloting, Republican stump speakers could hardly resist resorting to the familiar antisouthern rhetoric. But when the extent of the conservative tidal wave became apparent in the October elections, southern Democrats crowed that the radical outrage mill had finally ground itself to pieces.[62] By November the full dimensions of the Republican disaster became clear. The Democrats gained eighty-five seats to capture control of the House of Representatives and did equally well in state and local contests. The southern Republican contingent in the Forty-Fourth Congress would be pitifully small.[63]

If the issue of southern violence had played itself out in northern politics, it was not because of tranquillity in the southland. Conservatives might claim that disturbances occurred only in those states still under Republican control, but events in Gibson County, Tennessee, proved otherwise. Reports spread in August 1874 that armed blacks

were planning to murder whites and burn the small town of Pickets-
ville. On August 24 and 25, local authorities rounded up the suspects
and placed them in the county jail at Trenton. After two unsuccessful
attempts, a mob of between 75 and 150 whites broke into the cells and
seized 16 prisoners. Roping them together, the mob dragged the men a
few hundred yards to a bridge and started shooting. Four blacks were
killed, two were wounded, and the rest miraculously escaped. Governor
John C. Brown offered a $500 reward for the capture of each guilty
party, and eventually forty-one persons were indicted in state courts.
Brown, however, mitigated his condemnation of this crime by blaming
the federal Civil Rights bill for spurring the blacks to insurrection. The
governor criticized the United States marshal for making arrests when
the state and local authorities were prosecuting the case to the best of
their ability. United States attorney W. W. Murray doubted it would be
possible to bring the accused men to trial in state courts and pushed
ahead with federal indictments, but Attorney General Williams ordered
the prosecutions dropped because of the difficulty in obtaining convictions under the Enforcement Acts in light of recent court decisions.[64]

The obvious failure of federal enforcement policy, the disaffection of
Republicans over Reconstruction issues, and the Democratic landslide
raised southern spirits. Ecstatic editors announced the death of war-
related issues in national politics and rejoiced that the army could no
longer prevent the overthrow of the remaining Republican state governments. With a Democratic majority in the House, the South would
have enough leverage to deter Grant from new military adventures
and elect a Democratic president in 1876.[65]

In the wake of an apparent revolution in national politics, a quiet
confidence spread across the South. The reaction to a threatened black
uprising in Georgia during 1875 illustrated most clearly this change in
atmosphere. The election of a black militia general in Hancock County,
southwest of Augusta, alarmed nervous whites. Rumors spread during
August that a black man named Candy Harris was mustering armed
Negroes in neighboring Washington and Jefferson counties to massacre
whites. Posses moved into Burke County, just south of Augusta, and
arrested Joe Morris (described as a "notorious negro agitator" by the
Augusta Chronicle and Sentinel) and several other reported ringleaders. All told, some forty blacks had been captured in Washington
and Jefferson counties, and local newspapers carried stories of a bloody
conspiracy extending to as many as twenty counties in central Georgia.
The arrests calmed the public mind, and many of the incarcerated Negroes blamed the affair on Harris and Morris. Despite thorough searching, white raiders never found the estimated five hundred to a thousand
blacks alleged to have been under arms. Although officials had jailed

one hundred blacks, they held only twenty-five for trial. Unlike insurrection panics of the past, there were no summary executions. Judge Herschel Johnson charged a state grand jury that the accused were presumed innocent and the jurors should not allow momentary passions to overcome their sense of justice. Even though several blacks were indicted, subsequent trials ended with the charges being dropped for lack of evidence.[66] Southern editors congratulated the people of Georgia on their calmness in dealing with such a dangerous situation.

For conservatives, these soothing words belied the work still to be done. Democrats in Louisiana, Mississippi, and South Carolina still seethed with discontent, ready to drive the hated Republicans from the halls of government. The course of the counterrevolution had thus far been tortuous; each state had taken its own sometimes halting path to redemption. Some states returned to the Democratic fold with little upheaval or bloodshed; in others, violence played a significant if not decisive role. Southern opponents of Reconstruction had found both national politicians and the hooded terrorism of the Ku Klux Klan ineffective instruments to overthrow Republican state governments. Although factionalism among their opponents had sped the course of redemption, impatient politicians refused to wait on such an evolutionary process. The year 1874 marked a turning point. The success of the Alabama plan and the new Democratic majority in the House inspired conservative leaders in the "unredeemed" states and gave them tactical instruction at the same time. The disorganization and uncertainty of the Klan period had gone. The weakness of southern Republicanism, the abandonment of federal law enforcement in the South, and the steady withdrawal of the soldiers made the completion of the counterrevolution only a matter of time.

8. Counterrevolution Aborted: Louisiana, 1871–1875

Louisiana symbolized the feebleness of radical Reconstruction and Republican southern policy. The factional quarrels between the state's young governor, Henry Clay Warmoth, and federal officials in New Orleans (the "Custom House" Republicans) were the most acrimonious in the South. Black Republicans, led by Lieutenant Governor Pinckney Benton Stuart Pinchback, often acted independently and resisted white domination. An 1871 Republican convention at which the Warmoth and Custom House factions had vied for control nearly ended in bloodshed. In January 1872 the Custom House men joined with the Democrats in a desperate scheme to suspend Warmoth from office. Again violence was narrowly averted, thanks in large part to the level-headed actions of General William H. Emory, then in command of federal troops in the state. While charges of corruption swirled around Warmoth's head, the unrelenting opposition of the Custom House Republicans and, of course, the Democrats steadily pushed Louisiana toward anarchy.[1]

The election of 1872 only increased this factional ferment. Although there were initially five parties in the field, eventually the contest narrowed to Fusionists and the Republicans. The former, consisting of Democrats, Warmoth backers, and a handful of old Whigs, supported a ticket led by Democrat John D. McEnery and Liberal Republican D. B. Penn. With Democrat McEnery of Ouachita Parish heading the coalition, many Republicans believed the old corrupt Democracy of John Slidell had been reborn. The Republicans patched over differences between the Custom House contingent and the blacks by nominating Vermont carpetbagger William Pitt Kellogg for governor and black Custom House supporter C. C. Antoine for lieutenant governor. Compared to the ebullient and skillful Warmoth, Kellogg struck people as a cold fish who was not at home in Louisiana's exotic political waters.

Nor was Kellogg an ardent supporter of Negro rights; one story circulated that he always wore a glove when he shook hands with a black man.[2]

There are no means short of necromancy to determine who won the election of 1872 in Louisiana. The campaign was quiet by the state's usual standards. Warmoth used his control of the election machinery to best advantage, and the returns showed that the Fusion ticket won the election. Republicans accused the governor's registrars of refusing to enroll black voters, of moving polling places to remote locations, of closing the voting early, and of stuffing the ballot boxes. They also claimed that Fusion supporters had used physical threats and economic intimidation against Negroes. Although some of these tales were obviously manufactured by United States Marshal Stephen B. Packard and his Custom House cohorts to buttress their case for overturning the results, there is no doubt that enough irregularities occurred to skew the outcome. Because both sides claimed victory, state law mandated that the Returning Board (consisting of the governor, lieutenant governor, secretary of state, and two state senators) would count the ballots and declare the winners.[3]

A comic opera of political and legal maneuvering followed that turned a state election into a national scandal. In all, four different Returning Boards met, three that declared in favor of the Fusionists and one in favor of the Republicans. Charges of bribery and double-dealing circulated freely; apparently a Kellogg supporter offered Warmoth a United States Senate seat if he would abandon McEnery and Penn.[4]

Into this labyrinthine confusion stepped the national government. On November 23, Kellogg wrote to ask Republican National Chairman William E. Chandler whether the federal government would furnish soldiers to execute any court orders issued against Warmoth. On December 3, Attorney General Williams telegraphed Packard ordering him to "enforce the decrees and mandates of the United States courts, no matter by whom resisted, and General Emory will furnish you with all necessary troops for that purpose." Secretary of War William W. Belknap sent similar instructions to Emory, who held his men in readiness, as yet unaware of the developing Republican scheme. On December 5, federal judge Edmund H. Durell, an old man in poor health and much under the influence of Kellogg's friends, issued a decree directing Packard to occupy the statehouse and disperse all illegal assemblies there. This directive meant the marshal could prevent the convening of any legislative body recognized by Warmoth's Returning Board and could himself, in effect, determine who had a "legitimate" claim to a seat in the legislature.[5]

The next morning, Packard had a military posse guarding the state-house, and Judge Durell declared Warmoth's Board illegal and ordered the Republican Returning Board to take possession of and canvass the returns. Since Warmoth refused to hand them over, the Republican board decided, without consulting any official documents, that Kellogg and a majority of the Republican legislative candidates had been elected. This new legislature then held an extra session on December 9 and impeached Warmoth, thereby making Pinchback acting governor of the state.[6] After Democrats held "indignation" meetings, Pinchback asked for military assistance, and General Emory kept his men ready in case of a clash between the rival claimants.[7]

Warmoth called the legislature recognized by his Returning Board into session at City Hall and proclaimed the body organized by Pinch-back and Kellogg to be illegal. After Attorney General Williams informed Pinchback on December 12 that the president recognized him and the Republican legislature, armed conflict between rival state militias seemed likely.[8] Pinchback wrote to Grant complaining that the Warmoth militia had taken over the state armory and was in open revolt against his government. Under orders from Washington, Emory came to Pinchback's aid and recaptured the armory, turning it back over to Pinchback's police. Kellogg, Pinchback, and other Republicans saw the assembling of the rival McEnery legislature as the first step toward an attempted coup against the state government. As the situation deteriorated, Republicans charged the McEnery forces with planning to assassinate Pinchback and blow up the statehouse with nitroglycerine.[9]

The climax to this fiasco came on January 13, when Kellogg and McEnery each held his own inauguration ceremony. Louisiana then had two governors, two legislatures, and two state governments. More than any other Republican regime in the South, the Kellogg government faced a chronic crisis of legitimacy. Many white natives would always see Kellogg as a usurper imposed on the state and kept in power by the force of federal bayonets. Conservative leader E. John Ellis urged a cheering crowd in New Orleans never to recognize Kellogg and do everything possible to install McEnery as governor.[10]

This deadlock revealed the problems faced by the national government in attempting to arbitrate state political quarrels. The Grant administration committed itself to upholding Kellogg without knowing the true situation in New Orleans. But no one in Washington proposed using military force against the McEnery forces. Instead, the administration's response to a revolutionary situation was telegrams and a minimal commitment of soldiers.

The fault lay in part with Kellogg, whose strategy in the crisis was to wait for the spring sunshine to melt away the opposition. He blithely informed Attorney General Williams that public sentiment, particularly among New Orleans businessmen, was running against McEnery.[11] Kellogg was either naive or deliberately deceptive, but this was not the last time he would mislead officials in Washington about the condition of affairs in Louisiana.

Despite Kellogg's optimism, both the conservative *New Orleans Picayune* and the fire-eating *Shreveport Times* called for unyielding resistance to the "illegal" Kellogg government. When McEnery organized his own state militia, the chance of civil war in the state dramatically increased. Ellis told an enthusiastic New Orleans audience at the end of February that he was tired of "truckling to the United States" and would ignore Grant's recognition of Kellogg. A popular motto recommended "no quarter for the usurpation." The Republicans discounted such threats because they were sure armed resistance would be crushed by the state militia and federal troops.[12]

On the night of March 5, a division of McEnery's militia attempted to capture a police station in the old Cabildo on Jackson Square in New Orleans. Citizens broke into a nearby gun store and distributed weapons to a crowd of some six hundred men, who then opened fire on the station house. General A. S. Badger, the commander of the Metropolitan Police, arrived with United States troops to disperse the mob. This attack shocked Kellogg into taking the blustering of the McEnery forces more seriously, and he decided the charade of dual governments had to end.[13]

Fearing a possible coup by the Fusionists, the governor moved against the McEnery "government." Police armed with Winchester rifles invaded the Odd Fellows' Hall, where the McEnery legislature had been meeting, and arrested sixty-five persons for their involvement in the assaults on the Cabildo. McEnery angrily berated the military for complicity in this action, but Emory replied that his men had had nothing to do with the dispersal of the Fusion legislature and informed the would-be governor that his orders required the protection of the legally recognized state government. Kellogg, obviously pleased and always optimistic, reported that "everything is quiet."[14]

The governor had again cried peace when there was no peace. As McEnery's shadow government disappeared, the cry still rose for resistance, and defiant conservatives threatened not to pay their taxes, which a "foreign" government had no legitimate right to collect from the people. Republicans calmly asserted that tax resistance was a great failure.[15] Perhaps to overthrow Kellogg by tax avoidance or striking a direct blow in New Orleans was not possible. The Republicans' real vulnerability lay in the country parishes, where local officials faced strong opposition and federal troops were miles away. Whether the state's Democratic leaders decided to shift the attack on Kellogg to the local level is impossible to determine because of the absence of surviving records from the conservative side. In any case, a series of incidents in the country parishes strikingly demonstrated Kellogg's inability to protect his political allies.

Grant Parish in central Louisiana 350 miles northwest of New Orleans became the scene of the bloodiest attack on local Republican power anywhere in the South. The legislature had created the parish in 1868, naming it after President-elect Grant and designating the parish seat of Colfax in honor of the new vice-president, Schuyler Colfax. Both geographically and socially, the parish contained two distinct areas: an alluvial plain along the Red River inhabited mostly by blacks and a hill country populated primarily by white farmers. The town of Colfax consisted of William Calhoun's plantation buildings near which most of the blacks lived; Montgomery, some twelve miles to the north, was the white settlement. The parish population of approximately forty-five hundred persons had roughly equal numbers of whites and blacks. Democrats believed the Republicans had established the parish to supply themselves with lucrative offices, particularly for Calhoun, who was considered both politically and morally corrupt because he cohabited with a black woman whom he had supposedly "purchased" in New Orleans. After the election of 1872, whites accused William Ward, a black member of the legislature, of promising Negroes that they would receive the lands of their former masters if they voted for Kellogg.[16]

The state election imbroglio resulted in two sets of local officials in Grant Parish. McEnery commissioned the Fusionist candidates, Alphonse Cazabat and Christopher Columbus Nash, as parish judge and sheriff respectively. At the urging of two white citizens, Kellogg recognized Cazabat and Nash but soon changed his mind and declared the Republican candidates for judge (R. C. Register) and sheriff (Daniel Shaw) legally elected. On March 31 Register and Shaw climbed in a window of the Colfax courthouse and took possession of their offices. Ward and other leaders summoned blacks into Colfax to defend these officials against an expected attack. Some armed whites approached the town on April 1 and 3 but turned back when they saw the large number of blacks. Most of the whites living in town left, and the *New Orleans Republican* warned that the blacks would no longer kowtow to the whites or be bullied into submission. Ward and another black leader, E. H. Flowers, later denounced Kellogg for deliberately recognizing two sets of officers in the parish and thereby stirring up racial strife to aid his own cause. Contemporary evidence, however, suggests that the governor was more indecisive than devious.[17]

The parish political conflict exacerbated already existing racial tensions. Democratic concerns extended far beyond merely seating Cazabat and Nash. The white farmers in the hills could not tolerate being governed by blacks such as Ward and Flowers. The struggle in Colfax exemplified what Roger Fischer has called the "unusual desperation" of white Louisianians to keep black people in their "proper" place.[18] Louisiana's free black population had long exerted more influence than that of any other state. It had aroused resentment among many whites, who were determined to crush black political, economic, and social power before it destroyed the foundations of white supremacy.

The blacks in Colfax seized the courthouse and made it their headquarters. They improvised two cannons from gas pipes and fired these off periodically, frightening the few whites still in the vicinity. Rumors spread that blacks were planning to kill all the white men, take the white women for themselves, and produce a "new race" of people. Some blacks broke into W. R. Rutland's deserted house and took a small coffin containing the body of his daughter, who had died in Lake Charles in 1867, that Rutland was preparing to reinter. As they hauled the coffin away, the corpse fell out on the ground. Passing steamboat captains reported armed Negroes along the banks of the river patrolling the outskirts of town. Kellogg considered sending Adjutant General James Longstreet and the Metropolitan Police to Colfax but did not act until it was too late. White Republicans unsuccessfully pleaded with the Negroes to disband and then fled with the other whites on a steamboat to New Orleans. The blacks picketed the roads for a twenty-mile radius around Colfax, and four to five hundred Negroes, many of them armed, occupied the town, throwing up crude breastworks to defend their stronghold.[19]

These actions frightened both the Democrats and Republican leaders, who seemed to be losing control of their black followers. In crises demanding bold action, white Republicans often timidly refused to countenance black retaliation against white aggression. Scalawags and carpetbaggers daily faced the dilemma of their dependence on black voters but were unwilling to share power with them. The failure to unite in the face of conservative hostility allowed Democratic terrorists to take the offensive.

Fusion sheriff Nash marched a group of armed whites toward Colfax, but blacks drove them away. On April 5 fifteen of these men shot black farmer Jesse McKinney as he was mending a fence. The murder further excited the Negroes in town. Nash called for aid from the surrounding parishes of Winn, Rapides, Natchitoches, and Catahoula, and by April 13 he had collected a force of between 125 and 300 men.[20]

On Easter Sunday, April 13, Nash and more than one hundred men moved toward Colfax; some whites returned to their homes rather than fight the entrenched blacks. The sheriff arrayed his forces along the east bank of the river, giving the defenders a half hour to remove their women and children. Levi Allen, the leader of the black forces (Ward had joined his white friends in New Orleans), placed 250 to 400 men behind the breastworks and refused to surrender. Around noon white skirmish lines engaged the blacks, and sporadic firing continued until about three o'clock in the afternoon. At that time a squad of thirty whites crept along the riverbank, found a gap in the breastworks, and poured through the opening to ambush the blacks from the rear. Panic-stricken, they fled in all directions; some 150 took refuge in the court-house. After the whites brought in a cannon and fired on the building, some blacks hoisted a flag of truce, and several whites moved forward. Nash's men later claimed that the Negroes had treacherously fired on them as they approached with their white flag, but the black survivors countered that the whites had murdered unarmed blacks rushing out of the building. In any case, the shooting of two whites near the courthouse further incensed the mob. The posse forced an old Negro to set fire to the courthouse and killed blacks trying to escape the flames. The whites chased blacks into the countryside and killed an unknown number. By the time thirty or forty prisoners were under guard, many of the men from the neighboring parishes returned home. Eyewitnesses later stated that young, impulsive whites had been left in charge of the cap-tured Negroes and that during the night these sentinels took the blacks away two by two and shot them. Some miraculously escaped by feigning death. Perhaps as many as one hundred blacks lay dead around the courthouse and in the woods.[21] The bloodshed at Colfax substantiates Richard Hofstadter's generalization that racial and ethnic conflict has produced the most lethal riots in American history.[22]

Louisiana whites believed Kellogg had engineered a Negro riot at Colfax for his own selfish purposes. Conservative editors favorably compared the slaughter to General Philip Sheridan's recent massacre of the Modoc Indians. The state's Republicans downplayed the local causes for the Grant Parish violence and interpreted it as part of a conservative conspiracy to subvert the state government.[23]

Federal soldiers arrived at Colfax on the evening of April 21 under orders to arrest the participants in the riot. Many of the guilty parties, including Nash and other ringleaders, left the parish. Armed men invaded Colfax in August, threatening the lives of anyone aiding in the prosecution of the rioters. Democrats charged that the defendants had been arrested on the basis of false affidavits signed by ignorant Negroes who had themselves been involved in the fighting and took up collections for the prisoners' defense. A federal grand jury originally returned indictments against seventy-two men under the Enforcement Acts, but on the advice of Attorney General Williams, prosecutor James R. Beckwith brought only nine of these cases to trial in early 1874. Black witnesses retold in detail the events of April 13, 1873, but the defendants produced a string of witnesses who swore that the accused had not been in Colfax on that Easter Sunday. Such conflicting testimony led to the acquittal of one man and a hung jury in the other cases, despite suspicions that many white witnesses had committed perjury. At a second trial for the remaining eight accused men in May and June, William Cruikshank and two others were found guilty of violating several conspiracy provisions of the Enforcement Acts.[24]

Cruikshank and his co-defendants appealed their convictions to the United States Circuit Court. The district judge, who had presided at the earlier trials, upheld the original verdict, but Supreme Court Justice Joseph P. Bradley wrote an opinion that virtually emasculated the Enforcement Acts. Bradley maintained that under the Fourteenth and Fifteenth amendments Congress could pass legislation prohibiting the states from infringing the rights of United States citizens but had no jurisdiction over the actions of private individuals and could not enact laws dealing with crimes such as murder, robbery, and assault, which normally fell under state jurisdiction. With the Circuit Court divided, the case went automatically to the Supreme Court. Chief Justice Morrison R. Waite's majority opinion agreed with Justice Bradley's position on the scope of congressional authority to enforce the postwar amendments. The Court affirmed Bradley's verdict of dismissal and ordered the defendants discharged. Beckwith had recognized the dangerous consequences of Bradley's opinion even before the Supreme Court heard the case. He warned that such a narrow interpretation of federal jurisdiction made armed bands in the South immune from prosecution and gave timid grand jurors a convenient excuse to avoid doing their duty. The significance of these decisions was not lost on white leaders in Alabama, Mississippi, and South Carolina.[25]

After Colfax, the counterrevolutionary offensive against Republican officials quickly spread to other parishes, where men elected on the McEnery ticket forced Kellogg's officers to resign their positions. Democrats seized power in Franklin Parish in northeastern Louisiana and organized a militia to protect themselves. In May 1873 a Fusionist tax collector in New Orleans stepped up to a carriage in which Kellogg was riding and fired a shot through the top of the vehicle as it sped away. Although the governor was unharmed, he must have finally realized the lengths to which his fanatical opponents would go in their efforts to seat McEnery.[26]

According to reports in the *New Orleans Republican*, Kellogg was gathering arms for the Metropolitan Police to oust the McEnery usurpers and reinstate Republican officials. The first test of this effort came in St. Martin Parish, located in the swampy Teche region of the state. Metropolitans commanded by General A. S. Badger left New Orleans on May 3 for St. Martinville to install the Kellogg officers and put down the tax resistance movement. Colonel Alcibiades DeBlanc, one of the founders of the Knights of the White Camellia, commanded the McEnery militia in the parish. When the Metropolitans approached the town, DeBlanc and his force of four to six hundred men offered only token opposition and retired from the field, allowing Badger's men to occupy St. Martinville. After the general had installed a Republican judge and district attorney in the courthouse, DeBlanc's men periodically fired off their two cannons. Emory sent troops to prevent a collision. Despite threats against Badger's men, after a brief skirmish on May 7, DeBlanc ordered his forces back into a swamp from which they later fled when federal troops finally arrived. A deputy United States marshal, who had accompanied the soldiers, brought a packet of arrest warrants with him but found few of the parties named in them. DeBlanc and ten other insurrectionists finally surrendered to federal officials and were taken to New Orleans, where a cheering crowd greeted them at the ferry landing. A United States commissioner later dismissed the charges, but both peace and Kellogg's officials had returned to the parish.[27]

Ironically, during the disorder, the state government undertook an ambitious reform program that included tax reductions, some lessening of corruption, lower state expenditures, and the establishment of a sound funding system for the state debt.[28] White Louisianians still saw Kellogg as a conscienceless carpetbagger kept in power by federal bayonets and had no interest in reforms. Although McEnery's government seems to have faded from the picture, resistance to the Republicans at the local level continued unabated. In Franklin Parish, armed men ambushed and killed District Judge T. S. Crawford and District Attorney A. H. Harris. When the guilty parties were arrested, a mob threatened to rescue them from the jail. A police juror in northern Louisiana returned his commission to the governor, saying, "I cannot with safety accept it." An Alexandria Republican claimed it was not uncommon for blacks to be hanged or shot in Rapides Parish and warned that they might have to take the law into their own hands.[29] Kellogg underestimated the strength of this opposition and greatly misled his northern friends about the vitality of his regime. At the end of 1873, the governor informed Senator Morton that conservative resistance was fading and that his government could maintain order in Louisiana without calling on federal troops. Claiming to have worked out a modus vivendi with the New Orleans business community, Kellogg naively predicted, "The prospects of the republican party are bright for the future." By February 1874, he was even more sanguine: "I repeat there is no contingency that I can at all imagine as likely to occur in the future in which we cannot sustain ourselves."[30]

But by the beginning of 1874 opposition to Republican rule had grown desperate. Arguing that defiance to tyranny was a citizen's most solemn duty, conservative leaders proclaimed that Kellogg and his minions stayed in power only because of the presence of federal soldiers. The *New Orleans Bulletin,* which was fast becoming the leading organ of the state's reactionary zealots, maintained that when all peaceful avenues of protest had been closed, there would be an "outburst of indignation against this usurping Government, as will sweep it from power and consign it, we trust, to the farthest depths of oblivion."[31] More important, white leaders watched carefully as large numbers of troops were withdrawn from the South, northern opinion turned against the carpetbag regimes, and Grant failed to sustain Republican governors in Texas and Arkansas. The time seemed ripe to strike a blow for liberty.

In the spring and summer of 1874 McEnery led a swelling chorus calling for the organization of all white people to overthrow Republican rule and drive the carpetbaggers from the state. Rabid conservatives emphasized the critical necessity of forming a solid phalanx against the tide of social equality and miscegenation brought on by radical oppression. Whites blamed the Negroes for voting against the best interests of the community, forming armed Black Leagues, and hatching vile conspiracies. Several northern Louisiana editors asserted that blacks had drawn the color line against whites and that the superior race would retaliate by mustering its strength to defeat these forces of barbarism.[32] This overblown rhetoric allowed whites of all social classes to feel persecuted and to credit their opponents with evil designs. From acceptance of this logic it was an easy step to justify violent insurrection against the "enemy."[33]

Heightened white paranoia produced new rumors of black organization for racial warfare. Newspaper reporters claimed to have discovered several insurrectionary plots in the country parishes during the summer. Even the usually restrained *New Orleans Picayune* carried chilling accounts of an armed Black League whose object was to kill white men and enslave white women. The editors published an alleged constitution of this society in which the members were pledged to total secrecy and given an elaborate series of secret passwords and handshakes. The insubstantial nature of this "evidence" made even racial fanatics question the danger.[34]

The flimsiness of this rationale was obvious because White Leagues began organizing in the rural parishes during the spring of 1874, long before any mention of Black Leagues appeared in the press. Starting in Opelousas these groups spread north into the Red River parishes. With pageantry and the enthusiastic participation of women and children, whites held large rallies whose festival atmosphere belied their serious purpose. Historians have not recognized the importance of these mass meetings in turning normally peaceful citizens into angry mobs; propaganda and hoopla are necessary precursors of revolutionary action. The resolutions adopted at these gatherings recited the familiar litany on the evils of the Kellogg administration, and the White League in St. Martin Parish compared its catalog of grievances against Republicans to those of the American colonies against Great Britain listed in the Declaration of Independence. Emboldened by the winds of political reaction blowing out of the northern states, Louisiana conservatives openly vowed to use intimidation to crush the black electoral majority. The White Leaguers shared a singular animus against the traitors to their race, both scalawags and carpetbaggers, who had alienated the black masses from them. They favored the social and economic ostracism of these white Judases and Benedict Arnolds, and many of their rasher statements contained faintly concealed threats against the lives of white Republicans.[35]

Although there is little reliable information on membership, the Louisiana White League seems to have been a broad-based movement among the state's white citizens. Yeomen farmers suffering from economic depression were eager recruits in the war against the Negro.[36] Unlike the Knights of the White Camellia or the Ku Klux Klan, the White League operated openly with extensive press coverage of its activities. Few persons tried to conceal their membership in the organization, perhaps because there was decreasing danger that the federal government would move against them. The White League began at the parish level, and there is no hard evidence of any statewide organization; newspaper accounts of White League rallies in one area seemed to inspire the formation of similar organizations elsewhere. The relationship between the White League and the Democratic party was simple: the party convention, which met in Baton Rouge in August, adopted a platform calling for all those opposed to the Kellogg "usurpation" to join together for the preservation of white civilization.[37] Even this document's hollow pledge to respect the rights of all citizens regardless of race was similar to those contained in many White League statements. As the Republicans quickly realized, the White League was the military arm of the Democratic party.

Perceptive conservatives feared the rash statements and violent acts of fanatical White Leaguers would injure Louisiana's cause in the eyes of the nation and delay redemption. They had good reason to be apprehensive. The *Natchitoches People's Vindicator* pledged that the whites would defy the Kellogg government "*with all the means the God of nature has placed within our reach.*" The fire-breathing editor of the *Shreveport Times* issued a solemn warning to the Republicans: "If a single hostile gun is fired between the whites and blacks in this and surrounding parishes, every carpetbagger and scalawag that can be caught, will in twelve hours therefrom be dangling from a limb."[38]

Such threats were not mere bluster. Republican officials in Natchitoches Parish received anonymous notices that "the people" would exterminate all thieving rascals. Conservative leaders clamored for the resignations of police jurors and other officials. District Judge Henry C. Myers and parish Judge D. H. Boullt, Jr., fearing for their lives, left the parish. An estimated thirteen hundred persons assembled in Natchitoches on July 27 to demand that Myers, Boullt, and several other parish officials surrender their positions. Parish attorney J. J. Bossier and the tax collector, D. H. Boullt, Sr., quickly succumbed to the pressure and resigned.[39] The expulsion of Kellogg's men in Natchitoches not only made it impossible for the Republicans to canvass the parish but also gave the White League encouragement to move against local officials elsewhere.

The redoubtable Alcibiades DeBlanc led an armed mob that forced the officeholders in St. Martin Parish to flee to New Orleans. DeBlanc made several blustering speeches urging the people to defy the Metropolitan Police if they dared to enter St. Martinville. The revolt spread north into Avoylles, Winn, Lincoln, and Webster parishes. A taxpayers' association in Caddo Parish (Shreveport) investigated local assessments and admittedly tried to frighten Republican "rogues and scoundrels." Although Republicans lamely contended that coerced resignations were pointless because Kellogg would never accept them, few officials would return to their parishes unless accompanied by United States troops.[40]

White League spokesmen dismissed Republican reports of violence as partisan attempts to manufacture outrages for campaign speeches,[41] but events in Red River Parish soon gave the lie to these statements. Marshall Harvey Twitchell was a Union army veteran from Vermont, who had settled in the small town of Coushatta about sixty-five miles below Shreveport. After being elected to the state senate, Twitchell convinced the legislature to create the new parish of Red River, in which he became the dominant power. Twitchell's brother Homer and several other relatives moved to Coushatta and received appointments to office from then Governor Warmoth. These carpetbaggers had grandiose plans for expanding the town and increasing their own assets and influence. Twitchell, who was a relatively poor man when he arrived in Louisiana, soon acquired substantial wealth. He made most of his money by purchasing land at tax sales, but the Democrats accused him of operating a lucrative "ring" in the parish that reaped large profits from the construction of the Coushatta courthouse. Twitchell's most bitter political and economic rival, T. W. Abney, resented the sudden prosperity of these new residents, but what most exasperated the conservatives was their own inability to win elections. With a parish population of three hundred whites and eleven hundred blacks, Twitchell's control of the Negro vote made him invincible at the polls. Since blacks virtually worshiped Twitchell because of his friendship for them and support for their schools, the whites could see no end to radical rule.[42]

Abney and other leading conservatives organized a White League and at a public meeting in July resolved to "persuade" Twitchell and his cronies to resign their offices. Although both Republicans and Democrats later agreed to eschew violence, Twitchell had good reason to distrust his rabid enemies, and he left for New Orleans to ask Packard and Kellogg for federal troops.[43]

On August 25 some blacks in the tiny settlement of Brownsville, ten miles below Coushatta on the Red River, argued with two white men and threatened their lives. One of the whites moved his family to Coushatta, after which armed blacks broke into and searched his home. The following day a posse arrested one of the blacks, Dan Wynn, and tried to arrest another, Tom Jones, but Jones opened fire on them, mortally wounding a young white man. The enraged whites then murdered both Negroes and raised the thread-bare cry of black insurrection. With Twitchell in New Orleans, whites suspected the carpetbaggers intended to stir up violence among the blacks to provide an excuse for calling in troops.[44]

Several white Republicans rode to Brownsville and assured the blacks that the murders committed by the posse would not go unpunished. Despite growing apprehensions of a Negro attack, the young people held a dance at Abney's new brick store in Coushatta. The occasion was far from festive; the men came dressed in rough clothes with weapons bulging beneath their coats, and the women noticed that their partners seemed distracted and kept nervously watching the door. Meanwhile, a number of blacks had gathered at Homer Twitchell's home, some hiding under the house and others concealing themselves in a nearby cotton field. Two white pickets, who had been posted on the roads leading into town, stopped a Negro carrying a load of buckshot, but he fled into the night. These sentries later met Homer Twitchell in the road. After speaking briefly with him, they returned to their posts, but the blacks in the cotton field opened fire. One of the men received five bullet wounds, but both escaped to warn those at the dance that the Negroes had risen in revolt.[45]

Having been alerted by couriers dispatched by Abney, a thousand armed men from the neighboring parishes poured into Coushatta on August 29. As the mob grew turbulent during the day, Abney and other Coushatta citizens decided to arrest six white Republicans for their own protection: Homer Twitchell, Sheriff E. S. Edgerton, Robert Dewees, the tax collector of De Soto Parish, W. R. Howell, Red River Parish attorney, registrar Clark Holland, and M. C. Willis, a justice of the peace. They also took a United States marshal, a deputy sheriff, and six Negroes into custody but later released them. At a public "trial" for the six prisoners held the following day, the White Leaguers failed to produce evidence linking any of the Republicans to a Negro insurrection plot but demanded that they resign their offices. All six men acceded and agreed to leave the state within twenty-four hours. Abney kept the prisoners under heavy guard and delayed their departure an additional day to allow the popular excitement to abate.[46]

The plan was to escort the men to Texas with a posse of their own choosing. The prisoners and twenty-five guards left Coushatta on Sunday morning, August 31, and rode hard but finally stopped to rest their horses about twenty miles from Shreveport. Back in Coushatta, some young firebrands, who suspected that the six Republicans were guilty of many more crimes than had been revealed and who disapproved of the "lenient" verdict, pursued the prisoners. They overtook their quarry as the posse was resting and killed all six Republicans, mutilating several of the bodies. The guards either could not or would not protect their charges. Although some witnesses claimed that the massacre was done by Texans, the finger of guilt more clearly pointed to White Leaguers from Red River and surrounding parishes, led by the bloodthirsty Dick Coleman of De Soto Parish, popularly known as "Captain Jack." Shortly afterward, a mob lynched the two Negroes charged with the earlier wounding of the white picket.[47]

With Republicans screaming about a reign of terror in Red River Parish, Kellogg sent an account of the murders to Washington along with a request for more troops. The governor had good reason to fear the Coushatta affair might be part of a larger conspiracy to murder Republican officials elsewhere because White League newspapers palliated the crime and blamed it on the state government. McEnery denied ever making a speech praising the Red River assassins, but he did assert that the people had the right to resort to the "paramount law of self-preservation to protect society against the ravages of official plunderers and spoliators."[48]

McEnery's statement demonstrates how mobs can cloak their most hideous acts behind noble-sounding goals.[49] These men were not conscious scoundrels but rather deceived themselves as well as others about their violent deeds. Throughout the Reconstruction period, a consistent pattern of murderous assault followed by mild regret or, more often, vigorous defense emerges. The historian listens for voices to be raised against these outrages but hears very little from the conservative ranks. In this atmosphere of revolution, ends and means become hopelessly muddled in the minds of ardent partisans.

As in other incidents of this period, the perpetrators easily escaped punishment. Kellogg offered a reward of $5,000 for the arrest of the Coushatta murderers, and federal soldiers arrived in late September to restore the Republicans to tenuous power. Major Lewis Merrill, who had tangled with South Carolina Klansmen in 1871, arrived in Shreveport on October 19 and arrested thirteen persons in connection with Red River violence as well as several other persons accused of intimidating blacks and Republican officeholders in neighboring parishes. Conservative editors denounced this latest act of military despotism, but the prisoners voted under guard on election day, and the charges against them were later dropped.[50]

For Marshall Twitchell, the Coushatta affair had a grisly sequel. Though he won reelection to the state senate, Twitchell was exhausted and understandably weary of politics. He appeared for the opening of the legislature in early 1876 and returned home to Coushatta in late April. On May 2, as Twitchell and his brother-in-law, George King, prepared to attend a police jury meeting in town, a stranger rode into Coushatta on a pony. Disguised in a rubber raincoat, his face concealed by a false beard, a pair of goggles, and a hat pulled down over his eyes, the man waited patiently near a blacksmith shop until he saw Twitchell and King board the ferry on the opposite bank. As they approached the shore, he leveled a rifle at the boat and opened fire; King shot back but soon fell dead in the boat. Twitchell was wounded in the leg and jumped into the water, holding onto the boat with first one hand and then the other as the disguised man mercilessly shot him in each arm. The assassin remarked to a horrified woman that he was shooting "a damned black alligator." He then mounted his pony and rode off. The black ferryman, though wounded, managed to pull Twitchell back into the boat and prevent him from drowning. Even though an army surgeon later amputated both of Twitchell's arms near the shoulder, he lived thirty years longer, serving as a consul at Kingston, Canada. Evidence pointed to the notorious Captain Jack as the would-be murderer, but the timid sheriff failed to summon a posse. The "stranger" returned to Coushatta years later for a hero's welcome.[51]

This tragedy pointed up the very real vulnerability of the Republicans in the hinterlands. Neither state forces nor federal soldiers could protect local officeholders from intimidation or worse in remote parishes. Although Joe Gray Taylor has described the Coushatta massacre as "one of the most senseless outbreaks of violence in Louisiana history," it was certainly not senseless in that it lacked a purpose.[52] Using classical guerrilla warfare strategy, the White League gained control of the countryside by terrorizing the representatives of the hated Kellogg regime. Much like Mao Tse-tung's soldiers or the Viet Cong, the White League steadily expanded its influence in rural areas and isolated the governor's supporters. Kellogg lacked effective authority outside of New Orleans, and it was questionable how long he could hold out there. In June the Crescent City Democratic Club rechristened itself the Crescent City White League, and its members committed all their resources to defending white civilization against radical tyranny. By July quasi-military organizations were arming and drilling, eager to take the field against the Republicans at the first opportunity.[53]

Many of the city's White League units attended a large rally on September 1 to endorse the Democratic platform drafted at the Baton Rouge convention. John McEnery asked his loyal supporters how long they were going to tolerate the Kellogg "usurpation" and predicted that Grant would soon stop using soldiers to prop up the carpetbaggers. Metropolitan policemen with Winchester rifles and a Gatling gun nervously watched the assemblage for any sign of trouble.[54] The War Department had sent additional soldiers to Louisiana after the Coushatta affair, but the more fanatical White Leaguers vowed that even federal troops could not stop a popular uprising against Republican oppression. With most of the soldiers normally in New Orleans stationed in Holly Springs, Mississippi, for the yellow fever season, Emory ominously informed Packard that he did not have an adequate force in the city to keep the peace.[55]

The White League militia in New Orleans had ordered Belgian and Prussian rifles from New York, but Republicans discovered the shipments. The Metropolitan Police seized several boxes of arms from a store on Canal Street under warrants charging that these weapons were to be used for an insurrectionary purpose. On September 10 more rifles arrived on the steamer *Dallas* in crates marked "machinery," though they had not been entered on the ship's manifest. Custom House officers and Metropolitans confiscated the boxes as they were being unloaded and hauled them to a nearby police station. Shortly thereafter, the steamer *Mississippi* docked with a large shipment of arms, and whites swore that they would prevent the Metropolitans from taking them. On the night of September 13, White Leaguers entered their armory at the Leeds Foundry. The officers distributed arms to their men in preparation for their duties the next day.[56]

With McEnery safely exiled to Vicksburg, Mississippi, awaiting the results of the impending revolution, his lieutenant governor, D. B. Penn, and military commanders, Frederick N. Ogden and John B. Angell, decided on a plan of attack. Penn had earlier considered stationing armed men near the statehouse (the old St. Louis Hotel), who would kidnap Kellogg, take him out to sea, and install McEnery as governor. McEnery, however, feared a violent conflict with the Republicans and vetoed this wild scheme. On September 12 Ogden and Penn determined to take over the state offices and seize the state records. As part of this plan, the leaders ordered the White League forces to be ready on Monday morning, September 14, to unload the arms from the *Mississippi,* by force if necessary. Conservative newspapers published a call for a mass meeting at the Henry Clay statue on Canal Street—the opening move in the attempted overthrow of the state government.[57]

At the appointed hour of 11:30, a crowd of five thousand persons gathered to hear fiery orators denounce Kellogg and call for his immediate resignation. A committee appointed to wait on the governor returned to report that he refused to receive any message from an armed mob, a decision that elicited cries of "Hang Kellogg." As part of the preconcerted plan, armed White Leaguers appeared on the streets and threw up barricades along the length of Poydras Street from Carondelet toward the river.[58]

General James Longstreet, the adjutant general of the state militia, who had been known during the Civil War as a masterful defensive general, took the offensive. Late in the afternoon he marched his black militiamen and the Metropolitans from the police station on Jackson Square and distributed them along Canal Street between the Custom House and levee. About 250 Metropolitans commanded by General Badger moved from the levee toward the right flank of the White League forces. As they approached Gravier Street, Ogden's men laid down a blistering fire, forcing the Metropolitans to beat a hasty retreat and to leave two Gatling guns and a twelve-pound artillery piece behind. At the Custom House, Longstreet heard the whites give the rebel yell as they charged, reportedly "blanched," and ordered his men inside the building. When the Negro militia saw the Metropolitans break and run, they, too, scattered in all directions. The insurrectionary forces now controlled the city and easily captured state buildings but wisely decided not to attack the Custom House because it was federal property. In the fight, the Metropolitans had lost eleven killed and sixty wounded, while the White Leaguers suffered twenty-one killed but only nineteen wounded. Badger had fallen seriously wounded, and Longstreet was also hit. The casualties could have been much higher because large numbers of people stood on the levee, stuck their heads out windows, or roamed the streets during the battle.[59]

On receiving word of the fighting, General Emory, who was still in Mississippi, ordered Lieutenant Colonel John R. Brooke and four companies of soldiers to New Orleans. The victorious White Leaguers cheered the arriving soldiers, never suspecting that the federal government would attempt to reinstate Kellogg. The War Department ordered a reluctant Emory to return immediately, assume command, and under no circumstances to recognize the insurgent government. Packard and other Republicans bitterly complained that the government would never have been overthrown had there been a sufficient number of federal troops in New Orleans.[60]

Conservatives jubilantly celebrated the demise of their archenemy; the leading White League organ proclaimed New Orleans "the happiest city in the universe." David F. Boyd, president of Louisiana State University, assured his friend General Sherman that there was "no hostility to the United States Government, or to the President" and said that even blacks rejoiced at Kellogg's downfall. If the administration would leave the state alone, Boyd advised, there would be no more trouble.[61]

An ominous quiet spread over the Crescent City on September 15 as the White Leaguers dismantled their barricades and Acting Governor Penn set up the new government in the statehouse. The Custom House was closed, and Packard reported that the insurgents had captured the police stations, the arsenal, and all other state buildings. White League supporters from neighboring parishes poured into the city to join the festivities. Informing President Grant that Louisianians had had no choice but to revolt against the "usurpers" who had oppressed and plundered the people, Penn promised to keep the peace, protect the blacks, and guard federal property from attack. The Republicans were confident Grant would again come to their rescue. Armed revolutionaries had overpowered state authorities, Kellogg wired the president, and all the resources of the federal government should be used to put down this "domestic violence."[62]

Contrary to conservative expectations, Grant issued a proclamation on September 15 calling on the rebellious citizens to disperse within five days and submit themselves to the legal (Kellogg) government of Louisiana. On the night of September 17, both McEnery and General Emory arrived in New Orleans. During their meeting the following morning, the general demanded that the "state" troops disperse and return all weapons to the armory. Evidently, a few irreconcilables

favored resistance, but General Ogden and his staff unanimously resolved "not [to] come in conflict with United States troops." McEnery,
trembling and nearly overcome with emotion, conferred with Colonel
Brooke and surrendered his forces to the military authorities. By September 18, the army had restored the government to Kellogg's hands,
and Emory reported all quiet in New Orleans. He doubted that the
participants in the rebellion could be prosecuted because "the outbreak
embraced nearly every white man in the community."[63] This statement accurately described Kellogg's shaky hold on the reins of power.

The initial success of the revolution confirmed conservative assessments of Republican impotency. Most White Leaguers favored continued resistance against the state government, and Kellogg, according to
the editor of the *Shreveport Times,* would receive the same obedience
as if Grant had placed a "toad" in the gubernatorial chair. The still
tense situation in New Orleans forced the War Department to keep
troops in the city even though it would have preferred transferring
them elsewhere during the violent 1874 southern election campaign.[64]

The initial success of the White League putsch marked the collapse
of Grant's policies in Louisiana and the failure of the Kellogg government to establish any degree of legitimacy. Even though federal troops
restored some Republican officeholders to power, forced resignations
continued. As the *New Orleans Bulletin* smugly pointed out, soldiers
would have to be stationed in all fifty-seven parishes to keep the Republicans in power.[65]

Armed whites still patrolled the streets of New Orleans, and General
Emory wondered if he had enough troops in the city and state to keep
the peace on election day. Much to Kellogg's chagrin, the White Leaguers never returned fifteen hundred stand of arms and two howitzers
captured from the state armory during the September rebellion, and
Emory refused to order his troops to search for these weapons. In this
tense atmosphere, Kellogg was in immediate personal danger. While
riding in a cab one day, the governor saw one of his bitterest political
enemies, E. A. Burke, and made a "gesture of derision" with his finger.
Burke grabbed Kellogg by the arm, apparently trying to pull him out
of the cab. As the two men struggled, Burke hit Kellogg several times
with a piece of cowhide. The driver of the cab whipped the horses,
leaving the enraged Burke sprawled on the ground. Kellogg fired at
Burke from the careening vehicle, and Burke got off several shots at
his departing foe, but neither was hit. Despite such ominous portents,
election day passed relatively peacefully. Major Merrill reported a
"quiet" election in Shreveport, where one person was killed and four or
five wounded.[66]

The Democrats immediately claimed victory, but they had learned through bitter experience not to underestimate the resourcefulness of their enemies. White Leaguers in northern Louisiana warned Republicans against any attempt to tamper with the returns, and the editor of the *Shreveport Times* vowed to use "hemp" on candidates illegally counted into office.[67] Just as in 1872, the election of 1874 was marred by enormous irregularities. Both parties vividly painted their opponents in the darkest hues before congressional committees, and there is no way to sort out the truths from the falsehoods. Obviously, fraud and intimidation were committed by both sides, but much of the testimony, particularly that before the Returning Board, reeks of perjury.

In such an environment, Republican leaders expected an attack on the Returning Board and admitted that without the support of Congress and the president, the Kellogg government was doomed. General Emory kept his men alert to prevent the outbreak of partisan warfare in New Orleans. President Grant secretly instructed General Philip Sheridan to travel quietly through Mississippi and Louisiana, and especially to New Orleans, and send back confidential reports on conditions there. Grant further authorized Sheridan to take command of the Military Division of the South (or any part of it) if necessary.[68]

On Christmas eve, the Returning Board issued its report, declaring the Republican candidate for state treasurer elected and seating fifty-three Republicans and fifty-three Democrats in the House with five seats to be decided after the body convened. Staggered terms in the Senate left a safe Republican majority there. Democrats denounced these decisions as subverting the idea of free elections and posing a dangerous threat to republican government in the United States. White Leaguers vowed that the people would never submit to such an outrage, and several country editors warned that candidates counted in by the Returning Board could never safely take office.[69]

When the legislature met on January 4, 1875, Democrats forcibly seized control of the House and proceeded to seat their own claimants to vacancies in the body. On Kellogg's request and with Sheridan's "advice," General Emory sent Colonel Regis de Trobriand to clear the House of all persons not recognized as members by the Returning Board. That afternoon General Sheridan assumed command of the Department of the Gulf.

"Little Phil" wasted no time in taking vigorous action (at least on paper) against the anti-Kellogg forces. The irascible general wired the secretary of war suggesting that Congress declare the White Leaguers "banditti" so they could be tried by a military commission. Sheridan confidently reported the settlement of matters in New Orleans and the imminent collapse of the White League. The general downplayed threats against his life and dismissed protests against his actions as not being worthy of serious consideration. According to his own estimate, nearly thirty-five hundred persons had been murdered in Louisiana since 1866, and at least twelve hundred of these had died for their political beliefs. Sheridan claimed, with little evidence, that the substantial and respectable citizens of New Orleans were opposed to the White League.[70]

Far from remedying the situation, when Sheridan's imprudent telegrams appeared in the newspapers, they greatly embarrassed the Grant administration and unleashed a new storm of controversy in Louisiana. By 1875, any suggestion of military trials for "banditti" merely handed the Democrats a new weapon to use against an already tottering president. The "military invasion" of the Louisiana legislature combined with Sheridan's ill-considered telegrams marked the final collapse of the administration's Louisiana policies.[71] In a clumsily mixed metaphor, Louisiana editors compared Kellogg to Oliver Cromwell and Grant to Caesar, but their seeming sense of outrage must have been tempered by the obvious discomfiture of the national Republican party. Nor did angry conservatives hesitate to vent their anger on their least favorite general. With Sheridan present at New Orleans' Varieties theater, actor Lawrence Barrett in the role of Cardinal Richelieu spoke the line, "Take away the sword; states can be saved without it," with special emphasis. The audience cheered wildly; the general glowered. Guests at the St. Louis Hotel sent abusive newspaper articles to Sheridan's breakfast table with pertinent passages underlined.[72]

Though some diehards denounced all talk of compromise as a pusillanimous surrender, Congressman William A. Wheeler of New York and his congressional subcommittee on Louisiana affairs worked out a shaky settlement. The Democrats agreed to help maintain law and order in the state and not to impeach Kellogg for any past misconduct. For their part, Republicans would allow a congressional committee to canvass the 1874 election returns and determine the actual composition of the House, a procedure that would ensure a Democratic majority. Although this agreement never received the hearty endorsement of either side and House Democrats later moved to impeach Kellogg, an uneasy peace had been restored.

Conservative politicians in other southern states followed the struggle in Louisiana with intense interest. In their more apocalyptic moments, some editors saw Grant's recognition of Kellogg as a threat to liberty in every state in the Union. What Josiah Turner labeled the "crime of this century" led influential Charleston editor Francis Dawson to cry out: "If this tyranny is sustained the empire is not many years off." To the paranoid mind, the threat was real even in states safely in Democratic hands; as an Augusta, Georgia, editorialist warned, "The fate of Louisiana to-day may be the fate of Georgia tomorrow. No state is longer safe from attack, and no local government secure from subversion."[73] Yet while excoriating federal policy in Louisiana, perceptive southerners recognized the fragility of "radical despotism." The September rebellion, claimed Ethelbert Barksdale, the editorial voice of conservative Mississippians, "has taught a wronged people what it is possible for them to do, if they but dare; and it has taught their oppressors that they are helpless as babes in a lion's den, unless defended by the strong arm of the National Government."[74]

When de Trobriand's men scotched the conservative coup in January 1875, southern Democrats decried the emerging reign of the new Roman tyrant Grant. "Despot" was too mild an epithet for a man who was plotting to use federal troops to hold onto the presidency for life. Readers of southern newspapers must have seen the specter of military dictatorship appearing over the horizon.[75] Many editorials of this period smacked of partisan gasconade because only the naive or the ignorant could fail to see that the days of the Kellogg government were numbered no matter which party was in power.

Contemporary commentators and later historians missed the twin ironies of the situation. In no other state had the administration given so much attention and assistance to the Republicans as in Louisiana, yet Kellogg was forced to board up and secure with iron stanchions the doors and windows of the statehouse, leaving only a back entrance open.[76] Grant's tenacity caused the undoing of his policy. After committing himself to supporting the Custom House Republicans without qualification, the president made a series of decisions, seemingly unimportant at the time, that in their cumulative effect destroyed public support for Reconstruction. By 1875, Louisiana had become the Republican party's albatross. Even though the counterrevolution in the state had been temporarily halted, first in Mississippi and later in South Carolina, Democrats found in the White League a model for successful guerrilla warfare against Republicanism.

9. Counterrevolution Triumphant: Mississippi, 1873–1876

No one could doubt the gallantry or courage of Adelbert Ames. Badly wounded at the first battle of Bull Run, for which he later received the Congressional Medal of Honor, he fought in the Peninsula campaign, at Fredericksburg, at Chancellorsville, at Gettysburg, and at Petersburg. By the end of the war he was a brigadier general and not yet thirty years old.

Ames's meteoric rise in the army was but a prelude to a stormy future. Remaining in service after the war, he became Mississippi's provisional governor in 1868, and was elected to the United States Senate in 1870 and to the governorship in 1873. Besides being a Yankee veteran and a carpetbagger, Ames labored under an additional handicap in Mississippi. After the war he had married Blanche Butler, the daughter of Benjamin F. Butler. The governor's enemies seldom hesitated to drag into political discussions his "infamous" father-in-law, who had a penchant for stealing silver and insulting southern womanhood.

Ames was a man of sterling character, as even his bitterest foes admitted. A native of Rockland, Maine, he brought to Mississippi a New England zeal to aid the loyal men of both races and to build a strong Republican party. He took great, though to some extent condescending, pleasure in the devotion of Negroes to the party of Lincoln and had few doubts about his own rectitude or ability to lead the black race into freedom's promised land. Ames firmly believed that men such as himself would save the benighted South: "The carpetbagger represents northern civilization, northern liberty and has a hold on the hearts of the colored people that nothing can destroy. He is the positive element of the party and if the south is to be redeemed from the way of slavery it must be done by him."[1]

The Mississippi scalawags, led by Governor James Lusk Alcorn, did not share this vision of the future. Bitter quarrels between the carpet-bag and native Republican elements erupted over patronage, how to suppress Ku Klux Klan violence, and the position of blacks in the party. Alcorn and his followers hoped to make the state Republican party into a broad-gauged conservative coalition, but Ames favored working closely with black leaders to move the state in a more radical direction.[2] Because of his popularity among black voters and the refusal of many Democrats to cast their ballots, Ames handily defeated Alcorn in the 1873 gubernatorial election.

In his inaugural address the new governor praised blacks for their peaceful adjustment to freedom and their continuing kindness toward whites. Most blacks were Republicans, he asserted, because they wished to avoid destruction at the hands of the Confederate Democracy, but both races had a mutual stake in the state's prosperity. Sensitive to conservative charges of corruption and extravagance, Ames called for reduced expenditures, a lower state debt, and measures to attract manufacturing. Yet he entered some harsh strictures against plantation agriculture and argued that the men who tilled the land should own the land, which made him sound like an agrarian radical.[3]

Conservatives agreed to give the new governor a chance to fulfill the promises of his inaugural address, but clearly their patience was wearing thin. White Mississippians had responded to the passage of the Reconstruction acts with surprising moderation, but their willingness to cooperate with or even tolerate the Republicans largely depended on the ability of the state's newly elected officials to improve the economy and end political and social disorder.[4] During the factional wrangling of Alcorn's administration, many scalawags left the Republican party. By 1874 the party consisted mostly of carpetbaggers and blacks; the color line in state and local politics was a fact of life.

As William Harris has cogently observed, the beginning of the Ames administration unhappily coincided with a severe economic crisis in the state. In the aftermath of the panic of 1873, planters, farmers, and poor men of both races could barely scratch out a living. Newspapers noted an increasing amount of petty theft. Reports spread of black men raping white women, and several lynchings took place.[5] Conservatives found it easy to credit their distress to high taxes, excessive public spending, and corruption in the state and local governments.[6]

In Vicksburg economic hardship, rampant official corruption, and the racial polarization of politics plagued a city long known as a rough-and-tumble river town with a well-deserved reputation for street brawling. Vicksburg and surrounding Warren County had a population with more than twice as many blacks as whites, and blacks ran both county and city governments. Like southern whites elsewhere,

Vicksburgers bemoaned the effects on blacks of emancipation and enfranchisement.[7]

Black sheriff Peter Crosby asked in April 1874 that troops be sent to keep the peace in the city, but the military commander in Jackson turned down his request. By July black and white military companies were drilling in the streets in anticipation of the approaching municipal election. Crosby and the mayor issued a proclamation calling on all armed men to disperse and for citizens to aid the civil authorities in maintaining order. In the absence of Governor Ames, the black lieutenant governor, A. K. Davis, informed President Grant that the white and black militias in Vicksburg were in rebellion and had refused to return state arms to the adjutant general. Other city officials wired Grant that the city was peaceful, convincing the president not to send troops. When Ames returned to Jackson, he, too, telegraphed Grant that an infantry and cavalry organization had brought artillery pieces into the city. Grant again declined to provide military assistance.[8]

Conservatives claimed Crosby had closed registration early to prevent more whites from being added to the voting rolls. Using the excuse that blacks would use force to carry the election, armed whites patrolled the city and countryside. Military companies filled the streets on election day, leading to Republican charges of intimidation. As the election officials were tabulating the result in one ward, the lights in the room suddenly went out, and someone threw the ballots and tally sheet out the window. Whether enough irregularities occurred to affect the outcome is unclear, but the conservative People's party won the election.[9]

Ames blamed this Republican disaster on Grant's refusal to provide troops to protect black voters. Rashly accusing the president of hoping to receive support from southern Democrats for a third term, Ames more reasonably concluded that a northern retreat from Reconstruction had begun.[10] His assessment of the drift of northern sentiment was correct, but Grant could hardly have justified federal intervention in a local election when the state government had taken no action to maintain order. Instead of relying on their own resources, Davis and Ames had called for federal assistance at the first sign of trouble. The parallels to Kellogg's situation in Louisiana are obvious, and conservatives certainly recognized the increasing powerlessness of the state government as well as the reaction against radicalism taking place in the North. White leaders became ever bolder in their statements and actions, vowing that their patience had worn thin and that forcible resistance to the public plunderers could break out at any time. Ames advised Republicans to prevent racial strife and avoid violent collisions, but one frightened black man in Meridian thought the Negroes "had better have Alcorn in power than to be killed up like hogs and cows the way the cuclucks [Ku Klux] is killing our men now."[11]

Heightened white militancy produced serious complications in the river counties of the black belt because there was always the possibility that blacks would resist white aggression. Nervous whites in Tunica County in the northwestern corner of the state believed the long-expected war of the races was about to erupt. When a white man who had killed a black girl at the county seat of Austin was released from jail by a white mob, angry, heavily armed blacks marched toward the town. The whites immediately threw up barricades to hold them off and wounded two of them. Fearing for the safety of their families in the countryside, whites left Austin, allowing the blacks to enter the town and ransack several stores. Armed whites from Memphis, Tennessee, killed a black picket and took possession of the town. The blacks had scattered by that time, and no further sign of "insurrection" could be found. After quiet was restored, conservatives sarcastically chided Ames for not calling for troops as he had done during the Vicksburg disorders.[12]

The summer of 1874 marked the beginning of the counterrevolution in Mississippi. At this early stage, conservatives were by no means united on strategy, nor did they have an organization comparable to the Louisiana White League to spearhead the drive against the Ames regime. As in most southern states, conservative forces began by attacking Republican power at the local level. Their success in the Vicksburg municipal elections exposed the vulnerability of local Republicans, but the radicals still ran Warren County. White hostility to black officials was intense, and in August and September a Taxpayers' League uncovered substantial evidence of corruption involving several black politicians. A racially mixed grand jury in November indicted three judicial officers for larceny, embezzlement, and forgery, but soon afterward a large body of important records relating to these cases mysteriously disappeared from the sheriff's office. Whites naturally suspected Sheriff Crosby had either hidden or destroyed these documents to protect himself and his political friends. By this time, however, the sheriff had other worries. After a lengthy examination of the security of Crosby's bond and despite its insufficiency, the county board of supervisors declined to require a new one. For white Democrats and some Republicans, this action was the crowning outrage (or a convenient pretext to justify action outside legal channels).[13]

On December 2 the Taxpayers' League resolved that several county officials must resign and sent ten men to the courthouse to deliver this ultimatum. Only Crosby was there, and he responded evasively to their demand. Several hours later, five to six hundred whites, many of them drunk and armed, milled around the courthouse and crowded into the sheriff's office. Crosby then signed a resignation but told those persons present that he had done so only under duress. The sheriff left Vicksburg the next day and rode to Jackson to consult with Governor Ames and other Republicans about what course to pursue.[14]

Ames advised Crosby to summon a *posse commitatus* to disperse the mob but offered little tangible assistance.[15] The governor issued a proclamation calling for all riotous persons to return to their homes and sent a militia captain, the state's adjutant general, and one of his own aides to Vicksburg to investigate the situation and help Crosby. Local citizens informed the governor's representatives that the people would no longer tolerate the peculation of the "ring" and insisted on the ouster of men they termed public thieves. Street loungers furtively discussed hanging Crosby. The sheriff meanwhile published a card in the local Republican newspaper detailing his coerced resignation and summoning the people in the country (that is, the blacks) to his defense.[16]

Negro preachers read Crosby's plea for assistance in church services on December 6, and some blacks gathered to help the sheriff. The governor's representatives advised Crosby not to bring his supporters to Vicksburg, but he never rescinded the earlier call. Anxious whites watched every move of the city's Negro militia company and prepared to repel the invaders with the assistance of armed whites from the countryside, including 160 Louisianians. Although there were only seventeen men on the city's police force, two white militia companies, commanded by Colonel H. H. Miller and Captain Warren Cowan, were available for duty. While many other citizens waited on the morning of December 7 for the advancing blacks to reach the city, conservative leaders wisely put Crosby in jail for his own protection. White patrols ordered blacks on the street to return to their homes or be shot. Reports came in around nine o'clock in the morning that three black columns were slowly approaching Vicksburg from the east.[17]

Andrew Owen led the main force of between 120 and 500 blacks (some armed) moving along the Grove Street Road. Colonel Miller and his men intercepted them on the outskirts of town and, after a brief discussion, escorted Owen into the city for a parley with Crosby. After the sheriff pleaded with Owen to disband his company, he sullenly returned to his men, feeling betrayed by Crosby. As the Negroes began to disperse, whites opened fire, mounted men pursued the fleeing blacks, and the militia wildly shot at any black in sight. Armed whites also attacked a group of blacks who were on the Jackson Road near the John C. Pemberton monument but abandoned this position when white militia approached. The third column of blacks moving toward the city on the Cherry Street Road fired at a policeman and other white bystanders but retreated when they ran into a band of armed whites. The governor's aide, O. S. Lee, reported ten to twelve blacks and one white man dead and probably twice that number wounded. That night armed men ransacked black homes, ostensibly searching for weapons but in fact stealing money and murdering black men in their own yards. No one knows how many died in this unprovoked slaughter.[18]

Responding to the persistent rumors of a possible lynching, Crosby resigned his office again on December 8, and the board of supervisors had little choice but to acquiesce. He remained in jail until December 16, when he boarded a train for Jackson. Despite the obvious occupational liabilities, several eager applicants asked Governor Ames to appoint them sheriff of Vicksburg. The governor declared that a rebellion was in progress in Warren County and asked for federal troops to put down the insurgents. So grave had the situation become that the War Department ordered the soldiers in Jackson to protect the governor and the legislature from attack, and the president issued a proclamation on December 21 commanding all disorderly persons to disperse. White conservatives held an informal election of questionable legality and chose one A. J. Flannigan as sheriff. On December 29 the board of supervisors rescinded all previous actions on Crosby's resignation because they had been made under threat of force. Although federal troops arrived in January to reinstate Crosby, his troubles were far from over. A disgruntled deputy whom the sheriff had fired shot him in the head. He resigned in October because "peculiar circumstances" made it impossible for him to perform the duties of his office.[19]

When the House of Representatives investigated the Vicksburg troubles, Congressman Lucius Quintus Cincinnatus Lamar, the state's most articulate conservative, directed efforts to provide the committee with a "proper" understanding of the outbreak. Lamar suggested that witnesses present detailed statements on corruption in the county government, on the necessity for Crosby's resignation, and on the complicity of Governor Ames in the entire affair. To coincide with these machinations, several newspapers published lengthy apologias for the Vicksburg rioters. Detailing a long train of abuses by dishonest officials in Warren County, editors attempted to prove that the citizens there had acted purely in self-defense against intolerable evils. Privately, some young firebrands regretted that the war against the blacks had not gone further and waited to fight them again in the near future. Conservative politicians charged the governor with intentionally provoking bloodshed for the greater glory of the Republican party, and one Vicksburger bitingly suggested a new inscription for the Pemberton monument: "Here surrendered the Confederate chieftain in 1863, and here fell 100 Dupes to the unhallowed ambition of Adelbert Ames in 1874."[20]

The temporary restoration of a Republican sheriff in Warren County resembled on a smaller scale Grant's support for Kellogg after the abortive revolt of Louisiana Democrats in September 1874. Again federal soldiers had rescued a tottering Republican regime, but Mississippi's Republicans must have recalled Talleyrand's famous aphorism about sitting on bayonets. Like Kellogg in New Orleans, Ames was isolated in Jackson, unable to respond to the desperate pleas for assistance from Republicans in the countryside and increasingly nervous about the prospects of a conservative coup d'etat. Whether the events in Vicksburg foreshadowed trouble in the 1875 election campaign was uncertain because Mississippi conservatives remained divided on strategy, despite their feeling of urgency for ending Republican rule.

The failure of the Republican legislature to enact Ames's reform program dealt a severe blow to white moderates, who had urged giving the governor a chance to fulfill his promises. As early as 1873 conservatives in Washington County, located along the Mississippi River where blacks outnumbered whites nearly six to one, had formed a taxpayers' league to protect their property from what they considered the ravages of Republican cormorants. By 1874 many citizens favored refusing to pay the "confiscatory" state and local taxes and clamored for a state taxpayers' convention. On January 4, 1875, such a body met in Jackson and drafted a strong appeal to the legislature. Claiming that the people grew more impoverished daily while corrupt officials luxuriated in wasteful splendor, these conservatives called for drastic retrenchment in state government by slashing public printing expenses, legislative budgets, official salaries, and school funds. Arguing that it was unfair for the people who bore most of the burden to be taxed by a legislature primarily representing nontaxpayers, they warned that the failure to enact reforms would greatly increase the strength of the tax resistance movement.[21]

When the legislature adjourned without taking action on the grievances listed in the taxpayers' petition, furious conservatives could barely find words to express their outrage. They accused Ames of reneging on his campaign promises, using public patronage to build a political machine, and failing to veto excessive appropriations bills passed by the legislature. The state's black representatives and senators, white editors cried, were as bad as the carpetbaggers in opposing honest and economical government and were therefore personally responsible for drawing the color line in state politics.[22]

The Republicans' response to the growing militancy of their opponents only fueled white fears. Resolving to take defensive action to prevent a White League–style revolution in Mississippi, Governor Ames proposed reorganizing the state's militia system by establishing a state police similar to that in Texas. Conservatives accused Ames of attempting to goad whites to retaliatory violence, thereby providing a pretext for federal intervention. Armed black banditti, editorialists claimed, would scour the state, break into homes, and assault innocent citizens. Furthermore, such a force would require vast expenditures and would place almost unlimited power in the hands of the governor and his black followers. The legislature passed a bill authorizing the governor to organize two militia regiments and to purchase four or more Gatling guns and requiring any existing military companies to turn in their weapons to the quartermaster general. White leaders berated Ames for appointing carpetbaggers and Negroes as officers and vowed never to pay taxes for this purpose. Some intemperate men advocated mustering private companies to protect the people from these state murderers, but one wag suggested that there would be little danger because most of the money appropriated would be stolen by radical officials.[23]

The passage of the militia act added further impetus to the movement for a white man's party. By 1874 leaders in several counties were pushing for local organizations to unite all white men in a crusade against radicalism. These "white liners" denied any hostility to the blacks but maintained that their nearly total allegiance to the "radical" party had forced the adoption of measures of self-defense. For many Mississippians, the time for compromise and political equivocation had ended—the blacks had thrown down the gauntlet, and whites were prepared to take it up.[24]

Such militant rhetoric undermined moderate efforts to promote sectional reconciliation and greater national sympathy for the South's plight. When Lamar delivered his famous eulogy of Charles Sumner, he was more interested in vindicating the South than extolling the virtues of the Massachusetts radical. The Mississippian took advantage of the public revulsion against the carpetbaggers to plead for the withdrawal of federal troops, pledging in return that Democratic state governments would fully protect the rights of blacks. Even Lamar's friends wondered whether he had made too many concessions, and certain extremists found him lax in defending southern rights in Congress. By 1875, Lamar himself was expressing similar doubts: "I think the future of Mississippi is very dark. Ames has it dead. There can be no escape from his rule. His negro regiments are nothing. He will get them killed up, and then Grant will take possession for him. May God help us!"[25]

This despair and gloom did not necessarily generate more support for the white liners. Cautious men still feared such a movement could only stir racial strife and probably would provoke federal intervention. Former United States Senator Albert Gallatin Brown, who had been a fiery southern nationalist in the 1850s, warned that a white line policy would force blacks to form similar organizations. Brown stood by the old strategy of winning blacks' votes by convincing them that southern whites could be trusted to safeguard their newly won rights. *Clarion* editor Ethelbert Barksdale, who was the strongest voice against the white line, favored bringing together all enemies of corrupt government regardless of race or party affiliation. Like Brown, he held out the hope of converting blacks to the cause of reform. In a state where blacks constituted a clear majority of the voting population, more proscriptive policies could lead to electoral disaster as well as to bloodshed.[26]

By the spring and summer of 1875 the counselors of moderation, though still powerful, were in retreat, and many had come to blame the Negroes for dividing the races in politics. When *New York Herald* correspondent Charles Nordhoff asked a white liner how he would deal with reluctant moderates, he replied: "We'll make it too damned hot for them to stay out."[27]

New trouble in Vicksburg gave this debate greater urgency and set the tone for the election campaign. On July 4 two black officials, Secretary of State James Hill and Superintendent of Education T. W. Cardozo, arrived to speak at a Republican meeting. Warren Cowan, famed for his role in the 1874 riot, hit Cardozo on the head with a revolver. When Hill later addressed the blacks at the courthouse, a scuffle broke out, someone shot and killed a black deputy sheriff, and the blacks fled from the building. Many blacks stayed away from the municipal election the next day for fear of their lives or voted for the white man's ticket.[28]

After a fair amount of jostling over the makeup and name of a new antiradical party, a group of Democrats and former Whigs, old leaders and young hotspurs, assembled in Jackson in August 1875. Calling themselves the Democratic and Conservative party, the delegates listened to Lamar deliver a lengthy diatribe against the Ames regime. After reviewing his state's troubles, Lamar urged the delegates to accept Negro suffrage and the postwar constitutional amendments as fixed facts and warned that the adoption of a color line platform would be a "suicidal policy." The delegates resolved to recognize the civil and political equality of all men and called on the state's citizens to redeem Mississippi in the November legislative elections. Although moderate leaders rejoiced over the seeming defeat of the white line forces, platform pledges are always more easily made than kept. Despite his conciliatory address, Lamar knew of the intimidation and terror being perpetrated by his party, and however repulsive these bloody deeds may have seemed to him, he must have recognized their necessity. The excitement of the rallies and the organization of Democratic clubs often made the canvass resemble a military campaign. Moreover, the Democrats had nominated no blacks for public office, and many country editors proclaimed that the party had adopted the white line policy in fact if not in name. The *Columbus Democrat* summed up the situation well:

> And the white men of Mississippi will do it [win] in spite of eloquent diatribes and sham platforms which represent nothing but a clique's notions of expediency. In the contest on which they have entered they mean something more than the election of certain men to office or the elevation of Lamar or Alcorn to the Senate. They mean the preservation of their constitution, their laws, their institutions, their civilization from impending ruin. They mean that white men shall rule Mississippi.

Such a ringing declaration portended anything but peace.[29]

Bourbon editors adopted the motto, "Carry the election peaceably if we can, forcibly if we must." At stake was not only the office of state treasurer (the only statewide contest) but the more vital control of the legislature. Rabid partisans spoke of using hemp during the canvass and warned white Republicans that they would be the first to die should there be racial disturbances. The revitalized Democracy announced there could be no middle ground: each white man must decide "yea" or "nay." The white liners harassed blacks who did not join Democratic clubs and support the party of "reform," apparently unaware of the frightening paradox in this appeal. The campaign soon took on the atmosphere of both a camp-meeting revival and a revolutionary crusade, wild enthusiasm coupled with a determination to achieve victory at all costs. Between July and October, gun dealers had difficulty keeping up with the demand for weapons; as one Republican later recalled, both races went about heavily armed: "It [Mississippi] is the greatest place on the face of the earth for pistols. No man is comfortable down there unless he has got a pistol." For the whites, the election of 1875 became a deadly struggle for self-government, a crusade to control their own destinies, and a war that could not be lost.[30]

As Governor Ames and other Republicans soon realized, no matter what their professions, the "true sentiment" of their opponents was the color line. Predicting fraud and murder during the approaching campaign, Ames lamented that "no class of Democrats, it matter not what may be their intelligence or position, frown upon these crimes, but on the other hand the higher orders are the leaders in that which is the most wicked." Democratic hypocrisy thus became a major Republican electioneering theme. While Lamar was preaching "peace" with his honey-tongued words, the state's leading Republican newspaper complained, his fellow partisans were using the whip, the rope, and the gun with abandon. Some frightened radicals thought the governor himself would not be immune from assassination.[31]

The Republicans entered the campaign against a united and determined opposition with serious intraparty divisions. As in the other states, the Mississippi Republican party contributed to its own demise through internal bickering. Bitter factional disputes in several counties led to "bolting" and separate Republican tickets, virtually assuring victory for the Democrats. The federal officeholders in Mississippi, normally unswerving party regulars, lashed out at corruption in the Ames administration. United States District Attorney G. Wiley Wells publicly accused the governor of remarking shortly after the Vicksburg troubles that the deaths of twenty-five or thirty Negroes would greatly help his cause. Ames gloomily observed shortly before the beginning of the canvass: "It is saddening, yet with ludicrous phases, to see the strifes, envies, jealousies, and animosities existing in our own ranks."[32]

The Mississippi white liners, following the lead of the Louisiana White League, began their assault on the state government by attacking Republicans at the local level. This policy received its first test in Yazoo County, directly northwest of Jackson. Wisconsin carpetbagger Albert T. Morgan had engaged in planting, established a school for Negroes, married a black woman, and become a dominant figure in Republican politics. He won election as sheriff in 1873, but the Republican incumbent and leader of a rival faction refused to vacate the office. When his opponents briefly relaxed their guard, Morgan took possession. The other claimant summoned a thirty-man posse to recapture the jail. Morgan stepped outside to warn them against trying to expel him, but they forced their way inside, where, in an exchange of gunfire, one of Morgan's deputies killed the former sheriff. Democrats accused Morgan of murder and would have arrested him had it not been for the sudden appearance of belligerent blacks in Yazoo City. Several white military companies from Yazoo had participated in the 1874 Vicksburg riot and undoubtedly stood ready to take the field again. During the summer of 1875, conservative newspapers, apparently seeking a pretext to justify an attack on Morgan, printed documents purporting to show that sixteen hundred rifles had been sent to blacks in the county.[33]

Amid rumors of a Negro insurrection, Morgan called a political meeting for September 1 in Yazoo City and invited both parties to attend. The blacks and a few white Republicans filled the second floor of Wilson's Hall along with a handful of Democrats who, perhaps by prearrangement, took seats in the front row. Whites later swore that

Morgan had warned the blacks that a Democratic election victory would return them to slavery and said they might have to use their guns during the campaign. Morgan, however, claimed he had always advised the blacks to come unarmed to political gatherings and to avoid conflicts with the whites. By his own account, the sheriff excoriated the white liners and defended the Republican record in Yazoo County but counseled the Negroes to give the Democrats some representation on the board of supervisors. The whites had brought along a black Democrat who kept interrupting Morgan's speech, much to the dissatisfaction of the audience. On several occasions, Democrats drew their revolvers and threatened to shoot anyone who tried to eject their black friend from the meeting. When Morgan praised the performance of the board of supervisors, one of the whites said they were all "damned thieves." A black man took umbrage at this outburst, and shooting broke out. Later testimony conflicted about who fired first. When Morgan pleaded for peace, several Democrats leveled their revolvers at him. The sheriff fired twice at his foes and then nimbly climbed out a rear window. After a black deputy was killed in the melee, whites sounded an alarm, and armed men roamed through Yazoo City searching for Morgan.[34]

The sheriff holed up in his own house while his black friends deceived whites into thinking he had left the county. On September 7 some Negroes ambushed a white posse near the settlement of Satartia, southwest of Yazoo City. Fearing a general uprising, white companies stepped up their patrols. Morgan kept out of sight but sent black couriers to the capital with messages for the governor begging for assistance. He left for Jackson in disguise on September 13, successfully evading pickets on the roads. After white bands hanged several radical leaders, Republicans abandoned the canvass, and in the November election they polled only seven votes in the entire county.[35]

Close on the heels of the Yazoo disturbances, a riot occurred near the small Hinds County town of Clinton, just west of Jackson. Some two to three thousand black men, women, and children and perhaps one hundred whites gathered for a political barbecue and joint discussion between the two parties. Some Negroes became boisterous during the Democratic speech but listened with marked interest to the address of white Republican Hiram T. Fischer. After Fischer had talked for about ten minutes, a disturbance broke out in the audience. A few young white men with a bottle of whiskey walked down a nearby hill for a drink, but when a black policeman told them that no drinking was allowed at the meeting, a scuffle ensued. Black state Senator Charles Caldwell rushed to the scene of the disorder, but Fischer pleaded with his listeners to pay no attention. Whites later claimed the Negroes began beating drums and shouting: "Kill the whites!" Several shots were fired, and the crowd scattered in all directions. The small group of whites retreated, with the Negroes pursuing and firing at them. Three whites were killed in the fighting, including one man who was sheltering frightened black women and children in his home when he was shot. Blacks reportedly mutilated the corpses and stole a diamond ring from one of the dead men. Four blacks died during the rioting, and several members of both races were wounded.[36]

As news of the fighting spread, white companies from Vicksburg and surrounding counties came into Clinton on the train. These men whipped and shot blacks in the countryside and killed several leading Republicans. At least thirty blacks died during this indiscriminate slaughter. Refugees jammed the roads leading to Jackson before a small detachment of federal troops arrived to stop the massacre. Fearing the Clinton riot would give Ames the excuse he needed to call for federal intervention, state Democratic chairman James Z. George cautioned whites to restore peace quickly. Editors mocked the fears of the refugees in the capital, blaming the riot on the Republicans. A grand jury investigated the affair but brought in no indictments. Enraged whites later wreaked vengeance for their fallen comrades by murdering Charles Caldwell and two other black leaders.[37]

Both the Yazoo and Clinton outbreaks, taking place so near to Jackson, demonstrated the weakness of the state government and Ames's inability to safeguard his supporters during the campaign. The governor, however, saw these disturbances as an opportunity to press for federal intervention. After issuing a proclamation on September 7 calling for all private military companies to disband, he sent Grant an official request for military assistance. Although General C. C. Augur in New Orleans wired his superiors in Washington that he had enough men to keep the peace, there were only 13 officers and 235 enlisted men in Mississippi. This force was probably not sufficient to garrison the troubled areas near Jackson, much less other parts of the state controlled by the white liners.[38]

Ames recognized the reluctance of the northern public to support further military interference in southern elections but was confident Grant would resist the appeals to political expediency. Under pressure from northern Republican leaders, including members of his own cabinet, Grant decided to turn down Ames's request for troops. His oft-quoted rationale for doing so was a fitting epitaph for radical southern policies: "The whole public are tired out with these annual autumnal outbreaks in the South, and the great majority are ready to condemn any interference on the part of the Government." Attorney General Edwards Pierrepont lectured the governor on the necessity for exhausting his own resources rather than calling for troops at the first sign of trouble. Ames glumly concluded that northern Republicans did not understand the persistent spirit of rebellion in the southern states.[39]

The governor's understandable bitterness against the Grant administration did not prevent him from trying to salvage the situation. County Republican leaders had advised him to put the state militia into the field against the white liners and crush out Democratic terrorism for good. The Republican party, these men argued, must show its foes it could not be cowed and that force would be met with force.[40] The mere mention of state militia, which both parties agreed would consist mainly of black units, caused Democratic editors to denounce Ames for attempting to carry the election by force and vow that the people would resist the militia. Such truculent statements reflected the whites' commanding position of power in the countryside, where they could easily beat back any militia forays. On September 2 about fifty white men boarded a steamer docked at Vicksburg, seizing five boxes of state arms. Elsewhere whites captured militia weapons, finally forcing Ames to remove matériel from Jackson to a nearby army camp for safekeeping.[41]

The attempt to arm and deploy the militia was ill-fated from the outset. The legislature appropriated only $60,000 for the purpose, and a Republican supreme court justice enjoined the governor from spending most of this money. White Republicans were less than wholehearted in their support for military measures, fearing black companies would spark racial warfare. While waiting for the militia to escort him back to Yazoo City, Sheriff Morgan talked with several black legislators in Jackson, who shared similar qualms and naively believed their old masters would not use violence against them. On the other hand, ardent radicals accused Ames of laxity in making military preparations, and the governor confessed to having little faith in either the efficiency or courage of Negro regiments. Ames finally sent a company of black militiamen on a short march to Edwards' Station in western Hinds County, an insignificant operation that marked the extent of militia activity during the campaign. The Democrats howled loudly and prepared to stop the blacks at the Yazoo County line, but the company quietly returned to the capital.[42] Without ever putting a firm policy to the test, Ames abandoned the field to the white liners. Like Republican governors in some other states, the Maine carpetbagger thought the use of black militia would lead to race war and refused to turn his loyal black supporters into blood sacrifices.

The Democrats, whose campaign of persuasion, intimidation, and terror had already been largely successful, now proposed a "compromise" with Ames. The governor's advisers warned there would be bloodshed in Jackson if he did not agree to a settlement, and Ames's own doubts about the effectiveness of the militia and the chances for federal assistance pushed him toward an accommodation with the opposition. After some preliminary discussions, and through the good offices of Justice Department detective George K. Chase, the governor met with General George and several other Democrats on October 15. The two parties signed a document in which Ames agreed to disarm the militia in return for a Democratic promise to keep the peace for the remainder of the canvass.[43]

Putting the best face possible on a humiliating agreement with rebellious citizens, Ames claimed he had conceded nothing and hoped the other side would abide by the terms of the settlement. Democratic leaders may have genuinely desired peace, and they urged their followers to remain quiet, but military companies continued to patrol the counties, and there was no abatement in voter intimidation. Ames received firsthand evidence of the value of conservative pledges when a howling mob in Jackson took potshots at the executive mansion for three consecutive nights and shouted for the "coward" to come out of his hiding place. Attorney General Pierrepont notified the governor less than a week before the election that a small number of soldiers would keep order at the polls if necessary, but such meager assistance meant little to beleaguered Republicans and came far too late to deter white liners from carrying the election.[44]

The Democrats conducted a brilliant campaign to mobilize their supporters and demoralize their enemies by holding mass meetings during the day and large torchlight parades at night. With bands playing, flags flying, and wagons carrying colorful transparencies satirizing prominent Republicans and suggesting their destination in the afterlife, the conservative organizations not only aroused the enthusiasm of their own followers but gave the blacks a powerful visual demonstration of white power and determination. Some leaders candidly admitted that the large bonfires, the fiery oratory, the frequent rebel yells, and the discharge of firearms were designed to make Negroes stand in fear. Some of the wagons in the parades carried empty coffins with the names of local carpetbaggers and scalawags written on them.[45] Such methods may not have been subtle, but no one could doubt either their meaning or effectiveness.

Several Democratic clubs purchased cannons, which they hauled to Republican meetings and fired off at appropriate interludes. One army captain allowed whites in Rankin County to borrow a federal cannon for a political rally, an act for which he was later court-martialed. With a mock tone of innocence, whites described how they fired off blank rounds to arouse the dythrambic passions of their followers and even allowed interested blacks to set off the charges. If cannons were unavailable, resourceful men placed one anvil on top of another with gunpowder in the crevice between them. When ignited, this crude device made a tremendous noise, but such a makeshift procedure was not without its hazards. A rural district during the 1876 campaign recorded a "premature" firing of anvils in which one man received severe powder burns and another had a hole torn in his pants.[46] William Harris has argued that conservative leaders such as James Z. George recognized the ineffectiveness of terror tactics and in many counties used more traditional campaign rallies to appeal to voters of both races.[47] Given the quasi-military character of these meetings, however, many Republicans, with the sound of cannon ringing in their ears, must have had difficulty distinguishing between such "peaceful" methods and the more violent means employed by the white liners.

Although there were scattered reports of economic coercion against Negro voters and some mention of it in conservative newspapers, black-belt planters were naturally reluctant to risk alienating their labor force. During the latter stages of the canvass, intimidation became increasingly selective. White marauders, borrowing the tactics of the Louisiana White Leaguers, forced Republican officials to resign. In counties where radical candidates stood a good chance of winning, conservatives bluntly informed them that they would never be allowed to take office.[48]

Across the state, Democrats heckled Republican speakers, demanded joint discussions, and appeared at every opposition meeting to expose radical falsehoods. Mounted men rode into the audience, fired cannon, cut the heads off the drums used by blacks, jeered at the speakers, and shoved pistols against their ribs or heads. Some Democrats denied Negroes had a right to hold Republican meetings, and those that did take place sometimes ended in a hail of gunfire.[49] Republicans in several counties had no choice but to support "compromise tickets" on which Democrats would replace certain Republican candidates in exchange for promises of peace before and during the election.[50]

White liners in the river counties and other black-belt areas fired into the homes of black and white radicals at night. Frightened Republicans charged that Democratic clubs were receiving large weapons shipments and disarming blacks. Prominent leaders received threats against their lives and hid in the woods and swamps. By Reconstruction standards, there apparently were few casualties, but assassination attempts against local party figures were not uncommon.[51] Along the eastern border of Mississippi from Aberdeen to Meridian, Alabama night riders joined in raids to force Republicans to abandon the canvass and leave their homes.[52] Disingenuous Democrats blamed any reported disturbances on radical agitators who encouraged blacks to come armed to political meetings. The real intimidation, according to conservatives, was perpetrated by Republicans against black Democrats.[53]

After the Yazoo and Clinton riots, no large outbreaks of violence occurred. In the southwestern county of Pike, armed "regulators," who had driven Republican officeholders out of West Feliciana Parish, Louisiana, moved into Mississippi to ambush and assassinate Republicans. At the small settlement of Rose Hill near the state line, an estimated five hundred armed whites broke up a Republican meeting and killed two blacks. The terrorism evidently continued until election day.[54]

At the northern end of the state in Coahoma County along the Mississippi River, Sheriff John Brown, a black carpetbagger, ran afoul of the Alcorn family and other scalawags. In October, James Lusk Alcorn delivered a blistering speech accusing Brown of pocketing public money. Several days later, the sheriff called a meeting at the county seat of Friar's Point to answer Alcorn's charges. Whites organized a militia company to protect themselves against country Negroes who were marching toward town. When the two forces clashed on the outskirts, one white and two blacks were killed. Brown and other radicals fled to Helena, Arkansas, hastily wiring Governor Ames about the reign of terror in Coahoma. These disturbances deterred many voters of both parties from casting their ballots, and the Democrats carried the county.[55]

Election day was relatively quiet, but the effects of the "Mississippi plan" were everywhere. Democrats in Aberdeen placed an old cannon on a hill ominously aimed toward the polls. White infantry, artillery, and cavalry companies allowed only those blacks with Democratic tickets to vote, forcing others to run for their lives. At Port Gibson in the southern part of the black belt, mounted men drove Negro voters out of town. Democrats in Amite County seized two ballot boxes and dumped their contents on the ground. That night drunken Louisianians chased terrified Republicans through the woods.[56]

Military companies in several counties threatened to hang anyone who tried to distribute Republican ballots, and many party workers had difficulty delivering tickets to all their assigned precincts. Yazoo County Democrats warmly greeted a man carrying Republican ballots and plied him with whiskey, thus preventing him from performing his original task.[57] When armed whites stampeded Republicans who tried to vote, many blacks decided it was not worth sacrificing their lives to cast their ballots. With Democrats giving the "rebel yell" and crowding the polls, the election of 1875 became a mockery of the democratic process. Angry mobs jostled election supervisors and forced them to sign false returns. If the Republicans seemed to be winning at a particular poll, Democrats stole the ballot box.[58]

The results reflected the effectiveness of these tactics. The Democrats turned the 1873 Republican majority of twenty-three thousand into a margin of thirty thousand for themselves, gained lopsided control of both houses in the legislature, elected a state treasurer, and carried four of six congressional districts. When Republicans examined the county returns, they could see all too clearly the manner of their downfall. Large majorities had vanished through intimidation, fraud, and blatant terrorism. Yet as Harris has shown in his careful analysis, the Democrats not only reduced the Republican vote but spectacularly increased their own totals by fully mobilizing the white electorate.[59]

Some conservatives immediately called for their party to carry out its pledges to the Negroes,[60] but Republicans of both races soon faced severe reprisals in the aftermath of the Democratic tidal wave. Disheartened and terrified Republican officeholders gave up the fight and left the state. In Issaquena County, one of the few carried by the Republicans, night riders in December 1875 drove newly elected officials away at gunpoint. A federal grand jury at Oxford received voluminous testimony of violence and intimidation before and during the election, but after receiving threats against their own lives, the jurors brought in no indictments.[61]

With letters from demoralized, bitter, and frightened Republicans pouring into his office daily, Ames used his annual message to the legislature to deliver a ringing condemnation of Democratic violence and to assert that the right to vote had become a nullity in Mississippi. Justice Department officers in the state readily corroborated the governor's statements. Conservatives issued the expected denials and kept up a steady editorial barrage against Ames.[62] Indeed, long before the election, Democratic leaders recognized that control of the legislature would mean the opportunity to impeach and remove the governor from office. After the house in March 1876 voted articles of impeachment against him, Ames resigned and left Mississippi, never to return.[63]

He lived quietly in Massachusetts and later moved to Florida, where he died in 1933. With such a long time to mull over his experiences, Ames's once buoyant optimism gave way to sour regrets. He told historian James W. Garner that he had arrived in Mississippi with a sense of "Mission with a large M," convinced he could guide the blacks toward freedom's golden shore while pacifying a still rebellious southland. These efforts, he sadly admitted, had been foredoomed because "at all times and places the inferior race must succumb to the superior race even though the latter be backed by such a power as the United

States."[64] This carpetbagger's capitulation to racism and his confession of failure not only reflect the disillusionment of an old man but also a realization of the true dimensions of his task. He had done his best, and he shared the onus of defeat with many lesser men. The swirling tide of reaction had swept away his dreams just as it had carried his enemies into power.

The Mississippi Democrats had conducted a classical counterrevolutionary crusade, their tactics paralleling those of earlier campaigns in Alabama and Louisiana. Beginning with newspaper invective and taxpayer protests, conservatives then turned to the white line organizations, which soon became the military arm of the Democratic party. While publicly professing peaceful intentions, Democrats selectively used armed intimidation to destroy the Republican party in the counties by keeping black voters away from the polls or forcing them to vote Democratic. Emboldened by the knowledge that the national Republican leadership no longer had much stomach for military intervention in the South,[65] angry whites engaged in terrorist activities with seeming impunity. The "redemption" of Mississippi pointed up the domino effect of the counterrevolution. By 1876, South Carolina, Louisiana, and Florida were the only Republican dominoes left standing, and each of these had begun to totter noticeably.

10. 1876: The Triumph of Reaction

hen 1876, the centennial year of American independence, opened, the question of southern Reconstruction had receded in importance in national politics but lingered like a drunkard's hangover after a week-long binge. Public attention turned to celebrating the nation's one hundredth birthday and electing a new president. Northern editors and stump speakers would still wave the now tattered bloody shirt during the fall election campaign, but their hearts were no longer in it. Governor Kellogg in Louisiana held onto his office but exerted little authority outside New Orleans. Endemic factionalism among Florida Republicans made a Democratic triumph in that state only a matter of time. In South Carolina there was a reasonably strong Republican regime, but conservative opposition was growing bolder, stronger, and more violent.

The Republicans in the Palmetto State were ripe for a fall. Corruption had become a byword in state politics; carpetbaggers and scalawags, whites and blacks, radicals and conservatives, Republicans and Democrats had shared in the rewards of public plunder. All factions of the Republican party conceded the need for changes in both state and local governments and sought to outdo each other in standing foursquare for reform.[1] When the "regular" Republicans nominated Massachusetts carpetbagger Daniel H. Chamberlain for governor in 1874, the prospects for routing the corruptionists seemed remote. Chamberlain had been attorney general during Governor Robert Scott's notorious administration, and most observers saw his election as a continuation of business as usual. Yet in his inaugural address the new governor called for economy and honesty in the administration of the state government, a fairer assessment of taxable property, and an end to the scandalously inflated public printing contracts. Chamberlain's evenhanded patronage policy, which included the appointment of white conservatives to

many offices, deeply offended members of his own party. Robert Brown
Elliott, black former congressman and then Speaker of the House of
Representatives, spearheaded the opposition to Chamberlain. Elliott
probably resented the governor's wrapping himself in the mantle of
reform and certainly feared, with good reason, that Chamberlain
might form an alliance with white conservatives, leaving blacks isolated and powerless. Chamberlain never established a working relationship with black leaders, who found him aloof and patronizing, and
his frequent vetoes of bills passed by the legislature antagonized party
stalwarts. This deadlock between the Republican majority in the legislature and the governor not only stymied Chamberlain's program but
further divided the party at both the state and local levels, at last
giving conservative whites a realistic hope of ending Republican
domination.[2]

As in other states, the conservative opposition to the Republican
regime was united on goals but deeply divided on means. Some moderates, led by the influential editor of the *Charleston News and Courier,*
Francis W. Dawson, were skeptical about reviving the state Democratic party, which had been disbanded since 1868, and favored an
alliance of convenience with Chamberlain. White county leaders, however, had little faith in the governor's reform promises and could
hardly conceive cooperating with a carpetbagger. This straight-out
element was particularly strong in Edgefield County in the midlands
region of the state. There former Confederate General Martin Witherspoon Gary led a group of violent fanatics who would brook no concessions to radicalism. So adamant was Gary in his opposition to any
milk-and-water ticket that he came close to fighting a duel with
Dawson over the issue.[3]

These questions of campaign strategy could not by themselves have
generated such furious passions; at the bottom of the disputes lay the
volcanic race question. Most white South Carolinians denounced the
Republican state government as rule by ignorant Negroes, but they
had to deal with the reality of a black electoral majority. Paternalists,
such as Dawson, favored bringing the two races together in a common
fight against radicalism. Making the hope father to the thought, optimistic newspaper editors reported that more and more Negroes were
waking up to their true interests and seeing Republican leaders as the
knaves they were. All these statements about racial political harmony
held one important caveat: earlier attempts at biracial coalitions had
all failed. White patience, Dawson warned, was growing thin, and
South Carolina would be redeemed "whatever the means or cost."[4] The
most rabid advocate of a color line policy could not have said it better.

In the hothouse political atmosphere of the Chamberlain years, sev-

eral racial disturbances occurred that further undermined the influence of white moderates. Whether these outbreaks were instigated by
extremists to discredit Dawson and other accommodationists is unclear. Each incident grew out of local problems, but straight-out Democrats seized on these disorders to demonstrate the futility of compromise with Republicanism.

When a Negro militia company began drilling in Ridge Spring, near
Augusta, Georgia, in 1874, panicky whites expected a bloody uprising.
Armed and mounted men scoured the countryside searching for insurrectionary Negroes. No fighting took place, but the Republican sheriff
fled for his life as whites raised the usual clamor about an impending
race war.[5] Such exaggerated reports may have served some unstated
political purpose, and they certainly fit well the conservative notion
that Republicans were desperate to supply fresh outrages for their
northern political allies.

Edgefield County, or "bloody Edgefield" as it was often called, had a
long and well-deserved reputation for violence.[6] The county has produced not only successful cotton planters but also a remarkable group
of exceptionally volatile politicians from Preston Brooks to Strom
Thurmond. A hotbed of secession sentiment before the war, during
Reconstruction Edgefield became a center of Ku Klux Klan activity
and a bastion of straight-out Democracy.

Ned Tennant, a black militia captain, exemplified the characteristics Edgefield whites feared most in a Negro leader—ability and assertiveness. After Tennant paraded his men on July 4, 1874, angry young
white men emptied their pistols into his house. A group of armed
Negroes were eager to retaliate, but cooler heads among both races
kept the peace. When a similar disturbance took place in September,
white military companies, commanded by former Confederate General
Matthew Calbraith Butler and former Confederate Colonel Andrew P.
Butler, surrounded about eighty blacks near a plantation. The timely
arrival of United States troops prevented a serious clash, and after a
parley, both sides agreed to disband. Shortly before the 1874 state
election, in a thinly veiled attempt to intimidate Negro voters, Gary
advised planters to reduce their labor force by one-third, and thereafter many blacks could not find employment. A citizens' meeting in
December resolved to lynch any person caught setting fire to a house,
gin house, or cotton gin and blamed Republican officials for not preventing acts of arson. The following month Matthew Butler's residence
burned to the ground, and suspicion immediately fell on Tennant's
militiamen. During a brief exchange of gunfire with a white posse sent
out to arrest the suspects, two blacks died. Finally, Governor Chamberlain ordered all state arms returned to Columbia and all private

companies in Edgefield to disband. But when one of the governor's aides tried to take possession of these weapons, he found local whites had already seized some of them. Unsubstantiated reports of Negroes arming and drilling circulated for the remainder of the year.[7]

Racial violence in Edgefield and surrounding counties continued during the 1876 election year. Unknown parties assassinated former militia officer Joe Crews, long suspected of having an incendiary influence among Negroes. Alarmed whites reported an epidemic of burned gin houses, robberies of local stores, and several murders of "respectable" citizens. When an old man and his wife were killed in May, the Edgefield sheriff arrested six black men, but a band of whites hauled the suspects from the jail and shot them all to death. Even those conservatives who opposed lynch law justified its use in this case because they claimed local authorities would never have brought the guilty parties to trial.[8] Much of this violence arose from long-festering economic, social, and racial grievances and in that way more closely resembles the disorders of early Reconstruction than post-1867 political disturbances. But almost all these incidents, no matter what their origins, would have political overtones in an election year.

Even before the 1876 campaign had gotten under way, a bloody riot occurred in Aiken County along the Georgia border. What began as a purely local affair quickly mushroomed into a massacre with national political repercussions. Hamburg was a small village on the Savannah River opposite Augusta. Once an important transport center for up-country cotton on its way to Charleston, after the war Hamburg became a somnolent community of only five hundred inhabitants, mostly Negroes. Whites deeply distrusted the village's black officials and in the spring of 1876 had suggested that several black politicians leave before the election. The racial disorders in nearby Edgefield made both races nervous, particularly after a black man named Doc Adams organized a militia company. Conservatives immediately charged that this body would intimidate Democrats and massacre innocent citizens. As Benjamin R. Tillman later recalled, the white military companies waited for an incident to give them an excuse to teach the Negroes a lesson written in blood.[9]

On July 4, Adams marched his company of about eighty blacks along a quiet Hamburg street. Two young whites, Henry Getzen and T. J. Butler, had driven their buggy into town, watched the drill for a short time, and then asked Adams to move his troops to one side so they could pass. Adams pointed to a wide path on either side of his columns and, according to the testimony of Getzen and Butler, cursed them and refused to move. The seriousness of what most white southerners considered a breach of racial etiquette became clear as the two whites angrily vowed to stay in their usual wagon rut and not be turned aside by any "damned niggers." When a rain suddenly came up, the blacks left the street, allowing Getzen and Butler to go on their way. After a complaint was made by young Butler's father, Robert J. Butler, a black local justice named Prince Rivers issued arrest warrants against Adams and the other militia officers on charges of blocking a public thoroughfare. When Adams swore at Rivers during a court appearance on July 6, he was declared in contempt of court and the proceedings were postponed for two days.[10]

The Butler family retained Matthew C. Butler of Edgefield (no relation) as its attorney. Butler and two to three hundred armed whites rode into Hamburg on July 8 for the trial. Butler demanded that the militia surrender its arms and probably threatened to burn the town (a reversal of the usual pattern in these racial conflicts). Apparently sensing that Adams would never give up the weapons, he nevertheless demanded that the militia captain personally apologize to his clients. Because armed men were milling about in the streets, Adams did not appear in the courtroom but cautiously sought a parley with Butler. They could not agree on a meeting place because both sides feared an ambush. Determined to disarm the militia at all hazards, Butler dropped all pretense of seeking legal satisfaction. With the white mob growing more belligerent, Adams and thirty-eight of his men took refuge in a brick building used as an armory. Shooting suddenly erupted. A black militiaman killed a young white man near the railroad bridge, and enraged whites hauled over a cannon from Augusta and fired four rounds into the black stronghold. Fearing the attackers might blow up the building, Adams ordered his men to escape out the back. The whites pursued the fleeing blacks, took some prisoners, and ransacked the homes of several Negroes and one white Republican. The mob murdered the black town marshal and killed at least one other Negro, but the bloodshed was not yet over.[11]

Having captured perhaps twenty-five blacks, Butler ordered his men to escort them to the Aiken jail. Tillman's company disapproved of such lenient treatment for Negro incendiaries and executed five of the prisoners, reportedly mutilating the bodies. Although Butler denied approving the merciless slaughter, he shared the ultimate responsibility for turning a minor traffic accident into a bloody riot.[12]

Dawson joined other conservative editors in roundly condemning the Hamburg massacre, particularly the killing of the black prisoners. Several newspapers sharply criticized Butler for attempting to disarm the blacks in the first place and especially for allowing his men to behave like savages. Even these editorialists, however, argued that such incidents arose inevitably from the evils of Republican rule.[13]

Black leaders responded to conservative evasiveness by holding a large indignation meeting in Charleston at which they detailed their long history of suffering at the hands of the "semi-barbarous whites" and accused Butler and his men of committing premeditated murder. Noting that there were eighty thousand black men in the state who could carry Winchester rifles and two hundred thousand black women who could use torches and knives, the speakers warned of a Democratic conspiracy to carry the approaching election by force. The meeting endorsed a ringing appeal to the "people of the United States" written by Robert Brown Elliott, which defended the right of black militiamen to carry arms and demanded protection from the state government.[14]

The blacks had reason to wonder if Hamburg was only the beginning of a terror campaign against Negroes and Republicans. The sheriff of Aiken County reported that armed bands were seizing black property and arms. White cavalry companies patrolled the countryside and sometimes rode through Hamburg.[15]

Governor Chamberlain sent President Grant a detailed account of the riot, interpreting it as part of a larger plot, already partially successful in Louisiana and victorious in Mississippi, to overthrow Republican state governments through intimidation and violence. Chamberlain asked for more troops and joined United States Marshal Robert M. Wallace in suggesting that soldiers be placed in the counties near Hamburg. Grant was shocked at the sickening details of the slaughter and, overcoming his reluctance to use military power in the southern states, ordered several companies of troops to Edgefield, Laurens, and Barnwell counties.[16] Angry conservatives uttered their usual maledictions against the "mailed fist" while portraying themselves as the most peaceful people in the world. Such protests rang hollowly because South Carolina Democrats were experienced politicians, who by this time recognized the uselessness of soldiers in propping up Republican regimes. When the troops arrived at Edgefield Courthouse, cheering whites lined the streets to greet them. Some of the men were embarrassed, but others grinned.[17]

In the aftermath of the Hamburg affair, desperate Republicans attempted to suppress what they saw as the beginnings of a terror campaign. A grand jury indicted sixty men, whom conservatives described as some of the state's "best citizens," but the prisoners openly boasted that they would never be brought to trial. United States Attorney David Corbin admitted that armed whites would probably intimidate witnesses and make the outcome problematical. Tillman's men donned their red shirts, the new badge of uncompromising resistance to radicalism, but quietly surrendered to state officials. State Attorney General William Stone ordered a continuance of the cases until after the election so passions could cool.[18] By that time, disputes over the election of 1876 forced Stone to drop the prosecution.

The Hamburg riot dealt a fatal blow to the cooperation movement for both Chamberlain and his conservative friends. With the Edgefield fireeaters leading the way, the upcountry was ablaze for uncompromising Democracy, while the lowcountry remained quietly moderate. The votes taken at the state Democratic convention, which met in Columbia from August 15–17, starkly revealed this sectional division. After a five-and-a-half-hour secret debate on the final day, the delegates agreed to select their own slate of candidates for state offices. General Butler and his allies pulled a coup before the convention by convincing Wade Hampton to accept the nomination for governor. The choice of the popular and moderate former Confederate general soothed the feelings of the losers and ended the debate over strategy.[19]

For the public record, the South Carolina Democracy committed itself to conducting a conciliatory and peaceful campaign. Its platform recognized the permanency of the postwar constitutional amendments and summoned all citizens regardless of color to join the cause of reform. Several planks lambasted the Republicans for corruption, exorbitant taxation, and inciting racial warfare, but the party eschewed the use of violence during the canvass. Hampton seemed the embodiment of reasonableness. Though a speaker of ordinary ability, he effectively addressed racially mixed audiences by denouncing political intimidation and emphasizing his long friendship for the Negro race. In particular, he pledged as governor to guarantee blacks impartial justice, to support free schools, and to protect Negroes in all their legitimate rights. Hampton advised the violent men of his own race not to vote for him and urged his supporters to maintain order during the campaign. The Republicans remained justifiably skeptical, and the party's leading newspaper cut to the heart of the issue:

> Meanwhile, General Hampton may be all that his friends claim him to be, but he is the representative of the hot heads and reckless hearts which dictated his nomination. The leading characteristics of the campaign thus far developed are those of the tiger policy in Edgefield. The Tillmans, the Butlers, the Garys, the [James N.] Lipscombs, are the ones to whom he would owe his election, and to them he must needs bow in shaping his policy. He submits to their dictation now, and the habit would have to be continued.

There is no evidence that Hampton ever tried to control the forces of violence; though no puppet of the wild men, he lacked both the will and the power to stop the bloodletting.[20]

Democrats exaggerated the number of voluntary black "conversions" and accused radical Negroes of persecuting their conservative brethren. Local Democratic clubs with great fanfare sought legal redress for their injured black friends.[21] Although the conservatives offered blacks little besides soothing words, they bemoaned their lack of success and raised continual alarms about armed Negroes. In August a box labeled "agricultural implements" arrived in Newberry, northeast of Edgefield. The chief of police opened it, found sixteen Remington rifles inside, and arrested the Negro to whom the box had been sent. Because of slipshod administration in the militia, many state arms had fallen into the hands of unauthorized persons, and Chamberlain tried to retrieve these weapons, but in Edgefield armed men broke into the jail and seized more than one hundred rifles. Frightened whites claimed that turbulent blacks were threatening the lives of peaceful citizens and following the advice of Republican speakers to engage in arson against the planters.[22] This widening paranoia gave white military companies an all too convenient excuse for their own excesses.

Democratic tales of intimidation were overblown but not without foundation; lowcountry Republicans effectively employed some of the same methods as their opponents. On September 6 Charleston Democrats held a political meeting, which was addressed by some Democratic Negroes. Unruly black Republicans gathered outside the hall, reviling the turncoats and brandishing heavy sticks. When the Democrats tried to escort their black allies home, the mob attacked them, killing one white man and inflicting head wounds on several others. For the next two days, rifle clubs guarded all Democratic meetings, but some blacks hurled brickbats at whites and assaulted lone pedestrians.[23]

Similar conditions prevailed in neighboring plantation areas. A steamer left Charleston on the morning of October 16 with about two hundred passengers aboard, mostly Democrats, for a joint political discussion at the small town of Cainhoy, about twenty miles to the northeast. Both parties came to the meeting armed, and fighting soon broke out. Whites and blacks grabbed their guns, but the numerically superior Negroes chased frightened Democrats back to their boat. One black man and at least six whites died in the riot. For once conservative editors were right: blacks had been the aggressors at Cainhoy. Troops arrived in time to prevent a white counterattack, but black violence continued through election day.[24]

Labor trouble in the rice fields added to lowcountry turmoil. In May 1876 black rice workers struck for higher pay. Planters complained that lower rice prices forced them to cut wages and that unscrupulous white storekeepers were stirring up discontent among the field hands. In the latter part of August, Negroes along the Combahee River demanded a 50 percent wage increase, refused to accept checks that could be redeemed only at planters' stores, and drove blacks who were still working from the fields. When a sheriff's posse arrested the ringleaders, a mob of three hundred Negroes overpowered them and released the prisoners. Congressman Robert Smalls and Lieutenant Governor R. H. Gleaves, both black, calmed the angry strikers and convinced them to allow ten of their number to be taken into custody. The charges against these men were eventually dropped, but many blacks still stayed away from the fields. Angry planters warned the governor that disastrous crop losses would result if these disruptions continued and asked for the arrest and punishment of the malcontents who abused and whipped Negroes working quietly at their tasks. Evidently, the planters finally agreed to a compromise to save part of their crop, but sporadic disturbances broke out through September.[25]

The incidence of black-initiated violence was higher in the South Carolina lowcountry than in any other part of the South. The area had been turbulent since the beginning of Reconstruction, when outraged blacks protested vigorously and sometimes violently against the federal government's return of confiscated land to white landowners. Negroes working for low wages in the disease-infested swamplands found their situation in life little improved from the days of slavery, and the rice workers' strike was only the most noticeable sign of this discontent. Many blacks recognized their stake in the election campaign and understandably feared the return of the old planter class to power; Negro political leaders naturally felt threatened not only by Democrats but by conservative Republicans, who seemed ready to sell out their black supporters. Perhaps tearing a leaf from the book of the Edgefield Democracy, some blacks in the lowlands used intimidation to frighten their opponents and assure racial solidarity on election day.

Whatever the extent of "radical" violence, South Carolina Democrats were hardly innocent victims. General Gary had followed the progress of the 1875 campaign in Mississippi with growing interest and used it as a model for what became known as the "shotgun policy." This plan called for the Democrats to form clubs and military companies, which would attend every Republican meeting to denounce the speakers and impress the Negroes. The voters who could not be won with persuasion would be won by fear. Every opposition leader would know that any disturbance would cost him his life, and Gary called for the assassination of particularly obnoxious Republicans. Although the party officially repudiated this program of terrorism, county Democratic clubs adopted many of Gary's recommendations. Whites openly threatened to murder Republican leaders and scoffed at the prospect of federal intervention.[26]

The crusade against radicalism generated enormous popular enthusiasm across the state. Hampton addressed large audiences of wildly cheering whites, many wearing red shirts. Democrats held grand torchlight processions, brightly illuminating the night with their fervor for "reform." Women and children prepared bunting and other decorations for the eagerly anticipated "Hampton day," when the general would speak in their community. Brass bands played, military units fired cannon, and Negro Democrats marched. Excited boys paraded about in red shirts; voices old and young sang the favorite refrain of the canvass: "We'll hang Dan Chamberlain on a sour apple tree." In South Carolina history the daring deeds of 1876 took on a legendary quality that for some eclipsed the heroism of the Civil War; to have ridden with Hampton and the red shirts became the proudest boast of many citizens.[27]

Beneath the oratory and pageantry lay the harsher reality of the Mississippi plan. There were, of course, the usual reports of economic intimidation. Even the *News and Courier* defended the right of employers to exercise political preference in hiring laborers and suggested special consideration for black Hampton supporters.[28] Another key element of the Edgefield policy was "joint political discussions." Democrats insisted that Republicans "divide the time" with conservative speakers. Red shirts claimed they attended these meetings to protect black Democrats from the wrath of desperate radicals, but the evidence suggests otherwise. In many instances, a Republican refusal to share the platform served as a convenient excuse for armed men to assault the spectators. Military companies surrounded the meetings, cursed the Republican speakers, and sometimes threatened their lives.[29]

Unlike Mississippi or Louisiana, where Republican campaigners dared not venture out into the countryside, in South Carolina the party conducted a vigorous, albeit abbreviated, canvass. Governor Chamberlain and other leaders stumped the state in August, September, and October, coming face to face with the white fury. When Chamberlain addressed a Republican ratification meeting in Edgefield, Butler and Gary stationed red shirts across the parade route, yelling at the top of their lungs and waving pistols in the air. Gary warned Republicans either to listen to the conservatives or cancel the gathering. As the governor spoke, whites hooted, jeered, and questioned his paternity. Gary and Butler then harangued the crowd at length on the evils of the Republican administration, and several rowdies suggested executing Chamberlain on the spot. In Barnwell County the son of William Gilmore Simms blasted the governor as a "carrion coward, a buzzard and a Puritanical seedy adventurer who came down here to steal our substance." Toward the end of the campaign, armed whites followed Republicans from town to town, heckling speakers and sometimes beating and killing blacks. Some county Republican leaders could not hold more than one rally during the entire canvass.[30]

The most effective agency of intimidation and terrorism was the rifle and sabre clubs, first organized during the 1874 militia turmoil and reactivated for the 1876 campaign. Chamberlain's private secretary found 290 such groups in the state with a membership of 14,350, a formidable private army. Francis Butler Simkins estimated from these figures that a majority of the white male population able to ride was under arms. Many companies carried weapons seized from the militia, and some had cannon. Members maintained that the rifle clubs were purely defensive organizations formed to quell black insurrections, but mounted men roamed the countryside, cajoling, threatening, and occasionally murdering Republicans. This night riding created panic among both white and black radicals, who feared the red shirts might storm the polls on election day or even attack United States troops.[31]

Nowhere were these squads more active than in Edgefield and Aiken counties, the centers of anti-Republican fanaticism. As early as June, white extremists had vowed to win the election or kill all Republicans. On September 15 near Silverton in Aiken County, two black men entered the home of Alonzo Harley, hit his wife and young son over the head with sticks, but fled when Mrs. Harley grabbed a gun. Taking off in pursuit, white horsemen caught Peter Williams and hauled him back to the scene of the crime. After Mrs. Harley identified Williams as one of the assailants, his captors shot him to death. They obtained an arrest warrant for the other suspect, Frederick Pope, and began to search for him. Republicans later charged that Williams had been dragged out of a sickbed and was innocent of the assault charges.[32] Whatever the truth, this minor incident was enough to send the rifle clubs into action.

With armed whites on the march, Negroes gathered at a church the next day to discuss a plan for defense. Reports quickly spread that black incendiaries were plotting to burn gin houses and murder innocent citizens. Men from Aiken and Edgefield, led by Andrew P. Butler, broke up a Republican meeting on September 16 and by the next morning had surrounded a large body of blacks in a swamp. Butler's officers met several Negroes who refused to hand over Pope to the enraged whites. After a brief discussion on this point, the parties agreed to disperse peacefully. As both sides departed, other blacks ambushed one of the white companies, and the rifle clubs galloped through the countryside shooting blacks in the cotton fields. Some red shirts forced terrified Negroes to fall on their knees and promise to vote Democratic.[33]

On September 20 the fighting spread to nearby Ellenton, a depot on the Port Royal railroad. Red shirts poured into Aiken to join the battle, but some blacks derailed their train near the station. The infuriated whites then murdered several Negroes, including state legislator Simon Coker, whom Tillman's men shot as he prayed for mercy. Military companies again besieged Negroes in a swamp, but a detachment of federal troops arrived in time to prevent an almost certain massacre. One belligerent white remarked to an army officer that he would have given $500 to have had the soldiers arrive an hour later.[34]

All told, a handful of whites and perhaps as many as one hundred blacks died in the rioting, but the disorders were so widespread that casualty figures are guesses at best. Ignoring the large number of black corpses, Democrats held the Negroes responsible for the outbreak and shed many crocodile tears for the "innocent" men arrested by United States Marshal David Corbin. Corbin imprisoned more than eighty whites before the election, but Chief Justice Morrison R. Waite, whose judicial circuit then included South Carolina, declined to hear the cases during the campaign excitement. Federal authorities, Democratic editors cried, had solicited thousands of false affidavits and had paid ignorant Negroes liberal per diem allowances for perjured testimony. When the accused finally came to trial in the spring of 1877, their attorneys argued that arrests had been made solely to intimidate Democrats. The defense raised numerous procedural objections, maintained that the indictments were legally defective, and used dilatory motions to delay the proceedings. Waite was disgusted with the distorted newspaper coverage of the trial, particularly the slanderous attacks on government witnesses. But such tactics proved effective as the jury deadlocked along racial lines. On the request of Governor Wade Hampton, President Rutherford B. Hayes ordered the charges dropped.[35]

Although historians of South Carolina Reconstruction have given the bulk of their attention to the Hamburg massacre, the Ellenton riot had greater significance for the state's Republicans. The violence in Aiken County forced Chamberlain's hand: he either had to take action to protect his friends in the midlands or become a governor without authority like Kellogg or Ames. Letters poured into the governor's office from all parts of the state and from both parties begging for soldiers to quell disturbances. General Thomas H. Ruger, the commander of federal troops in South Carolina, did not have enough men to garrison all possible flashpoints. On October 7 Chamberlain issued a proclamation declaring that "unlawful combinations" in Aiken and Barnwell counties were hindering the enforcement of the law and ordering all rifle clubs to disband immediately.[36]

The disingenuous howls of protest from conservatives were deafening. The Democratic executive committee issued an address disputing the governor's assertions and produced statements from the state's circuit judges, including several Republicans, to prove that peace prevailed. According to Hampton and several Democratic editors, the real intimidation came from radicals trying to prevent the Negroes from breaking loose from partisan shackles. The rifle clubs calmly received Chamberlain's decree and reorganized themselves into such unlikely groups as the Allendale Mounted Baseball Club and the First Baptist Church Sewing Circle.[37]

Such ploys did not amuse Chamberlain, who informed President Grant that violence still plagued South Carolina. Desperate Republicans believed that only troops and the declaration of martial law could save them from being trampled into the dust under the thundering hooves of mounted red shirts. Although Grant and his advisers had hoped to avoid using the army during the campaign, the president issued a proclamation on October 17 calling on all rifle clubs to disband and ordered more soldiers to South Carolina. Federal intervention undoubtedly convinced Democrats to moderate their behavior; perhaps they believed that night riding had already done its work. Republicans at last held their meetings with relatively little interference, and Chamberlain optimistically predicted that his party would carry the election with large majorities. The soldiers found little evidence of hostilities. Ruger cautiously confined his men to their barracks but kept them close enough to the polls to render assistance in the event of a disturbance.[38]

Election day was comparatively quiet; army officers encountered scuffling between the parties in scattered precincts but little violence. Deputy marshals met with some resistance and feared to make arrests with armed red shirts riding about. The Democrats were convinced that federal troops were now on their side.[39]

After feeling the force of Edgefield tactics firsthand, it is not surprising that many Negroes doubted Hampton's soothing promises. One black man remarked after a meeting in Beaufort: "Dey say dem *will do* dis and dat. I ain't ax no man what him *will* do—I ax him what him *hab* done."[40] The paucity of voluntary conversions led Democrats to use trickery, intimidation, and occasional violence to win black votes. Ballots that looked like Republican tickets but contained the names of Democratic candidates were distributed to illiterate Negroes. Red shirts rode into villages, hooting, hollering, and threatening to kill all the radicals if the Democracy did not carry the day. Belligerent whites crowded ballot boxes, brandishing their pistols and preventing Republicans from depositing their tickets. Deputy marshals in several precincts had to flee for their lives when Democrats took control of the polls. Armed Georgians crossed the state line and not only voted themselves but helped rifle clubs cow Republicans.[41]

Not unexpectedly, election day in Edgefield more nearly resembled a military engagement than an exercise in American democracy. Armed men arrived in town the night before and rode around giving the rebel yell, firing their pistols, and hurling bloodcurdling epithets at local Republicans. Gary and M. C. Butler brought their rabid followers out in full force very early in the morning to beat blacks to the polls as well as to beat them at the polls. Red shirts formed a solid line around the ballot boxes and prevented Negroes without Democratic tickets from approaching. Some Democrats, including helpful Georgians, voted several times during the day. Federal troops finally cleared a path to the polls for the blacks, but by that time many had gone home.[42]

The only serious disturbances occurred in Charleston. The day after the election, November 8, some white men gathered around a bulletin board in front of the *News and Courier* office to read the latest returns. When a drunken man fired a pistol, several blacks ran through the streets screaming that a leading white Republican had been murdered. A crowd of Negroes, including several policemen, then began shooting at the whites. The rifle clubs and United States troops restored order, but one white man was killed and several men of both races were wounded in this last riot of the Reconstruction era in South Carolina.[43]

The outcome of the South Carolina election was uncertain, but the Hampton forces quickly claimed a victory. The campaign had been a counterrevolutionary one modeled on those in Alabama and Mississippi but with some peculiar twists. Factionalism in the Republican party centered around the administration of a Republican governor who actively solicited the support of conservative whites and ignored the interests of black leaders. The usual carpetbagger-scalawag division was absent in South Carolina, where black politicians exercised more power than in any other southern state. Yet the Republicans seemingly surrendered without putting up much of a fight. Neither Chamberlain nor his radical opponents proposed using militia to stop the red shirts. Grant immediately sent additional troops to the state, without suggesting as he had to Adelbert Ames that the state government must first exhaust its own peacekeeping resources. More than in any other state, black South Carolinians struck back at violent Democrats but with only limited success. Though able to maintain their strength in the lowcountry, Republicans stood little chance in the midlands and upcountry. Whatever its unusual features, the campaign taught southern Democrats a familiar lesson: what cannot be won through the normal political process can be secured by terrorism.

In contrast to South Carolina, Louisiana in 1876 was almost tranquil. Although there was some talk of employing the Mississippi plan, cooler heads initially prevailed. Democrats officially repudiated the use of violence though they would admittedly employ any other means, including fraud and intimidation, to redeem the state. The party platform, drafted at a July convention in Baton Rouge, accepted the postwar constitutional amendments and made reform the central issue of the campaign. The Democrats nominated Francis T. Nicholls for governor, a choice reflecting tactical shrewdness as well as a relaxation of political tensions in the state. A former Confederate general who had lost an arm during the war, Nicholls was the epitome of southern respectability and a man who could appeal to old soldiers and former slaves alike. In classic paternalistic fashion, Nicholls promised blacks that he would abide by his party's pledges and would ensure both races equal protection of the law. To their opponents, the Louisiana Democracy's only fixed principle remained hostility to the Negro. Governor Kellogg accurately observed that Nicholls, despite his own conciliatory attitudes, would never be able to tame the racial extremists in his own party, a relationship similar to those between Hampton and Gary in South Carolina and between L.Q.C. Lamar and the white liners in Mississippi. The *New Orleans Republican* sarcastically remarked: "Take away from the Democrat his shotgun, and he becomes as weak as Samson with his head shaved."[44]

Factionalism continued to erode the strength of Louisiana Republicans. The Custom House contingent controlled a tumultuous convention in New Orleans that nominated Stephen B. Packard for governor on a ticket with three black men. Packard had long experience in backroom politics, and for many members of both parties his candidacy signified a victory for political machination over reform. With Pinchback and Warmoth sulking on the sidelines, the Republicans entered upon a desperate contest. One overzealous partisan offered to bring in blacks from Arkansas to swell the Republican vote. Throughout the campaign, party speakers charged Nicholls with lacking both the will and the power to restrain his bloodthirsty followers. If the violence continued much longer, one Republican facetiously suggested, the state would not have enough Negroes left for a good race riot. More realistically, Packard supporters gloomily predicted that a Democratic triumph would force white Republicans into exile and lead to the disfranchisement of the Negroes.[45]

Frightened by violent outbreaks in several parishes, Republicans pressed their northern friends for more military assistance. Governor Kellogg requested that black cavalry troops be stationed around the state—a plan surely guaranteed to produce racial warfare. General Christopher Columbus Augur, who had succeeded Emory in command of the Department of the Gulf, deployed his men discreetly and unobtrusively. Despite screams of anguish, the Democrats knew that under recent judicial interpretations of the Enforcement Acts, the troops could do little but observe the voting. Augur stationed soldiers in sixty-two locations across the state on election day, but Republicans in New Orleans expected trouble, and Kellogg wanted General Philip Sheridan back in command.[46]

Election day in Louisiana was exceptionally peaceful by the state's usual standards. Enthusiastic Democrats turned out in large numbers; more blacks voted conservative than in any previous election. The question, of course, was whether these Negroes had voluntarily deserted the Republicans. Even revisionist historians have argued that many blacks had become so dissatisfied with the patronage and educational policies of the Kellogg government that they responded favorably to Democratic appeals.[47] The preponderance of evidence, however, not only from Republican sources but from army officers and government officials in Louisiana, shows that intimidation played a decisive role in "persuading" black men to vote Democratic. This generalization was particularly true in the five "bulldozed" parishes.[48]

Bands of regulators infested East Baton Rouge Parish as well as those areas lying immediately to the north. They claimed to be dispensing justice to thieving blacks and unscrupulous white storekeepers who trafficked in stolen seed cotton. The area had suffered from economic hard times since 1873, some of the best agricultural land was exhausted, and sharecropping arrangements were not entirely satisfactory to either blacks or planters. The regulators, more commonly called "bulldozers" by 1876, burned several stores and whipped and hanged Negro farmers. Blaming Republican officeholders for failing to arrest black criminals, angry Democrats forced the black sheriff, the tax collector, and the parish judge to resign and leave the parish. Once the campaign got under way, "bulldozers" rode through the countryside beating and murdering Republicans. Wild young men, many of respectable lineage, threatened to kill anyone who dared vote for the radical ticket and even abused black women. The coroner, who held inquests over the bodies of several slain Negroes, received notice either to leave the parish or suffer a similar fate. Mounted vigilantes broke up Republican meetings and forced blacks to attend Democratic rallies; two men who tried to organize a Republican club were later found hanging from a gatepost. On election day, whites handed Negroes Democratic tickets and herded them to the polls while armed men harassed election commissioners and seized control of the ballot boxes. The mayor and city police allowed Democrats to picket the roads leading to Baton Rouge, thus preventing many blacks from voting.[49]

Just to the north, rumors of a Negro insurrection had spread through East Feliciana Parish in July 1875, leading to the murders of several black "incendiaries." In October a sheriff's posse arrested a black man and woman on charges of poisoning a doctor, but vigilantes seized the pair, shooting the man to death and lynching the woman. When a district judge arraigned several members of this mob, armed whites entered the court and forced the judge to leave the parish. In March 1876 bulldozers hanged two young black girls, one of whom was pregnant, on a plantation near the parish seat of Clinton. By that time Democrats had decided the Republican majority in the parish could be reversed only by preventing Negroes from voting. Armed men visited blacks at night and warned them against going to the polls. When Packard spoke at Clinton in September, bulldozers jeered and interrupted his address; Republicans abandoned the canvass, and many slept out of doors until after election day. Negroes who had been threatened or whipped joined the Democratic clubs and voted the conservative ticket.[50]

Regulators in West Feliciana Parish assaulted a German storekeeper who was an active Republican, hanged two planters for living with black women, and whipped several Negroes for stealing cotton. Only the presence of federal troops in Bayou Sara kept Republicans from leaving, but they still complained that the post commander had Democratic sympathies. With assistance from Wilkinson County, Mississippi, vigilantes "persuaded" four police jurors to resign their offices. Refugees crowded the roads, fleeing from the plantations in fear of night riders. Since Republicans had no opportunity to canvass the parish, many blacks joined Democratic clubs in order to receive protection from the bulldozers. Economic and physical threats against Negroes who failed to vote the Nicholls ticket continued on election day. Republicans often could not distribute their ballots and failed to poll a single vote in a parish where they had previously won sizable majorities.[51]

Democrats were equally determined to carry the election in the northern parish of Morehouse. Regulators visited Negroes at night, sent coffins to Republican candidates, and whipped blacks who refused to join a Democratic club. Republicans held meetings at the risk of their lives, and when Packard delivered a speech in Bastrop, angry whites hanged him in effigy and shouted him down. Similar acts of intimidation continued through election day.[52]

Terrorism was more serious in adjoining Ouachita Parish. Regulators strung up Negroes to a tree until they agreed to join the Democratic clubs. Republicans could hold meetings only with the protection of federal troops; black leaders fled into the swamps to escape bulldozers. In August a man in a slouch hat and false whiskers (perhaps the infamous Captain Jack) assassinated parish tax collector Bernard H. Dinkgrave, whose dead body served as a grisly warning to others. Rumors circulated in Monroe that armed Negroes planned to march into the city on election day to create a disturbance. The mayor issued a proclamation and called out special policemen, whose main duty apparently consisted of driving black men away from the polls. After the ballots were cast, future governor Samuel D. McEnery and other prominent Democrats forced blacks to sign affidavits swearing there had been no intimidation in the parish.[53]

The terror in Louisiana in 1876 was less extensive and more selective than in 1874. Confident of winning the governorship and control of the legislature, the Nicholls forces used White League tactics when necessary while publicly proclaiming a policy of peace. Both Kellogg and Chamberlain faced the wrath of white men determined to complete the return of home rule in the southern states, but election violence did occur elsewhere. Historians have naturally focused on the larger and more bloody disorders in South Carolina and Louisiana, but disturbances took place in Florida and in several states already under Democratic control.

Like their brethren elsewhere, Florida Republicans entered the 1876 campaign deeply divided. Because blacks constituted 49 percent of the voting population, the party needed white support. Republicans of various stripes accused their rivals, often with some truth, of collaborating with Democrats. Initially there were two Republican candidates for governor, but the party's national committee pressured both sides to back a single ticket headed by incumbent Governor Marcellus L. Stearns. Seeing an excellent chance to throw out their enemies, Democrats eagerly rallied around the candidacy of the bland and conservative businessman George F. Drew.[54]

Anxious Republicans charged that Georgians were preparing to invade the state to intimidate blacks and incite race riots, but there were few disturbances during the campaign. Although several rifle clubs organized, apparently in the hope of receiving arms from South Carolina's disbanded companies, none were active. Political discussions were interrupted by only scattered incidents of gunfire. Some economic intimidation took place, and Democratic clubs forcibly exacted pledges from blacks to vote the Democratic ticket. Fraud rather than violence characterized the canvass and the election.[55] Despite bitter controversy over the outcome of the state races, Drew was quietly inaugurated in January 1877, but the disposition of Florida's electoral votes remained in dispute.

After the campaign of 1875, Mississippi Republicans realized the conservatives were determined to carry the state again. Democratic Governor James M. Stone dismissed reports of terrorism and claimed that both parties were conducting their canvasses with perfect freedom.[56] Country editors urged Democratic partisans to attend Republican meetings and prevent radical speakers from slandering the white people of Mississippi; behind such advice lay the implicit threat of physical assaults against Republicans of both races.[57]

Historians have generally seen the return of the Democrats to power as marking the end of Reconstruction in the various southern states and have treated this event with a finality that ignores contemporary complexities. Even though the Democrats had carried Mississippi in 1875, the state's black electoral majority led many Republicans to believe that they could regain political control if the federal government could provide protection for Negro voters. Angry Republicans, many of whom had grown bitter and cynical about Grant's southern policies, wrote to the president and Attorney General Alphonso Taft demanding that the administration either support the southern wing of the party with troops or stop pretending to be concerned about that wing. As one dismayed old soldier put it, "I am willing to take my chances . . . but [not] to put up a few men and have them killed for party purposes. I am getting tired of it." Although several hundred deputy marshals were stationed at various precincts on election day, this token force met verbal abuse and physical intimidation and was powerless to stop the Democratic clubs from controlling the ballot boxes.[58]

In counties where Republicans dared hold political gatherings, armed Democrats either heckled the speakers or demanded a division of the time. Angry young men chased one Republican canvasser through the streets of Natchez with shouts of "Hang the carpetbagger," "Shoot the radical," and "Rail-ride the son of a bitch." Just as in 1875, Democratic clubs used shotguns and cannon to cow voters and drive Republican leaders from their homes.[59]

At Hernando in the far northwestern corner of the state, United States Attorney Thomas Walton attempted to speak at a joint political rally. The seating arrangements were rigidly segregated both by party and by race (which in 1876 were identical), but a scuffle broke out over some chairs. A Democrat waved a stick at the blacks, and shooting erupted, leaving five blacks and two whites wounded.[60] In Lowndes County on the Alabama border, black men brought a wagonload of arms to a debate between congressional candidates. Democrats attempted to seize these weapons, and in the ensuing exchange of gunfire, six Negroes fell wounded.[61]

Determined to carry all six congressional districts, Democrats were particularly anxious to unseat black Congressman John R. Lynch. A few federal soldiers were stationed in Claiborne County along the Mississippi River, but local Republicans suspected them of harboring Democratic sympathies. When armed men appeared at a Republican rally in Port Gibson, Lynch thought it best to cancel the meeting rather than risk bloodshed. A white posse later exchanged gunshots with several of Lynch's black followers.[62] Besides intimidating voters, these tactics forced Republicans to curtail their campaign activities. As a result, the Democrats easily swept the state, thus completing the process of redemption and for the time being eliminating the Negro as a political force.

"The late election in this state," Republican State Executive Committee Chairman H. R. Ware lamented, "was but a medley of tragedy, comedy, and farce, the most shameless and unblushing outrage ever enacted in a free country." Federal officials agreed; Marshal J. H. Pearce described the white population as "one vast mob." Asserting that they would have easily won a fair election, Republicans vainly pleaded with administration officials to send more soldiers to prevent the extinction of their party in Mississippi.[63]

Alabama Democrats stood ready to abort any revival of the Republican party. Carpetbag Senator George Spencer and deputy United States marshals were threatened with assassination if they interfered with the canvass. Desperate Republicans begged for protection and encouraged their northern friends to wave the bloody shirt during the presidential campaign, but there were few disturbances in the state. At both the August gubernatorial election and the federal election in November, armed Democrats prevented the polls from being opened in many predominantly Republican precincts.[64]

Republicans reported scattered incidents of intimidation against black voters in other states, but in most areas the balloting proceeded quietly. In part, this sense of calm reflected the belief of conservative whites that redemption was about to be completed, but it may also have reflected a certain apathy about the presidential race. Although southern Democrats supported their presidential nominee, Samuel J. Tilden, their interest in the national election was distinctly secondary to their concern about state and local contests. The redoubtable Zebulon Vance of North Carolina bluntly dismissed the presidential election as "small potatoes." Even before election day, South Carolina Democrats admitted their willingness to concede the presidency to Hayes in exchange for control of their own state government.[65]

In both Louisiana and South Carolina, intimidation and terrorism placed the outcome of the election in doubt. The infamous Louisiana Returning Board and the State Board of Canvassers in South Carolina would scrutinize the returns and not only declare the state winners but also award their electoral votes to either Hayes or Tilden. With the outcome of the national election in doubt, there was greater than usual partisan pressure on these bodies to make the "correct" determinations.[66]

Grant took the growing number of threats made against the Republican state governments seriously and authorized additional troops for Louisiana and South Carolina. He also sent that old nemesis of southern firebrands, General Philip Sheridan, to New Orleans. Sheridan found the Crescent City surprisingly quiet, and his soldiers received a warm welcome from the White Leaguers. In the countryside, however, armed Democrats persecuted witnesses who had testified before the Returning Board. Nicholls-appointed local officials expelled Republicans from their offices, and White Leaguers patrolled several northern parishes.[67]

As expected, the Returning Board threw out enough ballots to give Hayes the state's electoral votes, to elect the Republican state ticket, and to establish a Republican majority in both houses of the legislature. Refusing to accept this result, Democratic leaders set up a de facto government and sought recognition from Grant. With arms seized from the state armory during the September 1874 rebellion, the Nicholls militia (White League units) paraded through New Orleans while General Ogden and his staff prepared to move against Packard. Early on the morning of January 9, armed men appeared on the streets, shops closed, and citizens braced themselves for battle. This time the outnumbered Metropolitan Police decided that resistance would be futile; the Nicholls militia captured the police stations and supreme court building and cut the telegraph lines. A mob surrounded the statehouse, where Packard and his friends had retreated to wait for help from Washington.[68] The hoped-for assistance never came.

Packard's position in New Orleans steadily deteriorated. In the scramble for state and federal patronage, some Republicans deserted to the Nicholls side. As observers on the scene noted, Democrats stood ready to fight for Nicholls, and a White League attack on the statehouse was expected at any time. A mysterious stranger from Philadelphia allegedly tried to shoot Packard at his office, but Democrats charged that this rumor had been concocted for northern edification. Had either Grant or Hayes recognized Packard, his assassination would have been highly probable. In contrast to their undying devotion to Nicholls, Louisianians attached little importance to the presidential question and were willing to accept Hayes in exchange for home rule.[69]

As the Republican era in Louisiana moved inexorably toward its close, Reconstruction in South Carolina entered its final phase. There, too, incomplete returns, charges of intimidation and fraud, and especially terrorism perpetrated by the rifle clubs, made an accurate determination of the results problematical. The State Board of Canvassers, protected by federal troops in Columbia, awarded the Republicans a majority of the seats in the legislature. That body would then determine who had been elected governor and lieutenant governor as well as ruling on disputed legislative seats from Edgefield and Laurens counties. To South Carolina Democrats, the presidential contest seemed inconsequential compared to the death struggle against radicalism at home.[70]

When the legislature assembled at the end of November, Republicans feared the Democrats might stage a coup. Although armed men moved into Columbia from the countryside, Hampton convinced his more fanatical friends to contain their outrage. For more than four days, both Republicans and Democrats attempted to conduct business in the House of Representatives, but on December 4 the Democrats withdrew to form their own house. With considerable difficulty, Hampton again dissuaded his supporters from storming the statehouse. General Gary and the Edgefield fire-eaters vigorously denounced this "retreat," but Hampton had wisely avoided precipitating a fatal collision with national authority.[71]

"We have the world, the flesh and the devil to fight," Chamberlain informed Attorney General Taft, "but think we shall pull through. The shotgun policy is . . . a success only with niggers." Such brave words hardly reflected the gravity of the situation. In his own inaugural address in early December, Chamberlain quoted Hampton as saying that he held the governor's life in his hands. Indeed, one word from Hampton, and the Massachusetts carpetbagger would have soon been dangling at the end of a rope. Angry Democrats drove local Republican officials from their offices, and the rifle clubs staged an effective campaign of economic and physical intimidation against the witnesses in the Hamburg and Ellenton riot cases.[72]

The countryside remained tense. Frightened Republicans reported a reign of terror, including several murders, against Chamberlain supporters. After a brief trip to South Carolina, veteran Ohio politico Samuel Shellabarger concluded that the rifle clubs would have easily taken over the state and assassinated Republican leaders had Hampton not restrained them. When President Hayes appeared to delay the withdrawal of military support for the Republican government, Hampton supposedly warned Hayes that every tax collector in the state would be hanged within twenty-four hours if the new president recognized Chamberlain.[73] This story is probably apocryphal, but it exemplifies the blind determination of South Carolina conservatives to triumph no matter what the cost.

In contrast to the passions generated by these state contests, only a few hotheads favored fighting for Tilden. Given their conspiratorial attitude toward national politics, many conservatives naturally suspected a radical plot by Grant and other Republicans to use federal troops to install Hayes as president. On the whole, however, the reaction in the southern states to the presidential election deadlock was surprisingly calm.[74] Still holding bitter memories from the 1860–61 period, southern conservatives had little faith in the northern Democrats and no great confidence in Tilden's abilities to meet the challenges of the electoral crisis.[75] With their primary objectives of home rule and white racial hegemony secure, southern Democrats could accept Hayes in the White House.

The election deadlock coincided with but had little influence on the ending of Reconstruction. The 1876 campaign merely marked the culmination of the counterrevolution and the completion of redemption. As the country argued over who had been elected president, few Americans paid much attention to the fraud, intimidation, and terrorism in the South that returned the region to conservative control and restored blacks to a condition more resembling serfdom than freedom.

Epilogue:
On the Inevitability of Tragedy

The violent overthrow of Republican state governments in the South and the subversion of the nation's Reconstruction policies raise several disturbing and timeless questions. The American nation was no more successful in resolving its sectional differences during Reconstruction than in the antebellum decades. The meaning and results of the North's battlefield victory remained unclear.

The tumult and bloodshed of Reconstruction were but a reflection of the period's revolutionary character. One need not accept Charles Beard's interpretation of the Civil War and Reconstruction as a "Second American Revolution" to demonstrate the reality of the upheaval.[1] To describe the era as a triumph of northern capitalism over southern agrarianism is too simple, although the revolutionary nature of emancipation is undeniable. In 1860 most southern blacks were slaves; by 1865 they were free; by 1867 they were citizens and voters; and by 1868 some were holding important public offices. Northern victory in the Civil War can be seen as the triumph of a modern society over a traditional one, of cosmopolitanism over provincialism, and of free labor over a quasi-feudal social order.[2]

To provide future security for a restored Union, the federal government attempted to supervise and shape the operations of state and local governments in the former Confederate states. Similar policies have often led to revolution in other parts of the world.[3] In this case I prefer to call it counterrevolution. Faced with the loss of their economic resources, political power, and racial hegemony, white southerners sought desperately to preserve as much of their traditional society as possible. Military Reconstruction forced politicians to reconsider their electoral strategy and make appeals to black voters, but it did little to change the ultimate direction of the region's politics. In the end, the white South threw off the yoke of "Jacobinical radicalism" and reestablished home rule and race control.

The myths and legends of Reconstruction, which have been exorcised by modern scholarship, still have a life of their own. Reconstruction was a great trauma that white southerners could not forget. The failure of the Republican party to remake southern society should not blind us to the fact that the attempt was made. Despite the North's abandonment of the crusade and the South's victorious guerrilla war, later storytellers greatly embroidered tales of carpetbagger knavery and black depravity.[4]

During the tumultuous decade following the war, a reactionary nationalism developed in the South that continued the war against the Yankee on several fronts. Antebellum southern nationalists had poured great energy into creating a sectional literature, a sectional idea of education, and above all an intellectual and moral defense of slavery. Northerners sought to destroy this world view, but they failed miserably. Instead, defeat produced a unity in the South that had never before existed, even during the halcyon days of the Confederacy.[5] The Reconstruction experience did not remake southern society in the image of the free North but reinforced regional distinctiveness. The nationalism that was shattered at Appomattox was reborn in the rocky soil of defeat and disillusionment.

The Confederacy never surrendered beyond the mere laying down of arms. An anonymous Georgian prophetically warned Thaddeus Stevens, "Your idea of governing the conquered states by the force of the bayonet may serve for a time, but it fills the future with blood. You are aware of the historical fact that no people have yet been satisfied with a single unsuccessful blow for independence." Even a moderate such as Ethelbert Barksdale asserted that an "army of one hundred thousand men" could not maintain the Reconstruction governments in the South. He predicted that the northern people would refuse to support a large military establishment and would abandon southern Republicans to their fate.[6] Albion Tourgée concluded from his own bitter experience in North Carolina that when southerners assaulted and killed white and black Republicans, they were really attacking the national government and the ideas it represented. Significantly, many of these acts of aggression took place near statehouses and courthouses, the symbolic centers of the revolutionary regimes.[7]

The violent episodes in the postwar South were not undifferentiated responses to defeat, racial competition, and sectional reunion. Rather, their character evolved from random outrages to systematic terrorism. During presidential Reconstruction, political, economic, and social turmoil produced disorders. Isolated assaults and murders, many against Union men and blacks, often had local or personal origins but also reflected a deep and general sense of frustration and anger among old

Confederates. Shifting population patterns, agricultural distress, and emancipation severely strained southern life both in the countryside and the cities. One result was the race riots in Memphis and New Orleans. These early outbreaks were indicative of the chaotic condition of the South during the early Reconstruction period.

The persistent tensions in southern society continued to produce individual acts of violence even after the passage of the Reconstruction acts. Yet by 1867 the violence became increasingly political as white southerners attempted to defy congressional mandates, overthrow the hated Republican state governments, and drive the "foreigners" from their soil. The lack of effective organization, however, blunted these counterrevolutionary thrusts. As a body designed to destroy Reconstruction and all its works, the Ku Klux Klan was a failure. Individual dens sometimes operated with frightening power, but there was never a wider "Klan conspiracy" in any real sense. Equally important, during the Ku Klux era the federal government was willing to take at least minimal action against southern terrorism.

By the mid-1870s changing political conditions and the redemption of several southern states had confined political violence to a smaller area but made it more desperate and intense. In states still governed by Republicans, white conservatives conducted a vigorous propaganda war against their foes and launched taxpayers' protests. Losing patience with slow and peaceful methods, many southerners eventually turned to the white line organizations. These groups sought to raise the color bar in southern politics and at the same time revive the state Democratic organizations. Applying lessons learned from the failure of the Klan, Democrats used intimidation and force in a way carefully calculated to sap the strength of their enemies without provoking federal intervention. This new strategy also benefited from the waning public support in the North for military interference in the South. A series of skillful and violent blows led to the final collapse of reconstruction, but all this activity took place behind a smokescreen of conservative alarms and hyperbole. As young Georges Clemenceau remarked about southern disturbances, "In all events of the kind, the remarkable feature is that according to telegraphic reports, there is always a band of heavily armed negroes attacking a handful of harmless whites. Then when it comes to counting the dead, a few negroes are always down, but of white men, not a trace."[8] As instances of violence mounted, both the magnitude of these disorders and the Lilliputian means available to suppress them became apparent.

From a modern perspective, the Reconstruction policies of the national government seem mild, timid, and too short-lived to produce significant changes in traditional southern society. Historians have therefore suggested that the South should have been kept out of the Union under military supervision for an indefinite period of time. Other scholars believe the distribution of land to the freedmen was essential because it would have given blacks an economic base from which to exercise and protect their newly won civil and political rights. Indeed, the conviction that land reform would have been the best solution has become, in Herman Belz's phrase, the "new orthodoxy in Reconstruction historiography."[9]

This faith in larger doses of radicalism may rest on questionable ideological assumptions, but, more important, it ignores both the size of the task and the context of the times. Tourgée later recalled that many southern Republicans had never realized that "the social conditions of three hundred years are not to be overthrown in a moment." The deeply conservative William T. Sherman agreed that the problems plaguing the South "will hardly disappear until a new generation is born and reach maturity." Ironically, even this pessimistic forecast underestimated the size of the task.[10]

In the middle decades of the nineteenth century, the American people and their political leaders were neither united nor patient enough to carry a radical policy to completion. The Yankees demanded both a thorough and a brief Reconstruction, but these goals were mutually exclusive. When a choice had to be made, the northern public preferred to wash its hands of the race question rather than follow a consistent program to a successful conclusion in the distant future. Historians who criticize the Republicans for not implementing more radical measures have neither demonstrated their workability nor shown that they could have been adopted, much less effectively administered.

Any Draconian policy would have had to rely on military force. The popular cry for slashing federal expenditures had already reduced the strength of the army, and it could barely handle its current responsibilities in the South and on the Great Plains. Both officers and enlisted men detested southern duty, and most seemed to prefer fighting Indians to dealing with recalcitrant and sometimes dangerous rebels. To effect a genuine reconstruction clearly would have required many more men than were available in the 1870s, and Congress was unwilling to expand the size of the army for this purpose. Finally, what would have been the long-range consequences for the American republic of keeping the southern states in a semicolonial status for a long period of time?

Popular antipathy to military measures and expenditures was part of a deeply rooted public philosophy. Few people advocated that an activist government reshape the South along the lines desired by radical Republicans or later historians. Despite the centralizing effects of the Civil War, retrenchment and limited functions became the hallmarks of government at all levels during the Gilded Age. President Ulysses S. Grant tried to administer the laws passed by Congress without actively participating in the legislative process. Grant's frequent vacation trips to the seaside resort at Long Branch, New Jersey, led James A. Garfield to remark, "The President has done much to show with how little personal attention the Government can be run." Garfield saw this attitude as the "drift of modern thought," and it was hardly fertile ground for a more vigorous southern policy.[11]

The desire to leave things alone coupled with the growing popularity of Social Darwinism precluded any substantial welfare assistance for blacks. Universal suffrage was the great panacea of the age, and many friends of the Negro believed he needed no further aid once he had acquired the sacred ballot. If, armed with this powerful weapon, the freedmen and their white allies lost elections to the southern Democracy, so be it. Northern radicals soon lost interest in the blacks and abandoned them to the tender mercies of the redeemers.[12]

The waning of northern commitment to Reconstruction was to be expected. The ability of any people to participate fully in a political or social crusade is sharply limited by time. In applying this generalization to the problem of revolution, Crane Brinton has argued that a Thermidorean reaction is a "universal" phenomenon that comes sooner or later in diverse settings under widely differing circumstances.[13] Therefore, to expect the American people to have sustained the commitment necessary for a radical transformation of the South is asking them to transcend their own humanity.

Historians have overemphasized the weaknesses of northern policy and ideology in explaining the failure of Reconstruction and have overlooked the persistence and strength of southern resistance.[14] Americans, like most other peoples, have been defensive about their violent past and have preferred to draw their moral lessons about brutality from the experiences of other cultures or to attribute all barbarisms to "outside" influences.[15] Conservative southerners, therefore, saw the Yankee as the embodiment of tyranny and the disorders in their region as instigated by foreign incendiaries.

Social scientists have long recognized the importance of violence as a catalyst for social change[16] but have neglected its role as a conservative or even reactionary instrument. The Reconstruction legacy legitimized the use of force in southern society.[17] By 1877 the magnitude of the terrorism and the success of the counterrevolution made the conclusion of the "tragic era" inevitably tragic.

Notes

Chapter 1: American Violence, Southern Violence, and Reconstruction

1. See David Potter, "Civil War," in C. Vann Woodward, ed., *The Comparative Approach to American History* (New York: Basic Books, 1968), 135–44.

2. W. Eugene Hollon, *Frontier Violence: Another Look* (New York: Oxford University Press, 1974), 5–15, 22–35; Richard Maxwell Brown, *Strain of Violence: Historical Studies of American Violence and Vigilantism* (New York: Oxford University Press, 1975), 3–4.

3. See Sheldon Hackney, "Southern Violence," in Hugh Davis Graham and Ted Robert Gurr, eds., *Violence in America: Historical and Comparative Perspectives* (Washington, D.C.: U.S. Government Printing Office, 1969), 387–401; Dickson D. Bruce, Jr., *Violence and Culture in the Antebellum South* (Austin: University of Texas Press, 1979), 4 and note 4. But one should be cautious about making too much of regional differences. As Michael Feldberg has pointed out, Americans in the Jacksonian period witnessed frequent riots and almost came to look upon violence as a natural part of the political process (*The Turbulent Era: Riot and Disorder in Jacksonian America* [New York: Oxford University Press, 1980], 4–7, 127–28).

4. Wilbur J. Cash, *The Mind of the South* (New York: Alfred A. Knopf, 1941), 32–35; Richard Slotkin, *Regeneration through Violence: The Mythology of the American Frontier, 1600–1860* (Middletown, Conn.: Wesleyan University Press, 1973), 552–56 and passim.

5. Bruce, *Violence and Culture*, 6–18, 44–72.

6. Ibid., 4–5, 91–98, 187–88.

7. The best critique of the ahistorical approach of many social scientists to the study of human aggressiveness is still Reinhold Niebuhr, *The Irony of American History* (New York: Scribner's, 1952), 60, 85–87.

8. For two concise expressions of this viewpoint, see Eric McKitrick, "Reconstruction: Ultraconservative Revolution," in Woodward, ed., *Comparative Approach to American History*, 151–54, and Michael Les Benedict, "Preserving the Constitution: The Conservative Basis of Radical Reconstruction," *Journal of American History* 61 (June 1974): 65–90.

9. C. Vann Woodward, *The Burden of Southern History* (Baton Rouge: Louisiana State University Press, 1968), 187–211.

10. A. C. McKinley to Kate McKinley Taylor, May 4, 1865, typescript, David C. Barrow Papers, Ilah Dunlap Little Memorial Library, University of Georgia; Arney R. Childs, ed., *The Private Journal of Henry William Ravenel,*

1859–1887 (Columbia: University of South Carolina Press, 1947), 241. In 1861 a fear of the future had produced secession and war. In 1865 it would produce resistance to federal policies and eventually bloodshed.

11. Alexander H. Stephens, *A Constitutional View of the Late War between the States,* 2 vols. (Philadelphia: National Publishing Company, 1868–70), 2:639; Benjamin H. Hill, Jr., *Senator Benjamin H. Hill of Georgia: His Life, Speeches, and Writings* (Atlanta: H. C. Hudgins, 1891), 48.

12. The classic expression of the frustration-aggression hypothesis is John Dollard, et al., *Frustration and Aggression* (New Haven: Yale University Press, 1939), with important modifications in Leonard Berkowitz, *Aggression: A Social Psychological Analysis* (New York: McGraw-Hill, 1962), 26–50. Critics of this approach have correctly observed that in many instances frustration does not lead to aggressive behavior. The historian can readily agree and add that the determining factor is the historical context. Frustrated white southerners did not always respond to feelings of powerlessness with violent acts, but they did so under particular conditions. Psychological theory can be firmly grounded in a historical setting, and the historian of Reconstruction can show how the psychology of aggression is applicable to a variety of violent episodes in the postwar South. See Arnold H. Buss, *The Psychology of Aggression* (New York: Wiley, 1961), 19–20, 27–32; Seymour Feshbach, "The Function of Aggression and the Regulation of Aggressive Drive," *Psychological Review* 71 (July 1964): 257–72; Feldberg, *Turbulent Era,* 86–87.

13. Ted Robert Gurr, *The Conditions of Civil Violence: First Tests of a Causal Model* (Princeton: Center of International Studies, 1967), 1.

14. *Georgia Senate Journal,* 1865–66, p. 63; William M. Browne to Howell Cobb, March 28, 1866, in Ulrich Bonnell Phillips, ed., "The Correspondence of Robert Toombs, Alexander H. Stephens, and Howell Cobb," *Annual Report of the American Historical Association* (1911), 2:678; *Raleigh Daily Sentinel,* July 5, October 31, 1866; Henry A. Wise to Nahum Capen, February 4, 1867, Henry A. Wise Papers, William R. Perkins Library, Duke University.

15. *New York Herald,* May 7, July 26, 1865; J. T. Trowbridge, *A Picture of the Desolated States; and the Work of Restoration, 1865–1868* (Hartford, Conn.: L. Stebbins, 1868), 188–89; Jason Niles Diary, July 12, 1865, Southern Historical Collection, University of North Carolina.

16. *Charleston Daily Courier,* June 5, August 31, 1865; William B. Campbell to William Shelton, May 25, 1865, Campbell Family Papers, William R. Perkins Library, Duke University; Henry Cleveland, *Alexander H. Stephens* (Philadelphia: National Publishing Company, 1866), 806–12; James Lusk Alcorn to Amelia Alcorn, May 16, 1865, P. L. Rainwater, ed., "Letters of James Lusk Alcorn," *Journal of Southern History* 3 (May 1937): 209.

17. Lee to C. Chauncey Burr, January 5, 1866, Robert E. Lee, *Recollections and Letters of General Robert E. Lee* (Garden City, N.Y.: Doubleday, Page, 1924), 225; Walter L. Fleming, *Civil War and Reconstruction in Alabama* (New York: Columbia University Press, 1905), 341–47; James Harrison Wilson, *Under the Old Flag,* 2 vols. (New York: D. Appleton, 1912), 2:347–56.

18. Michael Perman, *Reunion without Compromise: The South and Reconstruction, 1865–1868* (Cambridge, England: Cambridge University Press,

1973), 26–39. Perman has brilliantly described southern resistance to northern Reconstruction policies, and my analysis follows closely his skillful treatment.

19. Alexander H. Stephens to Linton Stephens, January 3, 1866, Alexander H. Stephens Papers, Manhattanville College.

20. Cash, *Mind of the South,* 46–60.

21. F. L. Claiborne to William N. Whitehurst, June 24, 1865, Whitehurst Papers, Mississippi Department of Archives and History; *Augusta Daily Constitutionalist,* April 26, 1865; Jubal A. Early to "Dear Goode," June 8, 1866, Jubal A. Early Papers, William R. Perkins Library, Duke University.

22. *Memphis Daily Avalanche,* January 1, 1866; Wade Hall, *The Smiling Phoenix: Southern Humor from 1865 to 1914* (Gainesville: University of Florida Press, 1965), 76; Gayarré to Evert A. Duyckinck, May 31, 1865, "Some Letters of Charles Etienne Gayarré on Literature and Politics, 1854–1885," *Louisiana Historical Quarterly* 33 (April 1950): 229–30.

23. Cash, *Mind of the South,* 44–45, 76; Bruce, *Violence and Culture,* 27–43; William J. Cooper, Jr., *The South and the Politics of Slavery, 1828–1856* (Baton Rouge: Louisiana State University Press, 1978), 241 and passim.

24. *Tallahassee Florida Sentinel,* June 2, 1866; *Charleston Daily Courier,* October 10, 1866; James L. Orr to Herschel V. Johnson, November 11, 1866, Herschel Johnson Papers. William R. Perkins Library, Duke University; E. P. Ellis to Thomas C. W. Ellis, December 4, 1865, E. John Ellis Papers, Department of Archives, Louisiana State University.

25. Thomas B. Alexander, "Persistent Whiggery in the Confederate South, 1860–1877," *Journal of Southern History* 27 (August 1961): 311—17; Donald H. Breese, "Politics in the Lower South during Presidential Reconstruction, April to November, 1865" (Ph.D. dissertation, University of California, Los Angeles, 1964), 381–84.

26. Edward McPherson, *Political History of the United States during the Period of Reconstruction* (Washington: Solomons and Chapman, 1875), 107–9; Salmon P. Chase to Andrew Johnson, May 17, 21, 1865, James E. Sefton, ed., "Chief Justice Chase as an Adviser on Presidential Reconstruction," *Civil War History* 13 (September 1967): 253, 261.

27. Joseph H. Parks, *Joseph E. Brown of Georgia* (Baton Rouge: Louisiana State University Press, 1977), 364–72; John H. Reagan, *Memoirs,* ed. Walter Flavius McCaleb (New York: Neale, 1906), 234, 288–95; Benjamin S. Ewell to Richard S. Ewell, February 7, 1867, Brown-Ewell Papers, Tennessee State Library.

28. Allan D. Candler, ed., *Confederate Records of the State of Georgia,* 6 vols. (Atlanta: Charles P. Byrd, 1909–11), 4:542–44; *Montgomery Daily Advertiser,* December 13, 1865; *Natchez Democrat,* December 19, 1865.

29. *New Orleans Daily Picayune,* January 25, 1867; *Raleigh Daily Sentinel,* April 26, August 21, 1866; *Memphis Daily Appeal,* January 13, 1867; Alexander W. Campbell to William B. Campbell, October 30, 1866, Campbell Family Papers.

30. Duff Green to "Colonel Dawson," October 30, 1866, Duff Green Papers, Southern Historical Collection, University of North Carolina; *Richmond Daily Dispatch,* August 21, 1866; "President Johnson's Policy of Reconstruction,"

DeBow's Review, After the War Series, 1 (January 1866): 19; J. G. de Roulhac Hamilton, ed., *The Papers of Randolph Abbott Shotwell,* 3 vols. (Raleigh: North Carolina Historical Commission, 1929–36), 2:201–2.

31. Alexander H . Stephens to Linton Stephens, April 8, 1866, Stephens Papers, Manhattanville College; Herschel Johnson to Alexander H. Stephens, May 31, 1866, Herschel Johnson Papers; *Richmond Daily Dispatch,* November 27, 1866.

32. Perman, *Reunion without Compromise,* 168–81; Charles Gayarre to James D. B. DeBow, July 4, 1866, James D. B. DeBow Papers, William R. Perkins Library, Duke University; *New Orleans Daily Picayune,* October 2, 1866.

33. Herschel Johnson to Alexander H. Stephens, September 25, 1866, Herschel Johnson Papers; O. M. Roberts, "Experiences of an Unrecognized Senator," *Quarterly Journal of the Texas State Historical Association* 12 (October 1908): 99–100.

34. Frank A. Montgomery, *Reminiscences of a Mississippian in Peace and War* (Cincinnati: Robert Clarke Company Press, 1901), 267–68; *Louisiana Legislative Documents,* 1866, p. 4; *Arkansas Senate Journal,* 1866–67, pp. 50–51.

35. Perman, *Reunion without Compromise,* 234–47; *North Carolina Senate Journal,* 1865–66, pp. 91–104.

36. Benjamin F. Perry to Andrew Johnson, November 10, 1866, Andrew Johnson Papers, Library of Congress.

37. Hannah Arendt, *On Violence* (New York: Harcourt, Brace and World, 1970), 63.

38. For the connection between arbitrary frustration and aggressive behavior, see, for example, Nicholas Pastore, "The Role of Arbitrariness in the Frustration-Aggression Hypothesis," *Journal of Abnormal and Social Psychology* 47 (July 1952): 728–31.

39. For the role of perception in determining whether frustration will produce aggression, see Nicholas Pastore, "A Neglected Factor in the Frustration-Aggression Hypothesis," *Journal of Psychology* 29 (April 1950): 271–79.

40. Rebecca Simms to Mrs. Barnsley, July 27, 1865, cited in Alan Conway, *The Reconstruction of Georgia* (Minneapolis: University of Minnesota Press, 1966), 30; J. E. Hilary Skinner, *After the Storm; or, Jonathan and His Neighbors in 1865–6,* 2 vols. (London: R. Bentley, 1866), 2:45.

41. Frank Vandiver, "The Southerner as Extremist," in Vandiver, ed., *The Idea of the South: Pursuit of a Central Theme* (Chicago: University of Chicago Press, 1964), 46–55.

42. *Nation* 2 (January 4, 1866): 18; Hampton to Lee, July 21, 1866, quoted in Allen W. Moger, "Letters to General Lee after the War," *Virginia Magazine of History and Biography* 64 (January 1956): 32; Early to D. H. Hill, December 4, 1866, quoted in Millard Kessler Bushong, *Old Jube: A Biography of Jubal A. Early* (Boyce, Va.: Carr Publishing Company, 1955), 293. The coolness of the southern response to northern migration should not be exaggerated. Lawrence Powell has recently shown that some southerners welcomed northern capital investment and northern planters. Powell's evidence, however, seems to indicate (contrary to his own conclusions) that a warm reception for the Yankees

was the exception rather than the rule (*New Masters: Northern Planters during the Civil War and Reconstruction* [New Haven: Yale University Press, 1980], 35–72).

43. The fact that most southerners had to change national allegiance three times in less than five years is but another indication of the revolutionary character of the Civil War era. This was particularly true because of the near mystical reverence for the Union in American thought. See Paul C. Nagel, *One Nation Indivisible: The Union in American Thought, 1776–1861* (New York: Oxford University Press, 1964).

44. Thomas North, *Five Years in Texas* (Cincinnati: Elm Street Printing Company, 1871), 188; Alvan C. Gillem to Joseph Smith Fowler, May 1, 1866, Joseph Fowler Papers, Southern Historical Collection, University of North Carolina.

45. A. C. Greene, "The Durable Society: Austin in the Reconstruction," *Southwestern Historical Quarterly* 72 (April 1969): 499; Paige E. Mulhollan, "The Arkansas General Assembly of 1866 and Its Effect on Reconstruction," *Arkansas Historical Quarterly* 20 (Winter 1961): 339.

46. Jeanie Chew Young to Louisa Wharton, January 16, 1866, Edward C. Wharton Papers, Department of Archives, Louisiana State University; *Florida House Journal,* 1866, pp. 9–10; Glenn Clift, ed., *The Private War of Lizzie Hardin* (Frankfort: Kentucky Historical Society, 1963), 246.

47. Alvin F. Sanborn, ed., *Reminiscences of Richard Lathers* (New York: Grafton Press, 1907), 250; William Physick Zuber, *My Eighty Years in Texas* (Austin: University of Texas Press, 1971), 230; *House Reports,* 39th Cong., 1st sess., No. 30, p. 151.

48. E. Merton Coulter, "Slavery and Freedom in Athens, Georgia, 1860–1866," *Georgia Historical Quarterly* 49 (September 1965): 285; James E. Sefton, *The United States Army and Reconstruction, 1865–1877* (Baton Rouge: Louisiana State University Press, 1967), 49–50.

49. *Memphis Daily Avalanche,* December 30, 1866. The record of civilian-military relations during Reconstruction was mixed. In many areas, citizens praised the soldiers for bringing order to their communities. Some southerners openly courted the favor of military commanders in order to win assistance against blacks and "northern adventurers." See Elizabeth Custer, *Tenting on the Plains, or General Custer in Kansas and Texas* (New York: Charles L. Webster, 1887), 161–64, 181–82, 229, 241–42; W. McKee Evans, *Ballots and Fence Rails: Reconstruction on the Lower Cape Fear* (Chapel Hill: University of North Carolina Press, 1966), 63–65.

50. Eric Hoffer, *The True Believer: Thoughts on the Nature of Mass Movements* (New York: Harper and Brothers, 1951), 45–46.

51. *Augusta Chronicle and Sentinel,* September 8, 1865; *Charleston Mercury,* December 22, 1866.

52. John Hope Franklin, *The Militant South, 1800–1861* (Cambridge, Mass.: Harvard University Press, 1956), 21, 34, 38–39. In most antebellum riots, the participants used rocks, clubs, knives, and slingshots rather than guns. Reconstruction disturbances are distinguished from earlier ones by the greater firepower of the perpetrators (Feldberg, *Turbulent Era,* 24–25).

53. See the discussion in Desmond P. Ellis, Paul Weinir, and Louie Miller, "Does the Trigger Pull the Finger? An Experimental Test of Weapons as Aggression-Eliciting Stimuli," *Sociometry* 34 (December 1971): 453–65.

54. John C. Gill to Mary A. Gill, July 7, 1865, Harry F. Lupold, ed., "A Union Officer Views the 'Texians,'" *Southwestern Historical Quarterly* 77 (April 1974): 485–86; Vernon Lane Wharton, *The Negro in Mississippi, 1865–1890* (Chapel Hill: University of North Carolina Press, 1965), 216–18.

55. Joe Gray Taylor, *Louisiana Reconstructed, 1863–1877* (Baton Rouge: Louisiana State University Press, 1974), 63–64.

56. Bruce, *Violence and Culture,* 73–80; Jack B. Scroggs, "Southern Reconstruction: A Radical View," *Journal of Southern History* 24 (November 1958): 408–9; George E. Spencer to Grenville M. Dodge, August 1, 1865, Stanley P. Hirshon, *Grenville M. Dodge: Soldier, Politician, and Railroad Pioneer* (Bloomington: Indiana University Press, 1967), 129.

57. *House Executive Documents,* 40th Cong., 2d sess., No. 57, p. 26; *House Reports,* 39th Cong., 1st sess., No. 30, p. 8; Otto H. Olsen, *Carpetbagger's Crusade: The Life of Albion Winegar Tourgée* (Baltimore: Johns Hopkins University Press, 1965), 54–55. The attempt here is not to argue that Tourgée's account is accurate (indeed, it smacks of exaggeration if not fabrication). Rather, the Tourgée incident illustrates how sensitive many conservative southerners were to charges about continued persecution and disorder in their region.

58. Thomas B. Alexander, *Political Reconstruction in Tennessee* (Nashville: Vanderbilt University Press, 1950), 57–68; Robert H. White, ed., *Messages of the Governors of Tennessee,* 8 vols. (Nashville: Tennessee Historical Commission, 1952–72), 5:535, 555.

59. E. P. Upton to William Pitt Fessenden, December 24, 1866, William Fessenden Papers, Library of Congress; Lewis E. Parsons to Andrew Johnson, August 29, 1865, Lewis Parsons Papers, Alabama Department of Archives and History; George F. Price to Henry P. Wade, October 20, 1866, Letters Received, Department of Tennessee, 1863–67, Record Group 393, National Archives.

60. Samuel L. Sumner to W. D. Whipple, October 22, 1866, Letters Received, Department of Tennessee, 1863–67, RG 393, NA; Ulysses S. Grant to Edwin M. Stanton, January 29, 1867, McPherson, *History of Reconstruction,* 298.

61. Perman, *Reunion without Compromise,* 145–55.

62. *Raleigh Daily Sentinel,* December 14, 1865; Wade Hampton to Andrew Johnson, August 25, 1865, Charles E. Cauthen, ed., *Family Letters of Three Wade Hamptons* (Columbia: University of South Carolina Press, 1953), 140–41.

Chapter 2: The Specter of Saint-Domingue

1. Cleveland, *Stephens,* 721; *House Reports,* 39th Cong., 1st sess., No. 30, p. 178.

2. Sidney Andrews, *The South since the War,* ed. David Donald (Boston: Houghton Mifflin, 1971), 154; *Charleston Daily Courier,* September 16, 1865.

3. Andrews, *South since the War,* 22; Alexis de Tocqueville, *Democracy in America,* 2 vols. (New York: Alfred A. Knopf, 1945), 1:370.

4. Kenneth Rayner to William A. Graham, September 4, 1865, J. G. de Rouhac Hamilton and Max R. Williams, eds., *Papers of William A. Graham,* 6 vols. (Raleigh: North Carolina Division of Archives and History, 1957–76), 6:350; Joseph C. Carter, ed., *Magnolia Journey: A Union Veteran Revisits the Former Confederate States* (University: University of Alabama Press, 1974), 127–28.

5. My analysis of race relations during Reconstruction follows the fine work of Leon Litwack and James Roark, both of whom argue that the death of slavery killed paternalism. Roark takes into account signs of survival and other ambiguities in the question but finally concludes: "Plantations survived, but plantation life was transformed." He overstates the case and his own evidence points to signs of continuity as well as change. See Litwack, *Been in the Storm So Long: The Aftermath of Slavery* (New York: Alfred A. Knopf, 1979), 193–99; Roark, *Masters without Slaves: Southern Planters in the Civil War and Reconstruction* (New York: W. W. Norton, 1977), 143–48, 197–209.

6. James D. B. DeBow to Benjamin F. Perry, October 12, 1865, *DeBow's Review,* After the War Series, 1 (January 1866): 7; Alexander H. Stephens to Montgomery Blair, February 5, 1867, Blair Family Papers, Library of Congress; James Lusk Alcorn to Amelia Glover Alcorn, August 26, 1865, James L. Alcorn Papers, Southern Historical Collection, University of North Carolina.

7. *Augusta Daily Constitutionalist,* September 14, 1866; Candler, ed., *Confederate Records of Georgia,* 4:359–62.

8. Trowbridge, *Desolated States,* 78–79, 134–35, 423; Farrar B. Conner to Lemuel P. Conner, November 30, 1866, Lemuel P. Conner Papers, Department of Archives, Louisiana State University; Isaac Erwin Diary, January 3, 1866, typescript, ibid.; Flavellus G. Nicholson Diary-Journal, January 22, 1866, typescript, Mississippi Department of Archives and History.

9. *House Executive Documents,* 39th Cong., 1st sess., No. 2, p. 16; Browne to Howell Cobb, March 20, 1866, quoted in Conway, *Reconstruction of Georgia,* 109; Mitchell to Joseph E. Davis, May 6, 1866, Lise Mitchell Papers, Howard-Tilton Memorial Library, Tulane University.

10. Gordon W. Allport, *The Nature of Prejudice* (Cambridge, Mass.: Addison-Wesley, 1954), 178–81; Howard J. Ehrlich, *The Social Psychology of Prejudice* (New York: Wiley, 1973), 21–31; Andrews, *South since the War,* 87; *Natchez Democrat,* December 28, 1865; J. Fraser Mathewes to Benjamin F. Perry, August 21, 1865, Benjamin Perry Papers, Alabama Department of Archives and History.

11. *Charleston Daily Courier,* July 25, 1865; Litwack, *Been in the Storm So Long,* 358–63; "Will the Negro Relapse into Barbarism?" *DeBow's Review,* After the War Series, 3 (February 1867): 179.

12. Litwack, *Been in the Storm So Long,* 255–61; Charles C. Soule to O. O. Howard, September 8, 1865, Letters Received, Bureau of Refugees, Freedmen and Abandoned Lands (BRFAL), 1865–72, RG 105, NA, microcopy 752, roll 17; *House Executive Documents,* 40th Cong., 2d sess., No. 57, p. 83; John William

De Forest, *A Union Officer in the Reconstruction,* ed. James M. Croushore and David Morris Potter (New Haven: Yale University Press, 1948), 28–29.

13. Allen Grimshaw, *Racial Violence in the United States* (Chicago: Aldine, 1969), 254–69, 490.

14. A. Toomer Porter, *Led On! Step by Step: Scenes from Clerical, Military, Education, and Plantation Life in the South, 1826–1898* (New York: G. P. Putnam's Sons, 1898), 192–93; John Witherspoon DuBose, *Alabama's Tragic Decade: Ten Years of Alabama, 1865–1874,* ed. James K. Greer (Birmingham: Webb Book Company, 1940), 33; Trowbridge, *Desolated States,* 239.

15. George A. Custer to Zachariah Chandler, January 14, 1866, Zachariah Chandler Papers, Library of Congress; Andrew Jackson Hamilton to Andrew Johnson, July 24, 1865, Andrew Johnson Papers; J. B. Rawles to O. D. Greene, November 21, 1866, Letters Received, Department of Tennessee, 1863–67, RG 393, NA; Thomas J. Wood to Benjamin G. Humphreys, June 4, 1866, Benjamin Humphreys Papers, Mississippi Department of Archives and History.

16. Roger L. Ransom and Richard Sutch, *One Kind of Freedom: The Economic Consequences of Emancipation* (Cambridge, England: Cambridge University Press, 1977), 56–80, 94–99; Roark, *Masters without Slaves,* 131–36, 141–43, 152–55, 157–70; Jonathan M. Wiener, *Social Origins of the New South: Alabama, 1860–1885* (Baton Rouge: Louisiana State University Press, 1978), 3–28, 35–73.

17. Orrin McFadden to Nathaniel Burbank, July 15, 1866, Philip Sheridan Papers, Library of Congress; N. B. Blanton to A. F. Hayden, August 31, 1866, Letters Received, Department of the Gulf, 1865–66, RG 393, NA; David G. Harris Books, November 24, 1865, Southern Historical Collection, University of North Carolina.

18. E. Whittlesey to O. O. Howard, April 4, 1866, Letters Received, BRFAL, RG 105, NA, microcopy 752, roll 29; John Young to Jane Young Simpson, November 30, 1865, William Dunlap Simpson Papers, William R. Perkins Library, Duke University.

19. C. M. Hamilton to S. L. McHenry, March 31, 1866, T. W. Osborne to O. O. Howard, May 8, 1866, Letters Received, BRFAL, RG 105, NA, microcopy 752, roll 27; W. T. Faircloth to Jonathan Worth, January 22, 1867, Worth Papers, Southern Historical Collection, University of North Carolina; Philip H. Sheridan to J. A. Rawlins, November 4, 1866, Sheridan Papers.

20. *House Reports,* 39th Cong., 1st sess., No. 30, pp. 10, 42, 59, 83; Philip H. Sheridan to Ulysses S. Grant, January 25, 1867, McPherson, *History of Reconstruction,* 298n.

21. Allen Grimshaw, "Urban Racial Violence in the United States: Changing Ecological Considerations," *American Journal of Sociology* 66 (September 1960): 110.

22. Donald P. Hartmann, "Influence of Symbolically Modeled Instrumental Aggression and Pain Cues on Aggressive Behavior," *Journal of Personality and Social Psychology* 11 (March 1969): 280–88; Seymour Feshback, William B. Stiles, and Edward Bitter, "The Reinforcing Effect of Witnessing Aggression," *Journal of Experimental Research in Personality* 2 (May 1967): 133–39.

23. Whitelaw Reid, *After the War: A Tour of the Southern States, 1865–1866,* ed. C. Vann Woodward (New York: Harper & Row, 1965), 84; John Richard Dennett, *The South as It Is, 1865–1866,* ed. Henry M. Christman (New York: Viking Press, 1965), 137; A. E. Niles to H. W. Smith, July 19, 1866, Letters Received, BRFAL, 1865–72, RG 105, NA, microcopy 752, roll 36.

24. *Augusta Daily Chronicle and Sentinel,* August 16, 1866; John Graham (?) to James M. Comly, February 5, 1866, James Comly Papers, Ohio Historical Society; Trowbridge, *Desolated States,* 270–71.

25. John Wallace, *Carpetbag Rule in Florida: The Inside Workings of the Reconstruction of Civil Government in Florida after the Close of the Civil War* (Gainesville: University of Florida Press, 1964), 24–25; *Richmond Daily Dispatch,* February 15, 1867.

26. William W. Hooper to James Buchanan, February 9, 1866, James Buchanan Papers, Historical Society of Pennsylvania; "The State of the Country," *DeBow's Review,* After the War Series, 1 (February 1866): 139–40; *New Orleans Times,* October 22, 1866.

27. David McCrae, *The Americans at Home* (New York: E. P. Dutton, 1952), 340; Fleming, *Civil War and Reconstruction in Alabama,* 446–48.

28. R. M. Smith to Stephen Duncan, December 3, 1865, Stephen Duncan Correspondence, Department of Archives, Louisiana State University; *Jackson Daily Clarion,* December 19, 1865; Kate McKinley Taylor to Middleton Pope Barrow, August 29, 1865, Barrow Papers; Mansfield French to J. B. Steedman, September 5, 1865, American Missionary Association Archives, Georgia, Dillard University.

29. *Flake's Weekly Bulletin* (Galveston), October 11, 1865; Sanford Barker to Benjamin F. Perry, July 10, September 8, 1865, Benjamin Perry Papers, Alabama Department of Archives and History; Childs, ed., *Journal of Henry Ravenel,* 258.

30. *Wilmington* (N.C.) *Daily Journal,* November 25, 1865; *Charleston Daily Courier,* October 28, 1865.

31. Evans, *Ballots and Fence Rails,* 23; John MacRae to Donald MacRae, June 22, 1865, Hugh MacRae Papers, William R. Perkins Library, Duke University; Dennett, *South as It Is,* 32–33; *Georgia Senate Journal,* 1865–66, p. 257; Reid, *After the War,* 213–14.

32. John W. Rutledge to Benjamin F. Perry, July 9, 1865, Benjamin Perry Papers, Southern Historical Collection, University of North Carolina; A. Gillespie to William Sharkey, July 29, 1865, William Sharkey Papers, Mississippi Department of Archives and History; *New Orleans Daily Picayune,* October 19, 1866; Childs, ed., *Journal of Henry Ravenel,* 245–46, 251.

33. H. Hanslow to Benjmain G. Humphreys, October 31, 1865, Andrew Johnson Papers; Pamela Cunningham to Benjamin C. Yancey, July 24, 1865, Benjamin Yancey Papers, Southern Historical Collection, University of North Carolina; A. M. Waddell to William W. Holden, June 18, 1865, William Holden Papers, North Carolina Department of Archives and History.

34. *House Executive Documents,* 40th Cong., 2d sess., No. 57, p. 34; *Charleston Daily Courier,* February 12, 1866; W. J. Abdill to G. M. Bascom, February 14, 1866, Letters Received, Department of Tennessee, 1863–67, RG 393, NA.

35. That bloody insurrection would surely follow emancipation had long been a staple argument of proslavery spokesmen. See Bruce, *Violence and Culture,* 114–36.

36. Dan T. Carter, "The Anatomy of Fear: The Christmas Day Insurrection Scare of 1865," *Journal of Southern History* 42 (August 1976): 351–57; Litwack, *Been in the Storm So Long,* 199–205, 425–30. A bloody uprising of Jamaican blacks in 1865 added to these apprehensions.

37. Samuel Agnew Diary, November 22, 1865, typescript, Southern Historical Collection, University of North Carolina; Andrews, *South since the War,* 36; J. Madison Wells to Andrew Johnson, July 29, 1865, Andrew Johnson Papers.

38. Erwin Diary, September 15, 1866; *Arkansas Gazette* (Little Rock), September 18, 1866; *Raleigh Daily Sentinel,* January 14, 1867. Dan Carter has found evidence of insurrection rumors in sixty counties and a half dozen parishes by November 1865. My research indicates the panic was even more widespread. Nor did these fears fade away at the end of 1865. Mississippi experienced similar scares in 1866 and 1867, and such apprehensions were never entirely absent from the Reconstruction South. Reported black uprisings served as a convenient pretext for white violence against Negroes. See Carter, "Anatomy of Fear," 348.

39. Rupert Sargent Holland, ed., *Letters and Diary of Laura Towne; Written from the Sea Islands of South Carolina, 1862–1884* (Cambridge, Mass.: Riverside Press, 1912), 165; Rev. S. H. Chester, "African Slavery As I Knew It in Southern Arkansas," *Tennessee Historical Magazine* 9 (October 1925): 181–82; Trowbridge, *Desolated States,* 375, 408.

40. Agnew Diary, November 3, 26, 1865; *Memphis Daily Appeal,* November 30, 1865; *Jackson Daily Clarion,* December 20, 1865.

41. *House Reports,* 39th Cong., 1st sess., No. 30, p. 30.

42. Agnew Diary, November 24, 1865; C. J. Pope to Lewis E. Parsons, December 11, 1865, Lewis Parsons Papers, Alabama Department of Archives and History; *Friar's Point* (Miss.) *Coahomian,* December 1, 1865; Petition of Colored Citizens of Apalachicola, Florida, to William H. Seward, January 25, 1866, Letters Received, BRFAL, 1865–72, RG 105, NA, microcopy 752, roll 19; Susan P. Lee, *Memoirs of William Nelson Pendleton* (Philadelphia: J. B. Lippincott, 1893), 410.

43. Carl Schurz to Andrew Johnson, August 29, September 4, 1865, William L. Sharkey to Johnson, August 20, 28, 30, 1865, Andrew Johnson Papers; *American Annual Cyclopedia and Register of Important Events, 1865* (New York: D. Appleton, 1866), 582–84; hereinafter cited as *Annual Cyclopedia.*

44. Various letters in Parsons Papers, September–December 1865; Thomas J. Moore and John C. Anderson to Benjamin F. Perry, September 27, 1865, Perry Papers, Alabama Department of Archives and History; Holden to Andrew Johnson, July 15, 1866, Elizabeth Gregory McPherson, ed., "Letters from North Carolina to Andrew Johnson," *North Carolina Historical Review* 27 (July 1950): 360–61.

45. E.R.S. Canby to Adjutant General, Washington, April 10, 1866, Letters

Received, Department of the Gulf, 1865–66, RG 393, NA; Thomas J. Wood to Benjamin G. Humphreys, December 20, 1865, January 8, 1866, Humphreys Papers; *House Executive Documents,* 39th Cong., 1st sess., No. 2, p. 36.

46. *Senate Executive Documents,* 39th Cong., 2d sess., No. 6, pp. 55, 113; *House Reports,* 39th Cong., 1st sess., No. 30, pp. 208, 227; *House Executive Documents,* 39th Cong., 1st sess., No. 70, p. 208.

47. Litwack, *Been in the Storm So Long,* 274–78; Charles Phillips to Kemp P. Battle, December 17, 1866, Battle Family Papers, Southern Historical Collection, University of North Carolina; Claude Elliott, "The Freedmen's Bureau in Texas," *Southwestern Historical Quarterly* 56 (July 1952): 6n.

48. Hortense Powdermaker, "The Channeling of Negro Aggression by the Cultural Process," *American Journal of Sociology* 48 (May 1943): 750–58; Herbert Shapiro, "Afro-American Responses to Race Violence during Reconstruction," *Science and Society* 36 (Summer 1972): 165–68; Edwin Fuller to Jones Fuller, September 14, 1865, Fuller-Thomas Papers, William R. Perkins Library, Duke University.

49. Fragmentary reports of outrages are scattered throughout the Freedmen's Bureau Records (RG 105) in the National Archives. Contemporary newspapers also published occasional statistical information. The lack of reliable quantitative data should make scholars wary both of trying to make sweeping generalizations about Reconstruction disorders and of drawing broad conclusions about regional violence.

50. John A. Carpenter, "Atrocities in the Reconstruction Period," *Journal of Negro History* 47 (October 1962): 234–47.

51. John Dollard, *Caste and Class in a Southern Town* (New Haven: Yale University Press, 1937), 368–71.

52. Andrews, *South since the War,* 28, 100, 219–20; George B. Farrar to Maggie Knighton, January 12, 1867, Josiah Knighton Papers, Department of Archives, Louisiana State University; *Daily Mississippi Clarion and Standard* (Jackson), June 14, 1866.

53. There is substantial disagreement over whether group conflict is more likely to become violent when group relationships are intimate or distant. The paradox of black-white relations in the South was that they were both at the same time. See Lewis Coser, *The Functions of Social Conflict* (New York: Free Press, 1956), 67–72; Harry Kaufman and Alan M. Marcus, "Aggression as a Function of Similarity between Aggressor and Victim," *Perceptual and Motor Skills* 20 (June 1965): 1013–20.

54. Cash, *Mind of the South,* 40.

55. *Raleigh Daily Sentinel,* September 25, 1866.

56. Ted Robert Gurr, *Why Men Rebel* (Princeton: Princeton University Press, 1970), 155–59, 168–77; Berkowitz, *Aggression,* 90–102; Buss, *Psychology of Aggression,* 198–203.

57. Gregory Bateson, "The Frustration-Aggression Hypothesis and Culture," *Psychological Review* 68 (July 1941): 350–55.

58. Dennett, *South as It Is,* 4–6; *House Executive Documents,* 39th Cong., 2d sess., No. 72, p. 3.

59. *House Executive Documents,* 39th Cong., 2d sess., No. 72, pp. 3–62; *New York Herald,* April 19, 1866.

60. *House Executive Documents,* 39th Cong., 2d sess., No. 72, pp. 4–7, 9, 11, 64; *Richmond Daily Dispatch,* April 20, 21, 1866.

61. Brown, *Strain of Violence,* 5, 205–18; Feldberg, *Turbulent Era,* 33–53.

62. H. Otto Dahlke, "Race and Minority Riots: A Study of the Typology of Violence," *Social Forces* 30 (May 1952): 419–25.

63. *New Orleans Daily Picayune,* August 31, 1865; *Montgomery Daily Advertiser,* August 16, 1866; *Richmond Daily Dispatch,* February 23, 1867.

64. William Faulkner, *The Unvanquished* (New York: Random House, 1938), 229.

Chapter 3: The Memphis Race Riot

1. Available secondary accounts of the Memphis riot ignore the modern aspects of this disturbance and focus too narrowly on causes without examining closely the course of the rioting itself. See Jack D. L. Holmes, "The Underlying Causes of the Memphis Race Riot of 1866," *Tennessee Historical Quarterly* 17 (September 1958): 195–221; Holmes, "The Effects of the Memphis Race Riot of 1866," *West Tennessee Historical Society Papers* 12 (1958): 58–79; James Gilbert Ryan, "The Memphis Riots of 1866: Terror in a Black Community during Reconstruction," *Journal of Negro History* 62 (July 1977): 243–58.

2. For suggestive remarks on the causes of twentieth-century racial disturbances, see Stanley Lieberson and Arnold R. Silverman, "The Precipitants and Underlying Conditions of Race Riots," *American Sociological Review* 30 (December 1965): 893–96; Bryan T. Downes, "Social and Political Characteristics of Riot Cities: A Comparative Study," *Social Science Quarterly* 49 (December 1968): 504–20.

3. Franklin, *Militant South,* 43; Gerald Capers, *The Biography of a River Town, Memphis: Its Heroic Age* (Chapel Hill: University of North Carolina Press, 1965), 162–63; Trowbridge, *Desolated States,* 333–35.

4. Reid, *After the War,* 426; Peter Eltinge to Kate Eltinge, March 18, 1866, Eltinge-Lord Family Papers, William R. Perkins Library, Duke University; John E. Smith to Elihu Washburne, December 8, 1865, Elihu Washburne Papers, Library of Congress; *Memphis Daily Post,* April 8, 1866.

5. Capers, *Biography of a River Town,* 163–64, 174–77; *Memphis Daily Appeal,* December 20, 1865; Trowbridge, *Desolated States,* 336; Alexander, *Reconstruction in Tennessee,* 50–51, 54–57. Overcrowding is a common characteristic of twentieth-century cities where civil disorders have occurred (Seymour C. Spilerman, "Causes of Racial Disturbances: A Comparison of Alternative Explanations," *American Sociological Review* 35 [August 1970]: 627–49).

6. W. C. Dunlap to Andrew Johnson, March 8, 1866, Andrew Johnson Papers; *Memphis Argus,* May 23, 1865; *Memphis Daily Commercial,* April 18, 1866. For examples of the role that reporting of black crime has played in modern racial conflicts, see Elliot Rudwick, *Race Riot at East St. Louis, July 2,*

1917 (Carbondale: University of Southern Illinois Press, 1964), 211–14; Arthur I. Waskow, *From Race Riot to Sit-In: 1919 and the 1960s* (Garden City, N.Y.: Doubleday, 1966), 22–23, 25, 110–11.

7. *Memphis Morning Post,* January 17, February 9, 1866; *Memphis Daily Avalanche,* January 13, 1866; Harry Wilcox Pfanz, "Soldiering in the South during Reconstruction, 1865–1877" (Ph.D. dissertation, Ohio State University, 1958), 56–57.

8. Capers, *Biography of a River Town,* 106–18; *House Reports,* 39th Cong., 1st sess., No. 101, pp. 90–91, 135, 191. The relationship between the blacks and the Irish contained all the elements commonly thought necessary to produce aggression. Both groups were highly visible and there was extensive contact and competition between them and substantial perceived differences in values and behavior (Berkowitz, *Aggression,* 168–77).

9. Capers, *Biography of a River Town,* 180–81; *Memphis Daily Argus,* May 16, August 12, 1866; George Stoneman to George H. Thomas, May 3, 1866, Telegrams Sent, Department of Tennessee, 1865–66, RG 393, NA: *Memphis Daily Appeal,* November 12, 14, 1865.

10. Feldberg, *Turbulent Era,* 104–5; Waskow, *From Race Riot to Sit-In,* 209–18; William R. Morgan and Terry N. Clark, "The Causes of Racial Disorders: A Grievance-Level Explanation," *American Sociological Review* 38 (October 1973): 611–24.

11. *House Reports,* 39th Cong., 1st sess., No. 101, pp. 156–58, 164, 326–27, 366–71; *Memphis Daily Argus,* October 15, 1865, February 23, 1866; *Memphis Daily Appeal,* December 15, 1865; *Memphis Daily Avalanche,* February 1, April 19, 1866.

12. *Memphis Daily Appeal,* December 10, 22, 1865, February 10, 1866; William L. Porter to J. G. Kappner, February 4, 1866, Letters Sent, Department of Tennessee, 1864–66, RG 393, NA; Holmes, "Causes of the Memphis Riot," 209–15; *Memphis Daily Post,* April 26, 1866.

13. Holmes, "Causes of the Memphis Riot," 215–20; *Memphis Daily Appeal,* December 29, 1865, January 14, 25, February 15, 1866; *Memphis Daily Post,* February 27, March 17, April 13, 1866; John E. Smith to William D. Whipple, January 9, 1866, Smith to W. L. Porter, January 26, 1866, Letters Received, Adjutant General's Office, Main Series, 1861–70, RG 94, NA, microcopy 619, roll 505.

14. *Memphis Daily Appeal,* December 1, 17, 1865, February 4, 1866; *Memphis Daily Commercial,* December 17, 19, 20, 1865; Special Orders, No. 84, Department of Tennessee, April 30, 1866, RG 393, NA.

15. *Memphis Daily Appeal,* December 14, 1865, March 6, 1866; *Memphis Daily Avalanche,* January 7, 14, February 9, 1866.

16. *Memphis Daily Appeal,* December 19, 21, 1865, February 22, March 1, April 20, 1866; *Memphis Daily Post,* February 25, March 18, 1866.

17. *Memphis Argus,* September 20, 1865; *Memphis Daily Commercial,* January 24, 1866; *Memphis Daily Avalanche,* January 4, 1866.

18. Report of Colonel Charles F. Johnson and Major F. W. Gilbraith on Memphis Riot, May n.d., 1866, Letters Received, BRFAL, 1865–72, RG 105,

NA, microcopy 752, roll 33; *House Reports,* 39th Cong., 1st sess., No. 101, pp. 64, 67–68, 245, 358.

19. *Memphis Daily Post,* May 3, 1866; *House Reports,* 39th Cong., 1st sess., No. 101, pp. 10, 88–89, 115–16, 182, 315–16, 318, 324, 346, 351; *Memphis Daily Appeal,* May 2, 1866; *Memphis Daily Avalanche,* May 2, 1866; *Memphis Daily Argus,* May 2, 1866. Secondary accounts erroneously begin with the traffic accident of May 1 rather than with the clashes between soldiers and police on the evening of April 30. See, for example, Holmes, "Causes of the Memphis Riot," 195.

20. *House Reports,* 39th Cong., 1st sess., No. 101, pp. 62–259, 295–96, 313–14, 336–58. From this point on the rioters fit the classic stereotype of the mob as an irrational body whose members lose their individuality in a carnival of fury against property and persons (Elias Canetti, *Crowds and Power* [New York: Viking Press, 1963], 19–20).

21. *House Reports,* 39th Cong., 1st sess., No. 101, pp. 50, 80, 122, 148–49, 227, 256, 355–56, 358–59.

22. *Memphis Daily Commercial,* May 3, 1866, quoted in *Arkansas State Gazette* (Little Rock), May 12, 1866; *House Reports,* 39th Cong., 1st sess., No. 101, 89–90, 119–20, 159, 194–248, 315, 322; *Memphis Daily Argus,* May 3, 1866.

23. *House Reports,* 39th Cong., 1st sess., No. 101, pp. 51–52, 80, 246, 359; *House Executive Documents,* 39th Cong., 1st sess., No. 122, p. 2.

24. *House Reports,* 39th Cong., 1st sess., No. 101, pp. 91–123, 161–200, 235, 247, 250, 320–51.

25. Alfred McClung Lee and Norman D. Humphrey, *Race Riot* (New York: Dryden Press, 1943), 102–3; Ralph W. Conant, "Rioting, Insurrection and Civil Disobedience," *American Scholar* 37 (Summer 1968): 423–26.

26. *House Reports,* 39th Cong., 1st sess., No. 101, pp. 34–36, 136, 153, 176, 260–62, 336, 341, 353; *Senate Executive Documents,* 39th Cong., 2d sess., No. 6, pp. 132–33. As measured by modern indexes of riot severity, Memphis was one of the worst riots in American history (Jules J. Wanderer, "Index of Riot Severity and Some Correlates," *American Journal of Sociology* 74 [March 1969]: 503).

27. *House Reports,* 39th Cong., 1st sess., No. 101, pp. 4, 50, 275, 361–62; William L. Porter to Sheriff, Shelby County, May 3, 1866, Stoneman to Mayor and City Council, Memphis, May 3, 1866, Letters Sent, Department of Tennessee, 1864–66, RG 393, NA; Witt Morgan to Elihu Washburne, May 11, 1866, Washburne Papers. James Gilbert Ryan severely censures Stoneman and the military for failing to stop the bloodshed, but his judgments are based more on hindsight than on evidence. His imputation of racist motives to Stoneman is particularly unfounded (Ryan, "Memphis Riots," 246–47, 251–53).

28. Stoneman to Thomas, May 3, 1866, Letters Sent, Department of Tennessee, 1864–66, RG 393, NA; Clinton B. Fisk to Elihu Washburne, June 21, 1866, Washburne Papers.

29. John E. Smith to William D. Whipple, January 9, 1866, Letters Received, Adjutant General's Office, Main Series, 1861–70, RG 94, NA, microcopy 619, roll 505; *Memphis Daily Avalanche,* May 3, 4, 1866; *Memphis Daily*

Argus, May 3, June 27, 1866; Ewing O. Tade to Michael E. Streiby, May 21, 1866, Joe M. Richardson, ed., "The Memphis Race Riot and Its Aftermath," *Tennessee Historical Quarterly* 24 (Spring 1965): 64–65.

30. *Memphis Daily Appeal,* May 3, 4, 1866; *Memphis Daily Avalanche,* May 5, 10, 1866.

31. *House Reports,* 39th Cong., 1st sess., No. 101, pp. 54–56, 74–77; Stoneman to Elihu Washburne, June 2, 1866, Washburne Papers; George H. Thomas to Adjutant General, Washington, June 15, 1866, Letters Received, Adjutant General's Office, Main Series, 1861–70, RG 94, NA, microcopy 619, roll 520; James Speed to Andrew Johnson, July 13, 1866, ibid.; Thomas to Ulysses S. Grant, August 15, 1866, Edwin M. Stanton Papers, Library of Congress.

32. Elihu Washburne to Thaddeus Stevens, May 24, 1866, Stevens Papers; *House Reports,* 39th Cong., 1st sess., No. 101, p. 5; *Memphis Daily Avalanche,* August 1, 7, 1866.

33. E. S. Garrett to Elihu Washburne, June 15, 1866, Washburne Papers; *Congressional Globe,* 39th Cong., 1st sess., 4159–60, 4266; *Chicago Tribune,* May 5, 1866; *Nation* 2 (May 15, 1866): 616.

34. For two remarkable parallels as well as insightful discussions of the causes of modern racial disorders, see Rudwick, *Race Riot at East St. Louis,* 217–33, and William M. Tuttle, Jr., *Race Riot: Chicago in the Red Summer of 1919* (New York: Atheneum, 1970), 263–65.

Chapter 4: New Orleans and the Emergence of Political Violence

1. All students of Reconstruction in Louisiana are deeply indebted to Joe Gray Taylor's skillful unraveling of the labyrinthine politics in that state in *Louisiana Reconstructed.*

2. Benjamin F. Flanders to Abraham Lincoln, January 16, 1864, Nathaniel P. Banks to Lincoln, March 6, 1864, Michael Hahn to Lincoln, September 24, November 5, 1864, Abraham Lincoln Papers, Library of Congress.

3. Taylor, *Louisiana Reconstructed,* 58–62; Walter McGehee Lowrey, "The Political Career of James Madison Wells," *Louisiana Historical Quarterly* 31 (October 1948): 995–1047; R. King Cutler to Carl Schurz, September 5, 1865, Michael Hahn to Schurz, September 6, 1865, Andrew Johnson Papers.

4. Taylor, *Louisiana Reconstructed,* 71–73; *Annual Cyclopedia,* 1865, pp. 512–13.

5. Henry Clay Warmoth, *War, Politics, and Reconstruction: Stormy Days in Louisiana* (New York: Macmillan, 1930), 32–33, 41–42; J. W. Shaffer to Lyman Trumbull, December 28, 1865, Lyman Trumbull Papers, Library of Congress; James G. Taliaferro to Susan B. Alexander, July 15, August 1, 1865, James Taliaferro Letters, Department of Archives, Louisiana State University.

6. *New Orleans Tribune,* August 23, September 23, December 13, 14, 1865; *New Orleans Times,* February 5, March 16, 1866.

7. Andrew Johnson to J. Madison Wells, March 2, 1866, Hugh Kennedy to Andrew Johnson, March 17, 1866, John T. Monroe to Johnson, March 17, 1866, Andrew Johnson Papers; E.R.S. Canby to Assistant Adjutant General, Divi-

sion of the Gulf, March 18, 1866, Letters Sent, Department of the Gulf, 1865–66, RG 393, NA.

8. John S. Kendall, *History of New Orleans,* 3 vols. (Chicago: Lewis Publishing Company, 1922), 2:305; *New Orleans Daily Picayune,* May 3, 1866; *House Executive Documents,* 39th Cong., 2d sess., No. 68, pp. 271, 277, 287.

9. Thomas W. Conway to Hugh Kennedy, July 7, 13, 17, 1865, Andrew Johnson Papers; *New Orleans Tribune,* June 22, 30, July 9, 19, 20, 26, 30, 1865. Although the riot has been briefly treated by several scholars, there is no adequate comprehensive account of the affair. Donald Reynolds ("The New Orleans Riot of 1866, Reconsidered," *Louisiana History* 5 [Winter 1964]: 5–28) narrowly focuses on disproving the old charge that the riot was a radical Republican conspiracy. Joe Gray Taylor (*Louisiana Reconstructed,* 106–13) deals with the notion of a radical conspiracy and ignores white perceptions or the motivation of the mob. Both Reynolds and Taylor depend entirely on published sources and contemporary newspapers and thereby miss some important information contained in several manuscript collections. Although sound in recognizing the importance of social and racial tension in causing the riot, Giles Vandal ("The Origins of the New Orleans Riot of 1866, Revisited," *Louisiana History* 22 [Spring, 1981]: 135–65) illustrates the limitations of quantification for this topic.

10. *New Orleans Times,* February 5, 1866; *New Orleans Daily Crescent,* February 14, July 7, 10, 28, 1866. It would be tempting to conclude that the fury of the New Orleans mob resulted from the white paranoia about black men raping white women, but there is no evidence to sustain such an inference. Both Wilbur Cash and Allen Trelease have argued that emancipation intensified the southern white rape complex, but I could find little evidence to sustain this assertion. Although the subject demands further study, the rape complex seems to be a far more important factor in the lynchings of the later nineteenth century than in the violence of the Reconstruction period (Cash, *Mind of the South,* 117–19; Allen W. Trelease, *White Terror: The Ku Klux Klan Conspiracy and Southern Reconstruction* [New York: Harper & Row, 1971], xx–xxi).

11. Kendall, *New Orleans,* 2:305–6; Taylor, *Louisiana Reconstructed,* 81–82, 103–4.

12. *Speech of the Honorable H. C. Warmoth at Economy Hall, on the 21st of March, 1866* (N.p.: N.p., n.d.), 1–8; Warmoth, *War, Politics, and Reconstruction,* 46–47; *New Orleans Tribune,* March 23–25, 1866.

13. Henry Clay Warmoth Diary, March 22, 28, 29, April 3, 29, June 30, 1866, Henry Warmoth Papers, Southern Historical Collection, University of North Carolina; J. Madison Wells to Andrew Johnson, April n.d., 1866, Andrew Johnson Papers; *New Orleans Tribune,* April 21, June 28, 1866.

14. Taylor, *Louisiana Reconstructed,* 104–5; *House Reports,* 39th Cong., 2d sess., No. 16, p. 262; Cyrus Hamlin to Hannibal Hamlin, June 25, August 19, 1865, Hannibal Hamlin Papers, University of Maine, Orono.

15. *House Reports,* 39th Cong., 2d sess., No. 16, pp. 56–57, 486–91, 500–503, 509–11, 513–14, 540–41; *New York Times,* July 16, 1866. The best analysis of this question is in Reynolds, "New Orleans Riot," 17–20. Reynolds is too quick

to assert that Republicans in Washington did not give direct approval and support to the plan to reconvene the convention. A more judicious conclusion would be the Scotch verdict, not proven.

16. Gordon Granger to Edmund Cooper, June 11, 1866, Albert Voorhies to J. A. Rozier, July 13, 1866, Andrew Johnson Papers; *New Orleans Daily Picayune,* July 8, 9, 11, 12, 21, 1866; *New Orleans Times,* April 24, June 11, 27, 28, 30, July 3, 8, 15, 1866.

17. *New Orleans Daily Picayune,* April 29, 1866; *New Orleans Times,* February 15, 24, 1866.

18. Admittedly the evidence on aggressive cues is largely experimental, and these conclusions should be applied to society, and particularly to the nineteenth century, with caution. See Russel G. Geen and Edgar C. O'Neal, "Activation of Cue-Elicited Aggression by General Arousal," *Journal of Personality and Social Psychology* 11 (March 1969): 289–92; Leonard Berkowitz, "Frustrations, Comparisons and Other Sources of Emotion Arousal as Contributors to Social Unrest," *Journal of Social Issues* 28, no. 1 (1972): 88–90.

19. *House Executive Documents,* 39th Cong., 2d sess., No. 68, pp. 72–75; Albert Voorhies to J. A. Rozier, July 13, 1866, Andrew Johnson Papers; *New Orleans Daily Picayune,* July 13, 28, 29, 1866. Recent secondary accounts of the New Orleans riot underestimate the intensity of conservative leaders' feeling about the convention. See Taylor, *Louisiana Reconstructed,* 105–6; Reynolds, "New Orleans Riot," 21–22.

20. *House Executive Documents,* 39th Cong., 2d sess., No. 68, pp. 6–7, 270; *House Reports,* 39th Cong., 2d sess., No. 16, pp. 5, 79.

21. *New Orleans Times,* July 28, 29, August 3, 1866; *House Reports,* 39th Cong., 2d sess., No. 16, pp. 16, 23–24, 32, 38–39, 66, 312, 476; F. D. Richardson to St. John R. Liddell, July 31, 1866, Moses Liddell Papers, Department of Archives, Louisiana State University.

22. This statement was incorrect. Wells had issued a proclamation calling for elections to fill vacancies in the convention. Judge Howell, president pro tem of the convention, had issued the proclamation for the meeting of July 30, 1866.

23. *House Executive Documents,* 39th Cong., 2d sess., No. 68, pp. 4, 56–57, 64, 97–98, 273–74.

24. Joseph Green Dawson, III, "The Long Ordeal: Army Generals and Reconstruction in Louisiana, 1862–1877" (Ph.D. dissertation, Louisiana State University, 1978), 70; *House Executive Documents,* 39th Cong., 2d sess., No. 68, pp. 4–5, 86–87, 269. Historians have long debated whether Stanton's failure to show Baird's dispatch to President Johnson was part of a political scheme. There is little evidence to sustain the often-repeated charge that Stanton was willing to provoke violence in New Orleans in order to undermine presidential Reconstruction, but he certainly exercised bad judgment, and his later testimony on the matter fails to exonerate him from charges of misfeasance if not malfeasance.

25. Acting Assistant Adjutant General, New Orleans, to G. C. Getchell, July 29, 1866, Letters Sent, Department of the Gulf, 1865–66, RG 393, NA.

26. *House Reports,* 39th Cong., 2d sess., No. 16, pp. 142–43, 190, 202–3, 210,

218, 285–86, 325–26, 384; *New Orleans Times,* July 30, 1866; *New Orleans Daily Picayune,* July 30, 1866; *House Executive Documents,* 39th Cong., 2d sess., No. 68, pp. 26, 112, 166.

27. *House Executive Documents,* 39th Cong., 2d sess., No. 68, pp. 6, 88, 168, 274; *House Reports,* 39th Cong., 2d sess., No. 16, pp. 221–22, 237–38.

28. *House Executive Documents,* 39th Cong., 2d sess., No. 68, pp. 39, 47, 177–78; *House Reports,* 39th Cong., 2d sess., No. 16, pp. 1, 11–12, 87, 232–33.

29. *House Executive Documents,* 39th Cong., 2d sess., No. 68, pp. 13–14, 39–42, 44, 49, 96–97, 114, 120–21, 142–43, 150–53, 175–96, 219, 244, 256, 264, 282–84; *House Reports,* 39th Cong., 2d sess., No. 16, pp. 188, 204–5, 253–54, 327, 401; *New Orleans Daily Picayune,* August 1, 1866; *New Orleans Times,* July 31, 1866; *Grand Jury Report and Evidence Taken by Them in Reference to the Great Riot in New Orleans, Louisiana, July 30th, 1866* (New Orleans: Daily Crescent Office, 1866?), 3–5, 14.

30. Unlike Memphis, conflicts between police and blacks were not the primary cause for the fighting, but in a pattern similar to several twentieth-century race riots, police not only failed to protect blacks' lives but cooperated with the white mob. Most nineteenth-century police forces received no riot training and had been singularly ineffective in controlling violence during the antebellum period (Allen D. Grimshaw, "Actions of Police and the Military in American Race Riots," *Phylon* 26 [Fall 1963]: 271–89; Feldberg, *Turbulent Era,* 27).

31. *House Executive Documents,* 39th Cong., 2d sess., No. 68, pp. 109–88; *New Orleans Times,* July 31, 1866.

32. *House Executive Documents,* 39th Cong., 2d sess., No. 68, pp. 47, 51, 91–285; Cyrus Hamlin to Hannibal Hamlin, August 19, 1866, Hamlin Papers; *House Reports,* 39th Cong., 2d sess., No. 16, pp. 77, 145; Warmoth Diary, July 30, 1866.

33. This description fits the classic picture of the mob participant as a rootless person on the margins of society. Young and restless individuals who are less likely to have a family or an economic stake in society are also more likely to become rioters (George Wade and James C. Davies, "Riots and Rioters," *Western Political Quarterly* 10 [December 1957]: 864–74).

34. *House Executive Documents,* 39th Cong., 2d sess., No. 68, pp. 55–56, 182, 216, 232–34, 240–41, 267; *House Reports,* 39th Cong., 2d sess., No. 16, pp. 171, 178, 215; Richard Taylor, *Destruction and Reconstruction: Personal Experiences of the Late War,* ed. Richard B. Harwell (New York: Longmans, Green, 1955), 305.

35. *House Executive Documents,* 39th Cong., 2d sess., No. 68, pp. 42, 51–52, 58–59, 110–238, 265; *Grand Jury Report,* 3.

36. At this stage, the riot resembled disturbances such as the Homestead and Pullman strikes in which the leadership of the mob was well-defined (in this case the police) and the targets of violence were likewise clear (in this case the convention delegates) (Peter Lupsha, "On the Theories of Urban Violence," *Urban Affairs Quarterly* 4 [March 1969]: 273–77).

37. *House Executive Documents,* 39th Cong., 2d sess., No. 68, pp. 44–45, 49–

50, 80, 108–229, 248, 258, 284, 286; *House Reports,* 39th Cong., 2d sess., No. 16, pp. 29, 35–36, 103, 120, 333, 356–57, 492; *Grand Jury Report,* 9.

38. *House Executive Documents,* 39th Cong., 2d sess., No. 68, pp. 46, 111, 121–23, 129–30, 165–217, 236, 242; *House Reports,* 39th Cong., 2d sess., No. 16, pp. 8, 70, 88, 106–7, 155, 164, 193, 341; Warmoth Diary, July 30, 1866.

39. *House Executive Documents,* 39th Cong., 2d sess., No. 68, pp. 70–71, 262–64, 285–86.

40. Ibid., 45–46, 176, 179, 219, 237, 242, 249, 257, 263, 288–89; *House Reports,* 39th Cong., 2d sess., No. 16, p. 478.

41. *House Executive Documents,* 39th Cong., 2d sess., No. 68, pp. 5–6, 8, 88, 160–61; General Orders, No. 60, Department of the Gulf, July 30, 1866, RG 393, NA; *New Orleans Daily Crescent,* August 1, 1866.

42. See Wanderer, "Index of Riot Severity," 503.

43. *House Executive Documents,* 39th Cong., 2d sess., No. 68, pp. 32, 93, 177. The casualty list reveals a preponderance of gunshot injuries and head wounds.

44. *House Executive Documents,* 39th Cong., 2d sess., No. 68, p. 2–3, 9, 11, 13–14, 22–23. Whatever the president's intentions, the strategy backfired, and Republicans accused him of intentionally releasing incomplete texts of Sheridan's telegrams to friendly newspapers (*The New Orleans Riot—Its Official History* [New York: Tribune Tracts, 1866?], 8).

45. *House Executive Documents,* 39th Cong., 2d sess., No. 68, p. 11; *New Orleans Daily Crescent,* August 1, 1866; James Harrison to Andrew Johnson, July 31, 1866, Jacob Parker to Johnson, July 31, 1866, Andrew Johnson Papers; O. O. Howard to Baird, August 8, 1866, Letters Sent, BRFAL, 1865–72, RG 105, NA, microcopy 742, roll 2.

46. *House Executive Documents,* 39th Cong., 2d sess., No. 68, pp. 12, 14–16, 75–77.

47. *New Orleans Times,* July 31, 1866; *New Orleans Daily Picayune,* July 31, August 1, 2, 4, 14, 1866; *Grand Jury Report,* 2–3; Jacob Barker to William A. Barker, October 2, 1866, Howard-Tilton Memorial Library, Tulane University.

48. "A Union Man" to Benjamin F. Butler, August 24, 1866, Benjamin Butler Papers, Library of Congress; *New Orleans Riot—Its Official History,* 8; *The New Orleans Riot: "My Policy" in Louisiana* (Washington: Daily Morning Chronicle Print, 1866), 13–15.

49. Thomas J. Durant to Henry Clay Warmoth, December 18, 31, 1866, January 21, 1867, Michael Hahn to Warmoth, December 27, 1866, Warmoth Papers; *House Reports,* 39th Cong., 2d sess., No. 16, pp. 4, 16–31, 37–40, 44–47, 51–54 (Majority and Minority Reports of the Committee); *New Orleans Times,* September 7, December 11, 22, 23, 25, 27, 1866, February 13, 1867.

50. *New York Tribune,* July 31, August 1, 1866; *Chicago Tribune,* August 27, 1866; *New York Independent,* August 30, 1866.

51. *Raleigh Daily Sentinel,* August 3, 6, 1866; *Richmond Daily Dispatch,* August 1, 2, 8, 1866; *Mobile Tribune,* n.d., quoted in *Raleigh Weekly North-Carolina Standard,* August 15, 1866. Despite the stridency of these voices, more thoughtful commentators saw the riot, in the words of a Memphis edi-

tor, as a political "godsend to Radicalism" (*Memphis Daily Argus,* August 1, 1866).

52. McPherson, *History of Reconstruction,* 137.

53. *Chicago Tribune,* August 1, 4, 1866; Joseph Holt to Henry Clay Warmoth, August 1, 1866, Warmoth Papers; *New York Tribune,* August 4, 1866; *Nation* 3 (August 30, 1866): 173.

54. Cyrus Hamlin to Hannibal Hamlin, August 19, 1866, Hamlin Papers.

Chapter 5: Military Reconstruction: The Triumph of Jacobinism

1. *Harper's Weekly* 10 (October 20, 1866): 658; *New York Tribune,* October 26, 1866.

2. Alfred R. Conkling, *Life and Letters of Roscoe Conkling* (New York: Charles L. Webster, 1889), 271–75; *Chicago Tribune,* August 10, 1866.

3. *Chicago Tribune,* February 26, 1867; *Nation* 3 (November 8, 1866): 371; *Harper's Weekly* 11 (February 23, 1867): 114.

4. *New York Times,* February 11, 1867; *Congressional Globe,* 39th Cong., 2d sess., pp. 116–17, 211, 251–52, 351, 560, 596, 815, 1076–77, 1098, 1178, 1186–90, 1213, 1375–77, 1462.

5. *Charleston Daily Courier,* March 15, 1867; Alexander Stephens to Walter R. Staples, March 8, 1867, Alexander Stephens Papers, Library of Congress; C. P. Culver to Jefferson Davis, March 12, 1867, Dunbar Rowland, ed., *Jefferson Davis, Constitutionalist: His Letters, Papers, and Speeches,* 10 vols. (Jackson: Mississippi Department of Archives and History, 1923), 7:92; Augusta J. Evans to P.G.T. Beauregard, March 30, 1867, P.G.T. Beauregard Papers, William R. Perkins Library, Duke University.

6. Charles F. Haner and Patricia Ann Brown, "Clarification of the Instigation to Action Concept in the Frustration-Aggression Hypothesis," *Journal of Abnormal and Social Psychology* 51 (September 1955): 204–6.

7. Gurr, *Why Men Rebel,* 24–30, 46, 52–56, 60–64. This is not to say that relative deprivation always produces violence or revolution, and white southerners responded to military Reconstruction in a variety of ways. Indeed, serious disorders did not begin until a year after Congress established military rule.

8. *Mississippi House Journal,* 1870, pp. 62–63; Notes for a speech at a Republican meeting in Rockingham County, North Carolina, March n.d., 1867, Thomas Settle Papers, Southern Historical Collection, University of North Carolina.

9. Robert M. T. Hunter, Plea to Congress for the relief of Virginia, n.d., 1868, Robert M. T. Hunter Papers, Alderman Library, University of Virginia; Benjamin G. Humphreys to Oscar J. E. Stuart, August 8, 1867, John B. S. Dimitry Papers, William R. Perkins Library, Duke University.

10. Gurr, *Why Men Rebel,* 66–73, 109–11.

11. John C. Moncure to his wife, January 6, 1870, Moncure Papers, J. Fair Hardin Collection, Department of Archives, Louisiana State University; *Ra-*

leigh Daily Sentinel, June 9, 1868; Alfred Huger to Thomas L. Wells, October 3, 1868, Daniel E. Huger Smith, Alice R. Huger, and Arney R. Childs, eds., *Mason-Smith Family Letters, 1860–1868* (Columbia: University of South Carolina Press, 1950), 277.

12. *Raleigh Daily Sentinel,* February 24, July 13, 1869; Stephens, *Constitutional View,* 2:639; *Augusta Daily Constitutionalist,* June 28, 1868; *Charleston Mercury,* March 16, 1868; Virginia Mason, *The Public Life and Diplomatic Correspondence of James M. Mason* (New York: Neale, 1906), 584.

13. Gurr, *Why Men Rebel,* 183–92.

14. Brown, *Strain of Violence,* 7; Edward A. Pollard, *The Lost Cause Regained* (New York: G. W. Carleton, 1868), 102; White League Resolutions, n.d., 1874, St. Martin Parish, Louisiana, Alexandre De Clouet Papers, Department of Archives, Louisiana State University.

15. George Rose, *The Great Country; or, Impressions of America* (London: Tinsley Brothers, 1868), 181; Childs, ed., *Journal of Henry Ravenel,* 348; *Charleston Mercury,* May 8, 1868.

16. Howard N. Rabinowitz, *Race Relations in the Urban South, 1865–1890* (New York: Oxford University Press, 1978); John W. Blassingame, *Black New Orleans, 1860–1880* (Chicago: University of Chicago Press, 1973), 173–201; Bushong, *Old Jube,* 295–96.

17. William Hand Browne to Alexander H. Stephens, July 9, 1873, Stephens Papers, Library of Congress; Agnew Diary, May 16, 1868; W. W. Sparks to James G. Taliaferro, April 5, 1868, Taliaferro Papers; *Mobile Daily Advertiser and Register,* November 30, 1867.

18. *Congressional Record,* 43d Cong., 1st sess., p. 421; *Augusta Daily Chronicle and Sentinel,* July 30, 1874.

19. Louis Hartz, *The Liberal Tradition in America* (New York: Harcourt, Brace, 1955), 167–72; C. Vann Woodward, *American Counterpoint: Slavery and Racism in the North-South Dialogue* (Boston: Little, Brown, 1971), 243–46; George M. Fredrickson, *The Black Image in the White Mind: The Debate on Afro-American Character and Destiny, 1817–1914* (New York: Harper & Row, 1971), 61–67.

20. *Jackson Daily Clarion,* January 8, 1868; Petition of Committee of Citizens of Columbia, South Carolina, to Jeremiah S. Black, September 20, 1867, Black Papers, Library of Congress; *Charleston Daily Courier,* September 21, 1868; Gurr, *Why Men Rebel,* 125–26. The tendency to see the future as one persecution piled on another led one South Carolinian to muse on the possibility of Congress passing a law requiring his daughter to marry a Negro (G. I. Crafts to William Porcher Miles, April 13, 1867, William P. Miles Papers, Southern Historical Collection, University of North Carolina).

21. Herschel V. Johnson to E. W. Johnson, May 15, 17, 1867, Herschel Johnson Papers; [George Fitzhugh,] "Exodus from the South," *DeBow's Review,* After the War Series, 3 (April and May 1867): 353, 355; *Charleston Mercury,* April 13, May 11, 1868.

22. H. H. Goodloe, "The Negro Problem," *Southern Magazine* 14 (April 1874): 373–76; Ethelred Philips to James Jones Philips, July 5, 1868, James

Jones Philips Papers, Southern Historical Collection, University of North Carolina; *Tuscaloosa* (Ala.) *Independent Monitor,* January 5, April 27, 1869.

23. Robert L. Dabney, *Defense of Virginia* (New York: E. J. Hale and Son, 1867); Ethelred Philips to James Jones Philips, December 1, 1867, Philips Papers; Augusta *Daily Constitutionalist,* August 16, 1868.

24. See, for example, *Raleigh Daily Sentinel,* February 25, March 6, 1867; *Montgomery Daily Advertiser,* February 27, March and April 1867.

25. James Longstreet to Robert E. Lee, June 8, 1867, James Longstreet Papers, William R. Perkins Library, Duke University; Parks, *Brown,* 376–80; Lillian A. Pereyra, *James Lusk Alcorn: Persistent Whig* (Baton Rouge: Louisiana State University Press, 1966), 90–93; *South Carolina House Journal,* Special Session, 1868, p. 9; *Proceedings of the Constitutional Convention of South Carolina, 1868* (Charleston: Denny and Perry, 1868), 45–55.

26. Hill, *Hill,* 740–47; William Gilmore Simms to William Hawkins Ferris, March 7, 1867, Mary C. Simms Oliphant, Alfred Taylor Odell, and T. C. Duncan Eaves, eds., *The Letters of William Gilmore Simms,* 5 vols. (Columbia: University of South Carolina Press, 1952–56), 5:22; Alexander H. Stephens to Herschel V. Johnson, July 17, 1867, Johnson to John G. Westmoreland, June 29, 1867, Herschel Johnson Papers.

27. My analysis of the debate among southern conservatives about political strategy is heavily dependent on three excellent treatments of the subject: Perman, *Reunion without Compromise,* 304–36; William C. Harris, *Presidential Reconstruction in Mississippi* (Baton Rouge: Louisiana State University Press, 1967), 237–45; Jack P. Maddex, Jr., *The Virginia Conservatives, 1867–1879* (Chapel Hill: University of North Carolina Press, 1970), 46–52.

28. The fatal flaw in political inaction was its divisive influence on conservative whites. As proponents of this strategy, such as Herschel Johnson of Georgia, recognized, "many good men take a different view. So that our division will work our ruin" (Johnson to Alexander H. Stephens, July 18, 1867, Stephens Papers, Library of Congress).

29. *Tallahassee Sentinel,* April 2, 1867; *Raleigh Daily Sentinel,* June 10, 1867; *Richmond Daily Dispatch,* April 2, 1867.

30. *Raleigh Daily Sentinel,* February 7, 1868; *Vicksburg Daily Herald,* April 7, 1868; *Augusta Daily Constitutionalist,* July 18, 1867.

31. *Charleston Daily Courier,* March 26, 1867; Jerrell H. Shofner, *Nor Is It Over Yet: Florida in the Era of Reconstruction, 1863–1877* (Gainesville: University Presses of Florida, 1974), 159–61; *Jackson Daily Clarion,* June 2, 1868.

32. *Jackson Daily Clarion,* July 3, 1868; *Louisville Courier-Journal,* June 29, 1870; *Memphis Daily Appeal,* July 9, 1875, January 9, 1876.

33. Myrta Lockett Avary, ed., *Dixie after the War* (New York: Doubleday, Page, 1906), 282–93; Francis Butler Simkins and Robert Hilliard Woody, *South Carolina during Reconstruction* (Chapel Hill: University of North Carolina Press, 1932), 83–85. Attempts to bring blacks and whites into more formal political alliances likewise failed. The Union Reform Movement in South Carolina in 1870 did not pick up enough black support to defeat the regular Republicans, and the Louisiana Unification Movement of 1873 could not overcome

the pervasiveness of white racism (R. H. Woody, "The South Carolina Election of 1870," *North Carolina Historical Review* 8 [April 1931]: 168–86; T. Harry Williams, *Romance and Realism in Southern Politics* [Athens: University of Georgia Press, 1961], 17–43).

34. John McCardell, *The Idea of a Southern Nation: Southern Nationalists and Southern Nationalism, 1830–1860* (New York: W. W. Norton, 1979), 277–335; Benjamin H. Hill to Mrs. M. D. Cody, October 30, 1868, Katherine Mood Chapman, ed., "Some Benjamin Harvie Hill Letters," *Georgia Historical Quarterly* 47 (September 1963): 312–13; Wade Hampton to John Mullaly, March 31, 1867, Cauthen, ed., *Letters of Three Wade Hamptons,* 142–43.

35. Joseph E. Brown speech, August 19, 1868, Joseph E. Brown Papers, Hargrett Collection, Ilah Dunlap Little Memorial Library, University of Georgia; *Tallahassee Sentinel,* August 27, 1868.

36. William Hidell to Alexander H. Stephens, August 4, 1868, Stephens Papers, Library of Congress.

37. *Atlanta Constitution,* August 20, 1868; *Tuscaloosa Independent Monitor,* September 1, 1868.

38. Trelease, *White Terror,* 3–27. The Klan's prescript is found in Walter L. Fleming, ed., *Documentary History of Reconstruction,* 2 vols. (Cleveland: Arthur H. Clark, 1906–7), 2:347–49.

39. Alexander, *Reconstruction in Tennessee,* 149–52; *Memphis Daily Post,* July 9, September 21, 1867; J. W. Brown to William G. Brownlow, June 18, 1867, William Brownlow Papers, Tennessee State Library. See also Trelease, *White Terror,* 28ff.

40. *Memphis Evening Post,* July 31, August 14, 1868; A.O.P. Nicholson to Andrew Johnson, July 24, 1868, Andrew Johnson Papers; John Lea to William G. Brownlow, July 29, 1868, White, ed., *Messages of the Governors of Tennessee,* 5:620; Trelease, *White Terror,* 28–46.

41. Trelease, *White Terror,* 49–64.

42. Ibid., 49–98; William C. Harris, *The Day of the Carpetbagger: Republican Reconstruction in Mississippi* (Baton Rouge: Louisiana State University Press, 1979), 172–75.

43. Trelease, *White Terror,* 92–109; S. L. Love to Mrs. S. V. Young, August 9, 1868, Burton-Young Papers, Southern Historical Collection, University of North Carolina; Charles W. Ramsdell, *Reconstruction in Texas* (New York: Columbia University Press, 1910), 230–31.

44. *Arkansas Daily Gazette* (Little Rock), August 31, 1868; Paul L. De Clouet Diary, De Clouet Papers, September 20, 1868.

45. W. M. Porcher et al. to Robert K. Scott, September 6, 1868, John B. Hubbard to Scott, September 3, 1868, Robert Scott Papers, South Carolina Archives; Milledge Luke Bonham to Scott, August 19, 1868, Milledge Luke Bonham Papers, South Caroliniana Library, University of South Carolina.

46. William Cauthorn et al. to William W. Holden, October 31, 1868, William Holden Papers, North Carolina Department of Archives and History; Ralph L. Peek, "Aftermath of Military Reconstruction, 1868–1869," *Florida Historical Quarterly* 43 (October 1964): 129–30, 132–35; Scott to J. Stuart Hanschel et al., September 1, 1868, Andrew Johnson Papers.

47. Trelease, *White Terror,* 149–55; A. E. Buck to C. A. Miller, November 2, 1868, William H. Smith Papers, Alabama Department of Archives and History; *Memphis Evening Post,* September 30, 1868.

48. A. C. Fish to William E. Chandler, August 24, 1868, John M. Morris to Chandler, September 14, 1868, William Chandler Papers; Library of Congress; Joseph Crews to Robert K. Scott, November 2, 1868, Lawrence Cain et al. to Scott, November 2, 1868, Scott Papers; Trelease, *White Terror,* 115–16, 120–24; Shofner, *Nor Is It Over Yet,* 227–28.

49. George Rudé, *The Crowd in History: A Study of Popular Disturbances in France and England, 1730–1848* (New York: Wiley, 1964), 237–58; Pauline Maier, "Popular Uprisings and Civil Authority in Eighteenth-Century America," *William and Mary Quarterly,* 3d ser., 27 (January 1970): 3–35.

50. Trelease, *White Terror,* 116, 154; *Anderson* (S.C.) *Intelligencer,* October 21, 1868; *Charleston Daily Courier,* October 22, 1868.

51. Sebastian Kraft to Robert K. Scott, August 5, 1868, Richard H. Cain to Scott, October 24, 1868, Mrs. John Cochran to Scott, October 27, 1868, Scott Papers.

52. Parks, *Brown,* 427–28; Foster Blodgett to William E. Chandler, September 13, 1868, Chandler Papers.

53. Thomas B. Fitz-Simons, "The Camilla Riot," *Georgia Historical Quarterly* 35 (June 1951): 116–25; *Georgia Senate Journal,* 1868, pp. 353–57; *Augusta Daily Constitutionalist,* September 23, 1868; Linton Stephens to Alexander H. Stephens, September 23, 1868, Stephens Papers, Manhattanville College.

54. *House Executive Documents,* 40th Cong., 3d sess., No. 1, p. 1044; P. James to John Emory Bryant, September 30, 1868, Bryant Papers, William R. Perkins Library, Duke University; *House Miscellaneous Documents,* 40th Cong., 3d sess., No. 52, pp. 12–23.

55. *House Executive Documents,* 40th Cong., 3d sess., No. 1, pp. xix–xx. General Robert Buchanan could find evidence of twenty-five murders, but it is not clear how many of them were related to politics (Buchanan to Adjutant General, Washington, August 19, 1868, Letters Received, AGO, Main Series, 1861–70, RG 94, NA, microcopy 619, roll 609).

56. Constitution and Ritual of the Knights of the White Camellia in Fleming, ed., *Documentary History of Reconstruction,* 2:349–54; *House Miscellaneous Documents,* 41st Cong., 2d sess., No. 154, pt. 2, pp. 321–24; James S. Robertson to Thomas Neill, September 22, 1868, Letters Received, Department of the Gulf, 1866–69, RG 393, NA.

57. *House Miscellaneous Documents,* 41st Cong., 2d sess., No. 154, pt. 1, pp. 74–87, 150–57, 198–211, 218–27, 236–38, 309–12, 319–22, 400–403, 505–7, 521–23, 527–29.

58. Ibid., 41–44, 66–74, 87–90, 135–43, 605–7, 634–42, pt. 2, pp. 154–62; Isaac N. Crawford et al. to Henry Clay Warmoth, August n.d., 1868, Letters Received, AGO, Main Series, 1861–70, RG 94, NA, microcopy 619, roll 609; *New Orleans Daily Picayune,* August 8, 1868.

59. *House Miscellaneous Documents,* 41st Cong., 2d sess., No. 154, pt. 1, pp.

125–32, 309–12, 355–68, 472–76. The information on the Bossier Parish troubles is sketchy. For differing accounts and varying estimates of the casualties, see Taylor, *Louisiana Reconstructed,* 168, and Trelease, *White Terror,* 130.

60. Carolyn E. DeLatte, "The St. Landry Riot: A Forgotten Incident of Reconstruction Violence," *Louisiana History* 17 (Winter 1976): 41–49; *House Miscellaneous Documents,* 41st Cong., 2d sess., No. 154, pt. 1, pp. 416–21, 454–57, 476–80, 495–501, 510–18, pt. 2, pp. 50–65.

61. Warmoth, *War, Politics, and Reconstruction,* 80; W. A. Smallwood to Andrew Johnson, September 6, 1868, Andrew Johnson Papers; *New Orleans Daily Picayune,* August 4, 1868.

62. H. A. Vaught to John R. Ficklen, May 8, 1894, Ficklen Papers, Department of Archives, Louisiana State University; *House Miscellaneous Documents,* 41st Cong., 2d sess., No. 154, pt. 1, pp. 17–28, 119–25, 253–56, pt. 2, pp. 183–200; W. C. Church to John M. Schofield, October 3, 1868, John Schofield Papers, Library of Congress.

63. E. D. Townsend to Robert C. Buchanan, August 10, 1868, Lovell H. Rousseau to Andrew Johnson, September 26, 1868, Andrew Johnson Papers.

64. *New Orleans Daily Picayune,* September 23, 25, 1868; Melinda Meek Hennessey, "Race and Violence in Reconstruction New Orleans: The 1868 Riot," *Louisiana History* 20 (Winter 1979): 78–79.

65. *House Miscellaneous Documents,* 41st Cong., 2d sess., No. 154, pt. 1, pp. 1–16, 44–51, 175–86, 245–53, 719–25; Hennessey, "Race and Violence in New Orleans," 81–82; Stephen B. Packard to William E. Chandler, October 20, 1868, Chandler Papers; Michael Hahn to Elihu Washburne, October 21, 1868, Washburne Papers.

66. Hennessey, "Race and Violence in New Orleans," 85–89; *House Miscellaneous Documents,* 41st Cong., 2d sess., No. 154, pt. 1, pp. 28–41, 58–62, 238–45, 743–68.

67. Frederick T. Wilson, "Federal Aid in Domestic Disturbances," *Senate Documents,* 57th Cong., 2d sess., No. 209, pp. 122–23, 144–45; John A. Rawlins to Ulysses S. Grant, August 4, 1868, George G. Meade to Rawlins, October 17, 1868, Letters Received, AGO, Main Series, 1861–70, RG 94, NA, microcopy 619, roll 609; John M. Schofield to Lovell H. Rousseau, October 27, 29, 1868, Andrew Johnson to Rousseau, October 31, 1868, Andrew Johnson Papers.

68. Thomas Settle to R. M. Pearson, August 8, 1868, Settle Papers; Joseph E. Brown to William E. Chandler, October 8, 1868, Chandler Papers.

69. W. F. DeKnight to William Stone, November 6, 1868, Joseph Crews to Robert K. Scott, November 4, 1868, Scott Papers; *House Miscellaneous Documents,* 40th Cong., 3d sess., No. 52, pp. 27–32, 35–38, 49–123; Francis H. Smith to Elihu B. Washburne, November 8, 1868, Washburne Papers.

70. *House Miscellaneous Documents,* 41st Cong., 2d sess., No. 154, pt. 1, pp. 62–66, 143–47, Appendix, x–xxxiii; DeClouet Diary, November 3, 1868.

71. *Tuscaloosa Independent Monitor,* August 17, 1869, November 15, 1870; E. John Ellis to Thomas C. W. Ellis, January 29, 1870, Ellis Papers.

Chapter 6: The Origins of the Counterrevolution

1. Gurr, *Why Men Rebel,* 144–48; Seymour Martin Lipset, *Political Man: The Social Bases of Politics* (Garden City, N.Y.: Doubleday, 1960), 79–80.

2. Gurr, *Conditions of Civil Violence,* 9; John P. Spiegel, "Psychological Factors in Riots—Old and New," *American Journal of Psychiatry* 125 (September 1968): 283–84.

3. George N. Appell, "The Structure of District Administration, Anti-Administration Activity and Political Instability," *Human Organization* 25 (Winter 1966), 312–20.

4. C. C. Clay to Jeremiah S. Black, July 11, 1869, Black Papers; Alexander H. Stephens, *The Reviewers Reviewed* (New York: D. Appleton, 1872), 243–44.

5. *Annual Cyclopedia,* 1868, p. 512; John C. Moncure to his wife, January 6, 1870, Moncure Papers.

6. *Wilmington* (N.C.), *Daily Journal,* April 25, 1873; Pollard, *Lost Cause Regained,* passim; A. Dudley Mann to Jefferson Davis, March 2, 1870, Rowland, ed., *Davis, Constitutionalist,* 7:261.

7. Gunnar Myrdal, *An American Dilemma: The Negro Problem and Modern Democracy,* 2 vols. (New York: Harper & Row, 1944), 1:446–48; Dollard, *Caste and Class in a Southern Town,* 50–51.

8. *Atlanta Constitution,* October 23, 1868; *Raleigh Daily Sentinel,* September 10, 1875.

9. Leonard Berkowitz and Dennis A. Knurek, "Label-Mediated Hostility Generalization," *Journal of Personality and Social Psychology* 13 (November 1969): 200–206.

10. *Raleigh Daily Sentinel,* August 6, 1869.

11. *Vicksburg Daily Herald,* September 22, 1868; *Tuscaloosa Independent Monitor,* August 17, 1869; Faulkner, *The Unvanquished,* 256–57. The social isolation of carpetbaggers could extend even to the second and third generations. In William Faulkner's fictional town of Jefferson, the spinster Miss Burden lives alone on the edge of town. Because her grandfather and brother had been Republican leaders during Reconstruction, vile gossip still attaches itself to her name, and even though she lives in the house in which she was born, she remains "a stranger, a foreigner" (Faulkner, *Light in August* [New York: Random House, 1932], 40–41).

12. Dollard, *Caste and Class in a Southern Town,* 60; Cash, *Mind of the South,* 119–20.

13. *Mobile Daily Register,* March 19, 1868; *Shreveport Daily Times,* January 10, 1875; W. S. Chaffin Journal, June 2, 1867, William R. Perkins Library, Duke University.

14. *Daily Arkansas Gazette* (Little Rock), September 4, 20, 1868; *Atlanta Constitution,* July 2, 1869; *Augusta Daily Chronicle and Sentinel,* August 22, 1868.

15. Agnew Diary, July 3, 1873; Herschel V. Johnson to Alexander Stephens, August 29, 1870, Herschel Johnson Papers.

16. Loyal League Catechism, 1867, in Fleming, ed., *Documentary History of Reconstruction,* 2:13–19.

17. Roberta F. Cason, "The Loyal League in Georgia," *Georgia Historical Quarterly* 20 (June 1936): 125–53; Frederick T. Wilson, "Federal Aid in Domestic Disturbances," *Senate Document,* 57th Cong., 2d sess., No. 209, p. 114; *Weekly North Carolina Standard* (Raleigh), November 6, 1867.

18. *Greenville* (S.C.) *Enterprise,* August 14, 1872; *Charleston Daily Courier,* May 29, August 17, 1867; *Augusta Daily Constitutionalist,* August 21, 1868.

19. Trelease, *White Terror,* xxx; Avary, ed., *Dixie after the War,* 263–68.

20. *Vicksburg Daily Herald,* June 26, 1868; *Charleston Daily Courier,* June 9, 1868; H. M. Cely et al. to William Dunlap Simpson, February 15, 1869, Simpson Papers.

21. James E. Sefton, "A Note on the Political Intimidation of Black Men by Other Black Men," *Georgia Historical Quarterly* 52 (December 1968): 443–48; Barbour Lewis to William E. Chandler, November 5, 1868, Chandler Papers.

22. Reports of Outrages and Arrests, June 1866–December 1868, Records of the Assistant Commissioner for the State of North Carolina, BRFAL, 1865–70, RG 105, NA, microcopy 843, roll 33; *Senate Miscellaneous Documents,* 40th Cong., 2d sess., No. 109, pp. 1–8; *House Executive Documents,* 42d Cong., 2d sess., No. 268, pp. 47–49.

23. *House Executive Documents,* 41st Cong., 2d sess., No. 142, p. 14; James H. Starr to William Pitt Fessenden, August 10, 1868, Fessenden Papers; *New Orleans Republican,* March 21, 1871.

24. George Forsyth to Charles Griffin, June 22, 1867, Letterbook, 1867–68, Fifth Military District Papers, William R. Perkins Library, Duke University; O. D. Barrett to Benjamin F. Wade, July 7, 1867, Benjamin Wade Papers, Library of Congress.

25. *Memphis Evening Post,* July 16, 27, 1868; William Hepworth Dixon, *White Conquest,* 2 vols. (London: Chatto & Windus, 1876), 1:330–31.

26. Shofner, *Nor Is It Over Yet,* 103–4; *Columbia Daily Union,* February 24, 1872.

27. *Daily Arkansas Gazette* (Little Rock), September 7, 1869; *Charleston Daily Courier,* October 21, 1869.

28. *Atlanta Constitution,* January 5, 1872; *Memphis Daily Appeal,* May 1, 1871, July 6, 1873; *Jackson Weekly Clarion,* May 1, 1873.

29. Harris, *Day of the Carpetbagger,* 251–53; John Gary to William G. Brownlow, July 8, 1867, Brownlow Papers; George H. Tracy to O. D. Kinsman, July 9, 1867, S. Moore to William H. Smith, July 13, 1867, Smith Papers.

30. Sarah Woolfolk Wiggins, "The 'Pig Iron' Kelley Riot in Mobile, May 14, 1867," *Alabama Review* 23 (January 1970): 45–55; *House Executive Documents,* 40th Cong., 2d sess., No. 342, p. 108; O. L. Shepherd to Acting Assistant Adjutant General, District of Alabama, May 17, 1867, Letters Received, BRFAL, 1865–72, RG 105, NA, microcopy 752, roll 41.

31. *New Orleans Republican,* July 9, December 25, 1870; C. W. Buckley to Elihu B. Washburne, January 9, 1868, Witt Gibbs to Washburne, July 11, 1868, Washburne Papers; Joseph McKee to Thaddeus Stevens, April 16, 1868, Stevens Papers.

32. *House Miscellaneous Documents,* 40th Cong., 3d sess., No. 53, pp. 93–95,

147–57, 171–84, 215–52; Kinsey Jones to William W. Holden, August 23, 1869, Holden Papers.

33. E. Merton Coulter, *The South during Reconstruction, 1865–1877* (Baton Rouge: Louisiana State University Press, 1947), 356–60; *Mobile Daily Register,* November 5, 1872; J. A. Yordy to Charles A. Miller, February 11, 1868, Wager Swayne Papers, Alabama Department of Archives and History; Edward C. Anderson Diary, October 12, 1869, Southern Historical Collection, University of North Carolina.

34. *New Orleans Daily Picayune,* November 11, 16–December 3, 1870; *New Orleans Republican,* November 10–12, 15, 17, 20, 26–December 4, 1870.

35. *Vicksburg Daily Herald,* June 16, 1868; *Mobile Daily Advertiser and Register,* December 27, 1867; John J. Ragin to John H. King, September 9, 1868, King Papers, South Caroliniana Library, University of South Carolina.

36. *Jackson Daily Clarion,* June 20, 1868; *Richmond Daily Dispatch,* June 22, 1869.

37. *House Executive Documents,* 40th Cong., 2d sess., No. 278, p. 36; Edward King, *The Great South,* ed. W. Magruder Drake and Robert R. Jones (Baton Rouge: Louisiana State University Press, 1972), 275; J. B. Killebrew Autobiography, 2 vols., 2:232–33, typescript, Southern Historical Collection, University of North Carolina.

38. Joel Williamson, *After Slavery: The Negro in South Carolina during Reconstruction, 1861–1877* (Chapel Hill: University of North Carolina Press, 1965), 98–100; *House Miscellaneous Documents,* 40th Cong., 2d sess., No. 111, pp. 1–46.

39. *Memphis Daily Post,* May 2, 1867; H. E. Sterkx, "William C. Jordan and Reconstruction in Bullock County, Alabama," *Alabama Review* 15 (January 1952): 68. White Republicans were divided on the effectiveness of economic coercion. Some pictured blacks as cowardly and overly dependent on their employers; others described them as steadfast and brave in the face of overwhelming pressure (Volney Spalding to William E. Chandler, September 1, 1868, Chandler Papers; William Hurter to Wager Swayne, October 10, 1867, Swayne Papers).

40. Ransom and Sutch, *One Kind of Freedom,* 149–71; Harris, *Day of the Carpetbagger,* 371–78, 481–514; Taylor, *Louisiana Reconstructed,* 358–63.

41. Gurr, *Why Men Rebel,* 46–50; Carl Hovland and Robert Sears, "Minor Studies in Aggression, VI: Correlation of Lynchings with Economic Indices," *Journal of Psychology* 9 (April 1940): 301–10; Shofner, *Nor Is It Over Yet,* 235.

42. Robert Somers, *The Southern States since the War,* ed. Malcolm C. McMillan (University: University of Alabama Press, 1965), 17, 60; [Horace Greeley], *Mr. Greeley's Letters from Texas and the Lower Mississippi* (New York: Tribune Office, 1871), 35–38; King, *Great South,* 89.

43. *Annual Cyclopedia,* 1867, p. 314; *Memphis Daily Appeal,* March 16, 1872; *Brookhaven* (Miss.) *Ledger,* November 2, 1876.

44. Somers, *Southern States since the War,* 130, 146; King, *Great South,* 274–75, 303; John Houston Bills Diary, July 30, 1867, typescript, Southern Historical Collection, University of North Carolina; Jones-Smith Plantation Diary, n.d., 1872, Mississippi Department of Archives and History.

45. Hill, *Hill*, 334–49; J. B. Killebrew to Kemp P. Battle, January 15, 1868, Battle Family Papers; Stephen Powers, *Afoot and Alone* (Hartford: Columbian Book Company, 1872), 35–36, 58.

46. Farrar B. Conner to Lemuel P. Conner, May 16, 1867, Conner Papers; *Austin Daily State Journal*, June 22, 1870; Shofner, *Nor Is It Over Yet*, 230.

47. Agnew Diary, November 3, 1868; *Edgefield* (S.C.) *Advertiser*, April 29, 1868; John Q. Anderson, ed., *Brokenburn: The Journal of Kate Stone, 1861–1868* (Baton Rouge: Louisiana State University Press, 1972), 368.

48. Francis B. Simkins, "The Ku Klux Klan in South Carolina, 1868–1871," *Journal of Negro History* 12 (October 1927): 629–39.

49. Hubert Howe Bancroft, *Popular Tribunals*, 2 vols. (San Francisco: History Company Publishers, 1887), 2:507–8, 639–63.

50. *Charleston Daily Courier*, November 29, 1870; Randolph A. Shotwell, "Three Years in Battle and Three Years in Federal Prisons," in Hamilton, ed., *Shotwell Papers*, 2:237–47, 256–57.

51. Otto H. Olsen, "The Ku Klux Klan: A Study in Reconstruction Politics and Propaganda," *North Carolina Historical Review* 39 (Summer 1962): 351–62; *Daily Arkansas Gazette* (Little Rock), April 30, 1871; *Columbia Daily Union*, January 1, 1872.

52. Olsen, "Ku Klux Klan," 342–51; Stephens, *Reviewers Reviewed*, 248–50.

53. Bancroft, *Popular Tribunals*, 1:513–14; Brown, *Strain of Violence*, 56–63.

54. Trelease, *White Terror*, 74, 349–61; *Raleigh Daily Sentinel*, July 1, 1871; *Austin Daily State Journal*, November 23, 1871.

55. Russel G. Geen, "Effects of Frustration, Attack and Prior Training in Aggressiveness upon Aggressive Behavior," *Journal of Personality and Social Psychology* 9 (August 1968): 316–21.

56. John A. Leland, *A Voice from South Carolina* (Charleston: Walker, Evans and Cogswell, 1879), 51–64; Mrs. J. Ward Motte to Robert Motte, September 3, 21, October 20, 22, 1870, Lalla Pelot Papers, William R. Perkins Library, Duke University.

57. Trelease, *White Terror*, 51–52, 199–200; Herbert Shapiro, "The Ku Klux Klan during Reconstruction: The South Carolina Episode," *Journal of Negro History* 49 (January 1964): 47–55; Harris, *Day of the Carpetbagger*, 385–90.

58. Bancroft, *Popular Tribunals*, 1:463, 2:84–140; Richard Maxwell Brown, "American Vigilante Tradition," in Graham and Gurr, eds., *Violence in America*, 148–52; Rudé, *Crowd in History*, 198–204.

59. *House Executive Documents*, 41st Cong., 2d sess., No. 288, pp. 16–19.

60. Feldberg, *Turbulent Era*, 54–75, 81–82, 96–99; Coser, *Functions of Social Conflict*, 33–38, 139–49.

61. Trelease, *White Terror*, 5–6, 28–35, 183–85, 332–33; Shotwell, "Three Years in Battle and Three Years in Federal Prisons," 279–80, 344–51; Brown, *Strain of Violence*, 103–8.

62. Norman R. F. Maier, "The Role of Frustration in Social Movements," *Psychological Review* 49 (November 1942): 586–99; Charles Stearns, *The Black Man of the South and the Rebels* (New York: American News Company, 1872), 455–56.

63. Trelease, *White Terror;* Berkowitz, *Aggression,* 182–85; Lewis A. Coser, *Continuities in the Study of Social Conflict* (New York: Free Press, 1968), 78–81, 93–110.

64. Trelease, *White Terror,* 226–38, 252–60, 310–12; Joe M. Richardson, *The Negro in the Reconstruction of Florida, 1865–1877* (Tallahassee: Florida State University Press, 1965), 167–72.

65. S. A. White et al. to William W. Holden, November 4, 1869, Holden Papers; Trelease, *White Terror,* 246–52; Shofner, *Nor Is It Over Yet,* 228.

66. Pauline Maier, "Revolutionary Violence and the Relevance of History," *Journal of Interdisciplinary History* 2 (Summer 1971): 119–35.

67. Trelease, *White Terror,* 362–80; Shofner, *Nor Is It Over Yet,* 228–34.

68. Max Beloff, *Public Order and Popular Disturbances, 1660–1714* (London: Oxford University Press, 1938), 154–55; Trelease, *White Terror,* 302–10, 318–35.

69. Wiener, *Social Origins of the New South,* 61–66; Trelease, *White Terror,* 242–45; Harris, *Day of the Carpetbagger,* 384–85, 396–98.

70. *Wilmington* (N.C.) *Daily Journal,* March 28, 1869; Ruth Watkins, "Reconstruction in Marshall County," *Publications of the Mississippi Historical Society* 12 (1912): 175–76; Trelease, *White Terror,* 318–35.

71. Henry Lee Swint, *The Northern Teacher in the South, 1862–1870* (Nashville: Vanderbilt University Press, 1941), 107–9, 129–33, 136–42.

72. Trelease, *White Terror,* 192–207; E. G. Robinson to Oscar J. E. Stuart, October 2, 1870, John B. S. Dimitry Papers; J. M. Dennis to John Y. Harris, January 14, 1868, Harris Papers, William R. Perkins Library, Duke University; George Petrie, "William F. Samford," *Transactions of the Alabama Historical Society* 4 (1899–1903): 484.

73. Wayne Guard, *Frontier Justice* (Norman: University of Oklahoma Press, 1949), 149–67.

74. Cash, *Mind of the South,* 116–17; John L. Lewis to Henry Clay Warmoth, July 10, 1868, Andrew Johnson Papers; Shofner, *Nor Is It Over Yet,* 235; Taylor, *Louisiana Reconstructed,* 420–21; Wade Hampton to Jeremiah S. Black, November 11, 1867, Black Papers.

75. Trelease, *White Terror,* 189–92, 261–70, 336–48; Shofner, *Nor Is It Over Yet,* 230.

76. Hall, *Smiling Phoenix,* 78–104; *Charleston Daily Courier,* September 27, 1871; N. J. Watkins, ed., *The Pine and Palm Gathering* (Baltimore: J. D. Ehlers, 1873), 37.

77. *Augusta Daily Constitutionalist,* January 16, 1871; *Louisville Courier-Journal,* February 13, 1872; *Augusta Daily Chronicle and Sentinel,* March 25, 1871.

78. Thomas Ruffin to John K. Ruffin, July 8, 1869, J. G. de Roulhac Hamilton, ed., *The Papers of Thomas Ruffin,* 4 vols. (Raleigh: Edwards & Broughton, 1918–20), 4:225–27; Alexander H. Stephens to William Hidell, January 26, 1869, Stephens Papers, Historical Society of Pennsylvania; Henry S. Foote, Jr., to Carl Schurz, November 13, 1871, Schurz Papers, Library of Congress.

Chapter 7: The Search for a Strategy

1. Trelease, *White Terror;* Harris, *Day of the Carpetbagger,* 381–83; Shofner, *Nor Is It Over Yet,* 226–27.

2. August Meier and Elliott Rudwick, "Black Violence in the 20th Century: A Study in Rhetoric and Retaliation," in Graham and Gurr, eds., *Violence in America,* 307–16; Stearns, *Black Man of the South,* 544–47. Some white Republicans mistakenly believed blacks were timid and cowardly and would never defend themselves against Klan attacks (Victor C. Barringer to Albion W. Tourgée, n.d., 1868, Albion Tourgée Papers, Chautauqua County Historical Society, Westfield, N.Y. [microfilm in Southern Historical Collection, University of North Carolina]; John Patterson Green, *Recollections of the Inhabitants, Localities, Superstitions and Ku Klux Outrages of the Carolinas* [Cleveland: N.p., 1880], 146–47).

3. Lawrence W. Levine, *Black Culture and Black Consciousness: Afro-American Folk Thought from Slavery to Freedom* (New York: Oxford University Press, 1977), 397–98; H. S. Baxham to William W. Holden, March 23, 1869, Holden Papers; George P. Rawick, ed., *The American Slave: A Composite Autobiography,* 19 vols. (Westport, Conn.: Greenwood Press, 1972), 6:136; Stearns, *Black Man of the South,* 404–5.

4. Parks, *Brown,* 432, 437–38; James Longstreet to Alexander H. Stephens, December 31, 1874, Stephens Papers, Library of Congress.

5. Sarah Woolfolk Wiggins, *The Scalawag in Alabama Politics, 1865–1881* (University: University of Alabama Press, 1977), 45–71; Elizabeth Studley Nathans, *Losing the Peace: Georgia Republicans and Reconstruction, 1865–1871* (Baton Rouge: Louisiana State University Press, 1968), 56–78; 129–32; H. L. Carroll to Henry P. Farrow, July 30, 1870, C. H. Hopkins to Farrow, August 12, 1870, Henry P. Farrow Papers, Ilah Dunlap Little Memorial Library, University of Georgia.

6. Carl N. Degler, *The Other South: Southern Dissenters in the Nineteenth Century* (New York: Harper & Row, 1974), 230–63; *Raleigh Daily Sentinel,* January 25, 1868, March 11, 1869.

7. Arendt, *On Violence,* 87; Edward N. Muller, "A Test of a Partial Theory of Potential for Political Violence," *American Political Science Review* 66 (September 1972): 928–59.

8. John Z. Sloan, "The Ku Klux Klan and the Alabama Election of 1872," *Alabama Review* 18 (April 1965): 116–23; Harris, *Day of the Carpetbagger,* 390–96.

9. *North Carolina House Journal,* 1869–70, pp. 17–18; *House Executive Documents,* 41st Cong., 2d sess., No. 288, p. 2; Albion W. Tourgée to Thomas Settle, June 24, 1869, Settle Papers; Tourgée to William W. Holden, June n.d., 1870, July 3, 1869, Holden Papers; Tourgée to Mrs. Tourgée, June 9, 1869, Tourgée Papers.

10. Otis A. Singletary, *Negro Militia and Reconstruction* (Austin: University of Texas Press, 1957), 15–16, 22.

11. *Jackson Weekly Clarion,* March 24, 1870; *Memphis Daily Appeal,* September 26, 1870; *Atlanta Constitution,* July 2, 1870.

12. *Charleston Daily Courier,* September 17, 1870; Williamson, *After Slavery,* 260–66.

13. Trelease, *White Terror,* 175–83; *Memphis Daily Avalanche,* February 24, 1869.

14. A. B. Laws to William W. Holden, July 23, 1868, Manuel W. Robinson to Holden, August 14, 1868, Holden Papers; James W. Osborn to William A. Graham, August 7, 1868, typescript, William Graham Papers, Southern Historical Collection, University of North Carolina; *Raleigh Daily Sentinel,* July 22, 24, August 7, September 7, 17, 1868.

15. *North Carolina House Journal,* 1870–71, pp. 22–30; William M. Moore to William W. Holden, June 24, 1870, Albert H. Darrell, Jr., to Holden, June 27, 1870, W. F. Henderson to Holden, July 9, 1870, Holden to George W. Kirk, August 3, 1870, Holden Papers; Trelease, *White Terror,* 208–25.

16. Powell Clayton, *The Aftermath of the Civil War in Arkansas* (New York: Neale, 1915), 40–41, 68–72; Howard C. Westwood, "The Federals' Cold Shoulder to Arkansas' Powell Clayton," *Civil War History* 26 (September 1980): 241–55.

17. Clayton, *Aftermath of the Civil War in Arkansas,* 119–22; Trelease, *White Terror,* 161–74.

18. *Austin Daily State Journal,* May 8, 19, August 11, November 12, 1870, July 28, 1873; Ann Patton Baenziger, "The Texas State Police during Reconstruction: A Reexamination," *Southwestern Historical Quarterly* 72 (April 1969): 470–91.

19. *Florida House Journal,* 1872, pp. 20–22; *Alabama State Documents,* 1869–70, pp. 5–13; Singletary, *Negro Militia,* 145–47. Allen Trelease is unsparing in his criticism of governors such as Smith who failed to launch vigorous campaigns in their states to suppress the Klan, but it is far easier to criticize than to suggest how state action could have been effective. Given the limited resources, factionalism, and racial tensions within the Republican party, in the absence of federal intervention, terrorism was bound to be at least partially successful (Trelease, *White Terror,* esp. 264–65).

20. *Congressional Globe,* 42d Cong., 1st sess., pp. 367–69, 389–95, 605–9, 653–55.

21. Stephens, *Reviewers Reviewed,* 228–30; *Memphis Daily Appeal,* April 2, 1871; *Wilmington* (N.C.) *Daily Journal,* April 20, 1871.

22. Bruce, *Violence and Culture,* 81–88; *New Orleans Daily Picayune,* August 12, 1868; Powhatten Lockett to Edward Hawthorne Moren, January 3, 1876, Moren Papers, Alabama Department of Archives and History.

23. *Jackson Weekly Clarion,* July 11, 1872, November 19, 1874; *Charleston Daily Courier,* November 27, 1871; C. Minaham to George P. Davis, February 17, 1872, David Davis Papers, Chicago Historical Society. Republican editors pointed out that the Democrats had barely raised their voices during the Klan terror, but they now protested the imprisonment of men who had committed numberless atrocities against both races. Conservative polemics were not only

false but lacked any sense of proportion (*Austin Daily State Journal,* November 10, 1871; *Columbia Daily Union,* May 10, 1872).

24. Edward C. Wade to Henry P. Farrow, May 6, 1873, Farrow Papers; A. T. Akerman to John E. Bryant, July 28, 1871, Letters Sent, Department of Justice: Instructions to U.S. Attorneys and Marshals, 1867–1904, RG 60, NA, microcopy 701, roll 2; Everette Swinney, "Suppressing the Ku Klux Klan: The Enforcement of the Reconstruction Amendments, 1870–1874" (Ph.D. dissertation, University of Texas, 1966), 184–88, 194–99.

25. A. T. Akerman to D. T. Corbin, November 10, 1871, Akerman to John A. Minnis, February 11, 1871, Letters Sent, Department of Justice: Instructions to U.S. Attorneys and Marshals, 1867–1904, RG 60, NA, microcopy 701, roll 2; Everette Swinney, "Enforcing the Fifteenth Amendment," *Journal of Southern History* 28 (May 1962): 205–18.

26. Sefton, *Army and Reconstruction,* 167–68; Pfanz, "Soldiering in the South," 536–64; John Robert Kirkland, "Federal Troops in the South Atlantic States during Reconstruction, 1865–1877" (Ph.D. dissertation, University of North Carolina, 1967), 220–21, 236–39.

27. Jonathan Worth to Andrew Johnson, December 31, 1867, Jonathan Worth Papers, Southern Historical Collection, University of North Carolina; *Augusta Daily Chronicle and Sentinel,* January 29, 1870; George H. Williams to John A. Minnis, January 25, 1872, Letters Sent, Department of Justice: Instructions to U.S. Attorneys and Marshals, 1867–1904, RG 60, NA, microcopy 701, roll 3.

28. *Richmond Daily Dispatch,* April 7, 1869; E. G. Higbee to J. R. Lewis, April 19, 21, 1868, Willard E. Wight, ed., "Reconstruction in Georgia: Three Letters by Edwin G. Higbee," *Georgia Historical Quarterly* 41 (March 1957): 84–88.

29. George S. Meade to Regis de Trobriand, August 28, 1867, Marie Post, *The Life and Memoirs of Comte Regis de Trobriand* (New York: E. P. Dutton, 1910), 347; John M. Schofield, *Forty-Six Years in the Army* (New York: Century Company, 1897), 395–404; *House Executive Documents,* 41st Cong., 2d sess., No. 1, vol. 1, pt. 2, pp. 17, 78; *Senate Executive Documents,* 41st Cong., 2d sess., No. 41, p. 6; Alfred H. Terry to William T. Sherman, January 19, 1870, Letters Received, AGO, Main Series, 1861–70, RG 94, NA, microcopy 619, roll 752; Kirkland, "Federal Troops in the South Atlantic States," 300.

30. Pfanz, "Soldiering in the South," 19; Trelease, *White Terror,* 384–85; Sefton, *Army and Reconstruction,* 223–24; Philip H. Sheridan to J. A. Rawlins, November 21, 1867, Sheridan Papers.

31. Buss, *Psychology of Aggression,* 53–55; Gurr, *Conditions of Civil Violence,* 11.

32. Trelease, *White Terror,* 419; Simkins, "Klan in South Carolina," 606–29; Ray Granade, "Violence: An Instrument of Policy in Reconstruction Alabama," *Alabama Historical Quarterly* 30 (Fall and Winter 1968): 181.

33. Ralph L. Peek, "The Election of 1870 and the End of Reconstruction in Florida," *Florida Historical Quarterly* 45 (April 1967): 353–62.

34. Trelease, *White Terror,* 223; Evans, *Ballots and Fence Rails,* 144–48.

35. Trelease, *White Terror,* 270–73; Smith Papers, September and October 1870, passim; John A. Moss to William W. Belknap, November 7, 1870, S. W. Crawford to Assistant Adjutant General, Department of the South, November 18, 1870, Letters Received, AGO, Main Series, 1861–70, RG 94, NA, microcopy 619, roll 775.

36. Nathans, *Losing the Peace,* 204–6; Trelease, *White Terror,* 238–42.

37. Ramsdell, *Reconstruction in Texas,* 301–18; William Gillette, *Retreat from Reconstruction, 1869–1879* (Baton Rouge: Louisiana State University Press, 1979), 99–102; *Austin Daily State Journal,* December 23, 1873, January 2, 3, 15, 17, 20–22, 30, 1874; T. B. Wheeler, "Reminiscences of Reconstruction in Texas," *Quarterly of the Texas State Historical Association* 11 (July 1907): 56–63.

38. George H. Thompson, *Arkansas and Reconstruction: The Influence of Geography, Economics, and Personality* (Port Washington, N.Y.: Kennikat, 1976), 97–123; *House Reports,* 43d Cong., 2d sess., No. 2; John M. Harrell, *The Brooks and Baxter War: A History of the Reconstruction Period in Arkansas* (St. Louis: Slawson Printing Company, 1893), 197.

39. Harrell, *Brooks and Baxter War,* 202–3, 214–15; *Daily Arkansas Gazette* (Little Rock), September 16–18, 1874; *House Executive Documents,* 43d Cong., 1st sess., No. 229, pt. 1, pp. 2, 4–8, 15, 17–19; *Senate Executive Documents,* 43d Cong., 1st sess., No. 51, pp. 2–3, 139.

40. *Daily Arkansas Gazette* (Little Rock), April 21–23, 25, 30, May 1, 5, 1874; *Senate Executive Documents,* 43d Cong., 1st sess., No. 51, pp. 5–8, 11, 137–44; *Senate Executive Documents,* 43d Cong., 2d sess., No. 25, pp. 21–22.

41. James D. Richardson, ed., *Messages and Papers of the Presidents, 1789–1897,* 10 vols. (Washington, D.C.: Bureau of National Literature and Art, 1897), 7:272–73; Thompson, *Arkansas and Reconstruction,* 135–58; Gillette, *Retreat from Reconstruction,* 136–44.

42. Gillette, *Retreat from Reconstruction,* 144–50.

43. *Tallahassee Sentinel,* December 19, 1867; *Charleston Mercury,* March 26, 1868.

44. Charles E. Kennon to Thomas C. W. Ellis, November 11, 1870, Ellis Papers; *Raleigh Daily Sentinel,* February 28, 1871; *Shreveport Daily Times,* July 4, 1874.

45. Wiggins, *Scalawag in Alabama,* 91–102; *Annual Cyclopedia,* 1874, pp. 15–16; *House Reports,* 43d Cong., 2d sess., No. 262, pp. 247–48, 1005–6.

46. *House Reports,* 43d Cong., 2d sess., No. 262, pp. 221–28, 252–53, 288–94, 299–304, 316–22, 710–16, 723–27, 771–72, 985–92, 1228–29, 1254–60; W. H. Black to David P. Lewis, August 25, 1874, David Lewis Papers, Alabama Department of Archives and History.

47. *Mobile Daily Register,* July 31, August 28, September 2, 23, 1874; Citizens of Baldwin County to David P. Lewis, October 4, 1874, G. B. Bryars to Lewis, October 8, 1874, Lewis Papers.

48. William Warren Rogers and Robert Davis Ward, *August Reckoning: Jack Turner and Racism in Post–Civil War Alabama* (Baton Rouge: Louisiana State University Press, 1973), 24–54; Edmund Turner and Jackson Turner to

David P. Lewis, August 21, 1874, Lewis Papers; *House Reports,* 43d Cong., 2d sess., No. 262, pp. 249, 251.

49. *House Reports,* 43d Cong., 2d sess., No. 262, pp. 232–36, 706–10, 751–60, 907–13; *Mobile Daily Register,* September 10, 11, 18, October 2, 1874.

50. *House Reports,* 43d Cong., 2d sess., No. 262, pp. 16–24, 243–47, 501–10, 547–54, 914–1233; W. H. Wayne to David P. Lewis, August 2, 1874, Lewis Papers; William B. Rochester to Assistant Adjutant General, Department of the South, September 22, 1874, Letters Received, AGO, Main Series, 1871–80, RG 94, NA, microcopy 666, roll 169; *Mobile Daily Register,* September 17, 20, October 3, 6, 7, 9, 25, 1874.

51. Harry P. Owens, "The Eufaula Riot of 1874," *Alabama Review* 16 (July 1963): 224–32; *House Reports,* 43d Cong., 2d sess., No. 262, pp. 1–9, 224–26, 838–48, 855–63, 1127, 1268; E. M. Kiels to Benjamin Gardner, August 25, 1874, David P. Lewis to Gardner, September 4, 1874, Lewis Papers.

52. *House Reports,* 43d Cong., 2d sess., No. 262, pp. 212–21, 793–825, 848–55, 966–84; Melinda M. Hennessey, "Reconstruction Politics and the Military: The Eufaula Riot of 1874," *Alabama Historical Quarterly* 38 (Summer 1976): 117–19.

53. *House Reports,* 43d Cong., 2d sess., No. 262, pp. 1–9, 427–33, 597–99, 1278; A. S. Daggett to Assistant Adjutant General, Department of the South, November 4, 1874, Letters Received, AGO, Main Series, 1871–80, RG 94, NA, microcopy 666, roll 170.

54. *House Reports,* 43d Cong., 2d sess., No. 262, pp. 9–16, 332–468; 590, 619–25.

55. *House Reports,* 43d Cong., 2d sess., No. 262, pp. 25–37, 111–16, 323–32, 877–90, 1218–49; E. R. Kellogg to Assistant Adjutant General, Department of the South, November 4, 1874, Letters Received, AGO, Main Series, 1871–80, RG 94, NA, microcopy 666, roll 171; *House Executive Documents,* 43d Cong., 2d sess., No. 110, p. 2.

56. *Senate Miscellaneous Documents,* 43d Cong., 2d sess., No. 107, pp. 1–11; *House Reports,* 43d Cong., 2d sess., No. 262, pp. i–xlv, 510–29, 701–4; W. B. Young to "Dear Aunt," December 3, 1874, Simpson Papers; George H. Williams to Robert W. Healy, November 24, 1874, Letters Sent, Department of Justice: Instructions to U.S. Attorneys and Marshals, 1867–1904, RG 60, NA, microcopy 701, roll 5.

57. Gillette, *Retreat from Reconstruction,* 211–35.

58. *New York Herald,* August 25, 1874; *Louisville Courier-Journal,* August 31, 1874.

59. *Natchez Daily Democrat,* September 24, 1874; *Memphis Daily Appeal,* August 4, 1874; *Augusta Daily Chronicle and Sentinel,* August 14, 1874.

60. Barbour Lewis to George H. Williams, October 3, 1874, Letters Received, AGO, Main Series, 1871–80, RG 94, NA, microcopy 666, roll 170; *House Reports,* 43d Cong., 2d sess., No. 261, pt. 3, p. 796; *Columbia Daily Union-Herald,* August 12, 1874.

61. *Augusta Daily Constitutionalist,* September 9, 1874; *Daily Arkansas Gazette* (Little Rock), September 18, 1874.

62. *Wilmington* (N.C.) *Daily Journal,* October 16, 1874; *Atlanta Constitution,* October 16, 1874.

63. Gillette, *Retreat from Reconstruction,* 236–58.

64. *Senate Executive Documents,* 43d Cong., 2d sess., No. 12, pp. 2–6; *New York Herald,* September 5, 1874; George H. Williams to W. W. Murray, May 4, 1875, Letters Sent, Department of Justice: Instructions to U.S. Attorneys and Marshals, 1867–1904, RG 60, NA, microcopy 701, roll 5.

65. *New Orleans Bulletin,* November 5, 1874; *Wilmington* (N.C.) *Daily Journal,* November 7, 1874; *Jackson Weekly Clarion,* November 12, 1874.

66. *Augusta Daily Chronicle and Sentinel,* July 16, August 19–22, 25, September 5, 11, 26, 1875; *Augusta Daily Constitutionalist,* August 19–21, September 1, 3, 7, 1875; Percy Scott Flippin, *Herschel V. Johnson of Georgia: State Rights Unionist* (Richmond: Dietz Printing Company, 1931), 306–8. Morris was later arrested, tried, and convicted on a charge of carrying a concealed weapon. As a prisoner, he worked in a pottery factory from which he was kidnapped in April 1876 and probably lynched (*Augusta Daily Chronicle and Sentinel,* April 19, 1876).

Chapter 8: Counterrevolution Aborted: Louisiana, 1871–1875

1. The best account of the enormous complexities of Louisiana politics in this period is Taylor, *Louisiana Reconstructed,* 209–52.

2. *New Orleans Republican,* July 26, 1872; John Edmond Gonzales, "William Pitt Kellogg: Reconstruction Governor of Louisiana, 1873–1877," *Louisiana Historical Quarterly* 29 (April 1946): 403–4.

3. *House Executive Documents,* 42d Cong., 3d sess., No. 91, pp. 2–7, 111–31; *New Orleans Republican,* November 8, 9, 14, December 1, 1872.

4. Warmoth, *War, Politics, and Reconstruction,* 205.

5. Kellogg to Chandler, November 23, 1872, Letters Received, Department of Justice, Louisiana, 1871–84, RG 60, NA, microcopy 940, roll 6; *House Executive Documents,* 42d Cong., 3d sess., No. 91, p. 13; William W. Belknap to E. D. Townsend, December 3, 1872, Letters Received, AGO, Main Series, 1871–80, RG 94, NA, microcopy 666, roll 93.

6. Under the constitution of 1868, once a governor was impeached, he was automatically suspended from office pending the outcome of a trial in the Senate.

7. *House Executive Documents,* 42d Cong., 3d sess., No. 91, pp. 13–14, 16; Emory to E. D. Townsend, December 11, 1872, Letters Received, AGO, Main Series, 1871–80, RG 94, NA, microcopy 666, roll 93.

8. *House Executive Documents,* 42d Cong., 3d sess., No. 91, pp. 18–21, 23. For the development of Grant's policy toward Louisiana, see George Rable, "Republican Albatross: The Louisiana Question, National Politics and the Failure of Reconstruction," *Louisiana History* 23 (Spring 1982): 109–30; but cf. Gillette, *Retreat from Reconstruction,* 104–35.

9. *House Executive Documents,* 42d Cong., 3d sess., No. 91, pp. 24–25; Emory

to Townsend, December 15, 1872, Letters Received, AGO, Main Series, 1871–80, RG 94, NA, microcopy 666, roll 93; *New Orleans Republican,* December 14, 17, 19, 1872.

10. *New Orleans Daily Picayune,* January 2, 3, 5, 8, 1873; *New Orleans Times,* January 3, 1873.

11. Kellogg to George H. Williams, February 8, 1873, Letters Received, Department of Justice, Louisiana, 1871–84, RG 60, NA, microcopy 940, roll 1.

12. *New Orleans Daily Picayune,* February 22, 1873; *Shreveport Daily Times,* February 27, 1873; *New Orleans Republican,* March 1, 1873.

13. *New Orleans Republican,* March 6, 1873. The Metropolitan Police was a force under the control of the governor that operated primarily in New Orleans but could be used anywhere in the state. Between 1869 and 1877, it became the military arm of the Republican party (Taylor, *Louisiana Reconstructed,* 177–78).

14. *New York Herald,* March 7, 1873; McEnery to Emory, March 6, 1873, Emory to McEnery, March 6, 1873, Letters Received, AGO, Main Series, 1871–80, RG 94, NA, microcopy 666, roll 93; Kellogg to George H. Williams, March 12, 1873, Letters Received, Department of Justice, Louisiana, 1871–84, RG 60, NA, microcopy 940, roll 1.

15. *New Orleans Daily Picayune,* March 17, 19, 1873; *New Orleans Republican,* March 19, 1873. Taylor has shown that the burden of taxation was not nearly so crushing as conservatives claimed and that Kellogg reduced state taxes. Yet many whites would still resent paying taxes to a government they considered to be the bastard offspring of federal tyranny. No one has closely examined the actual operation of the tax system in Louisiana, but certainly the panic of 1873 must have made even reduced rates seem oppressive. In attempting to rescue the Kellogg government from obloquy, Taylor exaggerates its virtues and downplays its vices (*Louisiana Reconstructed,* 257–67).

16. Manie White Johnson, "The Colfax Riot of April, 1873," *Louisiana Historical Quarterly* 13 (July 1930): 398–99; *New Orleans Daily Picayune,* April 16, May 22, 1873; "My Reconstruction Days: Ride to Colfax," John R. Ficklen Papers; Kate Kingston Boyd Grant, "From Blue to Gray or the Battle of Colfax," Ms novel in Layssard, Papers Department of Archives, Louisiana State University. This romantic novel, which weaves a melodramatic love story around a factual account of the Colfax riot, is a valuable source because the author apparently interviewed a number of the participants.

17. Johnson, "Colfax Riot," 399–400; *House Reports,* 43d Cong., 2d sess., No. 261, pt. 3, pp. 261–64, 409–10, 858; *Shreveport Daily Times,* May 3, 1873, October 11, 1876; *New Orleans Republican,* April 10, 12, 22, 1873; *House Miscellaneous Documents,* 44th Cong., 2d sess., No. 34, pt. 2, pp. 482–85.

18. Roger A. Fischer, *The Segregation Struggle in Louisiana, 1862–1877* (Urbana: University of Illinois Press, 1974), 156–57.

19. Grant, "From Blue to Gray," 131–37; *New Orleans Daily Picayune,* April 5, 7, 8, 10–13, May 6, 1873; Johnson, "Colfax Riot," 402–3; "My Reconstruction Days."

20. Grant, "From Blue to Gray," 111–14, 135, 149–61; *House Reports,* 43d Cong., 2d sess., No. 261, pt. 3, pp. 858–59; Johnson, "Colfax Riot," 407–9.

21. Johnson, "Colfax Riot," 409–16, 418; "My Reconstruction Days"; *New Orleans Daily Picayune,* April 16, 30, May 2, 1873; Grant, "From Blue to Gray," 170–84; *Colfax Chronicle,* June 3, 1882; J. H. Smith to Acting Assistant Adjutant General, Department of the Gulf, April 29, 1873, Letters Received, AGO, Main Series, 1871–80, RG 94, NA, microcopy 666, roll 93. When the Metropolitan Police and soldiers arrived a few days later, they found sixty or more mutilated corpses near the courthouse. The soldiers buried the bodies (Stephen B. Packard to George H. Williams, April 17, 1873, Letters Received, Department of Justice, Louisiana, 1871–84, RG 60, NA, microcopy 940, roll 6).

22. Richard Hofstadter, "Reflections on Violence in the United States," in Hofstadter and Michael Wallace, eds., *Violence in America: A Documentary History* (New York: Alfred A. Knopf, 1970), 13–17.

23. *New Orleans Daily Picayune,* April 17, 22, 1873; *New Orleans Republican,* April 17, 23, 26, 1873.

24. J. Ernest Breda to George H. Williams, August 11, 1873, J. Ernest Breda Letters, Howard-Tilton Memorial Library, Tulane University; James R. Beckwith to Williams, June 17, 1873, Letters Received, Department of Justice, Louisiana, 1871–84, RG 60, NA, microcopy 940, roll 1; *New Orleans Daily Picayune,* January 18, February 22, 27–March 12, May 19–June 12, 1874; *New Orleans Republican,* November 2, 11, 1873. These convictions did not end the violence in Grant Parish because the conflict over local offices continued. A former sheriff murdered the Republican tax collector, and unknown persons assassinated Judge Register (R. C. Register to Kellogg, June 20, 1875, Kellogg Papers, Department of Archives, Louisiana State University; T. H. Page to Kellogg, March 14, 1876, Louisiana State Executive Department, Governors' Correspondence, ibid.).

25. *U.S.* v. *Cruikshank, et al.* 25 Fed. Cas. 707 (1874); *U.S.* v. *Cruikshank, et al.* 92 U.S. 542 (1876); Beckwith to George H. Williams, October 27, 1874, Letters Received, Department of Justice, Louisiana, 1871–84, RG 60, NA, microcopy 940, roll 2.

26. W. H. McVey to Charles Clinton, April 29, 1873, Isaac H. Crawford to Kellogg, May 7, 1873, Letters Received, Department of Justice, Louisiana, 1871–84, RG 60, NA, microcopy 940, roll 1; *New Orleans Republican,* May 8, 1873.

27. *New Orleans Republican,* April 17, May 4, 6–10, 13, 15–16, 18, 27, 1873. Taylor exaggerates Kellogg's forcefulness in moving against tax resisters. The governor acted in only a few parishes, and there is no evidence that any of the persons arrested were ever brought to trial (*Louisiana Reconstructed,* 274–76).

28. Taylor, *Louisiana Reconstructed,* 204–8, 258–67.

29. George Wear to Kellogg, September 12, 1873, S. H. Cardill to Kellogg, October 20, 1873, Kellogg Papers; Jefferson McKinney to Jeptha McKinney, December 14, 1873, Jeptha McKinney Papers, Department of Archives, Louisiana State University.

30. Kellogg to Oliver P. Morton, December 8, 1873, January 7, 17, February 23, 1874, Morton Papers, Indiana State Library.

31. *New Orleans Daily Picayune,* March 22, 1874; *New Orleans Bulletin,* April 14, 1874.

32. *New Orleans Daily Picayune,* June 10, 1874; *Natchitoches People's Vindicator,* August 29, 1874; *Shreveport Daily Times,* July 25, 1874; *Alexandria Caucasian,* May 23, 1874.

33. Everett Dean Martin, *The Behavior of Crowds: A Psychological Study* (New York: Harper and Brothers, 1920), 92ff.; Canetti, *Crowds and Power,* 22–24. This reasoning also allowed conservatives to defend the abandonment of all appeals to black voters for support of the Democratic party (*Alexandria Caucasian,* April 25, June 13, 1874).

34. *Natchitoches People's Vindicator,* July 4, August 15, 1874; *New Orleans Daily Picayune,* July 4, 1874; *New Orleans Bulletin,* July 4, 5, 1874.

35. Martin, *Behavior of Crowds,* 37ff.; White League Resolutions, St. Martin Parish, n.d., 1874, De Clouet Papers; *Shreveport Daily Times,* July 8, 15, August 13, 15, 1874.

36. On the farmers' economic woes, see Taylor, *Louisiana Reconstructed,* 382–406. There is no adequate study of the White League—particularly its social base. The secondary accounts are either sketchy or partisan.

37. *Annual Cyclopedia,* 1874, p. 477. There was a congressional election in 1874, but for Louisiana Democrats the main prize to be won was control of the state legislature. With a majority in that body, they could impeach Kellogg and drive the carpetbaggers from the state. This need explains the great desperation of the struggle.

38. E. John Ellis to Thomas C. W. Ellis, June 24, 1874, Ellis Papers; *Natchitoches People's Vindicator,* June 20, 1874; *Shreveport Daily Times,* July 9, 1874.

39. *House Reports,* 43d Cong., 2d sess., No. 261, pt. 3, pp. 214–30, 276–98, 302–4, 536–54; *Natchitoches People's Vindicator,* June 20, July 11, August 1, 1874.

40. *New Orleans Republican,* August 22, 25, 29–30, September 1, 1874; *House Reports,* 43d Cong., 2d sess., No. 261, pt. 3, pp. 346–52, 581–87; *New Orleans Bulletin,* August 9, 22, 1874; *Shreveport Daily Times,* June 6, July 12, 1874.

41. *Shreveport Daily Times,* July 28, August 22, 1874; *New Orleans Bulletin,* August 29, 1874.

42. Jimmy G. Shoalmire, "Carpetbagger Extraordinary: Marshall Harvey Twitchell, 1840–1905" (Ph.D. dissertation, Mississippi State University, 1969), 62, 99–105, 107–10, 115–39; Mary Edwards Bryan, *Wild Work: The Story of the Red River Tragedy* (New York: D. Appleton, 1881), 51–54, 82–83, 130–45. Bryan's "novel" about a carpetbagger named "Marshall Witchell" is a valuable factual account of the Coushatta affair that fills in important gaps in other sources.

43. Shoalmire, "Carpetbagger Extraordinary," 139–51; *Shreveport Daily Times,* June 16, 1874.

44. Shoalmire, "Carpetbagger Extraordinary," 152–55; Bryan, *Wild Work,* 12–14, 24–30, 102–28, 204–9, 214–15.

45. Bryan, *Wild Work,* 236–45; Shoalmire, "Carpetbagger Extraordinary," 155–62; *Shreveport Daily Times,* September 2, 5, 1874; *House Reports,* 43d Cong., 2d sess., No. 261, pt. 2, pp. 386–99, 903–6.

46. Shoalmire, "Carpetbagger Extraordinary," 162–69; Bryan, *Wild Work,* 247–53, 265–83; *House Reports,* 43d Cong., 2d sess., No. 261, pt. 3, pp. 489–505.

47. Shoalmire, "Carpetbagger Extraordinary," 170–78; Bryan, *Wild Work,* 311–15; Oscar H. Lestage, Jr., "The White League in Louisiana and Its Participation in Reconstruction Riots," *Louisiana Historical Quarterly* 28 (July 1935): 677–78n.

48. *Senate Executive Documents,* 43d Cong., 2d sess., No. 13, pp. 11–12; *Shreveport Daily Times,* September 3, 1874; *New Orleans Daily Picayune,* September 3, 1874.

49. Canetti, *Crowds and Power,* 51ff.

50. Shoalmire, "Carpetbagger Extraordinary," 178–80, 185–93; *Senate Executive Documents,* 43d Cong., 2d sess., No. 17, pp. 2, 4–7, 12–16; *Shreveport Daily Times,* October 20, 23, 25, 27, 29, 1874; Bryan, *Wild Work,* 359, 384.

51. Shoalmire, "Carpetbagger Extraordinary," 194–229; *House Reports,* 44th Cong., 1st sess., No. 816, pp. 645–57, 660–61, 667–70; Unknown to "Dear Brother Mike," May 5, 1876, "Lagniappe," *Louisiana Studies* 15 (Summer 1976): 178; *New Orleans Republican,* June 23, 1876.

52. Taylor gives a detailed account of the Coushatta massacre but misses its significance by dealing with it only as prelude to the battle of Liberty Place (*Louisiana Reconstructed,* 287–91).

53. *New Orleans Daily Picayune,* June 24, July 1, 1874.

54. *New Orleans Daily Picayune,* September 3, 1874; *New Orleans Bulletin,* September 2, 1874.

55. *New Orleans Bulletin,* September 5, 1874; Emory to Packard, September 11, 1874, Letters Sent, Department of the Gulf, 1871–78, RG 393, NA.

56. Walter Prichard, ed., "Origins and Activities of the 'White League' in New Orleans (Reminiscences of a Participant in the Movement)," *Louisiana Historical Quarterly* 23 (April 1940): 533–38; *New Orleans Bulletin,* September 9–12, 1874.

57. W. O. Hart, "History of the Events Leading up to the Battle," *Louisiana Historical Quarterly* 7 (October 1924): 578; *New Orleans Times,* September 23, 1874; *New Orleans Daily Picayune,* September 13, 1874.

58. *New Orleans Daily Picayune,* September 15, 1874.

59. Penn to Ogden, September 14?, 1874, Frederick N. Ogden Papers, Howard-Tilton Memorial Library, Tulane University; Ella Lonn, *Reconstruction in Louisiana after 1868* (New York: G. P. Putnam's Sons, 1918), 271n.; *New Orleans Daily Picayune,* September 15, 1874; Kendall, *New Orleans,* 1:370–71.

60. Dawson, "Long Ordeal," 329–35; *House Reports,* 43d Cong., 2d sess., No. 101, pt. 2, pp. 26–29.

61. *New Orleans Bulletin,* September 16, 1874; David F. Boyd to Sherman,

September 16, 1874, Walter L. Fleming Collection, Department of Archives, Louisiana State University.

62. Packard to Williams, September 15, 1874, Letters Received, Department of Justice, Louisiana, 1871–84, RG 60, NA, microcopy 940, roll 2; *Annual Cyclopedia,* 1874, p. 481; Kellogg to Grant, September 15, 1874, Kellogg Papers.

63. Richardson, ed., *Messages and Papers of the Presidents,* 7:276–77; Unsigned resolution, Adjutant General's Office, September 17, 1874, Ogden Papers; E. John Ellis to Thomas C. W. Ellis, September 21, 1874, Ellis Papers; Emory to Grant, September 17, 1874, Letters Sent, Department of the Gulf, 1871–78, RG 393, NA.

64. *Shreveport Daily Times,* September 19, 20, 22, 1874; Irvin McDowell to Assistant Adjutant General, Washington, September 22, 1874, Emory to Assistant Adjutant General, Division of the South, September 22, 1874, Letters Received, AGO, Main Series, 1871–80, RG 94, NA, microcopy 666, roll 169.

65. *House Executive Documents,* 44th Cong., 2d sess., No. 30, pp. 215, 302, 358–59; *New Orleans Bulletin,* September 19, 1874.

66. *New Orleans Daily Picayune,* October 30, 1874; *Senate Executive Documents,* 43d Cong., 2d sess., No. 17, pp. 61, 63; Emory to Kellogg, October 11, 1874, Letters Sent, Department of the Gulf, 1871–78, RG 393, NA; Merrill to Adjutant General, Department of the Gulf, November 4, 1874, Telegrams Received, Department of the Gulf, 1874–75, ibid.

67. *Shreveport Daily Times,* November 15, 1874.

68. *Senate Executive Documents,* 43d Cong., 2d sess., No. 13, p. 16; *Senate Executive Documents,* 43d Cong., 2d sess., No. 17, pp. 19–20, 65–66.

69. Taylor, *Louisiana Reconstructed,* 302–3; *New Orleans Bulletin,* December 30, 1874; *Shreveport Daily Times,* December 25, 1874.

70. *Senate Executive Documents,* 43d Cong., 2d sess., No. 13, pp. 23–31; Sheridan to Orville Babcock, January 25, 1875, Sheridan Papers.

71. Taylor's defense of Grant and Sheridan is unpersuasive. With no one prepared to take vigorous action against the White League, idle threats were not only useless but politically foolish. Elsewhere, I have argued that the Republican fiasco in Louisiana was the pivotal event in the undoing of the party's southern policy (Rable, "Republican Albatross," 129–30; cf. Taylor, *Louisiana Reconstructed,* 307; Gillette, *Retreat from Reconstruction,* 123–35).

72. *New Orleans Bulletin,* January 7, 1875; George F. Hoar, *Autobiography of Seventy Years,* 2 vols. (New York: Charles Scribner's Sons, 1903), 1:208; James Ford Rhodes, *History of the United States from the Compromise of 1850 to the Final Restoration of Home Rule at the South in 1877,* 7 vols. (New York: Macmillan, 1896–1906), 7:125.

73. *Raleigh Daily Sentinel,* April 23, 1873; *Charleston Daily News,* January 4, 1873; *Augusta Daily Chronicle and Sentinel,* March 1, 1873.

74. *Jackson Weekly Clarion,* September 24, 1874.

75. *Atlanta Constitution,* January 10, 1875; *Memphis Daily Appeal,* January 6, 1875.

76. Dixon, *White Conquest,* 2:50.

Chapter 9: Counterrevolution Triumphant: Mississippi, 1873–1876

1. Adelbert Ames to William Claflin, November 8, 1869, William Claflin Papers, Rutherford B. Hayes Memorial Library; Ames to Blanche Butler Ames, July 30, October 1, 1873, Jessie Ames Marshall, ed., *Chronicles from the Nineteenth Century: Family Letters of Blanche Butler and Adelbert Ames*, 2 vols. (N.p.: Privately printed, 1957), 1:503, 585; Ames to Justin S. Morrill, October 20, 1871, Justin Morrill Papers, Library of Congress.

2. Harris, *Day of the Carpetbagger;* Harris's book supersedes all previous treatments of the Republican era in Mississippi politics.

3. *Mississippi House Journal,* 1874, pp. 27–32.

4. *Jackson Weekly Clarion,* January 22, 1874; Harris, *Day of the Carpetbagger,* 206–63, 287–90.

5. Harris, *Day of the Carpetbagger,* 605–7.

6. *Jackson Weekly Clarion,* 1874.

7. King, *Great South,* 288–89; *House Reports,* 43d Cong., 2d sess., No. 265, pp. 26–73; 474–81; Charles Nordhoff, *The Cotton States in the Spring and Summer of 1875* (New York: D. Appleton, 1876), 75–76.

8. Peter Crosby to Ames, April 9, 1874, Ames to Crosby, April 10, 1874, A. K. Davis to Grant, July 20, 1874, Ames to Grant, July 29, 1874, Adelbert Ames Papers, Mississippi Department of Archives and History; *Vicksburg Daily Times,* July 14, 20, 1874; *New York Times,* July 23, 1874.

9. James Madison Batchelor to Albert A. Batchelor, September 6, 1874, Albert A. Batchelor Papers, Department of Archives, Louisiana State University; *Vicksburg Daily Times,* August 6, 1874; *House Reports,* 43d Cong., 2d sess., No. 265, pp. 128–31, 177, 192, 223, 361–63, 369, 463–64.

10. Ames to Blanche Butler Ames, July 31, 1874, August 2, 5, 1874, Marshall, ed., *Chronicles from the Nineteenth Century,* 1:693, 695, 698–99.

11. *Jackson Weekly Clarion,* August 6, 1874; J. Z. George to L.Q.C. Lamar, April 15, 1874, Lamar-Mayes Papers, Mississippi Department of Archives and History; Ames to M. Howard, August 18, 1874, L.W.S.E. Franklin to Davis, August 30, 1874, Ames Papers.

12. *Jackson Weekly Clarion,* August 13, 27, 1874; *Natchez Daily Democrat,* August 15, 1874. Harris's account of the Tunica war makes it into a comic opera farce and fails to recognize that local blacks, whom he condescendingly calls "dusky warriors," in fact did take over the town because of a perceived lack of justice for their race. He is on more solid ground in arguing that this "black insurrection" made some black-belt whites more cautious about launching a white supremacy campaign against the state government (Harris, *Day of the Carpetbagger,* 640–41).

13. *House Reports,* 43d Cong., 2d sess., No. 265, pp. 11, 215–20, 252–72, 302–3, 311–17, 328–29, 399; *Report of the Joint Special Committee Appointed to Investigate the Late Insurrection in the City of Vicksburg, Warren County* (Jackson: Pilot Publishing Company, 1875), 42–44, 58–59; hereinafter cited as *Insurrection in Vicksburg.*

14. *Insurrection in Vicksburg,* 168–82; *House Reports,* 43d Cong., 2d sess., No. 265, pp. 131–32, 135–36, 329–31, 385–87, 400–401, 445–49, 495–507.

15. Harris provides a careful account of this meeting in Jackson. Ames rejected the idea of sending the militia to Vicksburg and thought a call for federal troops would be futile. Harris accepts a contemporary canard hurled against the governor that at this meeting he talked of the necessity for sacrificing the lives of a few blacks for the good of the Republican party. The governor's intentions remain murky, but there is little evidence to sustain such a serious attack on his moral character (Harris, *Day of the Carpetbagger,* 646–47).

16. *Insurrection in Vicksburg,* 44–47, 86–95, 220–29, 253–72; *House Reports,* 43d Cong., 2d sess., No. 265, pp. 10, 48–49, 173, 401–5, 459, 538–39.

17. *House Reports,* 43d Cong., 2d sess., No. 265, pp. 1–26; 87–520.

18. *Insurrection in Vicksburg,* 66–242; *Vicksburg Herald,* n.d., quoted in *Jackson Weekly Clarion,* December 10, 1874; *House Reports,* 43d Cong., 2d sess., No. 265, pp. 8–113, 140–222, 275–469. Harris accepts Ames's estimate of three hundred black casualties, but such round figures are generally suspect, and the testimony from both sides cited above indicates that the conflict was not that sanguinary (Harris, *Day of the Carpetbagger,* 648).

19. Richardson, ed., *Messages and Papers of the Presidents,* 7:322–23; E. D. Townsend to William H. Emory, December 19, 1874, Letters Received, AGO, Main Series, 1871–80, RG 94, NA, microcopy 666, roll 172; *Jackson Weekly Mississippi Pilot,* June 12, 1875; *Jackson Daily Mississippi Pilot,* December 30, 1874, January 20, 1875; Ames Papers, December 1874, passim; Crosby to Ames, January 20, October 28, 1875, ibid.

20. *Jackson Weekly Clarion,* December 24, 31, January 14, 1875; Lamar to E. D. Clark, December 21, 23, 1874, James H. Stone, ed., "L. Q. C. Lamar's Letters to Edward Donaldson Clark, 1868–1885, Pt. II," *Journal of Mississippi History* 37 (May 1975): 189–93; James Madison Batchelor to Albert A. Batchelor, January 4, 1875, Batchelor Papers; Singletary, *Negro Militia,* 85–86.

21. *Jackson Weekly Clarion,* May 8, 1873, November 26, December 3, 10, 17, 24, 31, 1874, January 28, 1875; *Jackson Daily Clarion,* January 6, 1875. Harris has effectively demonstrated that as a result of Mississippi's extreme poverty, taxes were burdensome (*Day of the Carpetbagger,* 626–27).

22. *Jackson Daily Clarion,* January 13, 14, 27–29, February 11, March 2, 1875.

23. Ames to A. T. Morgan, August 14, 1874, Ames Papers; *Jackson Daily Clarion,* January 7, 13, 28, February 1–5, 22, 1875; *Mississippi Senate Journal,* 1875, pp. 28–29, 147–49.

24. Edward Mayes, *Lucius Q. C. Lamar: His Life, Times, and Speeches* (Nashville: Publishing House of the Methodist Episcopal Church, South, 1895), 243–47; *Hinds County Gazette* (Raymond), September 23, 1874, April 7, 1875.

25. J. Z. George to Lamar, May 3, 1874, Lamar-Mayes Papers; Mayes, *Lamar,* 211–12, 216–17.

26. Harris, *Day of the Carpetbagger,* 641–45; Mayes, *Lamar,* 246; *Jackson Weekly Clarion,* September 3, 24, December 10, 1874; *Natchez Daily Democrat,* April 13, 24, 1875.

27. Jackson *Weekly Clarion,* July 7, 21, 1875; Nordhoff, *Cotton States,* 77.

28. *Jackson Weekly Mississippi Pilot,* July 10, 1875; *Senate Reports,* 44th Cong., 1st sess., No. 527, pp. 1316–17, 1350–1404, 1407–29.

29. Harris, *Day of the Carpetbagger,* 652–55; Mayes, *Lamar,* 252–54, 258–59; *Annual Cyclopedia,* 1875, p. 514; clippings from various newspapers in "Documentary Evidence," *Senate Reports,* 44th Cong., 1st sess., No. 527, pp. 160–63 (hereinafter cited as "Documentary Evidence"); *Columbus Democrat* n.d., quoted ibid., 163.

30. *Hinds County Gazette* (Raymond), September 22, October 20, 1875; "Documentary Evidence," 17–19, 25, 44, 63–64, 69, 162–67; *Senate Reports,* 44th Cong., 1st sess., No. 527, pp. 56, 1144, 1274–77.

31. Ames to Blanche Butler Ames, August 4, 31, 1875, Marshall, ed., *Chronicles from the Nineteenth Century,* 2:124, 153; *Jackson Weekly Mississippi Pilot,* July 31, October 2, 1875; "Documentary Evidence," 91.

32. Harris, *Day of the Carpetbagger,* 658–60; *Jackson Weekly Mississippi Pilot,* August 14, 21, 1875; Ames to Blanche Butler Ames, July 29, 1875, Marshall, ed., *Chronicles from the Nineteenth Century,* 2:115.

33. A. T. Morgan, *Yazoo; Or, On the Picket Line of Freedom in the South* (New York: Russell and Russell, 1968), 370–400, 428–32, 439–56, 461–64; *Senate Reports,* 44th Cong., 1st sess., No. 527, pp. 1729–56, 1765–73; A. T. Morgan to Ames, September 24, 1875, Ames Papers.

34. Oscar J. E. Stuart to J. A. Mitchell, September n.d., 1875, Dimitry Papers; Morgan to Ames, September 4, 24, 1875, Ames Papers; *Jackson Weekly Clarion,* September 15, 1875; J.W.C. Smith to Edwards Pierrepont, October 4, 1875, Letters Received, Department of Justice, Mississippi, 1871–84, RG 60, NA, microcopy 970, roll 3.

35. Morgan to Ames, September 24, 1875, Ames Papers; *Senate Reports,* 44th Cong., 1st sess., No. 527, pp. 1647–63, 1672–98, 1756–60; Morgan, *Yazoo,* 481–85.

36. *Jackson Weekly Mississippi Pilot,* September 11, 1875; *Jackson Weekly Clarion,* September 8, 1875; *Senate Reports,* 44th Cong., 1st sess., No. 527, pp. 303–29, 359–78, 429–33, 441, 445–47, 492–507, 520–25; Arthur W. Allyn to E. R. Platt, September 5, 1875, Letters Received, AGO, Main Series, 1871–80, RG 94, NA, microcopy 666, roll 228.

37. *Senate Reports,* 44th Cong., 1st sess., No. 527, pp. 228–489; 540–68; Arthur W. Allyn to E. R. Platt, September 7, 1875, Letters Received, AGO, Main Series, 1871–80, RG 94, microcopy 666, roll 228; *Jackson Daily Clarion,* February 9, 1876; W. B. Sibley to Kate Power, October 22, 1937, J. L. Power Papers, Mississippi Department of Archives and History.

38. *Annual Cyclopedia,* 1875, p. 516; Augur to Adjutant General, Washington, September 9, 1875, Statement of U.S. Troops Stationed in the Department of the Gulf, September 9, 1875, Letters Received, AGO, Main Series, 1871–80, RG 94, NA, microcopy 666, roll 228.

39. *Annual Cyclopedia,* 1875, p. 516; Gillette, *Retreat from Reconstruction,* 155–60; Ames to Blanche Butler Ames, September 10, 19, 1875, Marshall, ed., *Chronicles from the Nineteenth Century,* 2:172, 186.

40. "Documentary Evidence," 25, 29–30, 46–47, 86–87, 102–3.

41. *Jackson Weekly Clarion,* October 6, 1875; *Natchez Daily Democrat,* October 7, 8, 1875; "Documentary Evidence," 83–84; *Senate Reports,* 44th Cong., 1st sess., No. 527, pp. 14, 1277–85.

42. Ames to Blanche Butler Ames, September 21, 22, 23, 24, October 4, 10, 12, 1875, Marshall, ed., *Chronicles from the Nineteenth Century,* 2:187–88, 192, 195, 205–6, 210–12, 215; Morgan, *Yazoo,* 456–57; J. Morgan to Ames, October 13, 1875, Ames Papers.

43. *Senate Reports,* 44th Cong., 1st sess., No. 527, pp. 357, 1215–18, 1801–19; Frank Johnston, "The Conference of October 15th, 1875, between General George and Governor Ames," *Publications of the Mississippi Historical Society* 6 (1902): 69–72.

44. Ames to Blanche Butler Ames, October 14, 20, 28, 1875, Marshall, ed., *Chronicles from the Nineteenth Century,* 2:217, 229, 244; *Senate Reports,* 44th Cong., 1st sess., No. 527, pp. 15–16, 425–28, 433–35, 440–41.

45. John W. Kyle, "Reconstruction in Panola County," *Publications of the Mississippi Historical Society* 13 (1913): 73–74; J. C. Brown, "Reconstruction in Yalobusha and Grenada Counties," *Publications of the Mississippi Historical Society* 12 (1912): 251–52; *Senate Reports,* 44th Cong., 1st sess., No. 527, pp. 277–82.

46. "Documentary Evidence," 53–57, 67–69, 73; *Jackson Weekly Clarion,* December 15, 1875; Agnew Diary, October 23, 1876.

47. Harris, *Day of the Carpetbagger,* 676–80.

48. *Senate Reports,* 44th Cong., 1st sess., No. 527, pp. 47–48, 221–23, 272–77, 589–600, 610–23, 637–58, 790–98; Kyle, "Reconstruction in Panola County," 74. This evidence also suggests that violence was sometimes used against Republicans who refused to resign their offices or persisted in making campaign speeches. Harris's failure to make extensive use of the massive amounts of documents and testimony gathered by the congressional committee set up to investigate the election of 1875 in Mississippi led him to underestimate the terrorism that took place after the Yazoo and Clinton riots (*Day of the Carpetbagger,* 682).

49. *Senate Reports,* 44th Cong., 1st sess., No. 527, pp. 238–43, 756–89, 859–62, 1021–1255; *Hinds County Gazette* (Raymond), August 4, 1875; Major S. W. Ferguson to T. G. Barker, January 7, 1876, Martin W. Gary Papers, South Caroliniana Library, University of South Carolina.

50. Henry R. Smith to Ames, November 2, 1875, Ames Papers; Report of the United States Grand Jury and accompanying affidavits, Oxford, Mississippi, July 8, 1876, Letters Received, Department of Justice, Mississippi, 1871–84, RG 60, NA, microcopy 970, roll 2.

51. "Documentary Evidence," 3, 10–12, 14–15, 19, 43, 47–49, 65, 72, 87, 92–93, 105–7; R. A. Simmons to Ames, October 26, 1875, Ames Papers.

52. "Documentary Evidence," 35–36, 70–72.

53. *Natchez Daily Democrat,* September 26, October 1, 1875; *Jackson Weekly Clarion,* September 15, 1875.

54. "Documentary Evidence," 5–6, 9, 12–13; *Senate Reports,* 44th Cong., 1st sess., No. 527, pp. 106–22.

55. John Brown to Ames, October 7, 8, 1875, Ames Papers; *Memphis Daily Appeal,* October 6, 9, 1875; *New York Tribune,* October 12, 1875; cf. Harris, *Day of the Carpetbagger,* 671–72, who claims there were no casualties.

56. "Documentary Evidence," 6–8, 23–24, 65–66; *Senate Reports,* 44th Cong., 1st sess., No. 527, pp. 74–106, 172–90, 199–204, 409, 1050–86, 1147–49.

57. *Senate Reports,* 44th Cong., 1st sess., No. 527, pp. 572–88, 883–89, 1669–71; Robert Bowman, "Reconstruction in Yazoo County," *Publications of the Mississippi Historical Society* 7 (1903): 130.

58. *Senate Reports,* 44th Cong., 1st sess., No. 527, pp. 125–35, 139–45, 508–14, 1270–74; Report of the United States Grand Jury and accompanying affidavits, Oxford, Mississippi, July 8, 1876, Letters Received, Department of Justice, Mississippi, 1871–84, RG 60, NA, microcopy 970, roll 2; Brown, "Reconstruction in Yalobusha and Grenada Counties," 255–56. Harris claims there were "only a few incidents of violence and blatant intimidation" on election day, but the evidence presented above indicates more widespread terrorism (*Day of the Carpetbagger,* 684–85).

59. Harris, *Day of the Carpetbagger,* 685–87.

60. See, for example, Oscar J. E. Stuart to A. G. Brown, November 4, 1875, Oscar Stuart Papers, Mississippi Department of Archives and History; *Brookhaven Ledger,* November 11, 1875.

61. "Documentary Evidence," 10, 61–63, 75–76, 150–51; William Breck to Frederick Douglass, September 15, 1876, Frederick Douglass Papers, Library of Congress; *Senate Reports,* 44th Cong., 1st sess., No. 527, pp. 600–610, 623–36, 719; *House Executive Documents,* 44th Cong., 2d sess., No. 30, pp. 115.

62. *Mississippi House Journal,* 1876, pp. 5–8; Henry B. Whitefield to Edwards Pierrepont, November 6, 1875, Letters Received, Department of Justice, Mississippi, 1871–84, RG 60, NA, microcopy 970, roll 2; *Jackson Daily Clarion,* January 5, 1876.

63. See the excellent discussion of the political maneuvering behind Ames's impeachment and resignation in Harris, *Day of the Carpetbagger,* 691–98.

64. Ames to Garner, January 17, 1900, Blanche Butler Ames, *Adelbert Ames, 1835–1933* (New York: Argosy-Antiquarian, 1964), 573, 576.

65. Unlike Louisiana to which Grant sent federal soldiers to prop up the chronically weak Kellogg regime, he responded to requests for aid from a much stronger state government with hesitation and finally passivity (Gillette, *Retreat from Reconstruction,* 164–65).

Chapter 10: 1876: The Triumph of Reaction

1. Two excellent discussions of the corruption issue are Williamson, *After Slavery,* 381–400, and Thomas Holt, *Black over White: Negro Political Leadership in South Carolina during Reconstruction* (Urbana: University of Illinois Press, 1977), 140, 147–48.

2. Walter Allen, *Governer Chamberlain's Administration in South Carolina* (New York: G. P. Putnam's Sons, 1888), 10–29, 66–67; Peggy Lamson, *The Glorious Failure: Black Congressman Robert Brown Elliott and the Recon-*

struction in South Carolina (New York: W. W. Norton, 1973), 154–55, 184–87, 208–14; Holt, *Black over White*, 175–207.

3. *Charleston News and Courier*, June 5, July 5–15, 1876; *Columbia Daily Register*, July and August 1876; Alfred B. Williams, *Hampton and His Red Shirts* (Charleston: Walker, Evans and Cogswell, 1935), 52–53.

4. *Columbia Daily Register*, May 14, 1876; *Charleston News and Courier*, January 21, April 22, 1876.

5. Deposition of O. F. Cheatham, August 19, 1874, Bonham Papers; L. Cass Carpenter to Ulysses S. Grant, August 26, 1874, Letters Received, Department of Justice, South Carolina, 1871–84, RG 60, NA, microcopy 947, roll 2.

6. Brown, *Strain of Violence*, 67–90.

7. Francis Butler Simkins, *Pitchfork Ben Tillman: South Carolinian* (Baton Rouge: Louisiana State University Press, 1944), 58–61; *Charleston News and Courier*, December 10, 1874, January 21, 22, 25, 28, 29, 1875; *Columbia Daily Union-Herald*, September 27, October 16, 1874, February 27, 1875.

8. *Columbia Daily Register*, March 7, 25, 27, 1876.

9. *New York Times*, July 14, 1876; *Senate Miscellaneous Documents*, 44th Cong., 2d sess., No. 48, 1:3–11, 2:447–76; Simkins and Woody, *South Carolina during Reconstruction*, 487n.

10. *Senate Miscellaneous Documents*, 44th Cong., 2d sess., No. 48, 1:34–37, 77–90, 145–60, 1050–69, 2:308–39.

11. Ibid., 1:37–77, 695–714, 2:490–98, 602–14; *Senate Executive Documents*, 44th Cong., 1st sess., No. 85, pp. 8–24; *Augusta Daily Chronicle and Sentinel*, July 9, 1876; *Charleston News and Courier*, July 10, 12, 14, 18, 1876.

12. *Charleston News and Courier*, July 11, 12, 15, 1876; Simkins, *Tillman*, 62–63.

13. *Charleston News and Courier*, July 10, 11, 13, 14, 28, 1876. Dawson reprinted editorial comments from the country papers on the Hamburg affair.

14. *Senate Executive Documents*, 44th Cong., 1st sess., No. 85, pp. 41–54.

15. H. Jordan to Daniel H. Chamberlain, July 9, 1876, Frank Arnim to Chamberlain, September 18, 1876, Daniel Chamberlain Papers, South Carolina Archives.

16. *Senate Executive Documents*, 44th Cong., 1st sess., No. 85, pp. 2–6; *Senate Miscellaneous Documents*, 44th Cong., 1st sess., No. 48, 3:89; *House Executive Documents*, 44th Cong., 2d sess., No. 30, p. 6. Grant acted so promptly because the Hamburg incident had produced great indignation in the North, even among men who were not generally sympathetic to either southern Republicans or blacks. For South Carolina Democrats, Hamburg must have also demonstrated the danger of allowing terror tactics to get out of hand (*New York Herald*, July 10, 1876; *Chicago Daily Tribune*, July 17, 1876).

17. *Columbia Daily Register*, July 23, September 3, 13, 1876; Sefton, *Army and Reconstruction*, 247.

18. *Charleston News and Courier*, August 12, 1876; *Senate Miscellaneous Documents*, 44th Cong. 2d sess., No. 48, 3:89–91, 497–98; Simkins, *Tillman*, 64–65.

19. Simkins and Woody, *South Carolina during Reconstruction*, 489–90;

Henry Tazewell Thompson, *Ousting the Carpetbagger from South Carolina* (Columbia: R. L. Bryan, 1926), 104.

20. John S. Reynolds, *Reconstruction in South Carolina* (Columbia: State Company Publishers, 1905), 354–55; *Senate Miscellaneous Documents,* 44th Cong., 2d sess., No. 48, 1:528–52, 984–92, 2:201–4, 3:445–49; *Columbia Union-Herald,* September 4, 1876.

21. *Charleston News and Courier,* September 22, October 23, 27, 1876; Richland Democratic Club Minutes, August 31, September 7, 28, 1876, South Caroliniana Library, University of South Carolina.

22. *Charleston News and Courier,* September 2, 23, 25, 27, October 11, 1876; J. Y. Pope, et al. to Chamberlain, September n.d., 1876, Chamberlain Papers; Williams, *Hampton and the Red Shirts,* 253–54.

23. *Charleston News and Courier,* September 7–9, 1876; James P. Low to Chamberlain, September 8, 12, 1876, Chamberlain Papers.

24. *House Miscellaneous Documents,* 44th Cong., 2d sess., No. 31, pt. 2, pp. 153–79, 214–26, 229–56; *House Executive Documents,* 44th Cong., 2d sess., No. 30, p. 58; *Charleston News and Courier,* October 17, 18, 1876; M. Laughlin to Assistant Adjutant General, Department of the South, October 23, 1876, Letters Received, Department of the South, 1868–83, RG 393, NA.

25. Allen, *Chamberlain's Administration,* 340–41; Davis McPherson to Chamberlain, June 30, 1876, Robert Smalls to Chamberlain, August 24, 1876, B. T. Sellers to Chamberlain, August 26, September 1, 1876, Chamberlain Papers; *Charleston News and Courier,* August 25, September 5, 13–15, 19, 21, 23, 1876.

26. Simkins and Woody, *South Carolina during Reconstruction,* 500, 564–69; Barnwell County, Democratic Executive Committee, Plan of Campaign, August 1, 1876, Ms in South Caroliniana Library, University of South Carolina; *Columbia Union-Herald,* October 12, 1876.

27. Williams, *Hampton and Red Shirts,* 104–5, 161–65; James Conner to Mrs. Conner, October 10, 1876, Hampton Family Papers, South Caroliniana Library, University of South Carolina; Loula Ayres Rockwell Recollections, 1, 4, typescript, Southern Historical Collection, University of North Carolina; Thompson, *Ousting the Carpetbagger,* 112–14.

28. *Charleston News and Courier,* October 4, 1876.

29. *Senate Miscellaneous Documents,* 44th Cong., 2d sess., No. 48, 2:85–93, 388–95, 438–47; *Charleston News and Courier,* September 1, 1876; *Columbia Union-Herald,* September 25, 1876.

30. *Senate Miscellaneous Documents,* 44th Cong., 2d sess., No. 48, 1:223–29, 2:3–12, 232–48, 542–46; L. Cass Carpenter to James A. Garfield, September 25, 1876, James Garfield Papers, Library of Congress.

31. *Senate Miscellaneous Documents,* 44th Cong., 2d sess., No. 48, 2:104–9, 3:91–92, 499–509; Francis B. Simkins, "The Election of 1876 in South Carolina," *South Atlantic Quarterly* 21 (October 1922): 337; Jacob Kline to Adjutant General, Department of the South, October 25, 1876, Letters Received, Department of the South, 1868–83, RG 393, NA.

32. *Senate Miscellaneous Documents,* 44th Cong., 2d sess., No. 48, 1:90–117,

168–76, 475–81, 495–501, 927–36, 997–1001, 3:316–41, 511–14, 523–24; *New York Herald,* October 11, 1876.

33. *Senate Miscellaneous Documents,* 44th Cong., 2d sess., No. 48, 1:124–38, 176–300, 622–40, 648–61, 1016–18, 1047–50, 2:261–91, 298–307, 3:215, 270–316, 519–22; *Charleston News and Courier,* September 26, October 4, 1876.

34. *Senate Miscellaneous Documents,* 44th Cong., 2d sess., No. 48, 1:11–23, 183–87, 281–86, 377–79, 779–88, 1001–6, 1028–36, 3:93–95, 231–70, 341–91, 514–15; *Charleston News and Courier,* September 20–23, 1876; Simkins, *Tillman,* 66.

35. *Charleston News and Courier,* September 25, October 2, 11, 12, 14, 1876; *Senate Miscellaneous Documents,* 44th Cong., 2d sess., No. 48, 2:47–62; fragmentary proceedings in the trial of the Ellenton Riot Cases, May 15–17, 22–27, 1877, Letters Received, Department of Justice, South Carolina, 1871–84, RG 60, NA, microcopy 947, rolls 8 and 9; C. Peter Magrath, *Morrison R. Waite: The Triumph of Character* (New York: Macmillan, 1963), 156–64.

36. Chamberlain Papers, October 1876; Thomas H. Ruger to Chamberlain, September 30, 1876, Letters Sent, Department of the South, 1868–83, RG 393, NA; *Senate Miscellaneous Documents,* 44th Cong., 2d sess., No. 48, 3:439–40.

37. *Charleston News and Courier,* October 9–11, 13, 21, 1876; Williams, *Hampton and the Red Shirts,* 246.

38. Richardson, ed., *Messages and Papers of the Presidents,* 7:396–97; William Stone to Alphonso Taft, October 21, 1876, Letters Received, Department of Justice, South Carolina, 1871–84, RG 60, NA, microcopy 947, roll 3; Chamberlain to Taft, November 4, 1876, William Howard Taft Papers, Library of Congress; *House Executive Documents,* 44th Cong., 2d sess., No. 30, p. 13.

39. H. C. Cook to Assistant Adjutant General, Department of the South, November 10, 1876, Letters Received, AGO, Main Series, 1871–80, RG 94, NA, microcopy 666, roll 298; *Senate Executive Documents,* 44th Cong., 2d sess., No. 6, pt. 2, pp. 18–19.

40. Holland, ed., *Letters and Diary of Laura Towne,* 253–54.

41. Ibid., 255; *Senate Miscellaneous Documents,* 44th Cong., 2d sess., No. 48, 1:118–24, 266–76, 327–44, 384–524, 686–95, 743–48; Frank H. Barnhart to Thomas L. Lloyd, November 9, 1876, Letters Received, AGO, Main Series, 1871–80, RG 94, NA, microcopy 666, roll 298.

42. *Senate Miscellaneous Documents,* 44th Cong., 2d sess., No. 48, 1:504–9, 843–67, 1094–97, 2:99–103, 117–19, 131–36, 623–31; Affidavit of Wiley J. Williams and Abraham Lauhaw, November 9, 1876, Deposition of 280 black men, November 14, 1876, Martin W. Gary Papers, William R. Perkins Library, Duke University.

43. *House Miscellaneous Documents,* 44th Cong., 2d sess., No. 31, pt. 2, pp. 200–205; *Charleston News and Courier,* November 10, 14, 1876.

44. *Annual Cyclopedia,* 1876, pp. 483, 485–86; *Chicago Daily Tribune,* September 10, 1876; *New Orleans Republican,* August 3, 1876.

45. C. McKinney to William Pitt Kellogg, March 7, 1876, Kellogg Papers; *New Orleans Republican,* May 16, July 26, October 28, 1876.

46. *House Executive Documents,* 44th Cong., 2d sess., No. 30, pp. 11–13, 40, 150–51; Kellogg to R. C. McCormick, October 16, 1876, Rutherford B. Hayes Papers, Hayes Memorial Library, Fremont, Ohio; *House Executive Documents,* 45th Cong., 2d sess., No. 1, vol. 1, pt. 2, pp. 99–100.

47. Taylor, *Louisiana Reconstructed,* 488–89; T. B. Tunnell, Jr., "The Negro, the Republican Party, and the Election of 1876," *Louisiana History* 7 (Spring 1966): 101–16.

48. There is no adequate study of bulldozing. Taylor's account is sketchy and thinly researched (*Louisiana Reconstructed,* 487–88).

49. *Senate Reports,* 44th Cong., 2d sess., No. 701, pp. 1557–1985, 2093–2113, 2186–2206, 2317–42; *New Orleans Republican,* March 29, June 22, July 20, August 6, 9, 11, 13, 29, 1876.

50. *New Orleans Daily Picayune,* July 10, October 15, 1875; *Senate Reports,* 44th Cong., 2d sess., No. 701, pp. 1019–1200, 1272–1330, 1446–49; *New Orleans Republican,* September 21, 30, 1876.

51. Joseph A. Armistead and George Swazzie to Kellogg, May 1, 1876, Kellogg Papers; *Senate Reports,* 44th Cong., 2d sess., No. 701, pp. 2342–86, 2401–33, 2446–51, 2565–86, 2619–20; *New Orleans Republican,* January 21, 25, May 16–18, 1876; Statements of Refugees from Mount Pleasant Plantation, June 24, 1876, Letters Received, Department of the Gulf, 1873–77, RG 393, NA; E. M. Gerald to James R. Beckwith, January 1, 1876, Letters Received, Department of Justice, Louisiana, 1871–84, RG 60, NA, microcopy 940, roll 2.

52. *New Orleans Republican,* August 4, September 26, 1876; James A. Denny to Thomas B. Pugh, October 31, 1876, W. W. Pugh Papers, Department of Archives, Louisiana State University.

53. *Senate Reports,* 44th Cong., 2d sess., No. 701, pp. 17–259, 330–662, 746–886, 996–1002; *New Orleans Republican,* September 5, 10, October 11, 27, November 7, 1876.

54. Shofner, *Nor Is It Over Yet,* 300–313.

55. Jerrell H. Shofner, "Florida's Political Reconstruction and the Presidential Election of 1876" (Ph.D. dissertation, Florida State University, 1963), 211–39; *Senate Reports,* 44th Cong., 2d sess., No. 611, pt. 2, pp. 44–48, 201–5, 241–48, 257–60, and passim.

56. James M. Stone to Alphonso Taft, October 4, 1876, Letters Received, Department of Justice, Mississippi, 1871–84, RG 60, NA, microcopy 970, roll 3.

57. *Hinds County Gazette* (Raymond), August 30, 1876; *Senate Miscellaneous Documents,* 44th Cong., 2d sess., No. 45, pp. 318–20.

58. *House Executive Documents,* 44th Cong., 2d sess., No. 30, pp. 112–13, 121, 129–30; *Senate Executive Documents,* 44th Cong., 2d sess., No. 6, pt. 2, pp. 14–15.

59. *Senate Miscellaneous Documents,* 44th Cong., 2d sess., No. 45, pp. 90–108, 136–89, 250–60, 489–553, 744–61, 764–84, 902–16, 924–28.

60. *House Executive Documents,* 44th Cong., 2d sess., No. 30, pp. 123–25, 128–29.

61. *Senate Miscellaneous Documents,* 44th Cong., 2d sess., No. 45, pp. 302–73; John J. Bishop to Assistant Adjutant General, Department of the Gulf,

November 1, 1876, Telegrams Received, Department of the Gulf, 1876, RG 393, NA; Bishop to Assistant Adjutant General, Department of the Gulf, November 2, 1876, Letters Received, Department of the Gulf, 1873–77, ibid.

62. John R. Lynch to J. L. Lake, September 27, 1876, F. E. DeCourcy to Assistant Adjutant General, Department of the Gulf, October 21, 1876, Letters Received, AGO, Main Series, 1871–80, RG 94, NA, microcopy 666, roll 298; *Senate Miscellaneous Documents,* 44th Cong., 2d sess., No. 45, pp. 109–35, 191–204, 895–902; John L. Lake to Alphonso Taft, October 24, 1876, Letters Received, Department of Justice, Mississippi, 1871–84, RG 60, NA, microcopy 970, roll 3.

63. *House Executive Documents,* 44th Cong., 2d sess., No. 30, pp. 131–32.

64. Jonathan Bragg to Matt W. Ransom, January 20, 1876, Matt Ransom Papers, Southern Historical Collection, University of North Carolina; R. C. Goodrich to Rutherford B. Hayes, August 30, 1876, Hayes Papers; *Senate Reports,* 44th Cong., 2d sess., No. 704, passim.

65. *New York Tribune,* November 6, 1876; *Charleston News and Courier,* July 27, August 5, 1876.

66. For a fuller treatment of the relation of southern home rule to the election deadlock, see George C. Rable, "Southern Interests and the Election of 1876: A Reappraisal," *Civil War History* 26 (December 1980): 347–61.

67. *House Executive Documents,* 44th Cong., 2d sess., No. 30, p. 41; *House Miscellaneous Documents,* 44th Cong., 2d sess., No. 34, pt. 2, p. 826; Clayton Hale to Assistant Adjutant General, Department of the Gulf, December 15, 1876, Letters Received, AGO, Main Series, 1871–80, RG 94, NA, microcopy 666, roll 300.

68. J.R.G. Pitkin to Alphonso Taft, January 6, 8, 9, 10, 1877, Letters Received, Department of Justice, Louisiana, 1871–84, RG 60, NA, microcopy 940, roll 3; Louisiana Militia and National Guard Orders, January–April 1877, Louisiana Historical Association Collection, Howard-Tilton Memorial Library, Tulane University.

69. L. A. Sheldon to James A. Garfield, January 20, February 10, 1877, Garfield Papers; J.R.G. Pitkin to Alphonso Taft, February 13, 1877, J. B. Stockton to Pitkin, February 15, 1877, Letters Received, Department of Justice, Louisiana, 1871–84, RG 60, NA, microcopy 940, roll 3; John B. Robertson to William D. Kelley, February 18, 1877, Hayes Papers; Nicholls to E. A. Burke, February 17, 1877, Nicholls Letterbook, 1877–79, Department of Archives, Louisiana State University.

70. John M. Bacon to William T. Sherman, November 17, 18, 1876, William T. Sherman Papers, Library of Congress.

71. Daniel H. Chamberlain to Ulysses S. Grant, November 25, 1876, Grant Papers, Rutherford B. Hayes Memorial Library, Fremont, Ohio; *Columbia Union-Herald,* November 28, 1876; Thompson, *Ousting the Carpetbagger,* 142–43, 149–51.

72. Daniel H. Chamberlain to Alphonso Taft, November 30, 1876, Taft Papers; *Columbia Union-Herald,* December 7, 13, 1876; Chamberlain Papers, November 1876–April 1877; David T. Corbin to Taft, January 13, 1877, Let-

ters Received, Department of Justice, South Carolina, 1871–84, RG 60, NA, microcopy 947, roll 3.

73. *Charleston News and Courier,* January 29, 1877, B. F. Whittemore to Chamberlain, January 29, 1877, Chamberlain Papers; Samuel Shellabarger to James M. Comly, December 12, 1876, Comly Papers; Simkins and Woody, *South Carolina during Reconstruction,* 541n.

74. *Memphis Daily Appeal,* November 15, 1876; L. A. Sheldon to James A. Garfield, December 12, 1876, Garfield Papers.

75. *Jackson Weekly Clarion,* February 28, 1877; E. John Ellis to Mr. and Mrs. E. P. Ellis, February 25, 1877, Ellis Papers.

Epilogue: On the Inevitability of Tragedy

1. Charles A. Beard and Mary R. Beard, *The Rise of American Civilization,* 2 vols. (New York: Macmillan, 1930), 2:115–16.

2. Paul H. Buck, *The Road to Reunion, 1865–1900* (Boston: Little, Brown, 1937), 27–29; Richard D. Brown, *Modernization: The Transformation of American Life, 1600–1865* (New York: Hill and Wang, 1976), 12–13, 114, 140–48, 159–86.

3. Frank Tannenbaum, "On Political Stability," *Political Science Quarterly* 75 (June 1960): 161–80.

4. Hodding Carter, *The Angry Scar: The Story of Reconstruction* (Garden City, N.Y.: Doubleday, 1959), 145; A. B. Moore, "One Hundred Years of Reconstruction of the South," *Journal of Southern History* 9 (May 1943): 156–64; Carl N. Degler, *Place over Time: The Continuity of Southern Distinctiveness* (Baton Rouge: Louisiana State University Press, 1977), 109.

5. Richard M. Weaver, *The Southern Tradition at Bay: A History of Postbellum Thought* (New Rochelle, N.Y.: Arlington House, 1968), 113; McCardell, *Idea of a Southern Nation,* 49–90, 141–226; Cash, *Mind of the South,* 105–9; Robert Penn Warren, *The Legacy of the Civil War* (New York: Random House, 1961), 14–15.

6. "A Georgian" to Thaddeus Stevens, March 21, 1866, Stevens Papers; *Jackson Daily Clarion,* February 7, 1868.

7. Albion W. Tourgée, *A Fool's Errand* (1879; rpr. New York: Harper and Row, 1966), 255; Gustav Bychowski, *Evil in Man: The Anatomy of Hate and Violence* (New York: Grune and Stratton, 1968), 38–39.

8. Georges Clemenceau, *American Reconstruction, 1865–1870,* ed. Fernand Baldensperger (New York: Dial Press, 1928), 229.

9. Perman, *Reunion without Compromise,* 6–7, 14; Herman Belz, "The New Orthodoxy in Reconstruction Historiography," *Reviews in American History* 1 (March 1973): 106–13.

10. Tourgée, *Fool's Errand,* 24–25; William T. Sherman to Philip H. Sheridan, January 2, 1875, Sheridan Papers. As one perceptive psychologist has noted, military Reconstruction was never severe enough to force very many white southerners to change their fundamental assumptions about race (Wil-

liam C. Capel, "Cognitive Dissonance, Reconstruction and Negro Civil Rights: Applications of a Theory," *Journal of Human Relations* 19 [Second Quarter 1971]: 225–38).

11. Harry James Brown and Frederick D. Williams, eds., *The Diary of James A. Garfield,* 3 vols. (East Lansing, Mich.: Michigan State University Press, 1967–73), 2:63.

12. Slotkin, *Regeneration through Violence,* 561–62.

13. Crane Brinton, *The Anatomy of Revolution* (Englewood Cliffs, N.J.: Prentice-Hall, 1965), 205–7, 236.

14. The best summary of the weaknesses in federal Reconstruction policies is in Gillette, *Retreat from Reconstruction,* 363–80.

15. Charles Tilly, "Collective Violence in European Perspective," in Graham and Gurr, eds., *Violence in America,* 5–9.

16. James H. Laue, "Power, Conflict and Social Change," in Bower and Masotti, eds., *Riots and Rebellions,* 85–88; Coser, *Study of Social Conflict,* 87–92.

17. Myrdal, *American Dilemma,* 1:448–51.

Bibliographical Essay

The difficulty of unraveling the story of violence in Reconstruction was best expressed by Georges Clemenceau more than a century ago: "Whatever the facts, it is practically impossible to know the truth, for both sides are interested in exaggerating the reports. The Democrats want to frighten the negroes, and prevent the more timid from voting, if possible; and the Republicans are forging a weapon against the conservatives, seeking to convince them that radicalism is the only way out of the horrors of a second rebellion" (Georges Clemenceau, *American Reconstruction, 1865–1870,* ed. Fernand Baldensperger [New York: Dial Press, 1928], 229). Although in reality Democrats consistently downplayed disorders in the South, Clemenceau's main point still holds. Testimony about almost all incidents of Reconstruction violence is highly partisan, confusing, and contradictory. Historians have often abdicated their responsibility in dealing with this mass of information, especially in treating the course and consequences of particular disorders. Instead of examining the breadth of evidence, scholars have followed their own ideological leanings in rejecting various sources as being unreliable and partisan yet relying on other sources no more reliable and no less partisan. The only way to evaluate the sources is by a thorough examination of a wide variety of sources in which their reliability is assessed using the normal standards of historical analysis.

Archival and manuscript materials relating to Reconstruction violence are voluminous and helpful. In the National Archives, the records of the Bureau of Refugees, Freedmen, and Abandoned Lands (Record Group 105) contain useful reports on local conditions. Department of Justice files (Record Group 60) include extensive correspondence with United States marshals and attorneys in the South as well as revealing instructions sent to those officials by the attorney general. Army officers sent numerous accounts of racial and other disturbances to their superiors in Washington, many of which were never published in the congressional serial set. The Adjutant General's Office (Record Group 94) correspondence is essential for understanding the relationship between the army, state politics, and Washington's Reconstruction policies. The records of the United States Army's Continental Commands (Record Group 393) contain valuable day-to-day information on military operations in the South. Though far from being entirely objective, military personnel often provide the most complete and most balanced accounts of southern violence.

Unfortunately, the correspondence of the state governors is much more uneven in quality. The most useful collections are at the North Carolina Department of Archives and History, the South Carolina Archives, the Alabama Department of Archives and History, and the Mississippi Department of Archives and History. A small but important collection of Henry Clay Warmoth papers is in the Southern Historical Collection at the University of North Carolina. Among the useful collections of the papers of southern Republicans are the John Emory Bryant Papers (William R. Perkins Library, Duke University), the Joseph E. Brown and Henry P. Farrow Papers (University of Georgia Library), the William Pitt Kellogg Papers (Department of Archives and Manuscripts, Louisiana State University), and the Thomas Settle Papers (Southern Historical Collection, University of North Carolina). For southern conservatives, the harvest is disappointingly meager. Only for Alexander H. Stephens are there truly voluminous materials (primarily at Manhattanville College of the Sacred Heart, Purchase, New York, and the Library of Congress). The Benjamin F. Perry Papers at the Alabama Department of Archives and History contain many letters expressing the reaction of former Confederates in South Carolina to early phases of Reconstruction. The Herschel Johnson Papers (William R. Perkins Library, Duke University) supplement the various Stephens collections in probing conservatism in Georgia. The E. John Ellis Papers (Department of Archives and Manuscripts, Louisiana State University) are the only valuable collection of papers of a Louisiana conservative during the counterrevolution in that state. The small group of Lamar-Mayes Papers (Mississippi Department of Archives and History) sheds considerable light on the political maneuverings in the Mississippi Democracy during 1874 and 1875. Even at the Southern Historical Collection, material on conservative politicians is fragmentary and scattered. The family correspondence and private diaries cited in the footnotes often provided illuminating comments on social and economic conditions and occasionally startling remarks on the legitimacy of violence.

The papers of northern politicians are a rich source of letters from the South. Of particular value are the Benjamin H. Bristow, William E. Chandler, James A. Garfield, and Andrew Johnson Papers at the Library of Congress and the superb collection of Rutherford B. Hayes Papers at the Hayes Memorial Library in Fremont, Ohio.

Many historians of Reconstruction have neglected the great quantities of information contained in the federal serial set. Although many investigations of conditions in the South were conducted with partisan axes to grind, the material that was collected remains invaluable. The reports of congressional committees are highly partisan, but the accompanying testimony and printed documents are indispensable and very revealing if used with caution. In even the most slanted of these investigations, testimony was usually taken from both sides.

Historians who chose not to make extensive use of the testimony taken before congressional committees have generally considered newspapers to be more reliable sources. Historians who have mined the federal documents have usually thought newspapers were untrustworthy. Republican and Democratic newspapers contain information found nowhere else, and their editorials often unconsciously reveal the bases for party action. The most useful Republican newspapers are the *New Orleans Republican,* the *Jackson Mississippi Pilot,* the *Raleigh North Carolina Standard,* the *Columbia Daily Union-Herald,* the *Memphis Daily Post,* and the *Austin Daily State Journal.* Conservative and Democratic newspapers were the most important sources for comments on political strategy and the efficacy of violence. The best of these are the *Mobile Daily Advertiser and Register,* the *Little Rock Daily Arkansas Gazette,* the *Augusta Daily Constitutionalist,* the *Atlanta Constitution,* the *New Orleans Daily Picayune,* the *New Orleans Bulletin,* the *Shreveport Daily Times,* the *Jackson Clarion,* the *Raleigh Daily Sentinel,* the *Charleston Daily Courier,* the *Charleston News and Courier,* the *Columbia Register,* the *Memphis Daily Appeal,* the *Richmond Daily Dispatch,* and the *Louisville Courier-Journal.* Of the northern periodicals and newspapers, the *Nation, Harper's Weekly,* the *New York Times,* the *New York Herald,* and the *Chicago Daily Tribune* contain important southern correspondence as well as editorial comment.

Published primary sources fall into several categories. The most important travel accounts are Sidney Andrews, *The South since the War,* ed. David Donald (Boston: Houghton, Mifflin, 1971); J. T. Trowbridge, *A Picture of the Desolated States; and the Work of Restoration, 1865–1868* (Hartford, Conn.: L. Stebbins, 1868); Edward King, *The Great South,* ed. W. Magruder Drake and Robert R. Jones (Baton Rouge: Louisiana State University Press, 1972); Charles Nordhoff, *The Cotton States in the Spring and Summer of 1875* (New York: D. Appleton, 1876); and William Hepworth Dixon, *White Conquest,* 2 vols. (London: Chatto and Windus, 1876). For an indispensable inside look at Reconstruction in Mississippi from the viewpoint of a bedeviled carpetbag governor, see Jessie Ames Marshall, ed., *Chronicles from the Nineteenth Century: Family Letters of Blanche Butler and Adelbert Ames,* 2 vols. (N.p.: Privately printed, 1957). Most Reconstruction memoirs are thin, but three useful ones are A. T. Morgan, *Yazoo; Or, On the Pickett Line of Freedom in the South* (New York: Russell and Russell, 1968); Powell Clayton, *The Aftermath of the Civil War in Arkansas* (New York: Neale, 1915); and Henry Clay Warmoth, *War, Politics, and Reconstruction: Stormy Days in Louisiana* (New York: Macmillan, 1930).

Although the number of secondary works on Reconstruction grows larger all the time, there is no comprehensive treatment of violence during that period. Allen Trelease's *White Terror: The Ku Klux Klan Conspiracy and Southern Reconstruction* (New York: Harper & Row, 1971) is a model of clear narration and thorough research with a sprinkling of interpretive insights. For presidential Reconstruction, see Michael Perman's first-rate treatment of recalcitrant conservatism in *Reunion without Compromise: The South and Reconstruction, 1865–1868* (Cambridge, England: Cambridge University Press, 1973). Two nicely complementary studies of the first phases of postwar race relations are James L. Roark, *Masters without Slaves: Southern Planters in the Civil War and Reconstruction* (New York: W. W. Norton, 1977) and Leon F. Litwack, *Been in the Storm So Long: The Aftermath of Slavery* (New York: Alfred A. Knopf, 1979). The social and economic problems of the period are well handled in Roger L. Ransom and Richard Sutch, *One Kind of Freedom: The Economic Consequences of Emancipation* (Cambridge, England: Cambridge University Press, 1977); Lawrence N. Powell, *New Masters: Northern Planters during the Civil War and Reconstruction* (New Haven: Yale University Press, 1980); and Jonathan M. Wiener, *Social Origins of the New South: Alabama, 1860–1885* (Baton Rouge: Louisiana State University Press, 1978). A competent treatment of the army's role in dealing with a variety of southern problems is James E. Sefton, *The United States Army and Reconstruction, 1865–1877* (Baton Rouge: Louisiana State University Press, 1967). William Gillette's *Retreat from Reconstruction, 1869–1879* (Baton Rouge: Louisiana State University Press, 1979), brilliantly treats the collapse of Republican southern policies.

Although some significant gaps remain, state studies are invaluable for any student attempting to study the entire South. The three best for my purposes proved to be Jerrell H. Shofner, *Nor Is It Over Yet: Florida in the Era of Reconstruction, 1863–1877* (Gainesville: University Presses of Florida, 1974); Joe Gray Taylor, *Louisiana Reconstructed, 1863–1877* (Baton Rouge: Louisiana State University Press, 1974); and William C. Harris, *The Day of the Carpetbagger: Republican Reconstruction in Mississippi* (Baton Rouge: Louisiana State University Press, 1979). Two exceptionally well-done studies of South Carolina are Joel Williamson, *After Slavery: The Negro in South Carolina during Reconstruction, 1861–1877* (Chapel Hill: University of North Carolina Press, 1965), and Thomas Holt, *Black over White: Negro Political Leadership in South Carolina during Reconstruction* (Urbana: University of Illinois Press, 1977).

A large number of articles relating to Reconstruction violence may be found in various professional journals. John A. Carpenter deals with the problem of numbers in "Atrocities in the Reconstruction Period," *Journal of Negro History* 42 (October 1962): 234–47. Two perceptive studies of individual states are Ray Granade, "Violence: An Instrument of Policy in Reconstruction Alabama," *Alabama Historical Quarterly* 30 (Fall and Winter 1968): 181–202, and Ralph L. Peek, "Lawlessness in Florida, 1868–1871," *Florida Historical Quarterly* 40 (October 1961): 164–85. The secondary literature on specific riots is weakly researched and not very interpretive, but the following are useful: Jack D. L. Holmes, "The Underlying Causes of the Memphis Race Riot of 1866," *Tennessee Historical Quarterly* 17 (September 1958): 195–221; Manie White Johnson, "The Colfax Riot of April, 1873," *Louisiana Historical Quarterly* 13 (July 1930): 391–427; Carolyn E. DeLatte, "The St. Landry Riot: A Forgotten Incident of Reconstruction Violence," *Louisiana History* 17 (Winter 1976): 41–49; Melinda Meek Hennessey, "Race and Violence in Reconstruction New Orleans: The 1868 Riot," *Louisiana History* 20 (Winter 1979): 77–91; and Hennessey, "Reconstruction Politics and the Military: The Eufaula Riot of 1874," *Alabama Historical Quarterly* 38 (Summer 1976): 112–25.

The best introductions to the social science literature on violence are Ted Robert Gurr, *Why Men Rebel* (Princeton: Princeton University Press, 1970); Hugh Davis Graham and Ted Robert Gurr, eds., *Violence in America: Historical and Comparative Perspectives* (Washington: Government Printing Office,

1969); and Allen D. Grimshaw, ed., *Racial Violence in the United States* (Chicago: Aldine, 1969). There are thoughtful considerations of nineteenth-century American violence in Richard Maxwell Brown, *Strain of Violence: Historical Studies of American Violence and Vigilantism* (New York: Oxford University Press, 1975), and Michael Feldberg, *The Turbulent Era: Riot and Disorder in Jacksonian America* (New York: Oxford University Press, 1980). The context for southern violence is established in two classic works: Wilbur J. Cash, *The Mind of the South* (New York: Alfred A. Knopf, 1941), and John Dollard, *Caste and Class in a Southern Town* (New Haven: Yale University Press, 1937). Antebellum southern violence is treated in John Hope Franklin, *The Militant South, 1800–1861* (Cambridge, Mass.: Harvard University Press, 1956), and Dickson D. Bruce, Jr., *Violence and Culture in the Antebellum South* (Austin: University of Texas Press, 1979).

Index